Interlocking Dimensions of European Integration

One Europe or Several?

Series Editor: **Helen Wallace**

The **One Europe or Several?** series examines contemporary processes of political, security, economic, social and cultural change across the European continent, as well as issues of convergence/divergence and prospects for integration and fragmentation. Many of the books in the series are cross-country comparisons; others evaluate the European institutions, in particular the European Union and NATO, in the context of eastern enlargement.

One Europe or Several?
Series Standing Order ISBN 0–333–94630–8
(*outside North America only*)

You can receive future titles in this series as they are published by placing a standing order. Please contact your bookseller or, in case of difficulty, write to us at the address below with your name and address, the title of the series and the ISBN quoted above.

Customer Services Department, Macmillan Distribution Ltd, Houndmills, Basingstoke, Hampshire RG21 6XS, England

Interlocking Dimensions of European Integration

Edited by

Helen Wallace
Co-Director, Sussex European Institute, University of Sussex
Director, Economic and Social Research Council 'One Europe or Several?' Programme

palgrave

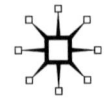

Editorial matter, selection and Introduction (Chapter 1)
© Helen Wallace 2001
Chapters 2–16 © Palgrave Publishers Ltd 2001

All rights reserved. No reproduction, copy or transmission of this publication may be made without written permission.

No paragraph of this publication may be reproduced, copied or transmitted save with written permission or in accordance with the provisions of the Copyright, Designs and Patents Act 1988, or under the terms of any licence permitting limited copying issued by the Copyright Licensing Agency, 90 Tottenham Court Road, London W1T 4LP.

Any person who does any unauthorised act in relation to this publication may be liable to criminal prosecution and civil claims for damages.

The authors have asserted their rights to be identified as the authors of this work in accordance with the Copyright, Designs and Patents Act 1988.

First published 2001 by
PALGRAVE
Houndmills, Basingstoke, Hampshire RG21 6XS and
175 Fifth Avenue, New York, N. Y. 10010
Companies and representatives throughout the world

PALGRAVE is the new global academic imprint of
St. Martin's Press LLC Scholarly and Reference Division and
Palgrave Publishers Ltd (formerly Macmillan Press Ltd).

ISBN 0–333–80296–9

This book is printed on paper suitable for recycling and made from fully managed and sustained forest sources.

A catalogue record for this book is available from the British Library.

Library of Congress Cataloging-in-Publication Data have been applied for.

10	9	8	7	6	5	4	3	2	1
10	09	08	07	06	05	04	03	02	01

Printed and bound in Great Britain by
Antony Rowe Ltd, Chippenham, Wiltshire

Contents

List of Tables and Figures	vii
List of Abbreviations	viii
Preface	x
List of Contributors	xii

1 Introduction: Rethinking European Integration 1
   Helen Wallace

Part I The Functional Dimension

2 European Union Trade Policy: Actually or Just
   Nominally Liberal? 25
   L. Alan Winters

3 Pan-European Industrial Networks as Factors of
   Convergence and Divergence Within Europe 45
   Slavo Radosevic

4 Functions, Levels and European Governance 68
   Ben Rosamond

Part II The Territorial Dimension

5 'You No Longer Believe in Us and We No Longer
   Believe in You': Russian Attitudes Towards Europe 87
   John Löwenhardt, Margot Light and Stephen White

6 New Forms of International Migration: In Search
   of Which Europe? 103
   Allan M. Williams

7 Regional Trajectories and Uneven Development in
   the 'New Europe': Rethinking Territorial Success and
   Inequality 122
   Adrian Smith, Al Rainnie and Michael Dunford

8 Enlargement and Regionalization: The Europeanization
   of Local and Regional Governance in CEE States 145
   James Hughes, Gwendolyn Sasse and Claire Gordon

9	Germany's Power in Europe *Charlie Jeffery and William E. Paterson*	179
10	Rethinking European Security *Lawrence Freedman*	215

Part III   The Affiliational Dimension

11	Imagining the Union: A Case of Banal Europeanism? *Laura Cram*	231
12	European Identity and National Identity in Central and Eastern Europe *Judy Batt*	247
13	EU Citizenship and Pan-Europeanism *Elizabeth Meehan*	263
14	Immigrants, Cosmopolitans and the Idea of Europe *Ash Amin*	280

Part IV   The Scope and Limits of Integration

15	Towards Post-corporatist Concertation in Europe? *Rory O'Donnell*	305
16	Organizing European Institutions of Governance ... A Prelude to an Institutional Account of Political Integration *Johan P. Olsen*	323

Index   355

List of Tables and Figures

Figures
8.1	Attitudes to regionalization in compliance with EU-funding criteria	170
8.2	The meaning of European Union	171
8.3	Key issues facing your city	171
8.4	Knowledge of EU-funded programmes	172
8.5	Perceptions of the benefits of EU membership	174

Tables
15.1	Traditional and new ideas of a social partner	314
15.2	Traditional and new roles of central government	316

List of Abbreviations

ACP	African, Caribbean and Pacific
ADB	Asian Development Bank
AFTA	ASEAN Free Trade Agreement
APEC	Asia–Pacific Economic Cooperation
ASEAN	Association of South East Asian Nations
ASEM	Asia–Europe Meeting
CAP	common agricultural policy
CEE	central and eastern Europe
CEECs	central and east European countries
CFSP	Common Foreign and Security Policy
CIS	Commonwealth of Independent States
CNPN	cross-national production network
CSCE	Conference on Security and Cooperation in Europe
DG	Directorate-General
EA	Europe Agreements
EBRD	European Bank for Reconstruction and Development
EC	European Commission
EC	European Communities
ECJ	European Court of Justice
ECSC	European Coal and Steel Community
EEA	European Economic Area
EFTA	European Free Trade Association
EMA	Euro-Mediterranean Agreement
EMU	economic and monetary union
ERM	exchange-rate-mechansim
ESDI	European Security and Defence Identity
EU	European Union
FDI	foreign direct investment
FSB	Federal Security Bureau
FTA	free trade agreement
FTAA	Free Trade Area of the Americas
GATT	General Agreement on Tariffs and Trade
GDP	gross domestic product
GDR	German Democratic Republic
GFR	German Federal Republic
GMO	genetically modified organism

GSP	Generalized System of Preferences
IMF	International Monetary Fund
LDC	less-developed country
mfn	most-favoured nation
MLG	multi-level governance
NAFTA	North American Free Trade Area
NATO	North Atlantic Treaty Organization
NGO	non-governmental organization
NESC	National Economic and Social Council
NPAA	National Programme for the Adoption of the *Acquis*
OECD	Organization for Economic Cooperation and Development
OSCE	Organization for Security and Cooperation in Europe
PNR	Programme for National Recovery
PPP	purchasing power parities
R & D	research and development
RDC	Regional Development Council
REPA	Regional Economic Partnership Agreement
RTA	reciprocal trading agreement
TNC	transnational corporation
UN	United Nations
WEU	Western European Union
WTO	World Trade Organization

Preface

This first volume in the 'One Europe or Several?' series brings together a variety of reflections about the phenomenon of European integration broadly construed. The introductory chapter was first written as the 1998 Stein Rokkan lecture for the European Consortium on Political Research. Its contents grew out of the discussions that had led to the devising for the Economic and Social Research Council in the UK of what became the programme on 'One Europe or Several? The Dynamics of Change in Contemporary Europe'. The programme opened in January 1998 and runs until December 2002. It directly funds 24 research projects and one Programme Fellowship; details can be found at http://www.one-europe.ac.uk.

Further volumes in this series will report the findings of individual projects within the 'One Europe or Several?' Programme. As the question mark in the title suggests, it is a deliberate aim of the programme to question many of the conventional wisdoms about how contemporary Europe is configured. Some of the broader reflections will be drawn together in further volumes that will address themes that run across the projects, in the hope of reformulating some of the intellectual puzzles about the character of European integration in the context of 'pan-Europe'.

For this first volume of essays we have brought together some members of the original Commissioning Panel, and of the Advisory Board, together with researchers involved in several of the 'One Europe or Several?' projects. The volume has a deliberately speculative character, raising questions, posing awkward issues, and reporting early work in some of the projects. Ash Amin, Lawrence Freedman, Elizabeth Meehan, Rory O'Donnell and Allan Williams were members of the Commissioning Panel and helped to shape the contours of the intellectual agenda for the programme. Johan Olsen, a member of the Advisory Board, has become a generous but tough mentor, while Ash Amin continues to offer provocative guidance. Alan Winters kindly allowed himself to be conscripted as a friendly goad. The other essays are all written bravely by members of the projects willing to share their early, still speculative findings from work in progress.

The shape of the volume follows my Rokkan lecture, which constitutes the first chapter. It was first published by the *European Journal of*

Political Research, 1999, 35 (3): 287–306. It is reproduced here, with only minor amendments, with kind permission of Kluwer Academic Publishers. Part I of the volume explores the functional, especially economic, dimension to integration and deliberately frames this in relation to both the wider European economy and the global context. Part II explores the territorial dimension, ranging across issues relating to the movement of persons and regional governance, as well as matters of military security and the interface with the former Soviet Union. A chapter is included addressing the specificity of the new Germany in its reconstituted European setting. Part III seeks to open up the debate on the affiliational dimension to integration, drawing on both deep-rooted understandings of Europe in central and eastern Europe and some of the new understandings of citizenship and society in western Europe. Part IV offers an insight into the new institutionalized partnership model of contemporary Ireland, of which perhaps there are mirrored versions elsewhere in other European countries. Alongside stands an essay on the challenge of how to understand the institutional dynamics of transnational Europe.

As always the production of a complex book depends on efforts of editing and manuscript management. Elizabeth Mellick has made a stalwart and skilled contribution to this process, ably complemented by Annie Bacon. I am grateful to them and to the authors for making this volume possible.

HELEN WALLACE

List of Contributors

Professor Ash Amin   University of Durham

Dr Judy Batt   University of Birmingham

Dr Laura Cram   University of Strathclyde

Professor Michael Dunford   University of Sussex

Professor Lawrence Freedman   King's College London

Dr Claire Gordon   London School of Economics and Political Science

Dr James Hughes   London School of Economics and Political Science

Professor Charlie Jeffery   University of Birmingham

Professor Margot Light   London School of Economics and Political Science

Professor John Löwenhardt   University of Glasgow

Professor Elizabeth Meehan   Queen's University of Belfast

Professor Rory O'Donnell   University College Dublin

Professor Johan P. Olsen   ARENA, Oslo

Professor William E. Paterson   University of Birmingham

Dr Slavo Radosevic   School of Slavonic and East European Studies

Dr Al Rainnie   Monash University

Dr Ben Rosamond   University of Warwick

Dr Gwendolyn Sasse   London School of Economics and Political Science

Dr Adrian Smith   University Southampton

Professor Helen Wallace   University of Sussex

Professor Stephen White   University of Glasgow

Professor Allan M. Williams   University of Exeter

Professor L. Alan Winters   University of Sussex

1
Introduction: Rethinking European Integration
Helen Wallace

Introduction

It is over a decade since the Berlin Wall came down – a decade in which there have been huge changes across the European continent. Yet it still remains very unclear what the shape of transnational relations will be in this new 'pan-Europe'.[1] It also remains very unclear whether a form of 'pan-European' integration is feasible or politically probable. The practitioners' debate remains rather conventionally focused on the questions of whether and how to extend eastwards the transnational organizations, built originally by and for west Europeans. Most of that debate is about the logistics of enlarging the European Union (EU) and the North Atlantic Treaty Organization (NATO), both set in train in early 1998. It is easy to criticize the practitioners for their unadjusted mindsets. But there are many in the academic community who are similarly groping for a new understanding of pan-Europe. It is tempting, and much easier, to stay locked into the familiar paradigms of the old – and divided – Europe.

The underlying puzzle to be resolved has at least three elements. First, how many Europes are we talking about? The Research Programme funded in Britain by the Economic and Social Research Council is for this reason entitled *'One Europe or several?'*. Second, what really is the distinctiveness of the model of *west* European integration, defined below as *deep* integration? An answer to this question seems a necessary preliminary to considering whether the same pattern of integration is feasible for pan-Europe. Third, what is the role of 'Europe' within the politics of individual countries. Or, in other words, how should we construe the domestication of Europe? This introductory chapter addresses each of these three elements in an effort to clarify the discussion about the emerging transnational features of the new Europe.

The discussion that follows is prompted in part by a personal intellectual journey, as well as by the experience of a citizen in Britain, a country that has not easily come to terms with Europeanization. My own starting position was sympathetic to the old neofunctionalist argument that west European integration was propelled by the interactions between political and economic elites across country boundaries in pursuit of some mix of shared ideas and complementary interests (Haas, 1968; and Lindberg, 1963). This presupposed that bargained reciprocities (diffuse and not just specific) could be sustained over time and facilitated by particular institutional processes. I was less persuaded by the argument that integration would lead to the creation of a supranational polity and I was always conscious of the *differences* between countries in the way that Europe was domesticated or instrumentalized. Nonetheless interest-based explanations seemed not to explain enough of the process to be wholly convincing.

However, I have become increasingly perplexed about what factors beyond the calculation of interests are necessary to permit – or to sustain – an interlocking of elite engagements, once the background conditions have altered. The issue here is less the 'turbulence' caused by 'dramatic political' personalities,[2] and rather what might be the impact on integration of the systemic turbulence in Europe over the past decade. It is this concern that has driven me back to contemplate Karl Deutsch's (1957) wide-ranging analysis of integration and the many factors which he argued were needed to create an 'amalgamated security community'. His argument both insisted on the importance of the societal dimension and asserted that extensive integration had to include some notion of a shared sense of security.

In a similarly ambitious vein Stein Rokkan (1975 – and more or less *passim*) evaluated a broad range of factors that shaped the political fabric of contemporary Europe. For him notions of territory and boundaries, and of core and peripherae, were crucial, as well as a daunting range of factors, from the military–administrative through the political and economic to the societal and cultural. For him the prefix 'geo' was crucial as a qualification of each of his key variables. It is a perplexing irony of post-cold-war Europe that we have all been forced to rediscover issues of territory and of boundaries, that the melting of that stark division between East and West should have revealed so many other disconcerting and difficult borders. It is a paradox too that so many practitioners should be tempted to create so many new borders. Hence the occasion of a lecture in memory of Stein Rokkan provided a particularly apt prompt for an effort to examine my puzzle about whose Europe and what kind of Europe and how many Europes.

How many Europes?

This question needs to be approached from two different angles, one more empirical and the other more analytical. The main empirical point is that we too easily exaggerate the simplicity of the transnational organization of western Europe. Hence we too easily transpose on to central and eastern Europe a reversed mirror image based on this misleading simplification, implying a contrast between a relatively homogeneous western Europe and a fragmented and segmented eastern Europe. But western Europe is also a set of multiple Europes, in which both the role of the EU as the predominant transnational organization and the coherence of west European integration and multilateralism are much overstated.

The oversimplified contrast of West and East disguises several important points. First, the EU has throughout its history coexisted with a different and larger transnational framework for managing west European security interests, namely NATO. There was always a relationship and, I would argue, an interdependence, between the two frameworks. This is not intended as a reductionist observation to adduce 'geopolitics' as the key variable, a position so fiercely attacked by Moravcsik (1998), but rather an insistence on a kind of synergy between the two domains. Moreover the defence relationships in western Europe have been underpinned by a whole array of other relationships, not only Western European Union (WEU), but other bilateral and multilateral linkages among individual countries. Recently, the interdependence of NATO and the EU has begun to be reconfigured as a more explicit complementarity through the creation of a so-called European Security and Defence Identity (ESDI).

Second, there have since the 1940s always been several 'outlier' countries in western Europe, not fully engaged in either the EU or NATO or outside both organizations. These outliers have been mostly located around the peripherae of western Europe, although Switzerland is a centrally located outlier. With the 'Eftan' (for members of the European Free Trade Association) enlargement of the EU and the arrangements for partial association of some 'non-aligned' countries' with WEU, the ranks of explicit outliers have shrunk.[3] Some would argue that the later-joiners of the EU include some outliers, inside more in form than in spirit. In contrast there is a west European core group of countries, larger in membership than the six founder members of the European Community (EC), but less than the current EU membership. The notion of a core western Europe, or 'little Europe' (Delors, 1992) has indeed been articulated by some practitioners, especially since 1989, as a operational organizing principle. In May 2000 Joshka Fischer (2000) attempted to launch a new debate on how to strengthen this core Europe. Also we might note that it is the south-eastern and north-western corners of western Europe that have been most difficult to embrace in the west European integration process. The north-west matters less in this context than the south-east, at the interface between Europe and 'non-Europe' and hence a real test for integration, as Rokkan (1975) might have argued.

Third, transnational western Europe has consisted of a series of interlocking relationships between particular neighbours, in groupings with different focal points and characteristics. Some are straightforward to list: Benelux, the Franco–German partnership; the Nordic family; the tangled British–Irish interdependency–each with varying degrees of organization and each marked by points of tension as well as by points of alignment. Others are less defined: the Dutch–German relationship; or almost invisible: the Portuguese–Spanish relationship; or marked by contestation: the Greek–Turkish relationship. These various groupings form the sub-structure of the wider west European pattern of relationships, and its external interfaces. Arguably without these interlocking groupings the fabric of broader integration would be less strong. The fabric of integration seems weakest in those parts of western Europe where the local connections are more differentiated, whether explicitly contested (Greece–Turkey) or ambiguously articulated (as in the Nordic region). Conversely the fabric of integration seems strongest in those parts where the links between neighbours have been most densely cumulative, mainly in the heartland of 'core' western Europe.

Fourth, over the past decade there have been both some newly emerging groupings between neighbours and some sharp fissures within previously coorganized countries. The dissolution of Czechoslovakia and of Yugoslavia are obvious, though different, examples of the latter. The disaggregation of Belgium is a west European example of fission. More encouragingly there is an engaging intensity of new linkages in the Baltic region. Less intense, but interesting, linkages are being built in the Black Sea region. In south-central Europe, some would say in Hapsburg Europe, another pattern of linkages is emerging. New channels of interaction are beginning to link Poland with Belarus, Ukraine and Lithuania. Each of Germany's eastern neighbours is feeling its way towards a more constructive relationship with Germany, echoing west European experiences of 50 years ago. These various forms of new bilateralism and multilateralism are perhaps the most dynamic feature of cross-border engagement, with echoes at the local (cross-border) and the private levels as well. Yet many of these new groupings straddle – and are perhaps in tension with – the planned phases of NATO and EU enlargement. These risk emphasizing borders counterproductively, for example to the east of Poland, or around Hungary. Boundary issues are thus crucial in the re-configuration of Europe.

This variegated pattern reveals several different transnational Europes, serving a mixture of functional, territorial and affiliational purposes. Where functional, territorial and affiliational purposes overlap and have been combined and institutionalized we can identify a pattern of *deep* integration. Part of the cement for this derives from bilateral relationships between countries, through 'multiple bilateralism', as Rummel (1982) phrased it. Elsewhere we observe forms of shallow or partial or soft integration.

In the analysis that follows these three categories are, first, briefly explained, and, second, interpreted in the context of systemic change in post-cold-war Europe. To stylize the discussion a little these three functions can also be related to particular schools of intellectual analysis. Thus the functional dimension comprises the areas of substantive concern across the arenas of public policy and private exchange, especially economic, commercial, industrial, environmental and physical resources, and some elements of social welfare. This is the ground defined by Haas and other neofunctionalists, now also claimed by those (such as Moravcsik) who assert that the collective regimes to serve national preferences on economic issues are at the heart of west European integration. The territorial dimension comprises: issues to do with security, internal as well as external; relations with contiguous neighbours; and the management of borders, within and at the edges of the system. This is where Rokkan has made such a large contribution to our understanding. The affiliational dimension includes questions of values, ideas, identity and culture, those factors that appear to distinguish the affiliated from the non-affiliated or 'other', and which feed into the societal dimension of politics. It was on these issues that Deutsch's transactional approach sought to clarify our understanding.

It is around these three dimensions that we can plot the different patterns of transnational linkages in western Europe. Some linkages have been mainly focused on one dimension, while others have been two- or three-dimensional. What is distinctive about the inheritance of west European transnationalism is that so much has been institutionalized across all three dimensions. However, we should still recall that this three-dimensional pattern has been articulated through different institutional frameworks and by different actors.

The functional dimension

What we now know as the European Union is the prime and most extended arena for functional cooperation. It is multi-scope and with extending and now extensive scope. It reflects the limits to the functional autonomy of individual countries, as Scharpf (1997 and 1998) has so elegantly argued. It has been responsive to changing definitions of functional needs emanating from both public policy debate and shifts in the patterns of private exchanges. It is also often analysed, we should recall, in the languages of agency and of interests.

Yet, we should remember, the EU does not monopolize functional cooperation between its member countries, nor are all of the boundaries to functional cooperation coterminous with the boundaries of EU membership. An array of other functional arenas coexist with the EU: some are a consequence of geography – for example, river and marine management; others relate to industrial and technological capabilities, as in European space cooperation; others are narrowly confined to a single technical sector, as in Eurocontrol for aviation traffic management. Throughout past decades the combining European economy always spread wider than the boundaries of the EU, hence the development in the 1980s of the European Economic Area or the various association arrangements between the EU and non-member neighbours. And, of course, hence a parallel array of private linkages between economic agents, and to a lesser extent social agents, what some have called informal integration (Wallace, 1991).

In addition some functional linkages have developed much more closely within smaller groups, reflecting differences in local interchange. Between Britain and Ireland or in the Nordic region there is, for example, extensive free movement of labour, in striking contrast to most of the rest of western Europe. Similarly we should note the lack of vigorous functional linkages between some immediate neighbours, notably in the Iberian peninsula and between Greece and Turkey. In the first of these cases functional interchange seems to have been prompted by EU membership (Inotai, 1997). In the second case, functional exchanges developed over many centuries have been severely disrupted in the twentieth century.

The territorial dimension

A neglected element in the commentary on European integration is the development of so many transnational linkages in western Europe to address the local territorial concerns of individual countries. Primary among these was the concern to regulate the boundary with immediate neighbours, a key concern for Germany and its neighbours, and an overriding concern for the west European neighbours of the Soviet Union. Both NATO and the EU have served as safety nets for the peaceful management of intra-west European borders, with distinctive forms of non-alignment in central and northern Europe as a reassurance *vis-à-vis* the Soviet Union. These border security issues, at least in the past, have been as pertinent as the conventional systemic security issues. Even today there are still tensions in the Dutch–German and Danish–German relationships, which weigh in the consideration of Dutch and Danish European policies. In the Nordic region borders between countries still represent borders between differences both of policy and of political culture.

A second territorial concern was propelled by the cold war, which promoted the consolidation of the various west European frameworks to defend western Europe as a whole against the *imperium* of the Soviet Union over the countries that it dominated in central and eastern Europe. Formally the west European alliance was orchestrated by NATO and the WEU, but the need to engage West Germany at the heart of this alliance was served by the role of the then EC as a reassurance mechanism for neighbouring countries *vis-à-vis* Germany. Somewhat different arrangements operated at the interface with the USSR in the Nordic region, where defensive non-alignment complemented and provided a buffer for NATO. It was in the south-eastern corner of 'western' Europe that the synergy between NATO and the EC failed to operate. Greece and Turkey both have long been full members of NATO, but have failed to find a *modus vivendi* within the contemporary EU. The consequence has been a persistently troubled relationship between Turkey and the rest of Europe (Barchard, 1998). The decision of the Helsinki Europe Council in December 1999 to confer on Turkey candidate status *vis-à-vis* the EU may offer in due course a constructive solution.

A third contribution was provided by these territorial safety nets in western Europe. With the benefit of hindsight it has become evident that the strong articulation of the military alliance, and the management of sensitive borders that accompanied it, also served to control borders for internal security purposes. The impermeability of the cold-war boundary along the central spine of Europe was a barrier against all kinds of potentially disturbing incomers, as was the active naval presence in the Mediterranean sea. Individual west European countries could pursue distinct national policies behind this shared set of territorial barriers. These barriers made unnecessary an explicit policy about the regulation of the eastern boundaries, and enabled west Europeans to be increasingly relaxed about their internal borders (comforted also by the low levels of labour movement inside western Europe).

The affiliational dimension

Western Europe, or most of western Europe, also developed several shared focal points of social and political affiliation in the period following World War II. These had three relatively explicit and distinct components. One was the shared value set around the variants of liberal democratic political systems that developed across western Europe, an important focus of transnational reassurance, and a guide for the management of relationships with west European countries emerging from authoritarian rule, especially relevant in southern Europe. In institutional terms this was expressed most explicitly through the Council of Europe and the European Convention on Human Rights.

The value set was only implicit and barely articulated within the EC/EU. The Treaty of Rome (1957) had simply noted that 'any European state' could apply for EU membership (Article 237, EEC). The 1977 *Joint Declaration by the European Parliament, the Council and the Commission on Fundamental Rights* was a rather feeble attempt at a rhetorical statement of shared democratic values. Not until the Treaty on European Union (Article F), agreed at Maastricht in 1991, did the member governments note that their states were founded 'on the principles of democracy' and their 'respect for fundamental rights'. Only in 1997 at Amsterdam did they further clarify Article F to read that the 'Union is founded on the principles of liberty, democracy, respect for human rights and fundamental freedoms, and the rule of law'. Applicants would have to respect these principles (Article O) and existing members might *in extremis* be suspended for breaching them. What a paradox that it should have taken so long to put this into treaty form. The current debate on the proposed EU Charter of Fundamental Rights is another illustration of these tensions.

A second shared affiliation was, to put it simply, around anti-communism as an ideological rallying point. This served a dual purpose. On the one hand it allowed the partial incorporation of autocratic regimes in Portugal, Greece and Turkey within various of the west European transnational organizations, especially NATO. On the other hand, there was an implicit warning against the inclusion of communist parties inside governing coalitions in west European countries, especially relevant at various moments in relation to Greek and Italian politics.

A third shared affiliation was linked to the socio-economic compacts developed within individual west European countries in complementarity with, and a stimulus to, the political economy mode of EC integration. In the 1950s and 1960s there was an apparent synergy between these and a shared goal of socio-economic modernization, for which the EC could be argued to be a vehicle. Initially, however, the narrative was more implicit than explicit. Again a paradox – the discourse about the 'European social model' began to be articulated only in the late 1980s in parallel with the shift towards a collective neo-liberal economic stance of market liberalization in the EC (Kapteyn, 1996; Leibfried and Pierson, 1995; Scharpf, 1997; Streeck, 1997).

It can be argued that these focal points of affiliation were vaguely stated and perhaps only ambiguously understood, not least in allowing important country variations to persist under the umbrella of apparent transnational cooperation. Much more evidence remains to be collated on the discursive narratives of the early years of west European integration, a field of enquiry which is beginning to yield valuable insights into the more recent period (see, for example, Diez, forthcoming; Risse *et al.*, 1998). Nonetheless the appeal to these focal points was a distinctive feature of efforts to integrate in western Europe. It particularly sharply distinguished western Europe from that *other* Europe to the east, an *other* Europe that also drew on, and was reinforced by, a whole series of images of 'otherness' in the eastern part of the continent and its peripheral yet further east, south-east and to the south. These focal points of affiliation were important constituents of the 'permissive consensus' from which west European integration for so long benefited.

On the other hand, the ambiguities in the articulation of these shared points of affiliation provided a base for only rather soft forms of collective policy. Within western Europe the freedom of social interchange, with its many manifestations of popular and cultural transactions, gave the impression, but perhaps only the impression, of a shared social and cultural space. Its force derived much from the contrast with that other Europe, with such opposite characteristics, namely of blocked social, cultural and popular transactions between west and east, as well as among the central and east European countries.

These caveats about the ambiguous affiliational dimension notwithstanding, it seems to be the combination of the three dimensions – functional, territorial and affiliational – that has induced a form of *deep* integration in western Europe. It has led many, both commentators and practitioners, to conflate the three dimensions into a single model of integration. Yet this seems to be an over-simplification. The argument in this chapter is rather that it was the ability to develop these three dimensions through an array of different frameworks that produced in western Europe specific transnational patterns of integration.

This is not to suggest that these different frameworks have necessarily been autonomous or that the different dimensions of integration have not impacted on each other. Many of the same west European states are involved in all of the frameworks and have built relationships with each other that operate on all three dimensions. There is thus an overlay of connections, as well as the utilization of parallel frameworks for differing purposes. Moreover, one can observe a pattern of 'club' behaviour – those within the west Europe transnational process have developed club privileges for insiders, and thus forms of discrimination against those beyond. The EU is by far the most articulated version of this – a transnational organization with clear functional goals, embedded in a wider setting with territorial and affiliational dimensions, but not able fully to absorb those territorial and affiliational dimensions. NATO was another club, its membership restricted to those prepared to go to war for and with each other.

One interesting feature of the past decade has been the debate over whether the shift from EC to EU should incorporate all three dimensions to integration within a single framework. Both the so-called second (common foreign and security policy) and third (justice and home affairs) pillars touch on the territorial dimension (both external and internal) outlined above. The recent articulation in the EU of some core principles of democracy and the sketching of elements of 'European citizenship' assert the importance of the affiliational dimension. The debate in 2000 over the drafting of an EU Charter of Fundamental Rights is an interesting further component. Indeed the effort to draw the three dimensions under one framework seems to have reinforced the 'club' characteristics of the EU. Nowhere is the case for retained club privileges more vehemently asserted than in the discussion of eastern and southern enlargement. This is a conservative and conservationist feature of the EU, technically articulated in the defence of the *acquis communautaire*, as shorthand for the club rules.

Contrasting legacies in central and eastern Europe

Before 1989 it is hard to find equivalent forms of transnationalism and multilateralism in central and eastern Europe. The cross-country *functional* linkages consisted of hub-and-spoke relationships to the Soviet Union; they were not productive of neighbour-to-neighbour contacts, interdependencies or agency relationships. Moreover the then economic system removed the scope for organic linkages relating to functional transactions. The cross-country *territorial* linkages and contestations were frozen within an oppressive and armed authoritarianism. This provided little opportunity for boundaries to be reconsidered or for societal connections to change the consequences of the inherited boundary structure. The *affiliational* dimension was subsumed within the tensions of an imposed ideology. Again here we should note the absence of vectors to carry across central and eastern Europe new and converging patterns of political and societal values and attitudes. Instead alternative focal points of affiliation were mostly country-bound or ethnic community-based, or sometimes underpinned by religion.

Central and east European countries have thus had to invent transnationalism more or less from scratch, with the apparent beacon of a multilateral Europe that they might join or rejoin, and with a horribly difficult set of eastern and south-eastern boundary questions to complicate the issues across all three dimensions of function, territory and affiliation. It was so much easier for west Europeans that they had a great stretch of ocean to the West!

To summarize, in western Europe we can observe the appearance of a single system, but one that was actually constructed through a series of interlocking and over-lapping groupings and institutions. The apparent coherence of those arrangements was partly a consequence of the distinction from the other Europe, a distinction that has lost its clarity since 1989. Meanwhile in central and eastern Europe we can observe a segmented history, followed by recent attempts to define European engagement by achieving incorporation within the west European-defined transnational system. This move 'towards' western Europe is now beginning, but only beginning, to be flanked by more local patterns of linkage. There are also the tragic instances of de-linkage where (joint functions) task, territory and (affiliation) trust are all contested.

How then should we characterize deep integration? what lessons can we derive for the feasibility of a pan-European variant?

West European experience reveals a distinctive pattern of integration: multi-framework, multi-layer, multi-lateral and multi-purpose. The pattern has included a variety of shared functional regimes; it has protected both individual and collective territorial boundaries; and it has built on several different focal points of affiliation, which were reinforced by the ideological and military division of Europe. Also, there were connections (see further below) between west European integration and wider global developments.

But it was not only the complementarity of the functional, territorial and affiliational dimensions that underpinned this deep integration. It was also nurtured by the particular pattern of institutionalization that was established, especially the dense institutional fabric of the EU. Within and through the EU institutions a variety of political, economic and even some societal actors were able to mobilize, to bargain, and to consolidate both prevailing ideas and specific interests (Jachtenfuchs and Kohler-Koch, 1996). European law emerged as a powerful instrument of discipline to induce persistent cooperation and to turn diffuse and diverse shared commitments into concrete rules of behaviour (Burley and Mattli, 1993). The EU arena proved especially apposite and useful as a way of mediating some west European relationships with the rest of the world, including with that other Europe to the east. And the EU arena also proved especially valuable as a framework for mediating relationships between EU countries. This EU arena was buttressed by an array of other institutionalized and especially elite-level connections. This amalgam of institutionalized engagements is now widely characterized as a special process of European governance (Armstrong and Bulmer, 1998; Kohler-Koch and Eising, 1999).

The way that the EU and its governance model developed had a number of important consequences for transnational linkages in western Europe. First, the EU provided a rather open opportunity structure for a variety of political, economic and societal actors to become engaged and to develop transnational connections. Societal linkages, however, were weakly developed, their sketchiness masked for a long time by the focal points of broader affiliation in western Europe. The EU's open opportunity structure particularly encouraged clientelistic and agency relationships, and ones that were more segmented in pursuit of particular shared functions than aggregating across functions (Wallace and Young, 1997). The relationships have been cognitive rather than affective in character.

Second, the EU did not need to be all-encompassing, since other west European frameworks and some of the smaller groupings of countries dealt with some of the other sensitive issues. Hence the curious dialectics of common foreign and security or defence policies in western Europe have, until recently, been spread across different frameworks of cooperation. These have included not only the obvious and publicly visible organizations (NATO, WEU and so on), but several more restricted and less public groupings. Both bilateral (notably Franco–German) and multilateral groupings have played a part, and there has been a kind of deliberate organizational redundancy, which has permitted choices among different frameworks.

Third, though wide-ranging in its scope, the EU has left protected domestic political spaces in which national actors could pursue different country-level trajectories. Latterly Ireland and the Netherlands have been positive examples of the differentiated use of this protected domestic space, while Greece is the frequently quoted negative illustration. To be sure where the line should be drawn between the country and the European arenas has been a recurrent subject of debate, but that different spaces should coexist has not as such been much contested. Within the jargon of the EU discussion about which level of governance is appropriate is channelled into the discussion of 'subsidiarity'. The academic literature contains competing accounts, some (such as Moravcsik, 1998) arguing that individual states are still able to exercise strategic choices about when to delegate to the EU, others suggesting that the state has lost capabilities without the EU acquiring comparable powers (Scharpf, 1997; Streeck, 1997), and yet others (Wessels, 1997) asserting that national systems have started to fuse at the transnational level.

Fourth, time scales and time perspectives have been important in conditioning attitudes about previous experiences and possible future behaviour. One part of the success of the EC in the early years was in establishing itself as a transformation-inducing framework for its participants. Another part of its success has been in structuring expectations about future cooperation, thus increasing the incentives for sustained engagement. Here too there are competing explanations in the literature, ranging between the more strategic manipulation of commitments (Moravcsik, 1998) and the development of a form of collective identity (Risse *et al.*, 1998; Sedelmeier, 1998).

Fifth, but much more contentious, has been the persistence of ambitions on the part of some to turn the EU into a form of polity. This ambition has led its proponents and apologists to seek to ratchet up the content of EU cooperation and its institutional features. Thus the extension from market integration to monetary integration signals an effort to endow the EU with more state-like features *vis-à-vis* the economy. The attempt to make the EU a security and defence arena implies taking on some of the territorial concerns hitherto addressed through the parallel NATO framework. Efforts to develop an EU capacity to address issues of justice and home affairs – and thus the internal security agenda – also suggest that the EU might become the focus for addressing much more explicitly some of the other territorial and boundary management concerns of its members. The discourse of polity-building implies that the EU itself could or should attract the transnational political and social affiliations hitherto more dispersed across different European arenas of cooperation (see, for example, Shaw, 1997; Wiener, 1998). This polity project presumes affective as well as cognitive loyalty on the part of its members, cognitive loyalty perhaps being sufficient to underpin shared governance.

Moreover by definition a polity-in-the-making becomes harder for others to join. Club privileges and club identity would logically have to be further reinforced; as Bartolini (1998) argues, the issues of exclusion and closure need much more thorough analysis. It is not so much that deep integration is incompatible with wide integration – the conventional argument – but that the concentration of all of the main dimensions of integration within a single EU framework reinforces the gulf between participants and non-participants *and* makes it harder to tolerate varying degrees of involvement. To make this leap towards a polity would indeed be to give the EU a quality quite different from other European frameworks and to presuppose that a more self-sufficient EU was no longer dependent on the coexistence and complementarity of other forms of transnational cooperation. Yet there is a historical paradox here, in so far as the deep integration experiment drew so much from territorial and affiliational elements built out of the division of Europe.

Thus we have two related and subversive issues before us. One is whether the deep integration model of western Europe can be sustained in western Europe, let alone transformed into a polity, in our much altered historical conditions. And the second is whether central and eastern Europe (or some of the CEECs) can be envisaged as sufficiently linked on the three dimensions of integration to make deep integration in pan-Europe seem feasible and be made operational through strong shared institutions. Both issues beg a further question about the disjunction in stages of development between western and eastern Europe. It is a demanding challenge to create a continent-wide process of integration across countries with contextually and temporally quite different sequences of political, economic and social development.

How then should we construe the domestication of Europe within the politics of individual countries?

It is self-evident that we cannot answer either the west European question or the pan-European question without more closely examining the way in which European integration plays into and emanates from the politics of individual west European countries. But the academic literature gives us inadequate handles on which to grasp. Let me target three deficiencies in the literature.

One is the overdrawn debate between those who see the European frameworks as essentially subordinate instruments for manipulation by national politicians and those who argue that European integration is the evidence of the lost autonomy of countries – intergovernmentalism versus fusion. My own preference is to navigate between these two camps rather to join either. To be sure, if countries had full autonomy and capability, European integration would be redundant. On the other hand if national politics were irrelevant European integration would not be so contested a process. A more satisfactory analysis must surely lie in a better understanding of the push–pull between the European and country levels of politics and governance.

A second deficiency in the literature lies in the absence of cross-country comparisons of the range of European connections and relationships that are pertinent to domestic politics. We can find comparisons of EU policies country by country, though not very many. We can find cross-country comparisons of foreign and defence policies, though again not very many. We can find cross-country comparisons in the patterns of ideological and political values and attitudes, but generally with slight references only to the European context. Studies of individual countries generally fail to address all the dimensions of European linkage that seep into national politics. Thus in my terms few national studies pay simultaneous attention to the transnational dimensions of function, territory and affiliation.

A third problem stems from the literature about globalization with its strong presumption that globalization erodes the political, economic and social options and opportunities available in national politics. We need to develop our understanding about how pressures of globalization are factored into national politics and how they interact with the different ways of construing Europeanization. Here, incidentally, we should also note the emerging fashion to conflate globalization and Europeanization, with Europeanization seen by many as essentially a medium of globalization rather than a differentiated phenomenon. There is a danger of misleading reductionism here.

Let me then attack my question about the domestication of Europe a different way. My earlier argument was that west European integration was composited from three dimensions of transnational linkage addressing questions of function, territory and affiliation. It follows that we should look for markers in domestic politics that relate to all three dimensions. Thus we might expect to find different patterns of European connection depending on how participants in a national polity have viewed the utility and pertinence of the European arena to each dimension and the relevant country-level preoccupations and predicaments. I also argued earlier that European integration was built out of a series of differentiated country groupings, which we should similarly expect to see resonate in country-level politics. Moreover I also indicated that, European linkages notwithstanding, there were protected and persistent domestic political spaces, within which we might expect to see differences between countries. Thus, for example, we might also expect to find more synergy between country and European levels for some countries and more tensions for others. I also suggested that there were differences between core and peripheral countries in terms of the intensity of their engagement in the different dimensions of integration. Hence we should expect to find significant differences in the way the symbols and substance of European integration are appropriated in domestic political discourse and in domestic political practice (a point made strongly by Risse *et al.* 1998), but which, as they indicate, needs further empirical and analytical investigation). In addition we should expect to observe variations between countries in the patterns of domestic preference formation on European issues and differences in the way in which agents from individual countries engage in the transnational institutional processes.

To cut a much longer story short, this is precisely what we can observe in ranging across the 15 member countries of the EU, the different membership of NATO, and the few countries that are currently in neither of these circles, although connected to several of the functional regimes or involved in other sub-continental groupings.

Essentially what we can observe is that in those west European countries for which the functional, territorial and affiliational linkages are densely correlated we can identify a three-dimensional and thus wide-ranging European engagement. Germany seems historically to be the clearest example of this, as Moravcsik (1998) hints, but does not spell out. In these countries the European context frames very many of the choices in domestic politics and on the whole issue-by-issue the debate is about *how* to utilize the European arena. In contrast in those west European countries where the linkages are strong on only one or two of my dimensions the political debate is about *when and whether* to utilize the European arena – not only about *how* to use it. A three dimensional engagement also generates more intensive elite interactions, which then become mutually reinforcing. Thus domestic preferences are more extensively conditioned by the interaction, the opportunities are greater to collude across country boundaries, and the voices from such countries are more influentially articulated in the European arena.

Here evidently the transnational institutionalization of western Europe has also made a difference to relative position and relative influence. It is with this in mind that we should appraise the scope for politicians from an individual country to situate themselves 'at the heart of Europe'. Domestic contestation of European engagements seems to reflect the weaker array of active transnational linkages.

One manifestation of this seems to be that for the countries that are outliers in the west European process of integration, the politically peripheral, there is a striking difference between incumbent politicians and opposition politicians. Incumbents for their period in office tend to become locked into the European arena (though the British provide inconsistent evidence), while opposition politicians reveal the weaker elite interactions imposed by an EU institutional system that privileges incumbents.

But we should add a couple of codicils here. One is that political peripherality and geographical peripherality do not necessarily coincide. Ireland and Finland both seem to exemplify strong utilization of the west European arena and a symbiosis between domestic and European opportunities, interestingly in both cases resolving territorial tensions with neighbours through a form of military neutrality. There is a longer story here in relation to Finland about the interdependence between its neutrality and the NATO alliance. A second codicil picks up the point about different qualities of voice within the west European institutions. For some west European countries there has been a closer *fit* or *congruence* than for other countries between collective west European regimes and prior national regimes or preferences. The political ability to exercise influence on, and structure, the negotiated collective outcomes helps to reinforce attachment to the European arena. One interesting footnote here – French governments are rarely no-sayers on EU Council decisions agreed by majority votes (Hayes-Renshaw and Wallace, 1997). There is much scope here for nuanced cross-country comparisons.

By way of interim conclusion

If we then look at both western Europe and central and eastern Europe we can see two contrasting patterns. Western Europe has a legacy of multiple, but overlapping and mutually reinforcing, European arenas. Plans are under discussion in effect to try to combine the arenas and, in particular, to make the EU the predominant arena, though this is a contested process, while several countries remain outliers. Meanwhile, there is also a new discussion about how to redefine the role of NATO and how to strengthen European defence autonomy in relation to NATO. In central and eastern Europe we can see emerging a scattering of different patterns of linkage; these are not combined and they are not clearly mutually reinforcing – or not yet. Indeed there is some contradiction between efforts to strengthen linkages with western Europe, while also encouraging firmer links within the region.

What then of the development of linkages across the continent more broadly? Here too we can see uneven patterns, with '*dysergies*' (to coin a word) as much as *synergies*. Let me summarize across the three dimensions of function, territory and affiliation.

Function

We can see several different kinds of functional linkage emerging – those promoted by and in relation to the EU, those emerging around groups of neighbours, and those stimulated by private actors. Of these the functional linkages around the EU seem by far the most potent, with many applicants for full EU membership and the EU endeavouring to divide (differentiate is the practitioners' more ambiguous term) central and east European countries into categories of accession, association and more distant partnership. Partnership in this context is the practitioners' euphemism. At the private level we can begin to see elements of organic linkages in the form of production and investment networks and we can observe that these are especially vigorous on the part of economic actors from particular west European countries: Germany, Austria, Finland and Italy.

Territory

The picture as regards territorial linkages is seriously confused. The decision to admit only three countries from central and eastern Europe to NATO – the Czech Republic, Hungary and Poland – leaves more questions open than it resolves about the emerging security system in Europe. Meanwhile the new territorial debate in western Europe is about the reinforcement of Schengen and the promotion within the EU of an 'area of justice, freedom and security' (to use the language from Amsterdam). This debate is, one can argue, a more or less direct consequence of the erosion of the old east–west border. It is already being played out as a constraint on the way that the central and east European countries deal with each other and on the scope for informal linkages to develop. Hence the recent difficulties between Poland and Belarus. This whole Schengen-plus discussion is perhaps the best example of how the territorial issues in pan-Europe are now being problematized. West Europeans should be very prudent here given their dismal record over the past century in establishing borders in those distant parts of central and eastern and especially south-eastern Europe which were poorly understood. Nonetheless it will be interesting to see how the groupings between neighbours develop to regulate contiguous borders – the policies and practices of Poland, Germany and Hungary will, for example, be especially interesting to watch.

Affiliation

It remains hard to discern the focal points of affiliation in pan-Europe and thus the scope for relevant linkages. Problems of state-building and post-communist adaptation are tough assignments for the countries in central and eastern Europe. Too much of the west European effort has been put into crude exports of fragments of a presumed west European model, much of this articulated around the statements of club membership rules by the EU. Similarly as regards the development of socio-economic patterns in the central and east European countries, west Europeans have been keen to export muddled preferences and off-the-peg arrangements. Their fit with the circumstances country-by-country is less clear. The need there too for a protected domestic space for experimentation and choice is surely important, otherwise the scope for constructive synergy between national and European arenas will be too cramped in central and eastern Europe. In the absence of synergy we might find the discourse of Europeanization becoming an obstacle, rather than a stimulus to transnationalism, let alone a support for modernization.

Institutions

We need to remind the practitioners of the importance of both formal and informal institution-building as instruments of integration. There is too much of the hub-and-spoke pattern in the current arrangements; too little opportunity for political and economic elites from central and eastern Europe to act as vectors of integration; too many limitations on the opportunity for central and east Europeans to speak with effective voices from which loyalties can be encouraged; and not much scope yet for the development of the rudiments of a shared social and cultural space.

I have argued in relation to west European integration that its simultaneous evolution on several different dimensions allowed scope for constructive ambiguities, for experimentation, and for differentiated dynamics. The process depended on a variety of building blocks, and changes over time allowed for creative engineering as well as organic linkages. It may be impatient and unrealistic to expect west European policy-makers to devise a comprehensive and coherent strategy in relation to central and eastern Europe. The logic of the argument in this chapter is to call for multiple arenas and opportunities for constructing linkages. What clearly does not make sense is to have the debate dominated by functional linkages, obstructed by new territorial segmentation, and weakly underpinned by shared focal points of affiliation.

The chapters that follow in this volume address a variety of the issues raised in this introductory chapter. Most are written by scholars who have been associated in one way or another with the development of the ESRC 'One Europe or Several?' programme. Some chapters throw down gauntlets by indicating challenges that need to be met, if pan-European integration is to be feasible and if the agenda of integration is to be renewed in the context of post-cold-war Europe. Other chapters present interim findings from some of projects funded under the 'One Europe or Several?' programme. The deliberately eclectic range of contributions reflects a judgement that we need to stretch our understandings to encompass the different dimensions of integration. Only then will we have a chance of grasping the nature of Europeanization.

Notes

1. The term 'pan-Europe' is used to connote the whole continent, irrespective of where its eastern boundary might be drawn. This reflects irritation at the way west Europeans appropriate the term 'Europe' to refer to their part of the continent, as well as at the frequent elision of Europe with the European Union.
2. Haas' account of west European integration was disturbed by his own observations about General de Gaulle (Haas, 1975), just as many British observers have been much preoccupied with the impact of Mrs Thatcher.
3. Norway, Iceland and Turkey inside NATO, outside the EU; Cyprus, Malta and Switzerland outside both; Austria, Ireland, Finland and Sweden inside the EU, but outside NATO.

References

Armstrong, K. and Bulmer, S. (1998) *The Governance of the European Single Market* (Manchester: Manchester University Press).
Barchard, D. (1998) *Turkey and the European Union* (London: Centre for European Reform).
Bartolini, S. (1998) *Exit Options, Boundary Building and Political Structuring* (Florence: European University Institute, Working Papers, SPS No 98/1).
Burley, A.-M. and Mattli. W. (1993) 'Europe before the Court: A Political Theory of Legal Integration', *International Organization*, 47 (1), 41–76.
Delors, J. (1992) *Le Nouveau Concert Européen* (Paris: Éditions Odile Jacob).
Deutsch, K. W. et al. (1957) *Political Community and the North Atlantic Area: International Organisations in the Light of Historical Experience* (Princeton: Princeton University Press).
Diez, T. (1999) *Die EU lesen: Diskursive Knotenpunkte in der Britischen Europadebatte.* (Opladen: Leske and Budrich)
Fischer, J. (2000) 'From Confederacy to Federation – Thoughts on the Finality of European Integration', speech at the Humboldt University, Berlin, 12 May.
Haas, E. B. (1968) *The Uniting of Europe: Politcal, Social and Economic Forces, 1950–1957* (Stanford: Stanford University Press).
Haas, E. B. (1975) *The Obsolescence of Regional Integration Theory* (University of California, Berkeley, Institute of International Studies).
Hayes-Renshaw, Fiona and Wallace, Helen (1997) *The Council of Ministers of the European Union* (London: Macmillan – now Palgrave)
Inotai, A. (1997) *Correlations between European Integration and Sub-regional Cooperation: Theoretical Background, Experience and Policy Impacts* (Budapest: Hungarian Academy of Sciences, Institute for World Economics, Working Paper No 84).
Jachtenfuchs, M. and Kohler-Koch, B. (1996) *Europäische Integration* (Opladen: Leske and Budrich).
Kapteyn, P. (1996) *The Stateless Market: The European Dilemma of Integration and Civilisation* (London: Routledge).

Kohler-Koch, B. and Eising, R. (eds) (1999) *The Transformation of Governance in the European Union* (London: Routledge).
Leibfried, S. and Pierson, P. (eds) (1995) *European Social Policy: Between Fragmentation and Integration* (Washington, DC: Brookings Institution).
Lindberg, L. N. (1963) *The Political Dynamics of European Economic Integration* (Stanford: Stanford University Press).
Moravcsik, A. (1998) *The Choice for Europe: Social Purpose and State Power from Messina to Maastricht* (Ithaca, NY: Cornell University Press).
Risse, T. *et al.* (1998) *To Euro or not to Euro? The EMU and Identity Politics in the European Union* (Florence: European University Institute Working Papers, RSC No 98/9).
Rokkan, S. (1975) 'Dimensions of State Formation and Nation-Building: a Possible Paradigm for Research on Variations within Europe', in Tilly, C. (ed.), *The Formation of National States in Europe* (Princeton: Princeton University Press).
Rummel, R. (1982) *Zusammengesetze Aussenpolitik* (Kehl am Rhein: N. P. Engel Verlag).
Scharpf, F. W. (1997) *Balancing Positive and Negative Integration: the Regulatory Options for Europe* (Florence: European University Institute, Policy Paper 97/4).
Scharpf, F. W. (1998) *Games Real Actors Play: Actor-Centred Institutionalism in Policy Research* (Boulder, CO: Westview Press).
Sedelmeier, U. (1998) *The European Union's Association Policy towards the Countries of Central and Eastern Europe: Policy Paradigms and Collective Identities in a Composite Policy* (Brighton: University of Sussex, Doctoral dissertation, mimeo).
Shaw, J. (1997) *Citizenship of the Union: Towards Postnational Membership?* (The Hague: Kluwer).
Streeck, W. (1997) 'German Capitalism. Does it Exist? Can it Survive?', *New Political Economy*, 2, 237–56.
Wallace, H. and Young, A. R. (eds) (1997) *Participation and Policy-Making in the European Union* (Oxford: Clarendon Press).
Wallace, W. (1991) 'Introduction: the Dynamics of European Integration', in Wallace, W. (ed), *The Dynamics of European Integration* (London: Pinter), 1–26.
Wessels, W. (1997) 'An Ever-Closer Fusion? A Dynamic Macropolitical View on Integration Processes', *Journal of Common Market Studies*, 35 (1), 267–99.
Wiener, A. (1998) *European; Citizenship Practice – Building Institutions of a Non-State* (Boulder, CO: Westview).

NB Extracts from cited works by Deutsch, Haas and Lindberg are helpfully reprinted in Nelson, B. F. and Stubb, A. C-G. (1998) *The European Union: Readings on the Theory and Practice of European Integration* (Boulder, CO: Lynne Rienner).

Part I
The Functional Dimension

2
European Union Trade Policy: Actually or Just Nominally Liberal?

L. Alan Winters[1]

Introduction

This chapter surveys the current state of European Union (EU) international trade policy and asks where it is going. Embedded in the latter is also a view about where it should go. By the standards of most countries, EU trade policy is pretty open, but it is not as open as is frequently thought. Moreover, EU institutions for making trade policy and the use of trade policy for tasks other than simply fostering economic welfare raise a doubt about whether, despite its liberal rhetoric, the EU will actually be able fundamentally to open trade.

The nominal liberalism of EU trade policy is easy to establish: tariffs are very low on imports of the majority of goods and there are few non-tariff barriers; the EU made one of the largest liberalizations of services in the Uruguay Round; the EU offers preferential access (that is, reduced tariffs) to all but ten of its trading partners; and the EU has relatively transparent and wholly law-based administrative procedures for trade. The other side of the coin is that agriculture is still hugely protected; traditional manufactures also have relatively high tariffs of 10 to 20 per cent; many services are subject to tight regulation which seriously handicaps foreign competitors; anti-dumping action allows 'surgical strikes' against competitive exporters; preferential trade agreements can shift trade in 'anti-liberal' directions – that is, towards inefficient suppliers; and most of the EU's trade agreements are selective, avoiding liberalization in precisely the sectors where it is most needed.

This is, of course, a half-full versus half-empty question, and in no way do I intend to denigrate the progress in European integration, still less to be 'anti-European' by pointing out what further remains to be done. Genuine trade liberalization is a politically difficult task, especially for a body lacking the cement of nationhood, but it is also an important one. It underpinned much of the prosperity of the old century and has much to offer in the new. I see my comments as an encouragement for those policy-makers who wish to take up that offer.

The chapter has four parts. 'Making trade policy' considers the EU's institutions for taking trade decisions; 'Most Favoured Nation trade policy' considers 'normal' – that is, non-preferential – trade policy; 'Preferential trade policy' reviews the Generalized System of Preferences (GSP), the EU's many reciprocal trade agreements and relations with the African, Caribbean and Pacific (ACP) countries; finally, there is a brief conclusion.

Making trade policy

At face value the nature of EU trade policy is quite straightforward. The Maastricht Treaty on European Union defines 'an open market economy' (Article 3a) as a principle, while Article 110 of the Treaty of Rome aims at 'the harmonious development of world trade, the progressive abolition of restrictions on international trade and the lowering of customs barriers'. However, these objectives are not expressed in operational terms, are not subject to transparent review, are not located unambiguously in the hierarchy of EU institutions and are not viewed as binding by the European Court of Justice (Pelkmans, 1997). Thus, while they are useful aspirations, they have rather little bite in defining the actual direction of current EU trade policy.[2]

On the ground, EU trade policy is influenced by a number of opposing forces. First, although the case that openness is generally beneficial for the economy is widely accepted, member states differ in the extent to which they believe that general exceptions are justified. This might be crudely caricatured, perhaps, by the contrast between the Gallic instinct towards interventionism and the Anglo-Saxon one towards *laissez-faire*. Moreover, every member state seeks exceptions for particular favoured sectors.

Second, the treaties governing the Union are implicitly strongly 'statist' (Messerlin, forthcoming). This is not surprising of Paris (1951) and Rome (1956), for they spring from a statist era, but even Maastricht prescribes active government almost everywhere. It introduces nine new areas of direct relevance to international trade, of which, according to Messerlin, none is couched in unambiguously market-oriented terms.

Third, the procedures and conventions for making trade policy are essentially consensual. This certainly helps to preserve the status quo, which in most cases is more restricted than reforms would imply. In Winters (1994), however, I argue that it also imparts a positively protectionist bias whereby, according to theories of universalism (for example, Shepsle and Weingast, 1981), packages tend to emerge that allow each participant (member state) to gain Union support for its favoured sectors. Bilal (1998) notes that in 1995, 92 out of 94 common trade policy decisions in the Council were unanimous. Given that trade policy is almost always redistributive within the Union (typically from consumers/users to producers, where different member states house these groups in different proportions) such unanimity clearly demonstrates something other than simple case-by-case voting.

Fourth, the division of competences between member states and the Commission complicates policy formation. During the 1980s the tussle over who actually controlled non-tariff barriers to imports certainly led to some barriers being imposed community-wide against the interests of many members, for example footwear restrictions on Korea and Taiwan (Winters, 1992). It is difficult for the political centre to claim control of policy instruments merely to prevent their use, so it seems likely that this tussle increased the tendency towards protection over that period. Similarly one of the attractions of using anti-dumping duties to head off members' protectionist desires was that it was substantially a Commission competence. A similar tussle may be in store over elements of services trade, for the decision by the European Court of Justice (ECJ) on competence (Opinion 1/94) in these areas was very indefinite (Johnson, 1998).[3]

A further complexity is that the Commission's aspiration to have a foreign policy is unmatched by its stock of instruments. Trade policy has, for many years, been its main foreign policy tool, and as a result receives more fine tuning than it otherwise would. Much trade-based foreign policy takes the form of trade preferences (for example, free trade agreements – FTAs); however, these are not necessarily desirable economically (see below) and one needs some basic trade restrictions if one is to exempt one's friends from them. Developmental objectives affect trade policy in a similar fashion. Of course, the EU is not unique in using trade diplomacy, and, if they controlled it, member states would also resort to it. But the larger menu of options open to sovereign states means that trade needs to bear less of the diplomatic burden.

A fifth, related, possibility is that trade policy plays a role in settling internal distributive questions – that is, losers in debates on internal policies might be compensated by a 'free kick' on the trade field. Of course, this might promote liberalization. However, for three related reasons, I suspect the opposite. First, governments are sensitive to adjustment costs; second, 'losing' governments are probably already facing more adjustment than they wish from the internal decision; third, the political returns to slowing down the decline of a sector are concrete and readily identifiable (you know who in your country benefits), while those of a liberalization are frequently not (you often do not know which sectors will expand, and even when you do, you cannot be certain that the expansion will benefit your nationals). It is an interesting topic for another paper whether enlargement will change these trade-offs.

Sixth, international factors influence trade policy. Obligations under the World Trade Organization (WTO) constrain options, sometimes in very uncomfortable ways, and, indeed, a major decision for the EU is how far it can live with this. The WTO also offers opportunities for trade liberalization in Rounds or sectoral negotiations, most dramatically, perhaps, by supporting European advocates of agricultural reform over the early 1990s. Perhaps because of its decision-making apparatus, the EU has not been good at exploiting these opportunities (Messerlin, forthcoming). The EU did press hard for the initiation of the so-called Millennium Round in Seattle, December 1999. Possibly this was only for the tactical reason of trying to shift the spotlight from agriculture in which negotiations were bound to start in 2000, but it may also reflect a greater willingness on the part of the world's largest trading entity to give leadership to the world trading system. If so, the opportunity could well enhance both European policy and bolster the WTO-system in an important fashion, now that the latter's traditional champion – the USA – has become so ambivalent.

From all this it should be clear that there is no simple determinism in the EU's future trade policy. Much will depend on the philosophy and vision that governs policy making. This chapter argues that the correct framework is the genuinely liberal one, in which the use of markets is the default, moderated only infrequently and cautiously when intervention can be shown to be desirable.[4] It is not clear, however, that this is what will actually happen.

'Most-favoured nation' trade policy

Since only nine out of about 180 customs entities in the world face most-favoured nation (mfn) tariffs in Europe (Sapir, 1998, updated by author), all the rest except one getting better treatment, one might be forgiven for thinking mfn is irrelevant.[5] That would be wrong, for these nine countries account for about 40 per cent of EU imports of goods. More importantly, mfn policy also defines the bench-mark against which other regimes are measured, and once we extend our view beyond tariffs and beyond goods, far more partners face the 'standard' package of measures.

The black-spot in mfn protection in the EU is agriculture, where high tariffs are a necessary prop for the common agricultural policy (CAP). Even after the transition period of the Uruguay Round agricultural tariffs will average about 16 per cent (Finger *et al.*, 1996).[6] This includes many low tariffs – for example, on tropical beverages – so that for temperate goods the average is much higher, including peaks of 82 per cent for wheat, 152 per cent for sugar and 178 per cent for dairy (Ingco, 1996). Agricultural protection imposes huge costs in several dimensions. It strains the EU budget, it complicates the accession of eastern partners, it taxes consumers and reduces real wages, and it sours international trading relations. As the debate at Seattle shows, while the EU remains defensive about agriculture, it is unlikely to achieve any of its other objectives in multilateral fora.[7] Even bilateral relations suffer from the agricultural virus as the difficulties of reaching trade agreements with, say the Republic of South Africa and Mercosur demonstrate. It is true that the South African agreement most nearly foundered on processed agricultural goods (beverages such as sherry and grappa), but it is precisely because of the huge protection further back in the production chain that these EU producers feel they require and are entitled to demand protection.

The combined pressure from all these problems seems likely to reduce agricultural protection in future. But if it is resisted at every step, agricultural reform could debilitate many other areas of policy. It would be far better – if not far easier for current politicians – to grasp the nettle sooner rather than later, pay such compensation as is necessary and get on with life in the post-agrarian, not to mention the post-industrial, era.

It is important not to confuse the CAP with the issue of standards in agricultural trade. Recent concerns over hormones in beef imports and genetically modified organisms (GMOs) are formally quite separate, and resolving them represents one of the major issues for the trading system over the next decade.[8] European resistance to imports of these goods lies in fears about their safety. These fears have not been scientifically substantiated, but given the long time scales over which problems could arise there is clearly some residual danger. The USA, in particular, has been prepared to bear these risks, Europe not. If the difference resides in different estimates of the risk, it may ultimately be resolvable through scientific work, discussion and arbitration. This is the interpretation of the problem implicit in the relevant WTO Agreements (on Sanitary and Phytosanitary Measures, and relatedly, on Technical Barriers to Trade), which call for scientific risk assessments (albeit with a very catholic definition of science).

An alternative view, however, is that there might be perfect agreement about the odds but different attitudes towards risk. This would reflect differences in utility functions – what people desire – respect for which is one of economists' fundamental precepts.[9] Where the risk involved was in consumption/use such a view would justify restrictions on imported goods so long as equal restrictions applied to domestic production. Where the risk was only in production – for example, a pollutant – on the other hand, this view would encourage international trade. If Americans are happy to risk the wild-life consequences of GMOs, Europe should be pleased to import those products in order to preserve their own wild-life from any possible dangers, at least in the absence of spillovers via concerns about biodiversity or transcontinental migration of species.

The correct degree of intrusiveness of international bodies into domestic regulation will become an ever more pressing question as disputes pile up in the WTO, and it is quite likely that it will have to be re-opened at some stage (Rollo and Winters, 2000). The European position is not untenable, it seems to me, but it is certainly confounded and obscured by the protectionist baggage it carries. Slashing agricultural protection would greatly strengthen the European hand on risk issues, which ultimately is a far larger issue.

Manufacturing generally has much less protection than agriculture in the EU, but there are nonetheless, several peaks. As Messerlin (forthcoming) observes, in addition to high mfn tariffs in areas such as footwear, leather, textiles and clothing, anti-dumping duties allow 'surgical strikes' against excessively competitive imports. Thus, according to Messerlin, fertilizers, VCRs, integrated circuits, photocopiers and clothing all have total rates of protection exceeding 30 per cent.[10] Once one allows for these peaks, the EU tariff structure imposes significant costs in manufacturing, preserving many sectors that should ultimately be allowed to decline.[11] Being explicit that such sectors must evolve, by time-limiting their protection, would be a great advantage. As with agriculture, if such declines impose great hardship on certain individuals it would be better to pay the necessary compensation than postpone adjustment indefinitely. The difficulty is that by a conspiracy of mutual non-interference in national trade policy objectives (universalism), each member government respects other members' support for their producers, even at the expense of its own consumers. Thus it is difficult to address these issues politically.

The EU has led the world in liberalizing internal services trade, and it has also been quite enthusiastic multilaterally. There is a huge distance to go in the latter dimension, however, and, because issues of domestic regulation are involved, progress is extremely slow even when there is a will for liberalization. In fact, however, in many cases, and for many different reasons, the will is lacking – for example, in film-making, where French and British firms are supported; air transport, where attempts to develop a European position have discouraged members states' liberalizations; and professional qualifications. While governments (at Community and national levels) clearly have fiduciary responsibilities in many services areas, many restrictions are clearly protectionist in nature. Subject to meeting fiduciary requirements, there are gains from trade in services just as in goods. The EU would benefit from its own liberalization as a service user, and if, via the WTO, it were to induce others to liberalize services it would gain exports as well. It may also reap a first-mover advantage (or reduce the USA's advantage) in terms of investment flows and/or technical advance.

A difficulty in liberalizing services (as in certain goods – agriculture, coal, steel) is that sectoral ministries and the Commission's specialized Directorates-General (DGs) are involved. Created to regulate and, frequently, promote their sectors, these bodies tend to have limited international horizons and to assess what they do see in mercantilist terms ('exports good, imports bad'). This, plus the fact that their narrow briefs discourage cross-sectoral trade-offs, generally makes them poor liberalizers. What is required, therefore, is a broad and political commitment at the highest level. Just as the single market emerged from the dispair of failing to grow out of the early 1980s recessions, so comparison between the dynamism of the service-driven US economy and European sedantry could fuel a future initiative in this field.

Preferential trade policy

As noted above, nearly all the EU's trading partners receive preferential tariff treatment, but this is far from implying that the EU effectively has free trade, or indeed, liberal trade. Slightly over a quarter of imports of goods come from countries that benefit from the Generalized System of Preferences (GSP), about a quarter from countries with reciprocal trading agreements (RTAs) with the EU (including South Africa and Mexico), and about seven per cent from countries with non-reciprocal trade agreements (in the Mediterranean and the ACP group) (Sapir, 1998, updated by the author).

The Generalized System of Preferences (GSP)

The GSP is a series of schemes operated by all developed countries to give trade preferences to developing countries. Provided that they do not discriminate between developing countries, these preferences are legal under the 'Enabling Clause' of the GATT, dated 1979. For products supplied just by developing countries, zero tariffs under the GSP could effectively provide a regime of free trade, but, in fact, its liberalizing effects are rather small. For the same reasons – which I discuss shortly – its value to the developing country recipients is also rather small. Hence, while it is presented as a major component of development policy, it is in fact very much less.[12]

Why does GSP count for so little? First, the amount of preference (that is, the reduction in the tariff) is graduated from 100 per cent to 0 per cent of the mfn tariff according to the 'sensitivity' of the products – that is, how much protection the EU feels it needs. Since mfn tariffs are also so graduated by sensitivity, developing countries typically receive proportionately little relief from high tariffs and much from low ones. In the latter cases mfn tariffs are so low that it is hardly worth doing the paper work necessary to avoid them. Second, very sensitive products – agriculture – are excluded altogether. Third, trade can be constrained by safeguards or anti-dumping action if imports grow 'too' large. Fourth, rules of origin impose both an administrative burden on exporters and exclude many developing country products from preferences because they are insufficiently processed in the exporting country. Fifth, uncertainty over rules of origin, product standards and other import regulations discourages developing country exporters. Sapir (1998) estimates (exact official figures are, unforgivably, unavailable) that 36 per cent of EU imports from GSP-eligible countries are in categories with zero mfn tariffs, and that of the remaining 64 per cent, only 24 per cent claim and qualify for preferences. Finally, it is worth observing that the complexities of preference regimes create rents in developing countries, which can be a ripe source of corruption.

Possibly more pernicious than these technical issues is the fact that GSP is a so-called autonomous concession, unilaterally withdrawable or modifiable at any time by the EU. Even setting aside such draconian measures, the GSP requires that countries providing one-quarter or more of the EU's imports of a 'four-digit' heading be 'graduated' out of receiving preferences.[13]

With so little assurance of access, the GSP provides a limited basis for investment in using and producing industries. Moreover, it has now acquired provision for deeper preferences where recipients meet EU-defined social and environmental conditions. These are currently not very demanding, but their potential for allowing EU influence on 'non-trade' issues is clear. Overall, for those EU producers whose goods compete with developing countries' exports, these technical and political conditions mean that the additional competitive pressure they experience through the GSP is minimal.

In Seattle, the EU suggested that the GSP be extended and legally bound at the WTO to guarantee duty-free and quota-free access for all least-developed countries' exports. This would remove many of the problems above, especially if importers also agreed to forego anti-dumping duties as well. It hardly represented a liberalization for the EU, however, first, since the USA (perfectly predictably) rejected the proposal, nothing happened; second, the less-developed countries (LDCs) are so small economically (with the possible exception of Bangladesh) that the measure would hardly affect EU supplies; and third, the LDCs produce almost nothing that is directly competitive with EU products, so the burden of the additional LDC sales would fall almost exclusively on the exports of countries whose incomes fell just outside the 'least developed' limits.

Preferences are great public relations, but they are not a great tool for development. If the EU is serious about helping developing countries and stimulating its own economy, it should guarantee access under the GSP – including freedom from anti-dumping duties and other contingent barriers – and then gradually reduce GSP tariff rates to zero (over, say, a 15 year period). It should simultaneously reduce mfn rates on products of interest to developing countries to ensure that where products are available from both industrial and developing country producers, the latter did not get too inefficient by virtue of having large margins of preference. This would gradually squeeze simple production industries within the EU, but with sufficient time to allow younger workers to divert to other sectors. Such a contraction in Europe need not be socially disruptive, even in the short run, for services will generate plenty of demand even for unskilled workers, provided that labour markets are not unduly constrained. In the long run, shifting workers to more modern industries should help to stimulate wages.

Reciprocal trade arrangements

This section considers the EU's reciprocal trade agreements (RTAs), including customs unions, many of which go beyond border measures to consider other factors affecting trade, such as standards and competition policy and contain financial protocols. At present these include the European Economic Area (EEA), plus arrangements with the central and east European countries (CEECs), including the Baltics, and the Mediterranean countries. It also considers 'non-traditional' RTAs, currently with Mexico and South Africa, and under negotiation with Mercosur and Chile, which are 'pure' trade agreements. With exception of the last category, the partners involved are pretty small economically.

The deepest of the EU's RTAs is the EEA – with Iceland, Liechtenstein and Norway.[14] These bring the partners under the full *acquis communautaire* except in agriculture, which, given restrictiveness on both sides, is excluded. The EEA is intended to deliver the economic benefits of the single market without the political ties that bind EU members. Effectively similar arrangements pertain to Switzerland.

The Europe Agreements (EAs), which effectively date from 1992, are also deep by the standards of North–South RTAs. They do not apply the *acquis*, but do require partners to adopt EU competition and intellectual property regimes and to make efforts to converge in other dimensions such as environmental standards. They permit virtually free flows of direct investment in both directions and underpin this with commitments to permit the mobility of key personnel. The latter refers to skilled workers; unskilled workers have no formal rights to move, although de facto, it seems that many do so. In addition to these elements of deep integration, the Europe Agreements provide for financial and technical assistance (considerably expanded since accession came onto the agenda), and for political cooperation.

Trade in goods was substantially liberalized under the Europe Agreements. However, although agricultural trade was relaxed, it remains significantly managed, and similarly, although EU industrial imports from EA members are free of tariffs, they can be subjected to emergency protection under less restrictive conditions than the GATT requires and subject to political-level arbitration in case of disputes. Thus market access remains somewhat conditional, although in practice interruptions have been relatively few. The EA members had longer to liberalize their imports than EU, and were also permitted temporary reversals in liberalization, so the EAs do not yet permit CEEC consumers/users totally free and secure access to EU goods. Similarly, although services trade has been significantly liberalized it is by no means completely free between the EU and EA members.

One of the least satisfactory aspects of the EAs is their bilateral nature – each partner has an RTA with the EU, but not with all other EA countries. This is a classic hub-and-spoke structure, which redounds substantially to the EU's advantage (Baldwin, 1994): the EU is a more attractive site for activity than any CEEC, because it grants access to EU and *all* EA markets; EA sites do not. The recent agreement for pan-European cumulation – whereby inputs from any EA member can be counted as 'local' for the sake of meeting EA rules of origin – has now removed the other highly pernicious aspect of the EA-system.

The Euro–Mediterranean Agreements (EMAs) vary. Long-standing RTAs with Cyprus and Malta were viewed as precursors to accession, now stutteringly underway. Similarly, the Ankara Agreement of 1963 and subsequent protocol of 1970 envisaged eventual Turkish membership of the EU, but appeared to get stuck in the customs union as an interim stage, given the difficulties of achieving accession. Customs union was achieved (on time) by 1996. At that time, however, accession looked most unlikely and it was only in December 1999 that, presumably mainly in return for foreign policy support over the 1990s, the EU conceded that Turkey should be treated as a candidate (McLaren, 2000). The customs union, which will rule until accession, is prospectively far-reaching in its treatment of Turkish trade policy with the EU and third countries and in introducing several aspects of the *acquis*, for example, competition policy, standards and intellectual policy. Frictions remain, however, such as the facility for levying anti-dumping duties on EU–Turkish trade and the absence of a timetable for freeing agricultural trade, which basically belie the title 'customs union'.[15] (Transition periods of up to 22 years are permitted in other elements of the agreement, so 'no time-table' does indeed look very slow.) Additionally neither capital nor, of course, labour mobility is allowed for, and neither is the liberalization of the Turkish service market required.

The 'ordinary' FTAs among the EMAs concern Israel and the Arab countries. That with Israel dates from 1975 and was updated in 1995, whereas the others are more recent: Morocco and Tunisia switched from non-reciprocal arrangements to FTAs in 1995, and those with other countries have yet to be signed. These FTAs have their origins in the Barcelona Convention of 1995, which sought to offer the Mediterranean countries (and their Latin champions among the EU membership) levels of commitment similar to those offered to the CEECs under the EAs. Relative to the RTAs discussed so far, the Tunisian FTA, and by inference the others, do not look very far-reaching: EU market access in agriculture is not substantially liberalized, and services, investment and establishment are effectively not included.[16]

Finally, the EU has negotiated or is negotiating, formally or informally, a series of FTAs with larger and more distant partners: South Africa, Mexico, Mercosur and Chile in order of appearance. These are restricted in coverage to goods and even here both sides exclude lists of sensitive products – mainly agricultural in the EU. These lists have been hugely contentious and may yet scupper the deals. The FTAs make no attempt to extend the *acquis* to the partners and, unlike the 'traditional' RTAs, there are no effective financial protocols. They are simple FTAs aimed at securing preferential market access.

As an economist, I view the EU's various RTAs as differing in degree rather than in nature. It is true that, once an RTA partner is accepted as an official candidate, the RTA becomes embedded in a larger and deeper process and that some of its conditions come to be regarded differently. However, most RTAs pre-date official candidature and, anyway, they continue to apply to countries eligible for membership until accession occurs. Thus as a source of evidence about EU trade policy it seems best to consider the pre-accession RTAs at their original face value. On this basis I would argue that the whole set of RTAs shows strong commonality. All are structured around trade and its ancillary requirements, all have extended into areas such as investment, and most include an aid or financial component. This similarity might *prima facie* suggest similar objectives, but in fact it arises because the EU's preferred instrument of diplomacy is commercial. Commercial instruments require the partners to deal with Brussels directly rather than with national capitals, and are much easier to use than more traditional instruments such as diplomatic support in world fora, monetary affairs, and security arrangements. I postulate four broad EU goals in the RTAs (Winters, 2000).

Community

For close neighbours in Europe the EU is prepared to contemplate accession. This is the area over which the EU seeks to extend the *acquis*.[17] One set of motivations for the EU is basically cultural and political, reflecting a vocation to unify. The EU may reap economic advantages, but these are minor, first because of the small size of the partners and, second, because of the exceptions to free trade. The partners, on the other hand, could reap large benefits from access to the large EU market, although, until accession occurs, these are also curtailed by the incompleteness of the arrangements. Recent extension of the official list of candidates to thirteen suggests that community is perhaps a more important motivation than previously thought by some.

Stability

The second motive for signing RTAs is to foster a band of stability and security around the EU's borders. This was evident with the EAs and EMAs and now applies further east, in the promises of agreements with Ukraine and Russia if they reform sufficiently. Serious peripheral disruption could disturb economic performance in neighbouring parts of the EU, and, more seriously, could spillover in the form of violence or migration. The EMAs are intended to address these problems by (a) increasing the returns to labour in order to reduce migratory pressure and (b) both directly and indirectly via increasing prosperity, fostering westernized political and social reform. For several reasons, however, success is far from assured. It is not guaranteed that increasing trade will raise (low-skilled) wages in the region, especially given the exclusion of most agriculture from the RTAs; there is not much sign of deep reform, even in trade areas such as services, let alone elsewhere such as labour markets or public ownership; and increasing prosperity might stimulate rather than discourage migration in the short run. Finally the popular notion that agreements provide an incentive for reform because they can be withdrawn if reform is baulked at, is not very plausible for the large economies like Russia and Ukraine. The EU has to deal with them whether they reform or not.

Development

The EU is concerned, for both humanitarian and geo-political (as opposed to Euro-political) reasons, that poverty be alleviated and economic development encouraged. This lies most obviously behind the GSP (above) and relations with the ACP countries (below), but also affects the EAs and EMAs too.

Defensive

The motivations above refer to partners that lie within EU members' traditional and local spheres of interest. Defensive RTAs, on the other hand, all of which are recent, aim to defend EU access to distant markets in the face of the latter's attempts at regional integration. It is most obviously present in the arrangements recently concluded or currently under negotiation with Mexico, Chile and Mercosur and I would also locate the FTA with South Africa in this group.[18] It also potentially applies to the Asia–Europe Meeting (ASEM) talks with the countries of the Association of South East Asian Nations (ASEAN) and to the TransAtlantic Market Place proposal with the USA, although these are not progressing very far in the direction of preferences and are not considered below.

Until the 1990s, the EU had grown up and pursued its trading arrangements with other countries in a world in which it was the only major regional bloc. Among other things, this gave it a relaxed attitude to the GATT's Article XXIV and meant that it was rarely on the exporting end of the trade diversion (see, for example, Nagarajan, 1998). Thus, the EU had never had to worry about market access except in an mfn fashion at the GATT. In return, through a slightly vague agreement with the USA in 1974 (the Casey–Soames Agreement), the EU agreed not to extend its preferential trading arrangements beyond its traditional borders. All this changed in the 1990s as regionalism took hold in a number of the world's major economies, leading to blocs such as the North American Free Trade Area (NAFTA), Mercosur and AFTA (the ASEAN Free Trade Agreement).

Although one can already identify some trade diversion in these blocs – see, for example, Yeats (1998) on Mercosur, and USITC (1997) and Nagarajan (1998) on NAFTA – the concern is more for the future, as the blocs come to the end of their transition periods and, potentially worse from the EU perspective, consider ever deeper or wider forms of integration. By negotiating FTAs with these various blocs or their members, the EU can reverse the discrimination it faces on tariffs and make a stronger case for concerning itself with their future development. Thus as a formal FTA partner of Mercosur or Mexico the EU feels that it may more legitimately comment on, or even participate in, talks on the evolution of Mercosur, NAFTA and the Free Trade Area of the Americas (FTAA). A good parallel is US demands for a 'seat at the table' as the Europeans discussed their single market programme in the 1980s, and, similarly to that case, although the EU will not obtain full access to western hemisphere talks, the more active its prior engagement, the more influence it is likely to be able to wield in regional talks. Exactly the same arguments apply to the ASEM relationship, which I see as basically an attempt at entryism to APEC.

It is less obvious that EU relations with South Africa fall mainly under the defensive heading. On balance, however, I suspect that the main motive was to bind the major political force and market in Africa into the European sphere rather than risk President Mandela's internationalist sentiment and the USA's evident interest in the region from leading it elsewhere. Whether the strategy will be successful remains to be seen, however, given the scars created by the negotiation.

Especially with the disappointments in Seattle, regionalism may surge in the near future, and with it EU defensive activity.[19] As with all regionalism, however, whether such agreements are beneficial is moot, especially given their selectivity, which tends to avoid concessions in the very sectors that require them. In fact, FTAs are probably less likely to be beneficial if the partner already belongs to other FTAs than if it does not. Partner FTAs have no effect on the net benefits flowing from the EU import side, but reduce the possibility of earning big rents on exports because they lower the partner's protective barriers. The EU would be far better to liberalize multilaterally and consistently than to pursue a plethora of ad hoc, exception-ridden, FTAs.

Relations with the African, Caribbean and Pacific (ACP) States

The Lomé Convention defines the EU's relationship with 71 small and mostly poor developing ACP countries, nearly all of which were formerly colonies of one of its members. Like the GSP, it too involves unilateral trade preferences – access to EU markets duty free and subject to no quantitative restrictions except for some tariff quotas – but here of a contractual nature. The EU cannot unilaterally withdraw Lomé preferences during the life of an agreed Convention (five to ten years). The Lomé Convention also involves special protocols for certain commodities – bananas, beef, sugar and rum – an aid protocol and a good deal of political cooperation.

Lomé is essentially a post-colonial policy aimed at helping development, securing supplies of raw materials and cementing EU influence around the world (Winters, 2000, a). The first objective has largely been a failure. With the exceptions of Botswana and Mauritius, none of the initially poor ACP countries has been conspicuously successful in development and several have been quite disastrous. Indeed, the record is so disappointing that one might wonder whether development really was the aim. Similarly, access to raw materials is much less of a concern now than two decades ago. The last objective, on the other hand, continues to be relevant, receiving several mentions in EU documents dealing with the Convention's successor (for example,

Commission, 1997). Developing countries are becoming increasingly important in the global economy both in terms of size, although the ACP group is still tiny economically, and in terms of institutions; hence a set of 71, albeit small, votes probably is a useful adjunct to EU diplomacy.

The current Convention runs until 2000 and its successor – the Cotonou Agreement – has been negotiated through an extremely fraught process. Major changes were required, since the Lomé arrangements had been ruled to be inconsistent with WTO obligations; however, to even adjustment strains and give time for details to be developed the, EU and ACP countries are seeking a waiver from WTO for something like the current arrangements. The EU's plans for renegotiation are to grant all least-developed countries (not just those in ACP) non-reciprocal preferences, and to require other ACP countries to sign a series of region–EU FTAs (so-called Regional Economic Partnership Agreements – REPAs), as is permitted (at least implicitly) by WTO. There are no models for these, but given the ACP countries' lack of development, the nature of the EMAs and the difficulties encountered in the non-traditional RTAs, one should not expect anything too far-reaching.

I have argued in Winters (forthcoming) that the REPAs offer little to either the EU or the ACP countries. A far better way of reconciling WTO commitments with access for ACP exports would be to take the issue to the next round of global trade talks and try to negotiate a multilateral deal. Acting only on a non-discriminatory basis and binding the results at the WTO, this deal would reduce EU tariffs on goods of the sort exported by ACP countries, significantly liberalize ACP imports (which in virtually everyone's view they desperately need), and seek some tariff cuts from other major importers in recognition of the increased access that they would receive to EU and ACP markets as a result of replacing preferences by non-discriminatory policy. Unfortunately, I do not predict success for these proposals unless the non-EU/ACP members of WTO press very hard: despite its obvious shortcomings, both parties to the Lomé Convention seem wedded to it and would rather beg for an extension in the WTO than contemplate radical solutions. Again EU policy seems more comfortable with 'managed' liberalization than the genuine article.

Conclusion

The EU makes the right noises for an effective international trade policy both in goods and services. Unfortunately, while it has arguably achieved much in terms of liberalization over the last four decades, it still has some way to go. The exceptions it has to liberal trade – agriculture, simple manufactures and many services – and the instruments it has to control trade – especially anti-dumping policy – are enough to refute the view that it is fundamentally liberal. And this is not reversed by the exceptions to the exceptions – that is, the many arrangements to allow imports in with reduced tariffs. These tend to distort the sourcing of imports and are, anyway, subject to many reservations. Overall, the EU's trade regime still entails a good deal of governmental management.

Of course, EU policies are not set in stone and, in particular, the process of enlargement could provide a stimulus to change. On the whole, however, it does not seem to me that in this area one should expect it to have a major impact. First, previous enlargements (for example, to include the UK) have not obviously changed trade policy much, although, of course, how it might have developed without enlargement is unknown. Second, although most have transformed themselves almost beyond recognition, the current candidates are not, on average, a particularly open set. Moreover, they will face adjustment strains from access for the foreseeable future and will not be anxious to create more pressure by forcing the pace of liberalization; besides, at least, at first they will be politically weak, supplicants rather than leaders, and will probably choose to use their limited influence on domestic and financial rather than trade issues. One of the major issues to confront the enlarging (and enlarged) EU will be how to treat Russia and the Ukraine, which are too large to ignore. The most likely outcome, I suspect, is that they will eventually be offered FTAs with the usual sectoral exceptions and strong reserve powers to restrict imports if they boom or if there are political frictions.

It would be hyperbole to talk of a cross-roads in the early 2000s, but there are important decisions to take about the future of trade policy. The complex and clumsy institutions for taking these impart a bias towards a residual protectionism, so taking the liberal option – living up to the rhetoric – will require strong political commitment. A willingness to remove the exceptions in the bilateral trading arrangements, coupled with an imaginative approach to future relations with the ACP countries would be a good start. Following that, non-discriminatory liberalization – especially in agriculture and services, and possibly in the context of the ongoing multilateral talks – would stimulate the economy and ultimately boost efficiency and real income.

Notes

1. I am grateful to Béatrice Harrison and Shoshana Ormonde for logistical assistance, and to Carl Hamilton, Christopher Stevens and Helen Wallace for excellent comments on an earlier draft. None of them should be held responsible for the chapter's remaining short-comings.
2. If policy-makers took a dramatically protectionist turn, these constitutional clauses may slow down their progress in that direction, but they do not influence current debate because they are so vague.
3. Interestingly, since the 'battle' for trade policy has been won, anti-dumping duties have become even easier to impose, being subject to simple majority voting in Council. Also interesting is that in this area contested votes have been quite common recently. Whether this reflects a passing attempt to curb this element of protectionism or a more fundamental shift remains to be seen.
4. Identifying market failure is not sufficient to justify intervention. One needs also to be sure that intervention will not fail more seriously.
5. The nine are Australia, Canada, Hong Kong, Japan, Korea, New Zealand, Singapore, Taiwan and the USA. North Korea is the exception.
6. This figure is only approximate because it relies on the conversion of many specific duties (ECU per kilogram) to *ad valorem* equivalents.
7. My message here is that the EU be more radical in reforming agriculture, not that it seek to get agriculture off the agenda.
8. There is, regrettably a covert practical link between these issues and the CAP. Hormones and GMOs both 'threaten' large increases in yields, immediately and directly in the case of beef hormones. If EU farmers adopted them, their extra output would bankrupt the CAP.
9. My neighbour backed Red Rum in the Grand National, but I, with an equal degree of (total) ignorance, did not. This must reflect different attitudes to taking risk.
10. Messerlin warns that his list is not exhaustive.
11. Simple economic theory suggests that the cost of a trade restriction rises with the square of its size: a 20 per cent tariff is four times more costly than a 10 per cent tariff on the same good, (for example, Winters, 1991).
12. See Wang and Winters (1998) for a discussion of preferences in general. Pelkmans (1997) discusses the EU's GSP briefly.
13. There are about 1,250 four-digit headings in the EU's trade classification.
14. In truth 'depth' is not single dimension: the EU's customs unions (Andorra, Cyprus, Malta and Turkey) are deeper in having a common external tariff, but less deep in permitting other restrictions on trade and other intercourse.
15. A customs union strictly requires all aspects of trade policy to be common.
16. The Israel FTA makes some progress in these areas.
17. There are cases of countries unilaterally adopting parts of the *acquis*, but that is a different matter.
18. In this last case, however, development and stability are also significant.
19. The surge is not inevitable, however, because regional liberalization may fall out of fashion as rapidly as multilateral liberalization.

References

Baldwin, R. (1994) *Toward an Integrated Europe* (London: Centre for Economic Policy Research).

Bilal, S. (1998) 'Political Economy Considerations on the Supply of Trade Protection in Regional Integration Agreements', *Journal of Common Market Studies*, 36 (1), 1–31.

Commission of European Communities (1997) *Communication from the Commission to the Council and the European Parliament: Guidelines for the Negotiation of New Cooperation Agreements with the African, Caribbean, and Pacific (ACP) Countries* (Brussels: European Commission).

Finger, J. M., Ingco, M. D. and Reincke, U. (1996) *The Uruguay Round: Statistics on Tariff Concessions Given and Received* (Washington, DC: The World Bank).

Ingco, M. D. (1996) 'Tariffication in the Uruguay Round: How Liberalization?', *World Economy*, 19 (4), 425–46.

Johnson, M. (1998) *European Community Trade Policy and the Article 113 Committee* (London: Royal Institute for International Affairs, International Economics Programme).

McLaren, L. M. (2000) 'Turkey's Eventual Membership of the EU', *Journal of Common Market Studies*, 38 (1), 117–30.

Messerlin, P. A. (forthcoming) *Measuring the Costs of Protection in Europe* (Washington, DC: Institute for International Economics).

Nagarajan, N. (1998) 'Regionalism and the WTO: New Rules for the Games?', *Economic Papers*, 128 (Brussels: European Communities).

Pelkmans, J. (1997) *European Integration: Methods and Economic Analysis* [Netherlands Open University] (Harlow, Essex: Longman).

Rollo, J. and Winters, L. A. (2000) 'Subsidiarity and Governance Challenges for the WTO: The Examples of Environmental and Labour Standards', *The World Economy*, 23 (4), 561–76.

Sapir, A. (1998) 'The Political Economy of EC Regionalism', *European Economic Review*, 42 (3–5), 717–32.

Shepsle, K. A. and Weingast, B. R. (1981) 'Political Preferences for the Pork Barrel: a Generalization', *American Journal of Political Science*, 25 (1), 96–111.

US International Trade Commission (1997) *The Impact of the North American Free Trade Agreement on the U.S. Economy and Industries: A Three-Year Review*, Publication 3045 (Washington, DC: US International Trade Commission).

Wang, Z. K. and Winters, L. A. (1998) 'Africa's Role in Multilateral Trade Negotiations: Past and Future', *Journal of African Economics*, 7 (1), 1–33.

Winters, L. A. (1991) *International Economics* (London: Routledge).

Winters, L. A. (1992) 'Trade Policy, Integration and the European Footwear Market', in Winters, L. A. (ed.), *Trade Flows and Trade Policy after 1992* (Cambridge: Cambridge University Press) 175–209.

Winters, L. A. (1993) 'Expanding EC Membership and Association Accords: Recent Experience and Future Prospects', in Anderson, K. and Blackhurst, R. (eds), *Regional Integration and the Global Trading Systems* (Hemel Hempstead: Harvest Wheatsheaf).

Winters, L. A. (1994) 'The EC and Protectionism: The Political Economy', *European Economic Review*, 38 (3–4), 596–603.

Winters, L. A. (2000) 'The EU's Preferential Trade Agreements: Objectives and Outcomes', in van Dijck, P. and Faber, G. (eds), *The External Economic Dimension of the European Union* (The Hague, London and Cambridge, MA: Kluwer Law International), pp. 195–222.

Winters, L. A. (forthcoming) 'Post-Lomé Trading Arrangements: the Multilateral Alternative', in von Hagen, J. and Widgren, M. (eds), *Regionalism in Europe* (The Hague: Kluwer).

Yeats, A. (1998) 'Does the Mercosur's Trade Performance Raise Concerns about the Effects of Regional Trade Arrangements?', *The World Bank Economic Review*, 12 (1), 1–28.

3
Pan-European Industrial Networks as Factors of Convergence and Divergence Within Europe

Slavo Radosevic[1]

Introduction

This chapter argues first, that the way in which central and east European countries (CEECs) integrate into the wider European economy will have important effects on the long-term growth of the European Union (EU) and central and eastern Europe. Their integration through production networks, formed through linkages within and between transnational corporations (TNCs), is an essential part of the wider European integration, which includes market, as well as institutional (or policy) integration. Next, I argue that micro-level integration in the wider Europe is neither automatic nor without its problems. Deep industrial integration is not the automatic outcome of deep institutional integration. How far institutional integration is compatible with micro-level integration is an issue that needs to be explicitly addressed – the ways in which the two processes interact will determine the emerging industrial architecture of the wider Europe and thus the growth prospects for Europe.

The beginnings of pan-European integration coincide with a period characterized by trade liberalization and the expansion of international financial markets. These processes are described in UNCTAD (1994: 118) as *shallow* international integration, meaning the spread of market linkages through greater trade and factor flows, and government action to reduce obstacles to these flows. In broader accounts of globalization the processes of financial and trade integration are closely linked to the processes of producing goods and services, that is, what happens at the micro-level of the individual enterprise. One of the features associated with globalization is that as a micro-phenomenon it facilitates production integration and networking. In this sense it creates opportunities for *deep* international integration at the firm level. Integration via international production goes beyond arm's length market exchanges by internalizing cross-border exchanges under the common governance of TNCs or through different forms of sourcing or network relationships.

Interlinkages between macro- and micro-processes of integration produce a specific economic and technological dynamic of globalization (Radosevic, 1999a). Interlinking produces unbalanced outcomes, with increasing integration of some geographic areas or dimensions (competition, production, demand, finance) within the world economy, while simultaneously leading to divergence or marginalization of others.

Although market integration is a necessary objective of eastwards enlargement of the EU, it is in no way a sufficient condition of dynamically efficient outcomes. The CEECs are much more likely to converge in terms of growth if market integration between the current EU and the CEECs is reinforced by production and technology integration. Otherwise, the CEECs could be integrated into the EU market, but remain isolated and marginalized in terms of production and technology linkages and excessively dependent on budgetary transfers. A proper understanding of the conditions for 'deep integration' demands a better understanding of supply-side phenomena and, in particular, of the extent and nature of production and technology linkages between the current EU and the CEECs.

The specificity of EU integration, when compared to other regional groupings in the world, is the strong policy and institutional integration. Its integration process is 'top-down' and aims at 'deep' institutional integration. However, the viability of political and institutional integration of the wider Europe cannot be separated from the breadth and depth of integration at the firm-level. Policy (macro) and production (micro) integration are driven by different forces and can, to a degree, be developed independently of each other. However, in the long-term one might expect them to be compatible and to reinforce each other. If the disparity between depth and breadth of micro/production and macro/institutional integration is too great, this will cause both economic and political costs for the EU and the accession countries, and could thus undermine the enlargement process.

The need to ensure compatibility between policy and production integration therefore raises a whole set of new policy and management issues. Will the compatibility between these two levels of integration emerge automatically? Is the policy of integration sustainable if micro-links are weak? Is the policy of integration necessary at all for micro-integration?

The analysis of these issues should shed new light on the potential and sustainability of 'deep' integration within the wider Europe. It could also provide a basis for evaluating the current EU policy towards the CEECs, which so far has had neither coherence nor any overarching strategy (Wallace, 1997).

Against this background this chapter explores the main issues posed by the problem of (in)compatibility between micro/production and macro/institutional integration of the wider Europe. In particular, it sketches a framework for research on how East/West industrial networks are shaped by the policy integration processes. This locates the problem within the discussion of growth as relevant to the convergence and divergence perspective, then looks at the specific context of industrial upgrading. This leads to the suggestion that an 'alignment of networks' framework (Kim and von Tunzelmann, 1998) provides a valuable conceptual approach for understanding the issues of industrial integration in the central and east European situation.

Industrial networks in the wider Europe

The extent and nature of the linkages that emerge between the east and west of Europe will strongly shape the competitive dynamics and industrial development in not only central and eastern Europe, but also in the EU. The prospect of the accession of the CEECs into the EU raises the issue of whether East/West industrial networks will be a factor in improving the growth prospects of the enlarged EU or whether they will deepen the differences in levels of development and undermine prospects for more balanced growth.

This requires some understanding about what central and eastern Europe bring to European industry and economy. With eastern enlargement, the heterogeneity of the EU in terms of output will increase. In general, the enlargement will lead to a lowering of the average GDP/per capita. Even the most developed CEE countries, like the Czech Republic, Hungary, Poland and Slovakia, are below southern EU countries in terms of GDP per capita. In this respect, the enlargement would lead to more heterogeneity in the EU. Also, in terms of trade competitiveness, other things being equal, the enlargement would lead to a weakened trade balance and export competitiveness of the EU. On the other hand, the variations in cost variables, such as wages, productivity levels, and labour unit costs, have also increased in the wider Europe and are now approaching the range of Asian economies (Landesmann, 1999: 5).

However, the enlargement would increase the coherence of the EU economy in terms of economic (EBRD, 1999; Mickiewicz and Bell, 2000) and industrial (Urban, 1999) structures, and research and development (R&D) (Radosevic and Auriol, 1998).[2] CEECs are in an intermediate position between the EU north and the EU south in terms of industrial structure, such as shares of labour-intensive and sophisticated engineering industries (Urban, 1999). In terms of industrial specialization, the CEECs and the less prosperous countries in the current EU are not targeting the same sectors. In this respect, they will not compete against each other but could be complementary. As Weber and Soete (1999: 8) point out, 'the specialization profiles of first-round eastern European enlargement countries and the main EU countries with less favoured regions indicate that this [competition] is generally not the case, with the exception of transport equipment'.

As a result of this intermediate position the opportunities in the CEECs for intra-industry trade and intra-industry production networks between the EU north and the future EU east are possibly greater than with the current EU south countries. Heterogeneity in terms of outputs, but increasing homogeneity in terms of structure and inputs, suggest that the prospects for EU enlargement may be much better than is commonly supposed. Significant cost differentials make more attractive opportunities for further expanding intra-industry trade and production networks.

Driven largely by integration into the supply chains of major European industrial firms, the economies of the CEECs are already showing signs of convergence to the industrial specialization profiles of the EU north countries (OECD, 1998). This comes through an increase in foreign direct investment (FDI) in CEECs, but also through complementary networks of non-equity links. Contrary to initial expectations, there has been no significant diversion of FDI from the EU south to the CEECs (Brenton *et al.*, 1998). Nevertheless, countries like Hungary and the Czech Republic seem to be already equally well, if not better, integrated into global production networks than some regions in the current EU (Weber and Soete, 1999).

So far, the increased heterogeneity in levels of development of a would-be enlarged EU has been perceived as a problem. However, based on the 'East' Asian experience, Zysman and Schwartz (1998: 17) argue that the 'heterogeneity of production functions' within the wider

Europe may offer a solution. East/West industrial networks could operate as a mechanism for industrial upgrading. Increased differences in levels of development are interpreted by Zysman *et al.* (1997) not as a liability, but as an asset. The advantages of divergence come from the opportunity to separate product development from production and to minimize radically the capital requirements and the range of in-house production skills needed for volume production and mass strategies (Zysman and Schwartz 1998; Zysman *et al.*, 1997).

Inspired to a great extent by the phenomenon of east Asian cross-national production networks Zysman *et al.* (1997) posed the question of whether East/West European production integration, if based on cross-national production networks (CNPNs), would represent a potential growth opportunity, not only for central and eastern Europe, but also for the developed EU economies. CNPNs are defined as 'relationships among firms that organize, across national borders, research and development activities, procurement, distribution, production definition and design, manufacturing and support services in a given industry' (Ernst, 1995, cited in Zysman *et al.*, 1997: 57).

Traditional analysis would suggest that differences in wage and development levels would structure the East/West relationship in terms of relative comparative advantages and that it would be confined to trade. However, the opportunity for the EU countries to incorporate economies with such different 'production functions' could generate technical dynamism through CNPNs. As Zysman *et al.* (1997: 59) point out, '(i)nstead of essentially labour intensive low or middle skill products in a mature or at least declining sector, we are talking about production arrangements in the core elements of the industrial economy, consumer durables, and in the most rapidly expanding set of the sector, electronics'.

Many of these observations are useful in generating hypotheses and in defining a research agenda, but they should not be taken for granted. The opportunities arising from differences between the CEECs and EU as regions may be undermined in several ways: first, differences between the European east and west may be similar to east Asian differences in terms of output (GDP *per capita*, wages, export unit prices, productivity). However, differences in terms of economic and industrial structure and of inputs (skills, R&D) have actually made Europe more homogenous. Whether this is a favourable basis or not for CNPNs is not yet clear. Second, the process of European integration and enlargement is also shaped by political integration. As Zysman and Schwartz (1998: 13) point out, legal restrictions on labour reorganization and layoffs deter European companies from expanding networked production arrangements. The institutional convergence and legal harmonization are certainly not favourable to such production arrangements as those that rest on technological and institutional diversity. Third, economic conditions in Europe over the past decade have not been conducive to rapid internationalization of production by EU firms, thereby slowing their expansion into foreign locations (Linden, 1998: 4). Finally, Zysman and Schwartz (1998) point out that the European TNCs have, to date, been slow to explore the new strategies or to exploit the possibilities for these CNPNs. Their limited involvement in production in Asia, or in Asian production networks, means that they have little experience in CNPNs. Those which have developed seem to be organized as closed networks, which hinder the development of contract manufacturing.[3]

International industrial networks and industrial upgrading

The crucial issue is thus whether the evolution of the wider European economy will, through some mixture of trade and foreign direct investment (FDI) lead to the industrial upgrading in central and eastern Europe as well as in the EU. More specifically, under what conditions can policy, trade and production-based integration become a vehicle for industrial upgrading. As Ernst (1999: 32) points out 'the dynamic coupling of domestic and international knowledge linkages is of critical importance for economic growth in a globalizing world'. Growth is dependent on the way countries integrate into the global economy, not only from national factors but also through the strategies of foreign enterprises. An understanding of this process is essential to gauge the prospects for 'catching up' in a globalized world economy. It follows that the emerging policy issue is under what conditions can international linkages be leveraged as carriers for industrial upgrading.

Participation in global commodity chains is a necessary step for industrial upgrading, because this is what puts firms and economies on a 'potentially dynamic learning curve' (Gereffi, 1999: 339) or generates 'dynamic learning' (Radosevic, 1999a). As Ernst (1999: 1) points out, '(i)nternational linkages can recharge domestic knowledge creation, provided appropriate policies and firm strategies are in place'. Also, 'under certain conditions, international linkages can compensate for initially weak domestic linkages' (1999: 32). However, there is nothing automatic about the coupling of domestic and foreign networks. Constraints on the knowledge flow and knowledge generation within international production networks can be due to a variety of factors specific to firms, as well as to other factors related to the role of the state or features of the market.

The economic and business literature on industrial networks is mostly focused on modes of entry (full ownership versus arm's length relationships versus alliances). The emphasis is on transaction costs and the theory examines the TNC as one of several possible ways of organizing economic activity and explains why and when this particular form will be chosen in preference to its various alternatives. The dominant explanation is the OLI-framework, or Eclectic Paradigm of International Production (Dunning, 1993). This holds that TNCs have a specific competitive advantage (O) that is better leveraged internally (I) by physically setting up a number of assets in the host country (L). Within this framework alliances are interpreted as cases of 'incomplete internalization'. TNCs are interpreted as economic institutions that internalize the nonpecuniary externalities resulting from 'natural' market imperfections. The basic concern within this framework is to understand when the markets for intermediate inputs will be subject to such high transaction costs that hierarchical coordination becomes more efficient than the market.

By focusing on markets and hierarchies as the fundamental modes of organization, transaction cost analysts often do not consider the diversity of organizational arrangements that are contained within the alliances. By focusing on given transactions, transaction analysis overlooks the dynamic interaction between organizations and transactions and the ways in which established organizations can develop new additional transactions (Meyer, 1998). The importance of the social networks in which alliances operate provides a much richer explanatory framework for understanding the growth and the issues of strategic management (Gulati, 1998).

The link between international industrial networks and growth has been dealt with only partially with relation to FDI (Dunning and Narula, 1996; Narula, 1996; Ozawa, 1992; Vernon, 1966). The problem with these explanations is that their limited number of explanatory variables especially neglect both broad political variables and the variety of country- and sector-specific factors. The complexity of variables that are relevant to the framework explains in part why research on these issues of global industrial trade and production networks and their linkages to growth and industrial upgrading lacks a coherent theory and is relatively under-developed.[4] These limits to the research so far are evident in accounts of both aspects of the problem: industrial upgrading; and international linkages to the national innovation systems. An important weakness of innovation system theory is its neglect of the international dimension (Ernst, 1999: 2), in particular how much international industrial networks matter for the process of national industrial upgrading and also which variables matter in this process of interaction. Similarly, the notion of industrial upgrading as such remains vague,[5] although it is said to go beyond R&D in explaining industrial progress.

It is usually assumed that, when integration takes place at the production level via the establishment of subsidiaries and link-ups through joint ventures, this will automatically bring some degree of integration at the technological level. This is not necessarily the case. The EU and central and eastern Europe are full of individual instances where production integration is not followed by technological integration. Hence this is one of the key issues in the cohesion debate.

If we start from an international industrial networks perspective, then our efforts to understand the industrial upgrading framework needs to focus on the relative position of firms or countries in international trade or supply networks. In order to apply this framework to central and east Europe we must first establish empirically which positions producers from CEE occupy in international production chains and how these positions can be explained. Only then can we attempt to understand the dynamics of these networks. Being plugged into the global production network and having access to world markets do not guarantee that a 'dynamic learning' capability is acquired.[6] Enterprises may remain in the same technological positions within production networks, because the structural barriers against moving upward are too high to overcome. This suggests that the learning process through international production networks is not a continuous, but a discontinuous, process. In technology 'catching up' enterprises have to pass through several distinct phases, each with specific learning and capability requirements.

Here two questions seem to be important for explaining the growth aspects of East/West industrial networks. The first, is whether opportunities and requirements for growth in central and eastern Europe via trade and international industrial networks depend on the position that domestic enterprises occupy in those networks. Are opportunities for technology transfer and growth determined by the 'club' or network to which the enterprise is attached? For example, are the opportunities for moving up the ladder of technological complexity the same for a central European component manufacturer as for one in western Europe when supplying Nissan or Ford? Second, how can domestic enterprises move from lower to higher value-added positions within production networks? For a domestic economy a higher value-added position should, in principle, ensure more spillovers and more technology inflows, as well as more opportunities for domestic clustering.

A better understanding of the nature of production networks in central and eastern Europe should tell us more about their dynamic potential. The discussion and research on this has already started. For example, Ellingstadt (1997) argues that we are witnessing the emergence of technologically stagnant East/West networks which resemble Mexican *maquilladora* types of relationships. Radice (1995: 307) makes a similar point in suggesting that the region will be a case of 'dependent national capitalism, integrated into the capitalist world economy on the now standard liberal lines, yielding a tolerable living standard for most of their citizens, but with the permanent high unemployment and inequalities typical of the semi-periphery'. In this version of the story central and eastern Europe can operate only as a low cost and low skilled labour base with limited possibilities for technological integration.

In an alternative story, some suggest that central and eastern Europe could complement western production in a different way. Zysman and Schwartz (1998: 15) point to the example of German firms, which are drawing on the low cost and low skilled labour, but in such a way as to develop 'distinctive complementary, production capacities', which enable them to develop 'distinctive product and market strategies'.

The testing of these two propositions requires far more empirical research, since it seems inappropriate to reduce the determinants of central and eastern Europe as a location to either market access or cost reductions. International production involves a much more complex agenda where market access and cost reduction have to be reconciled with other requirements, such as operational flexibility, services, delivery, quality and technology.

However, even when we get a rough picture of the factors behind the individual positions of central and east European industries in international production networks we may still miss the most important aspect of the problem: the dynamic potential of the initial positions and factors that influence industrial upgrading. Factors relevant to the static requirements for efficiency in resources allocation (cf. make or buy framework) tell us little about the dynamic requirements of learning and innovation.

A further issue relates to the mechanisms of interactive learning, or diffusion of knowledge to domestic companies from foreign affiliates or from other domestic companies, which are plugged into international sourcing networks. The dynamic effects for the economy are stronger when related domestic suppliers or buyers are involved. The integration of sectoral technological flows with individual production capability comes from the clustering of firms and from network externalities. Globalization may weaken this integration through different forms of 'enclaves' (*maquilla*, export processing zones, subsidiaries highly isolated from the host economy) unrelated to domestic sectors. The gain of world market share through 'enclaves' is not necessarily related to an improvement in productivity or to a structural change in the pattern of industrialization.[7] Finally, if the Canadian experience can be of relevance to central and eastern Europe, then it shows that there the positions of firms within international production chains are changing, mainly due to the capabilities of local subsidiaries. On the sample of Canadian world product mandates, (defined as any subsidiary responsibility that extends beyond its own market) Birkinshaw (1996) and Birkinshaw and Morrison (1995) come up with several important conclusions. First, mandates are usually earned, not given. Second, mandate development is fundamentally subsidiary driven. Third, responsibility over several production or business management functions gives a subsidiary more control over its destiny than managing a single function. Fourth, the sustainability of mandates depends on the strength of a firm and country-specific advantages.

This brief overview of the conceptual understanding of the linkages between industrial upgrading and international industrial networks shows that we still lack a comprehensive conceptual framework.[8] However, a range of concepts and theories can illuminate different aspects of industrial networks.

Networks and their alignment: a framework for research

An approach that could take into account the diversity of factors that shape industrial integration of the wider Europe would need to be based on the three basic assumptions set out in the following sections.

Industrial organization and political economy perspectives merged

The internationalization of production networks cannot be explained only through an economics or business economics perspective. In particular the understanding of alliances and more broadly of industrial networks cannot be framed within the purely economic 'make or buy' framework, which is rooted in the transaction cost perspective.[9]

Variables that might be considered 'political', in the broadest sense of the term, must be taken into account. These variables include institutions, whether economic or political, systems of innovation, different political and corporate governance regimes, and socio-political coalitions (Hall, 1997).

The classical choice posed in the literature is between arranging to produce some good or service 'in house' and acquiring it elsewhere through the market. An increasingly common third option is to enter an alliance or network. From an economic perspective these choices are seen as being based on cost efficiency criteria. TNCs are very rarely seen as agents with market power whose expansion can be explained by collusion or monopoly power (Hymer, 1972). TNCs are too often seen as organizations that take country factors as given, and that try to internalize specific locational advantages or to avoid locational disadvantages. The mainstream interpretation of FDI is as an internalization framework, following transaction costs theory. As Dunning (1991) argues, internalization theory is a leading explanation of why a firm should engage in FDI rather than the market.

However, we contend, this approach cannot explain the level, structure and location of international production as claimed. If we are to understand the emerging industrial architecture of the wider Europe, the internalization framework, with its 'make or buy' dichotomy seems far from sufficient to explain country and sectoral differences in the extent and structure of industrial networks. Even though the internalization framework can illuminate the choices between make or buy, it cannot say much about the growth of a particular firm or a group of firms (Cantwell, 1991). The growth of the individual firm is to a great extent a result of internally generated growth associated with firm-specific advantages. Nevertheless, within a Coasian or transaction costs framework ownership-or firm-specific advantages are not essential. Firms basically adjust to external conditions and are not able themselves to shape the modes of entry. However, empirical research anchored to a resources-based theory of firms suggests that firms can actively shape their industry environment. This is indeed the case in central European industries, where the entry of large investors has changed the nature of competition in the sector.

All this points to the insufficiency of a 'make or buy' framework to understand the changing emerging international industrial networks in central and eastern Europe. As pointed out by Kim and von Tunzelmann (1998: 4), '[t]he "make or buy" decision may however be amalgamated with the political governance perspective, and the decision seen as one that may take place variously in firms, networks or countries'. The variety of 'make or buy' decisions will be seen as shaped not only through OLI (ownership–location–internalization) variables, but also by a broader set of political variables. The point is that TNC networks will be determined not only by the 'make or buy' decisions of foreign enterprises, but will also be formed in interaction with a larger set of external variables in both the host country and the world market. This suggests that we should merge the approach based on industrial organization with a political economy perspective.

Multi-level factors that shape industrial networks

The inclusion of political variables into the analytical framework inevitably requires an understanding of different levels of analysis. In a review of different theoretical approaches to FDI and TNCs, Cantwell (1991) concluded that they addressed different questions and levels of analysis, even though in addressing different aspects of the question each approach – market power, internalization, macro and business administration – claimed to be comprehensive. There is not as yet a consensus on the full range of factors that shape industrial networks. In what follows here we implicitly accept the contingency-based view of alliances or industrial networks of Lorange and Roos (1992). This assumes that no particular type of network is better, nor universally more correct, than another (Britto, 1998). The choice of networks is dependent on the particular conditions at hand. Furthermore, in contrast to the international business literature, which finds contingency considerations only within the set of strategic features related to partner firms, we propose a framework in which variables that influence the formation of networks are broader in scope and include state actions by governments in central and eastern Europe, sectoral features and EU policies. This need for the inclusion of different levels is necessary because of the proliferation of actors, which influence how international production networks are shaped.

As Strange (1996: 189) argues very persuasively we live in a world of diffused power. '(T)he power had shifted upward from weak states to stronger ones with global or regional reach beyond their frontiers, that power had shifted sideways from states to markets and thus to non-state authorities deriving power from their market shares, and some power has "evaporated", in that no one was exercising it'. Similarly, Dunning (1997) argues that contemporary capitalism has changed towards alliance capitalism, where the relationship between governments and TNCs has turned from being hostile to more cooperative and more interdependent. This requires us to take into account the actions of many more actors (TNCs, international organizations, national and local governments, non-governmental organizations), if we are to understand the patterns of the international production and knowledge linkages. Each level (national, global, local or firm) plays a role in shaping global industrial networks. For example, country factors in central and eastern Europe can explain functional types of FDI, but not its extent, volume and structure (Lankes and Venables, 1996). Since there is not a smooth functional relationship between levels of FDI and a country's progress in economic transformation this suggests that sectoral, firm and other institutional variables play a role.

The strategies of large firms, for instance, may often be more decisive than country-specific variables in shaping the sectoral patterns of international production networks. As von Tunzelmann (1995: 10) points out, 'by endogenously changing their circumstances through technological accumulation, firms may ultimately alter the national system itself'. New systems of innovation in central and eastern Europe will be strongly shaped by the way enterprises develop and integrate their business functions. Hence the analysis should extend to the level of the individual firm, especially in those cases where large foreign investors can change the entire structure of the industry.

Globalization is also relevant. As Chesnais (1995: 85) put it: ' "global markets" are exclusively markets where purchasing power and intermediate inputs are effectively located'. This implies that the scope of 'globality' is relative to each specific case and differs across different dimensions. Financial markets and competition are more globalized than production and sourcing networks. An industry can be global in the sense that the industrial competition is global, that is, a situation of 'mutual global market dependence', although this does not imply that production, let alone technology, in that industry is globalized.

Alignment of various networks

The pattern of industrial relationships can be seen as an alignment of various networks. Ernst (1999: 32) points to the 'co-evolution of international and domestic knowledge linkages that explains Korea's extraordinary success in information industries'. Kim and von Tunzelmann (1998) stress the alignment of networks as an explanation for the Taiwanese success in information technology. Network alignment comes as a result of effective coupling between nationally specific systems and the global (regional) production networks. The issue is not only 'developing networks, but of integrating locally and nationally emerging networks with global network structures' (Kim and Tunzelmann, 1998: 1). Hence we need to examine the ways in which markets, firms, governments in central and eastern Europe and EU actions can bring about the 'alignment' of these networks.

By plugging themselves into global supply networks domestic firms in central and eastern Europe can externalize their disadvantages in accessing markets, technology and finance by surrendering control to foreign owners. Foreign investors then operate as compensatory mechanisms for weakened domestic firms. Weak national networks are likely to have small growth potential if not aligned to foreign networks.

However, whether an alignment of networks will take place depends not only on such linkages, but also on the nature of each individual network. For example, robust industrial networks elsewhere have developed political governance and corporate governance that match each other, but this is not the case in central and eastern Europe. An overview of corporate governance in the former Soviet Union by Estrin and Wright (1999) shows that slow progress in transition arises from weaknesses in implementing effective corporate governance, as well as from weaknesses in the broader economic environment (capital markets, banks, product markets). In this case, weakness of national industrial networks hampers their alignment with global networks.

The more national and local networks are developed the more sustainable will be their alignment with foreign firms and networks. Following Kim and von Tunzelmann (1998) a comprehensive analytical framework should include all three dimensions – global, national and local networks – as well as their interactions. The major problem here is methodological – how to combine systematically and integrate research on all three dimensions. A mechanical combination of sector, country and micro studies is unlikely to be sufficient.

Network actors and linkages

From a business studies perspective global production networks are primarily seen related to firms' strategies and the role of cooperative alliances (see, for example, Dussauge and Garrette, 1999). Indeed, corporate behaviour and strategies are essential for understanding the dynamics of production networks. However, if we are to understand the role that networks play in growth then we should not ignore the wider relationships within which corporate decisions are taken, for example government strategies, especially privatization, and EU policy interventions.

Another very important element is to understand which the main network organizers are, potentially or actually, that could undertake the task of organizing cross-national production networks.

Foreign multinationals often act as focal points within networks as the key actors controlling and directing other players. On other occasions, a domestic player may emerge in that role. Sometimes, it is a combination of the two. Where foreign firms take the lead role, there are often immediate advantages in terms of finance and access to technology, but these may be offset by limited long-term growth potential; the lack of endogenous R&D, for example, and implicit market-sharing with existing European operations both set clear limitations. Domestic-led modernization is likely to be slower, but promotes the development of indigenous capabilities, which grow 'from within' and are, therefore, deeply implanted into the process. However, lack of finance and difficulties in accessing state-of-the-art technical skills (which have to be learned from foreign firms) make such a process hazardous. This explains why the modernization process often ends up being led by a combinations of foreign and domestic players. A review of industry studies in six industrial sectors across central and eastern Europe suggests that the incidence of foreign-led modernization is much more frequent in central Europe than in Russia and eastern Europe (Romania, Bulgaria) (Radosevic, 1999b).

Another way of addressing this issue is through the notion of lead firms, an idea developed in a different context. In a different context but with similar concerns, this issues has been addressed through the notion of lead or flagship firms. Rugman (2000) points out that the flagship firm stands at the hub of an extensive business networks, or cluster. The flagship has long-term relational contracts with the key suppliers, key customers, key competitors and the non-business infrastructure. The strategy of the lead company thus directly affects the competitive position of other network participants. Ernst (1999: 15–16) points out that '(t)he lead company derives its strength from its control over critical resources and capabilities, and from its capacity to coordinate transaction between different network nodes. Both are the sources of its superior capacity for generating economic rents. Growth and strategic direction of suppliers is heavily determined by the lead firm'.

Gereffi (1999) echoes our concerns about central and eastern Europe in highlighting points to the key question of who will be the main 'organizing agents' in modernizing commodity chains in Mexico due to NAFTA.[10] At the core of this are the problems of coordination among, and complexity of, production networks. Thus it is mainly the simple production networks, that is, woodworking, the garment industry, or bulk commodities, that are re-orienting themselves relatively easily to world markets. In foreign trade this shift is found in the strong rise of labour-intensive, supplier-dominated and commodities-based sectors (see Guerrieri, 1999a,b; Kubielas, 1999; Landesmann, 1997).[11] Elsewhere (Radosevic, 1999c) we argue that the prospects for rebuilding the economies of central and eastern Europe are not only conditioned by (dis)economies in production, but can also result from the inability of actors in production networks to self-organize due to institutional uncertainty and coordination failures, which hinder the self-organization of industry.[12] This process affects whether or not network organizers emerge to promote trade, production or innovation linkages.

Who is likely to be a network organizer in the post-socialist context? Limited and unsystematic evidence shows that there is a wide diversity of network organizers. Network organizers are any actors with the necessary capability and resources – a user or supplier firm, a bank, a holding company or a financial-industrial group, a foreign trade organization, a design institute, a foreign firm or, in some cases, even the state. Given the management, finance and technology gaps in central and eastern Europe described in Radosevic (1999b) it is foreign companies that, for the time being, seem to be the most active network organizers.

However, network restructuring is not the result of the activities of foreign investors alone. As Tulder and Ruigrok (1998: 36) show in the case of car industry, a tiered structure of countries developed in the region is triggered by an interaction of firms' strategies and governments' policies mediated by trade and industrial policies. In some cases, for instance the case of Suzuki in Hungary, the network alignment is very weak and might be better defined as a network failure (Swain, 1998).

Conclusions

With the reintegration of central and eastern European countries, the European economy has become much more diverse and varied in terms of production and technology structures. Also, the process of EU enlargement is taking place at a time when trade patterns are being strongly shaped by the complex integration strategies of TNCs, involving the construction of international production networks across national boundaries. This brings together issues relating to trade policy, FDI and other forms of linkage in the production and technology field. The chapter discussed the role of East/West industrial networks in reinforcing the competitive advantages of the EU and CEECs. However, we also stressed that it is not inevitable that the process of industrial integration will be positive, integration could also lead to the erosion of the national, or even regional, bases of competitiveness. This raises the question of what the requirements would be for a 'win–win' situation.

The literature on national systems of innovation shows that the roots of technological competitiveness remain distinctly national (Lundvall, 1992; Nelson, 1993). What we may expect to see over the next period, therefore, is a new emerging European economic architecture which will be shaped by a multiplicity of corporate linkages and the interaction of corporate and national competitive strategies. How this evolves will depend on the modes and patterns of production and technology integration of central and eastern Europe into the wider European economy, phenomena that we still do not understand well enough. Although market integration is a necessary objective of EU enlargement, it is in no way a sufficient condition for dynamically efficient outcomes. The chances of convergence by the economies of central and eastern Europe in terms of growth are much more likely if market integration ('shallow integration') between them and the current EU is reinforced by production and technology integration ('deep integration'). Otherwise, these countries could end up politically integrated into the EU, but isolated and marginalized in terms of production and technology linkages and excessively dependent on budgetary transfers.

Given that the specificity of European integration, as defined by EU membership, is 'deep' institutional integration, the issue of its links with industrial integration warrant more attention. A proper account of the conditions for deep integration demands a better understanding of supply-side phenomena, in particular of the extent, factors, and nature of production and technology linkages between the current EU and the countries of central and eastern Europe. This chapter has developed a line of analysis that could help to resolve some of the 'blank spots' indicated.

We examined how best to understand the role of global industrial networks in central and eastern Europe and the way in which they are contributing to growth in the region, as well as in the EU. The opportunities for, and constraints in, industrial upgrading are particularly important. Our conclusion is that if we want to understand the emerging industrial architecture of the wider Europe, then perspectives drawn from industrial organization have to be combined with political economy perspectives. Different theoretical approaches to FDI, among which the 'make or buy' perspective is dominant, have been distinguished from political economy approaches.

The basic difficulty with combining these different approaches is to define which variables should be taken into account (Hall, 1997). Our unit of analysis is industrial dynamics and this is necessarily an 'open system'. As Lundvall (1998) points out '(I)industrial dynamics is not linked to one specific level of aggregation in terms of micro-, meso-, and macro-analysis (b)ut present a specific perspective on the firm as an open system that is affected by and affects wider systems' (p. 2–3 cited in Ernst, 1998). To get to grips with this requires both multi-level and multi-dimensional investigation. The intersection between different networks is either nationally or sectorally specific and involves a variety of the governance factors that hinder or facilitate alignment of different networks. Kim and von Tunzelmann (1998) offer a valuable framework for analysing the (mis)alignment of networks. However, this does not solve the problem of how to understand the nature and quality of networks that (mis)align. Differences in types and qualities of national, global and local networks influence how this alignment will take place. In the context of central and eastern Europe, even though governments are not able to fully enforce property rights, this alignment does sometimes take place, although with important effects on the ways in which firms from the region become integrated into global networks[13]. As the formal processes of accession move forward, EU decisions on policy alignment will increasingly impact on the economic processes.

Notes

1. This chapter draws on a project on 'The Emerging Industrial Architecture of the Wider Europe' funded by the ESRC 'One Europe or Several?' Programme, award number L213252037.
2. According to EBRD (1999: 89) in the more advanced central European countries, industrial employment as a share of the total had stabilized by the mid-1990s at a level above that in comparable market economies.
3. While the first argument is valid, the second may not reflect what seems to be happening. Research by Tulder and Ruigrok (1998) on strategies of EU companies in the car industry of central and eastern Europe shows that the majority operate as open networks.
4. For modelling of the backward and forward linkages through which domestic firms can overtake and force out FDI, see Markusen and Venables (1997).

5. Gereffi (1999: 51, 52) defines industrial upgrading as 'a process of improving the ability of a firm or an economy to move to more profitable and/or technologically sophisticated capital and skill-intensive economic niches'.
6. By this we understand learning through continuous access to markets and technology which puts a firm on the path of technology accumulation and enables its 'catching-up' or 'forging ahead'. This is in contrast to the one-off import of technology and subsequent learning behind the protective barrier. The experience of developing countries suggests that the learning behind the barrier is inferior in a dynamic sense to learning which is linked to continuous access to foreign markets (Radosevic, 1999a).
7. For example, the Mexican *maquilla* specialization has not been followed by changes in either the development of production capacity or technological capabilities (Capdeville et al., 1996).
8. For example, Caves (1996: 237) concludes that 'the relationship between an LDC's stock of foreign investment and its subsequent economic growth is a matter on which we totally lack trustworthy conclusions'.
9. See Kay (1991) for the critique of this perspective in the case of TNCs.
10. Gerrefi (1999: 67) defines organizing agent as 'those firms, foreign and domestic, that could enhance the competitiveness of the apparel commodity chains in Mexico through backward or forward linkages with major producers and retailers'. 'The lead firms in manufacture centered and retailer centered networks in the North American apparel commodity chains are in a position to play a direct role in upgrading Mexican domestic industry' (68). He predicts that 'sourcing intermediaries will emerge in Mexico to perform the same kind 'full package' services that trading companies and integrated manufacturers provided in 'East' Asia' (68).
11. For evidence in the case of Baltic economies see Radosevic, 1997b.
12. The difficulty with the empirical testing of this argument is that in real life self-organization ability may not be the only constraint; the state of demand, domestic and foreign, may also be an influence. Also, strong import competition or export restrictions from EU in 'sensitive sectors' like agriculture may hinder self-organization of an industry.
13. For example the enforcement of property rights in Ukraine is much less effective than in central Europe. Under the conditions of little property rights security and third party enforcement Pivovarsky (1998: 33) concludes that 'MNEs that were successful in establishing production in Ukraine utilised strategies that aligned their interests with those of the discretionary government. They choose integration with the government bureaucracy by sharing part of the cash flow rights on their assets with the government agents. Joint ventures with local state owned enterprises were one avenue for integration with the government agents and aligning their interests with those of the MNE's owners'.

References

Birkinshaw, J. (1996) 'How Multinational Subsidiary Mandates are Gained and Lost', *Journal of International Business Studies*, 27 (3), 467–95.

Birkinshaw, J. and Morrison, A. J. (1995) 'Configurations of Strategy and Structure in Subsidiaries or Multinational Corporations', *Journal of International Business Studies*, 26 (4), 2729–53.

Brenton, P., Di Mauro, F. and Lucke, M. (1998) 'Economic Integration and FDI: An Empirical Analysis of Foreign Investment in the EU and in Central and Eastern Europe', *Kiel Working Paper*, 809, Institute for Economy of the Kiel University.

Britto, J. (1998) 'Technological Diversity and Industrial Networks: An Analysis of the Modus Operandi of Co-Operative Arrangements', *SPRU Electronic Working Paper*, 4, University of Sussex.

Cantwell, J. (1991) 'A Survey of Theories of International Production', in Pitelis, N. and Sugden, J. (eds), *The Nature of the Transnational Firm* (London: Routledge).

Capdeville, M., Cimoli, M. and Dutrenit, G. (1996) *Specialization and Technology in Mexico: a Virtual Pattern of Development and Competitiveness*, Nota di Lavoro, 96.09, Department of Economics, Universita Ca-Foscari di Venezia.

Caves, R. (1996) *Multinational Enterprise and Economic Analysis, Cambridge Survey of Economic Literature* (Cambridge: Cambridge University Press).

Chesnais, F. (1995) 'World Oligopoly, Rivalry between "Global" Firms and Global Corporate Competitiveness', in Molero, J. (ed.), *Technological Innovation, Multinational Corporations and New International Competitiveness: The Case of Intermediate Countries* (Reading: Harwood Academic Publishers).

Dunning, J. H. (1991) 'The Eclectic Paradigm of International Trade', in Pitelis, N. and Sugden, J. (eds), *The Nature of the Transnational Firm* (London: Routledge).

Dunning, J. H. (1993) *Multinational Enterprise and the Global Economy* (Reading: Addison Wesley).

Dunning, J. H. (1997) *Alliance Capitalism in Global Business* (London: Routledge).

Dunning, J. H. and Narula, R. (1996) 'The Investment Development Path Revisited: Some Emerging Issues', in Dunning, J. and Narula, R. (eds), *Foreign Direct Investment and Governments: Catalysts for Economic Restructuring* (London: Routledge).

Dussauge, P. and Garrette, B. (1999) *Co-operative Strategy. Competing Successfully Through Strategic Alliances* (Chichester: John Wiley & Sons).

EBRD (1999) *Transition Report 1999. Ten Years of Transition* (London: European Bank for Reconstruction and Development).

Ellingstadt, M. (1997) 'The Maquiladora syndrome: Central European Prospects', *Europe–Asia Studies*, 449 (1), 7–21.

Ernst, D. (1995) 'Mobilizing the Region's Capabilities. The East Asian Production Networks of Japanese Electronics Firms', in Doherty, E. (ed.), *Japan's Investment in Asia* (Berkeley, CA: BRIE).

Ernst, D. (1998) 'Catching-up, Crisis and Truncated Industrial Upgrading: Evolutionary Aspects of Technological Learning in "East" Asia's Electronics Industry', paper presented at the UNU INTECH Lisboa Conference, September.

Ernst, D. (1999) 'Globalization and the Changing Geography of Innovation Systems. A Policy Perspective on Global Production Networks', paper presented at the International Workshop 'The Political Economy of Technology in Developing Countries', Isle of Thorns Training Centre, Brighton, 8–9 October, UNU INTECH, Maastricht.

Estrin, S. and Wright, M. (1999) 'Corporate Governance in the Former Soviet Union: An Overview', *Journal of Comparative Economics*, 27 (3), 398–421.

Gereffi, G. (1999) 'International Trade and Industrial Upgrading in the Apparel Commodity Chain', *Journal of International Economics*, 48, 337–70.

Gulati, B. (1998) 'Alliances and Networks', *Strategic Management Journal*, 19, 293–317.

Guerrieri, P. (1999a) 'Technology and Structural Change in Trade of the CEE Countries', in Dyker, D. and Radosevic, S. (eds), *Innovation and Structural Change in Post-Socialism: A Quantitative Approach* (Dordrecht: Kluwer Academic Publishers).

Guerrieri, P. (1999b) 'Technology, Structural Change and Trade Patterns of Eastern Europe', in Hutschenreiter, G., Knell, M., and Radosevic, S., (eds), *Restructuring of Systems of Innovation in Eastern Europe* (Aldershot: Edward Elgar) (forthcoming).

Hall, A. P. (1997) *The Political Economy of Europe in an Era of Interdependence* (Cambridge MA: Center for European Studies, Harvard University, mimeo).

Hymer, S. A. (1972) 'The Internationalisation of Capital', Collogues Internation aux du CNRS. *The growth of the Large Multinational Corporation*. No 549, Rennes.

Kay, N. (1991) 'Multinational Enterprise as a Strategic Choice', in Pitelis, N. and Sugden, J. (eds), *The Nature of the Transnational Firm* (London: Routledge).

Kim, S. Ran and von Tunzelmann, N. (1998) *Aligning Internal and External Networks: Taiwan's Specialization in IT*, SEWP 17, May 1998, SPRU, mimeo.

Kubielas, S. (1999) 'Transformation of Technology Patterns of Trade in the CEE Countries', in Dyker, D. and Radosevic, S. (eds), *Innovation and Structural Change in Post-Socialist Countries: A Quantitative Approach* (Dordrecht : Kluwer Academic Publishers).

Landesmann, M. (1997) 'Emerging Patterns of European Industrial Specialization: Implications for Labour Market Dynamics in Eastern and Western Europe', Research Reports, 230 (The Vienna Institute for Comparative Economic Studies [WIIW]).

Landesmann, M. (1999) 'The Shape of the New Europe: Vertical Product Differentiation, Wage and Productivity Hierarchies', in Knell, M., Hutschenreiter, G. and Radosevic, S. (eds), *Restructuring of Innovation Systems in Central Europe and Russia* (Cheltenham: Edward Elgar).

Lankes, H. P. and Venables, A. J. (1996) 'Foreign Direct Investment in Economic Transition: the Changing Pattern of Investments', *Economics of Transition*, 4, 331–47.

Linden, G. (1998) 'Building Production Networks in Central Europe: The Case of the Electronics Industry', BRIE, Working paper 126. Online at: http://socrates.berkeley.edu/~~briewww/pubs/wp/wp126.html

Lorange, P. and Roos, J. (1992) *Strategic Alliances: Formation, Implementation, and Evolution* (Cambridge, MA: Blackwell Publishers).

Lundvall, B. (ed.) (1992) *National Systems of Innovation – Towards a Theory of Innovation and Interactive Learning* (London: Pinter Publishers).

Lundvall, B-A. (1998) 'Defining Industrial Dynamics and its Research Agenda', paper presented at DRUID Winter Conference, January.

Markusen, J. R. and Venables, A. J. (1997) 'Foreign Direct Investment as a Catalyst for Industrial Development' NBER Woromg paper series, Working Paper 622411, on line at: http://www.nber.org

Meyer, K. (1998) *Direct Investment in Economies in Transition* (Cheltenham: Edward Elgar).
Michalet, C. A. (1994) 'Transnational Corporations and the Changing International Economic System', *Transnational Corporations*, 3 (1), February, 9–21.
Mickiewicz, T. and Bell, J. (2000) *Transitional Unemployment or Transition to Unemployment* (Reading: Harwood Publishers).
Narula, R. (1996) *Multinational Investment and Economic Structure: Globalisation and Competitiveness* (London: Routledge).
Nelson, R. (ed.) (1993) *National Systems of Innovation: A Comparative Study* (Oxford: Oxford University Press).
OECD (1998) *The Competitiveness of Transition Economies* (Paris: OECD, WIFO and WIIW).
Ozawa, T. (1992) 'Foreign Direct Investment and Economic Development', *Transnational Corporations*, 1 (1) February, 227–54.
Pivovarsky, A. (1998) 'Multinational Enterprise Entry Under Unstable Property Rights: The Case of Ukraine', *Ukrainian Economic Review*, 4–5, 1997–98, 65–91.
Radice, H. (1995) 'The Role of Foreign Direct Investment in the Transformation of Eastern Europe', in Chang, H. J. and Nolan, P. (eds), *The Transformation of Communist Economies* (London: Macmillan).
Radosevic, S. (1999a) *International Technology Transfer and Catch-Up in Economic Development* (Cheltenham: Edward Elgar).
Radosevic, S. (1999b) 'Restructuring and Reintegration of S&T Systems in Economies in Transition', Final Report, TSER project, SPRU, University of Sussex, Brighton.
Radosevic, S. (1999c) *Growth of Enterprises Through Alliances in Central Europe: the Issues in Controlling Access to Technology, Market and Finance*, UCL, School of Slavonic Studies, mimeo.
Radosevic, S. and Auriol, L. (1998) 'Patterns of Restructuring in Research, Development and Innovation Activities in Central and Eastern European Countries: Analysis Based on S&T Indicators', *Research Policy*, 28, 351–76.
Rugman, Alan (2000) *The End of Globalization* (London: Random House Business Books)
Strange, S. (1996) *The Retreat of the State: The Diffusion of Power in the World Economy* (Cambridge: Cambridge University Press).
Swain, A. (1998) 'Institutions and Regional Development: Evidence from Hungary and Ukraine', *SEI Working Paper*, 28, Sussex European Institute, University of Sussex, Brighton.
Tulder, R. and Ruigrok, W. (1998) 'European Cross-National Production Networks in the Auto Industry: Eastern Europe as the Low End of European Car Complex', *BRIE Working Paper*, 121, May, online at: http://brie.berkeley.edu/~~briewww/pubs/wp/wp121.html
UNCTAD (1994) *World Investment Report*, UNCTAD, Geneva.
Urban, W. (1999) 'Patterns of Structural Change in Manufacturing Industry in Central and Eastern Europe', in Dyker, D. and Radosevic, S. (eds), *Innovation and Structural Change in Post-Socialist Countries: A Quantitative Approach* (Dordrecht: Kluwer Academic Publishers).
Vernon, R. (1966) 'International Investment and International Trade in the Product Cycle', *Quarterly Journal of Economics*, 80, 190–207.

von Tunzelmann, G. N. (1995) *Technology and Industrial Progress: the Foundations of Economic Growth* (Cheltenham: Edward Elgar).
Wallace, H. (1997) *Coming to Terms with a Larger Europe: Options for Economic Integration*, SET Working Paper No. 23, Sussex European Institute, Falmer.
Weber, M. and Soete, L. (1999) 'Globalization, Digitization and the Changing European Context: Impacts on Regional Economies', *The IPTS Report*, 39, November, 3–9.
Zysman, J., Doherty, E. and Schwartz, A. (1997) 'Tales from the "Global" Economy: Cross-national Production Networks and the Reorganization of the European Economy', *Structural Change and Economic Dynamics*, 8, 45–85.
Zysman, J. and Schwartz, A. (1998) 'Reunifying Europe in an Emerging World Economy: Economic Heterogeneity, New Industrial Options, and Political Choices', BRIE, Berkeley Roundtable in the International Economy, in *Journal of Common Market Studies*, (36), 3, Sept. 38, pp 405–429 on line at: http://brie.berkeley.edu/BRIE/pubs/wp/wp.113.html

4
Functions, Levels and European Governance

Ben Rosamond[1]

Introduction

The period since 1945 has seen the remarkable growth of a set of institutions associated with the processes of European integration. At one level, the informal dynamics and formal decisions that have together resulted in the contemporary European Union (EU) can be thought of as the product of one of the most sustained attempts to 'think otherwise' about one of the most perplexing problems of human governance. For the purposes of this chapter, this problem will be labelled the 'functions/levels dilemma', though beneath that convenient term sit many complex and contested issues.

In essence the functions/levels dilemma invites us to think about the most appropriate way of delivering authoritative policy outputs. The term 'governance' is useful here because it does not necessarily associate regulation, stabilization, distribution and other authoritative functions with the formal institutions of government. Moreover, it is not only the way in which authority is exercised that is at stake, but also the level at which it is exercised. Thus, it may be that some areas of economic and social activity are more effectively regulated beyond the conventions of national territory.

That said, (western) Europe has gone further than any other region in 'thinking otherwise' about the functions/levels problem. It is perhaps the place where serious questions about governance are most frequently posed. Is the nation-state the most effective capsule to secure peaceful coexistence among states, and to what extent does the nation-state, and the states system it spawns, contribute to efficient and prosperous allocation of resources? The European Communities (EC) emerged out of these impulses at a time – in the wake of World

War II – when creative thinking about governance was decidedly plausible. What emerged was a developing system of supranational governance whose inspiration was the resolution of the first of these imperatives, but which seemed to possess an in-built dynamic towards further economic and political 'enmeshment' (or in French, *engrenage*).

Whether the architects of the European Coal and Steel Community (ECSC) had these longer-term implications in mind is debatable. But as the Communities evolved over five decades, west Europeans might have been forgiven for thinking that they had arrived at a set of institutions with at least a fair chance of meeting the needs of advanced industrial societies in the context of the international political economy of the late twentieth century.

In this context the battle lines of the 'European debate' seemed to be locked into a discussion about the continued efficacy of national economic management versus the utility of 'Europeanizing' governance functions. This has always been a particularly crude antinomy, especially when boiled down to the nation-state versus super-state dichotomy favoured by many politicians and journalists. The emergence of debates about globalization has added piquancy to the functions/levels dilemma, not least because of the challenges globalization is said to pose for conventional forms of authority. In addition, the theory, practice and rhetoric surrounding globalization raise a series of intriguing puzzles for students of European integration that tend to emphasize the complexity of the nature of contemporary European governance.

In pursuit of this argument, this chapter begins with a deeper discussion of the functions/levels issue and the way that this has fed into thinking about the processes of European integration. The following section inserts a discussion of globalization, especially in terms of its relationship to forms of regionalization and to matters of authority. The final section explores the significance of globalization for our understanding of the EU and European integration.

Thinking about functions and levels

Serious thinking about the functions/levels question emerged in the aftermath of the extreme violence of World War I. Politicians and scholars alike began to question the extent to which governance based on the conventions of the territorial nation-state was both necessarily efficient and peaceful.

Such concerns drove writers like David Mitrany to reject the norm of national, territorially based governance as dogma. In his classic book

A Working Peace System, first published in 1943, Mitrany argued that the primary purpose of government should be the maximization of human welfare and the fulfilment of human need. The organization of human affairs should not be governed by the pursuit of a particular ideological credo, but rather should be a matter for rational and technocratic insight. Mitrany's functionalism refused to offer a blueprint for the organization of authority. Indeed the functionalist *mantra* became 'form follows function'. Quite simply, human needs vary across policy areas and will change over time. Understanding these needs rationally would produce a flexible and variegated pattern of organizations charged with supplying governance for identifiable policy domains (Mitrany, 1966).

Mitrany's key message for anyone thinking about European integration was that fixing territorial boundaries on any scheme of governance and bundling together functions within a single organizational form amounted to a dangerous type of closure. It would have the effect of reproducing the faults of the states system, albeit on a grander scale. Mitrany's critique of the EC (Mitrany, 1975) developed two lines of criticism, which he labelled the 'federal fallacy' and the 'regional fallacy'. The latter described the tendency to predefine membership of the regional organization, thereby doing violence to the functionalist claim that some human needs transcend territory. Efficient and rational governance would not be possible in the EC, a tragedy reinforced by the 'federal fallacy' where Mitrany held that the Communities arose out of 'political' impulses rather than a concern for the real welfare dilemmas arising from World War II. 'A political union must be nationalistic', he wrote, 'as such it must impede, and it may defeat, the great historic quest for a general system of peace and development . . . it is bound to shape towards a centralized system . . .' (Mitrany, 1975: 72). All-encompassing regional integration schemes mimic processes of (nation) state-building, but in the absence of the natural cohesiveness that enables the successful imagining of community in nation-states. Finally, because they create a supra-territorial community out of pre-existing national communities, entities such as the EC leave the (erroneous) policy-making mechanisms of the nation-state intact (if somewhat circumscribed).

These powerful criticisms aside, the discussion of Mitrany's functionalism is useful because of its relationship to some of the sentiments resident in the minds of the architects of contemporary European unity. Of course, there are persuasive arguments to suggest that the ECSC and its successors arose from one of: (a) a classic series of international trade-offs; (b) a concerted attempt to rescue the policy capacities of European governments; or (c) an expression of the interests of powerful elements of European and American capital. But it is clear that in terms of both institutional design and integrative strategy, the Communities owe a significant debt to functional and technocratic impulses. The rationale for creating a 'High Authority' – what became the European Commission – was precisely that a body of knowledgeable technocrats operating at the European level (and thereby lacking the baggage of national interests) would be best placed to initiate and manage the integration of economic sectors across countries. Moreover the Monnet – Schuman method of integration was designed to yield long term political union out of inconspicuous economic beginnings. Neofunctionalists – in many ways the 'authorized theorists' of European integration – came to call this process 'spillover'. Integration in modest but strategically significant sectors would create the pressures for the integration of cognate sectors, which – egged on by the High Authority – would be accompanied by the shift in the loyalties of key producer groups away from national authorities. Their instrumental rationality would ensure that shifts in the locus of authority quickly became significant. As they came to operate within an integrating transnational economy, so they would increasingly demand more supranational rules – something that only supranational authorities could supply effectively.

The neo-functionalist explanation for integration held that these processes of 'politicization' could come into play in instances where certain background conditions prevailed. Roughly these amounted to the existence of pluralistic polities among putative member states with a degree of elite complementarity and a significant rate of transactions already in existence between the countries. The discussion of necessary background conditions came to be used as an explanation for why the west European model of integration had not been reproduced elsewhere (Haas and Schmitter, 1964).

Globalization

The relationship between European integration and other forms of regionalism is now once again a major preoccupation that feeds into the long-standing functions/levels problem identified above. In a sense this is a policy question: Does the EU as presently configured offer a reasonable framework for the management of the types of problems now confronting Europe? For those in extra-European regions, the status of the EU as a model of regional institution-building becomes a matter of debate. But it is also an intellectual question: can we meaningfully conceptualize the EU and the North American Free Trade Area (NAFTA), Mercosur, or the Asia–Pacific Economic Community (APEC) within the same intellectual breath? (Rosamond, 2000: ch 7).

These questions have been given added poignancy in light of recent debates about the relationship between governance and globalization. Globalization provides a compelling if sometimes confusing motif for the present period. Apart from its status as a (rather slippery) analytic category, the term has a real world policy presence given substance by its regular appearance in the public discourses of politicians, journalists, business executives and policy professionals. The invocation of 'globalization' conjures up a world without borders, where the economic fates of distant localities are rendered radically interdependent. In much public and academic discourse, the idea of globalization is reduced to the discussion of intensified interaction along a series of economic circuits, notably finance, production and trade with the image of a worldwide convergence of policy priorities around a neoliberal agenda.

This is not the place for a full-scale engagement with the many debates about globalization (for which see Scholte, 2000). But if nothing else, the vigorous discussions that have accompanied the entry of the concept of 'globalization' into the academic, policy and journalistic lexicons have forced us to think carefully about cherished and seemingly immutable concepts. Whether or not we accept that 'globalization' is bringing about radical transformations, it is certainly the case that there has been a widespread expansion in the capacity to once more 'think otherwise' about world order and the bases of economic, political, cultural and social life (Immerfall, 1998). At the heart of these deliberations again lies the question of the integrity and sustainability of the international system of sovereign states. Rather than the avoidance of war, the dilemma now revolves around the knotty question of how to govern globalization and how to capture its benefits and/or how to resist its debilitating consequences. In particular, much of the literature on globalization sees the executive capacities of the modern state becoming chronically constrained or at the very least refined, 'residualized' or 'hollowed out' (Cerny, 1995; Jessop, 1994; Strange, 1996). Moreover, the literature invites us to think in terms of the increasing irrelevance of borders, the dissolution of territorial ties and the growth of transnational transactions.

The alleged incapacitation of the state 'from the outside' inevitably raises questions about the internal dimensions of authority. The more extravagant claims about 'globalization' present an image of the progressive marginalization of virtually all aspects of *national*, territorially based governance. In its keynote report *Our Global Neighbourhood*, the Commission on Global Governance (1995) identified a series of distinct changes to the fabric of the global political economy of the late twentieth century and raised questions about how these complex challenges (such as economic globalization, rapid technological change, environmental degradation, altered security structures and the like) had undermined the guiding logics of the UN system. The new world defined in such policy-oriented work resonates with many academic studies. James Rosenau defines governance as '[encompassing] the activities of governments, but it also includes any actors who resort to command mechanisms to make demands, frame goals, issue directives and pursue policies' (1997: 145). In Rosenau's view the fragmented and turbulent world we inhabit has spawned a multiplicity of such actors that, in turn, contribute to both the dispersal and privatization of authority. Moreover, patterns of authoritative governance – hitherto routinized in the authority structures of the nation-state – have become dynamic, evolving and elusive.

In this context the rebirth of the 'region' as a feature of a globalizing world presents a powerful contribution to the image of a 'neomedieval' image of world order favoured by some analysts of globalization (Cerny, 2000). To an extent, this intellectual move 'anticipates a return to the region as the basic unit of economic, cultural and political organization, as a result of the crisis of the national state-based system of capital accumulation, identity formation, institutional representation and political governance which dominated the post-war era' (Amin and Thrift, 1994: 7). Hyperbole aside, it has become commonplace to identify the increased salience of regional economies and (thus) to ask questions about the relationship between regionalization and globalization. The debate has two dimensions. The first concerns the rebirth or increasing salience of subnational or local regions (which may indeed cross formal national borders). The second is connected to the wider discussions about the growth of super-regions, such as the EU, where questions of institutionalization and identity formation are equally pertinent (Storper, 1999).

Europe, multi-level governance and globalization

Contemporary Europe provides particularly fertile ground for such debates. The processes of European integration and the growth of EU-level governance capacities offer some of the starkest examples of the drift from national modes of authority. Yet there remains serious debate about the extent to which this represents a significant diminution of national executive autonomy. Moreover, the nature of the relationship between 'Europeanization' and 'globalization' is at best ambiguous and for the most part downright confusing. Finally, the (sub) regional dimensions of European integration have come to increasing prominence. So-called 'cohesion policy' has become the second largest line item in the EU budget and the powerful discourse of 'Europe of the Regions' (emanating from both supranational institutions and subnational actors) has shown how the image of a radical reconfiguration of territory can become a discernible political project serving particular strategic ends.

There are multiple questions here, all worthy of extensive investigation. The extent to which 'Europe' is 're-territorializing' on a post-national regional basis with meaningful forms of emergent regional governance is much discussed (Harvie, 1994; Hooghe, 1996; Keating, 1998; Le Galès and Lequesne, 1998), as is the importance of EU cohesion policy and structural funding for the consolidation of sub-regional identities (Amin and Tomaney, 1995; Hooghe, 1996). But we are still some distance from a full understanding of how this connects with a series of concerns to do with globalization and governance. There is an impressive range of literature on the economic geography of local economic development in Europe (Amin and Thrift, 1994a; Hudson and Williams, 1999), but this often 'brackets' European integration and the growth of the EU. One of the core problems is that there is – as yet – no serious attempt to account for the complex relationship between the global, European, national and local/regional levels of action.

The complexity of the task is heightened by the fact that each level can be thought of in terms of both structure and agency. In other words, all four levels are populated by forms of collective agency, but all four constrain and structure the capacities for human agency through the operation of – among other things – economic imperatives, institutional logics and prevailing discourses of the politically possible. Perhaps a more modest – but still daunting – task is to think about the connections between Europeanization and globalization where the former is treated in terms of the compelling and increasingly pervasive metaphor of 'multi-level governance' (Marks, Hooghe and Blank, 1996).

The recent literature dealing with multi-level governance (MLG) is designed to avoid two prominent analytical traps: state-centrism and the treatment of the EU polity as only operating at the European level in the formal institutional arenas of Brussels and Strasbourg:

The point of departure for [the] multi-level governance (MLG) approach is the existence of overlapping competencies among multiple levels of governments and the interaction of political actors across those levels. Member state executives, while powerful, are only one set among a variety of actors in the European polity. States are not an exclusive link between domestic politics and intergovernmental bargaining in the EU. Instead of the two level game assumptions adopted by state-centrists, MLG theorists posit a set of overarching, multi-level policy networks. The structure of political control is variable, not constant, across policy areas (Marks, Nielsen *et al.*, 1996: 41).

MLG analysis amounts to the claim that the EU has become a polity where authority is dispersed between levels of governance and among actors, and where there are significant sectoral variations in governance patterns. The MLG metaphor refuses to deal with the politics of endpoints, where 'integration' or the 'drift of governance capacity' is leading to the transformation of authority structures in a particular direction. Moreover, debates about authority and sovereignty cannot be zero-sum. Intergovernmentalists may capture certain truths about the operation of particular segments of the EU policy process, but these insights cannot be generalized.

The appearance of MLG as a defining metaphor for the EU polity takes us away from thinking about the EU as simply the product of a formal act of institutional design or the deliberate creation of sets of decision rules. Rather it is re-imagined as the complex consequence of the actions of multiple political and economic agents within the formal confines of the EU's institutions and the changing fabric of national policy-making processes. In a sense MLG could be read as the latest policy-making pattern to have arisen in the EU context. Yet, the emergence of MLG seems to reflect a qualitatively different set of processes from the trade-offs between broadly intergovernmentalist and supranationalist forces that characterized the transition from the Monnet partnership method to the so-called Gaullist method in the 1960s (Wallace, 1996).

Expressed in radical language, the MLG literature could even give substance to John Ruggie's claim that 'the EU may constitute nothing less than the emergence of the first truly postmodern international political form' (Ruggie, 1998: 173). Territoriality, rule-bound closures and tight definitions of authority characterize modernist forms of politics. This means that the evolution of transnational political space takes a new and distinctive form. For Ruggie it is limiting to talk about the EU solely in terms of the familiar (modernist) vocabulary of political organization. So while there may appear to be echoes of a federalist vocabulary in MLG language about tiers of authority, MLG does not denote a polity governed by clear constitutional rules about the location(s) of power (Warleigh, 1998: 11).

MLG writers have suggested that the configuration of the Euro-polity in this way will have particular effects. For example, Gary Marks and his colleagues note substantial variation in the representation of subnational governments within the EU policy process, and treat this as a consequence of the playing out of the logic of multi-level governance rather than a product of the differential resource capacities of local and regional authorities (Marks, Nielsen *et al.*, 1996). Indeed, they argue that the mobilization of subnational representation has virtually nothing to do with the availability of EU-level financing – partly because the EU has much more purchase as a regulatory state than as a traditional interventionist/redistributive state (Majone, 1996). Rather '[w]e find that the broader the competencies of a subnational government and the more intense its conflicts of interest or identity with the national state, the more likely it will be to mobilize in Brussels' (Marks, Nielsen *et al.*, 1996: 62). This is facilitated by the multiple points of access afforded by the multi-level polity. This makes admission to the EU game easier for those authorities (such as German *Länder*) that have considerable authoritative capacity, or for authorities in significant disagreement with their national governments.

Research such as this shows the value of MLG as an organizing metaphor, but there is no necessary explanation of how 'multi-levelness' and the fluidity implied therein came to replace (or at least supplement) more hierarchical versions of governance structure. One answer might be to see MLG as the evolutionary or path-dependent consequence of the particular institutionalized form taken by the European Communities. Yet it is not difficult to make connections with the broader literature on the transformation of governance in the international system (Jachtenfuchs, 1997). Here the issue again becomes how patterns of governance evolve in the light of globalization. This does not necessarily mean that the state is redundant, but there is often recognition that formal government is constrained and limited. What emerges is a depiction of diverse sites of intergovernmental cooperation, networks of exchange, the increased use of regulatory modes of enforcement, the growth of functionally specific institutions and the widespread dispersion of authority to various state and non-state bodies (Rosenau and Czempiel, 1992). The tempting conclusion, therefore, is to relate the emergence of MLG to the impact of globalization upon Europe (or at least the EU).

However, a simple assertion will not do, because there are various ways in which the link can be made. One argument might be that the crisis of the Fordist/Keynesian welfare state forced the withdrawal of government from several spheres of action. The moves towards regional empowerment and devolution apparent throughout the 1970s in Europe could be seen as an attempt to re-order the functions of government in the light of global challenges (Mény, 1982). Regions would become a crucial site of regulation and the regional/meso level would become an important level of authoritative action. However, most regional specialists seem to agree that this scenario has failed to transpire (Keating, 1998). This is not necessarily because regions have 'false started'. Globalization can be read as inducing not just a crisis of formal state authority but also a radical alteration in the way in which governance is delivered. Formal projects of regionalization and devolution seek to reallocate (rather than transform) the functions of hierarchical, territorially based governance. Therefore, the 'second sweep' of globalizing logic could be seen as undermining the ability of regions to grasp formal authoritative competence: '[t]here is no level of regional government in Europe because such a level is not conceivable in a world where the link between . . . territory and political power has been so attenuated' (Keating, 1998: 28). However, the 'failure' of formal regionalization does not indicate a return to the *status quo ante*. As Keating argues, old territorial hierarchies may be dissolving, but new territorial forms of action are emerging.

The question then becomes, how does this happen? And what place does European integration have in the process? If MLG represents the (perhaps unintended) product of the (west) European attempt to grapple with globalization, then this raises issues about the extent to which MLG will become widespread as a governance form. It might be that the crises of the capitalist state and the reordering of the territorial bases of political action are generic phenomena. But MLG 'European style' may owe much to the intervening variable of EU institutionalization.

Governing globalization?

At least one thing is clear from the foregoing. The thrust of the current literature makes clear that the appearance of a system of multi-level governance in Europe cannot be explained as a formal attempt to tussle in a rational way with the functions/levels dilemma. It is also evident that many of the themes that emerge in these discussions about MLG replicate ideas raised by discussants of the dilemmas of governance under conditions of globalization. The significance of private (non-state) action, the problematization of territory, the redefinition of political space, the recalibration of the tools of national governance and the sheer multiplicity of significant actors are common themes. This begs the obvious question (raised above) about the relationship between globalization and the emerging regime of European governance. The argument here is that we could read MLG as the complex product of the exertions of multiple actors, operating within institutional limits, to come to terms with globalization. This may manifest itself in at least three ways: (a) efforts to capture or extract the benefits of globalization; (b) efforts to resist the costs of globalization; and (c) efforts to develop particular discourses about globalization.

An immediate rider is necessary. It would be foolish to attribute too much explanatory power to globalization. As recent literature in EU studies has been at pains to show, much of the politics taking place within the EU begins with nothing less than the traditional 'who gets what, when, how?' question. Actors participate within the EU polity, neither to influence the trajectory of integration nor to make claims about the appropriate levels at which authority should reside. Rather they are there because of they are pursuing their perceived interests in often heavily circumscribed policy domains (Hix, 1999). The intention here is to speculate about the reasons for the emergence of the EU polity in the particular form of MLG – and it is here that the connection to globalization is important. Also, it should be understood that 'globalization' is not just an 'exogenous variable' in discussions about governance dilemmas. The resultant reconfiguration of authority is also part and parcel of many definitions of globalization. So globalization is not just something 'out there' to which actors respond; it is also something that arises out of their actions.

In the context of the EU, it is clear that different actors position themselves differently in relation to globalization. Even within the European Commission, it is clear that there is some variance between Directorates General (DGs). For some, notably in the core economic DGs, globalization is presented both as an external challenge to the European political economy and as a set of largely desirable neoliberal economic practices that the EU should position itself to enable. Elsewhere, in DGs dealing with social policy, environmental policy and energy policy for example, the presentation of globalization shifts to 'external threat', contained 'out there' in the impersonal logic of markets. In both cases the deployment of the concept is used to justify the furtherance of European-level action (Rosamond, 1999). Thus 'globalization talk' is a convenient way of resolving the functions/levels question in favour of the Europeanizing claims of the Commission.

But there are some deeper points about globalization and the usage of the term within European policy circles. For one thing, there are quite different claims about the extent to which globalization amounts to a process within the control of policy actors. In EU terms this translates quite neatly into the issue of the relationship between globalization and both (a) European economic integration and (b) the Europeanization of governance functions as represented by the EU. Does European integration represent resistance to or facilitation of globalization? Does economic globalization move outwards from intensive regional integration? Alternatively do the regionalizing actions of private economic actors represent large scale corporate repositioning in an increasingly globalized economy? On the governance front, does the form of authority structure developed in the EU represent an engagement with globalization?

These questions are not easily dealt with, but they are some of the most important intellectual and policy questions of the present period in Europe. The extent to which authoritative political actors control or influence the broad behavioural patterns of private economic actors cuts to the heart of many debates about the EU. Writers like Andrew Moravcsik (1998) have argued consistently that the key to understanding the trajectory of the EU is through an analysis of the inter-state bargains occurring at key nodal points in the EU's history (such as Treaty revisions). Thus, to use terms coined by William Wallace (1990), 'formal' integration precedes 'informal' integration. Decisions made by governments create the space for cross-border activity to occur. Of course, it may be that governments are pressurized into the pursuit of such bargains by the demands of powerful domestic economic constituencies which, for example, perceive material gain from operating in transnational space (finance capital is the obvious example). A corollary might be the demand for transnational regulatory structures, not as a form of 'state intervention', but as a necessary prerequisite for a viable, rule-bound field of action (Sandholtz and Stone Sweet, 1998). The extent to which national governments remain in control thereafter is also a serious matter for debate. For many, governmental actors then find themselves locked into a two-level game where there is an intimate relationship between the strategies pursued in international bargaining situations (such as those provided by the EU) and the regular affairs of domestic politics (from which authority continues to derive) (Milner, 1998). Comparative work suggests that region-building elsewhere might derive from the growth of *de facto* regional economies (Higgott, 1997), but the fact remains that the EU experiences these recent regionalizing and globalizing tendencies quite distinctively through the framework of a set of pre-existing institutions.

A popular argument is that the EU's present set of institutions derives from a set of bodies constructed in the context of the particular problems faced by a small group of west European states in the 1950s. The inevitable bureaucratic 'lock-in' of institutions means that the mechanisms for intercepting contemporary challenges remain wedded to institutional choices made by policy-makers half a century ago. Change and adaptation is thus 'path dependent' (Pierson, 1998), so that the choices of current authoritative actors are – to an extent – constrained by their predecessors, who in turn were largely unaware of the long-run implications of their acts of institutional architecture. This powerful argument goes some way to explaining the variance between European and other regional responses to globalization. We might extrapolate further and identify multi-level governance as a path-dependent consequence of institutional and policy trajectories set long ago.

Alternatively, the negative effects of lock-in can be offset by the positive effects of institutionalization. Institutions, defined here as both formal venues and routinized practices, are often read as facilitators of effective dialogue between policy actors and therefore as the basis for effective positive-sum policy outputs. Read in rational choice terms, this means that the institutionalization of the EU lowers transaction costs and (potentially) enables actors to produce the trade-offs necessary to govern globalization. Put more sociologically, institutions act as venues for socialization where common interests *vis-à-vis* identifiable external challenges can be formulated.

None of this is to suggest that the EU lacks formal efforts to 'constitutionalize' globalization (Elazar, 1998), or at least to capture formally the evolving multi-level polity. The gleaming example is 'subsidiarity'. John Peterson and Elizabeth Bomberg (1999) identify subsidiarity as a norm of EU decision-making. They recognize that the term is deeply contested, but note that understandings seem to have converged so that it means that decisions should be taken wherever possible at the national or subnational levels (1999: 57). Subsidiarity limits the capacity of the Community to act. As clarified at the Edinburgh European

Council in 1992 the doctrine states that 'national powers are the rule and the Community's the exception', and that 'this has always been a basic feature of the Community legal order' (cited in Church and Phinnemore, 1994: 538) and that action should take place only within the established corpus of the *acquis communautaire*.

However, the enactment of the formal idea of subsidiarity as an attempt to resolve the functions/levels question leaves space for a lot of politics. In particular, it is often a matter for the inventiveness of the Commission to define an area as appropriate for Community competence. With or without 'subsidiarity' as a guide, the evolution of Community policy competence into new areas has frequently relied more upon the definitional dexterity of the Commission as much as the formal sanction of treaties. Also, understandings of 'subsidiarity' vary widely. For some it is a doctrine which has the effect of preserving national governments at the centre of the EU system; for others is a route to a decentralist federal polity.

Conclusions

The creation of the doctrine of subsidiarity may have given constitutional purchase to the multi-level polity, but this does not mean that the EU system has evolved into a system characterized by rigid layers of authority. As we have seen, writers on multi-level governance highlight the fluidity and non-hierarchical aspects of this layer cake. Authority is dispersed rather than concentrated. Therefore, the stretching of the polity over several layers of action has been accompanied by the disappearance of identifiable sites of absolute authority. For many, in turn, this has been an accompaniment to the widespread displacement of traditional/hierarchical authority configurations to non-state/non-traditional forms of authority.

While these processes may be evolving largely beyond the wit of deliberate human design, this does not stop widespread creative thinking about the extent to, and the ways in which, authority structures can and should be adapted. The argument here is that we can gain access to these contemporary problems through the functions/levels dilemma that perplexed policy-makers and academics alike throughout much of the twentieth century. The distinct take on this issue now is the problem of how to govern globalization. With globalization meaning not only the growth of a single global economic space, but also the radical alteration of patterns of governance, the dilemma of how to 'capture' and manage this phenomenon becomes all the more acute.

This is amplified by the fact that different actors experience globalization differently and thus appear to have alternative conceptions of the possibilities for agency in this context. If the functions/levels dilemma has a problem, it is that it is usually phrased in largely technocratic terms. Where the complex processes identified here leave concerns about democracy is, of course, another matter altogether.

Note

1. Elements of this chapter first appeared as 'Globalization and Multi-Level Governance in Europe', a paper presented to the EU Center of Georgia conference on 'Globalization and its Implications for Europe and the United States', Sheraton Buckhead Hotel, Atlanta, 12 March 1999. I am grateful to the European Union Center of New York, where I was Marshall-Monnet Visiting Professor, for logistical support in the early stages of writing. The present version is written with the financial support of the ESRC 'One Europe or Several Programme' (award number L213 252 024).

References

Amin, A. and Thrift, N. (1994) 'Living the Global', in Amin, A. and Thrift, N. (eds), *Globalization, Institutions and Regional Development in Europe* (Oxford: Oxford University Press), pp. 1–22.

Amin, A. and Tomaney, J. (eds) (1995) *Behind the Myth of European Union: Prospects for Cohesion* (London: Routledge).

Cerny, P. G. (1995) 'Globalization and the Changing Logic of Collective Action', *International Organization*, 49 (4), pp. 595–625.

Cerny, P. G. (2000) 'The New Security Dilemma: Divisibility, Defection and Disorder in the Global Era', *Review of International Studies*, 26 (4) pp. 623–46.

Christiansen, T. (1997) 'Reconstructing European Space: From Territorial Politics to Multilevel Governance', in Jørgensen, K-E. (ed.), *Reflective Approaches to European Governance* (Basingstoke: Macmillan – now Palgrave), pp. 51–68.

Church, C. H. and Phinnemore, D. (1994) *European Union and European Community: A Handbook and Commentary on the Post-Maastricht Treaties* (New York: Harvester Wheatsheaf).

Commission on Global Governance (1995) *Our Global Neighbourhood* (Oxford: Oxford University Press).

Elazar, D. J. (1998) *Constitutionalizing Globalization: the Postmodern Revival of Confederal Arrangements* (Lanham, ML: Rowman & Littlefield).

Haas, E. B. and Schmitter, P. C. (1964) 'Economics and Differential Patterns of Political Integration: Projections About Unity in Latin America', *International Organization*, 18 (4), pp. 705–37.

Harvie, C. (1994) *The Rise of Regional Europe* (London: Routledge).

Higgott, R. (1997) '*De Facto* and *De Jure* Regionalism: The Double Discourse of Regionalism in the Asia Pacific', *Global Society*, 11 (2), pp. 165–84.

Hix, S. (1999) *The Political System of the European Union* (Basingstoke: Macmillan – now Palgrave).

Hoffmann, S. (1966) 'Obstinate or Obsolete: the Fate of the Nation State and the Case of Western Europe', *Daedalus*, 95 (3), pp. 862–915.
Hooghe, L. (ed.) (1996) *Cohesion Policy and European Integration: Building Multi-Level Governance* (Oxford: Oxford University Press).
Hudson, R. and Williams, A. M. (1999) *Divided Europe: Society and Territory* (London: Sage).
Immerfall, S. (1998) *Territoriality in a Globalising Society: One Place or None?* (New York: Springer).
Jachtenfuchs (1997) 'Conceptualizing European Governance', in Jørgensen, K-E, (ed.), *Reflective Approaches to European Governance* (Basingstoke: Macmillan – now Palgrave), pp. 39–58.
Jessop, B. (1994) 'Post-Fordism and the State', in Amin, A. (ed.), *Post-Fordism: A Reader* (Oxford: Blackwell), pp. 251–79.
Keating, M. (1998) 'Is There a Regional Level of Government in Europe?', in Le Galès, P. and Lequesne, C. (eds), *Regions in Europe* (London: Routledge), pp. 11–29.
Le Galès, P. and Lequesne, C. (eds) (1998) *Regions in Europe* (London: Routledge).
Majone, G. (1996) 'A European Regulatory State?', in Richardson, J. (ed.), *European Union: Power and Policy-Making* (London: Routledge), pp. 263–277.
Marks, G., Hooghe, L. and Blank, K. (1996) 'European Integration from the 1980s: State-Centric v. Multi-Level Governance', *Journal of Common Market Studies*, 34 (3), pp. 341–378.
Marks, G., Nielsen, F., Ray, L. and Salk, J. (1996) 'Competencies, Cracks and Conflicts: Regional Mobilization in the European Union', in Marks, G. *et al.*, *Governance in the European Union* (London: Sage), pp. 40–63.
Marks, G., Scharpf, F., Schmitter, P. C. and Streeck, W. (1996) *Governance in the European Union* (London: Sage).
Mény, Y. (1982) *Dix ans de régionalisation en Europe: bilan et perspectives* (Paris: Cujas).
Milner, H. V. (1998) 'Regional Economic Co-operation, Global Markets and Domestic Politics: A Comparison of NAFTA and the Maastricht Treaty', in Coleman, W. D. and Underhill, G. R. D. (eds), *Regionalism and Global Economic Integration: Europe, Asia and the Americas* (London: Routledge), pp. 19–41.
Mitrany, D. (1966) *A Working Peace System* (Chicago: Quadrangle Books) [first published 1943].
Mitrany, D. (1975) 'The Prospect of Integration: Federal or Functional', in Groom, A. J. R. and Taylor, P. (eds), *Functionalism: Theory and Practice in International Relations* (London: University of London Press), pp. 53–78.
Moravcsik, A. (1998) *The Choice for Europe: Social Purpose and State Power from Messina to Maastricht* (London: UCL Press).
Peterson, J. and Bomberg, E. (1999) *Decision-Making in the European Union* (Basingstoke: Macmillan – now Palgrave).
Pierson, P. (1998) 'The Path to European Integration: A Historical-Institutionalist Analysis', in Sandholtz, W. and Stone Sweet, A. (eds), *European Integration and Supranational Governance* (Oxford: Oxford University Press), pp. 27–58.
Rosamond, B. (1999) 'Discourses of Globalisation and the Social Construction of European Identities', *Journal of European Public Policy*, 6 (4), pp. 652–668.
Rosamond, B. (2000) *Theories of European Integration* (Basingstoke: Macmillan – now Palgrave).

Rosenau, J. N. (1997) *Along the Domestic-Foreign Frontier: Exploring Governance in a Turbulent World* (Cambridge: Cambridge University Press).
Rosenau, J. N. and Czempiel, E-O. (eds) (1992) *Governance Without Government: Order and Change in World Politics* (Cambridge: Cambridge University Press).
Ruggie, J. G. (1998) *Constructing the World Polity: Essays on International Institutionalization* (London: Routledge).
Sandholtz, W. and Stone Sweet, A. (1998) 'Integration, Supranational Governance, and the Institutionalization of the European Polity', in Sandholtz, W. and Stone Sweet, A. (eds), *European Integration and Supranational Governance* (Oxford: Oxford University Press), pp. 1–26.
Scholte, J. A. (2000) *Globalisation: A Critical Introduction* (Basingstoke: Macmillan – now Palgrave).
Storper, M. (1999) *The Regional World: Territorial Development in a Global Economy* (New York: Guilford Press).
Strange, S. (1996) *The Retreat of the State* (Cambridge: Cambridge University Press).
Wallace, H. (1996) 'The Institutions of the EU: Experience and Experiments', in Wallace, H. and Wallace, W. (eds), *Policy-Making in the European Union* (Oxford: Oxford University Press), pp. 37–68.
Wallace, W. (1990) 'Introduction: the Dynamics of European Integration', in Wallace, W. (ed.), *The Dynamics of European Integration* (London: Pinter/RIIA), pp. 1–24.
Warleigh, A. (1998) 'Better the Devil You Know: Synthetic and Confederal Understandings of European Unification', *West European Politics*, 21 (3), pp. 1–18.

Part II
The Territorial Dimension

5
'You No Longer Believe in Us and We No Longer Believe in You': Russian Attitudes Towards Europe

John Löwenhardt, Margot Light and Stephen White

Introduction

Ten years after Hungarian border troops started cutting the Iron Curtain, new borders are emerging that threaten to create dividing lines almost as forbidding as the old. For several decades, barbed wire prevented the citizens of communist states from leaving for the 'capitalist abroad'. The Curtain was the ultimate frontier, a 'territorial based code of obedience in a binary form'.[1] Now freshly installed barbed wire and 'Schengen' borders again prevent them from entering our prosperous Europe. With central and east European states at various stages of transition, three groups are emerging in relation to the entry to NATO and the EU: the 'ins', the 'pre- or perhaps ins' and the 'definitely outs'. For the third category, the prospect is that a prosperous and impregnable 'Fortress Europe' will rise up with steep, unassailable walls at the western frontiers of Russia, Belarus, Ukraine and Moldova's inhospitable wastelands.

The Iron Curtain and the Berlin Wall were intended to 'protect' people from democracy. With few exceptions, in Soviet times Russians were allowed to travel to the West only in carefully supervised tourist groups. In a sense they did not cross the frontier, for while on 'enemy territory' the Soviet state with its informers still surrounded them. The new fortress that we are building is to keep them from harming *our* democracies and *our* economies. It encapsulates the inherent tension between the concepts of democracy and borders. Democracy is a set of rules of the game operated by the government of a state. The state, by definition, has borders, and where they coincide with the dividing lines between different types of political–economic systems they are invested with a powerful symbolism. Democracy assumes a free society – and a free society, in the words of Didier Bigo, has 'open borders, open minds and plural identities'.[2] Crossing a boundary, the anthropologist Anthony Cohen has stated, 'stimulates the awareness of a person *as an individual*, as someone who can step back and reflect on his or her position with respect to society'.[3] Russians can now travel on their own – if they have the money – and, in pursuit of a visa, they are prepared to endure what they consider degrading treatment by the embassy officials representing our democracies in Moscow.

Partnership across new borders?

In an effort to soften the blow of exclusion, western governments and international institutions are indulging in new 'post-wall' vocabulary. 'Partnership' has become, in the words of one of our interviewees in Moscow, the 'diplomatic cliché' of the day. From 1995 NATO has offered Partnerships for Peace to those waiting for, or excluded from, its membership, and in their 'Founding Act' of 1997 NATO and the Russian government promised each other to work 'on the basis of common interest, reciprocity and transparency' towards a 'strong, stable and enduring' or even 'enduring and equal partnership'.[4] The European Union has offered Partnership and Cooperation Agreements[5] and, in its Common Strategy on Russia of June 1999, it presents a 'Vision of the EU for its partnership with Russia'.[6] The document refers to a 'strategic partnership' twice.

The invocation of partnership is clearly meant as a remedy against feelings of international exclusion. But can it work? And does it work in Russia? Going by NATO and EU usage, and by definitions in common dictionaries (including Russian), one would assume that parties see each other as at least potential partners who are in a common business and 'share the profits and losses, esp. equally'.[7] They need not consider each other as partners for life, but the use of the word 'partnership' evokes at the very least a commitment to work with (and not against) each other towards common goals. In the context of EU enlargement, the Russian scholar Yuri Borko has stated that, in contrast to cooperation (limited to a set of pragmatic interests and aims),

> Partnership is based on three prerequisites: respect for and the full implementation of all basic principles as defined in the Helsinki

Final Act and the Charter of Paris for a New Europe; a broad spectrum of common long-term interests that can only be secured through cooperation and, if necessary, joint action; and a very high degree of mutual understanding and confidence.[8]

It was doubtful that by the year 2000 public opinion in EU member states would display such a degree of understanding and confidence towards the Russians and their state. In sharp contrast to the Gorbachev period, in recent years Russia has become 'bad news'. Observers sometimes wonder whether organized crime has not become a convenient *ersatz* for the now obsolete 'enemy image' of the cold war period.[9] One of our interviewees, a leading journalist dealing with Russia's image abroad, said that 'Russia used to have the face of an enemy. Now it is that of a criminal.' Can we have partnership with criminals?

But what we are interested in is not how west or central European publics feel about Russia. Our subject is Russian attitudes towards and perceptions of NATO and the EU in a period when, partnership declarations notwithstanding, Russia is being more and more excluded from mainstream European developments. We draw, in this connection, upon the first phase of a two-year project funded by the British Economic and Social Research Council under its *One Europe or Several?* programme.[10] This chapter is based on 25 elite interviews and two focus group discussions, all of which took place during the first two weeks of September 1999 at a time when the war in the northern Caucasus was increasing in intensity and Moscow was in the grip of a terror campaign directed indiscriminately at the population in which nearly 300 people died.[11] Soon after, Moscow started its campaign in Chechnya. Faced with criticism from European governments and institutions such as the EU and the OSCE, the Russian leaders were insistent that they were engaged in a domestic struggle against 'terrorism' in which the intervention of outside powers would not be welcome. Another issue dominating Russian public debate during the period of our interviews concerned Western allegations of money laundering and the diversion of IMF credits to Russia through the Bank of New York and several European banks.

These 25 elite interviews were organized by our partner institution in Moscow, the Department of Elite Studies at the Institute of Sociology of the Russian Academy of Sciences, and were conducted by us under Chatham House rules. The interviewees were assured that they would not be identifiable from published texts. With the exception of an anonymous colonel from the Federal Security Bureau (FSB), however, none of the interviewees objected to our taping the conversation and it was our impression that none of them would, in practice, have objected to having their names published, as well.

Through these interviews we hoped to get an impression of the diversity of opinions on foreign and security policy among members of the Russian political elite in Moscow. Among our interviewees were members of the State Duma; representatives of Duma committees and their apparatus; advisors to the Federation Council; a member and a former member of the Presidential Administration; department heads of the Ministry of Foreign Affairs; representatives of the security apparatus (FSB) and the military; businessmen; journalists; and academics affiliated with various research institutions. Several of these were policy advisory bodies attached to state institutions. The chapter also makes use of the transcribed results of the first two focus groups conducted for our project in Moscow and in the town of Dolgoprudnyi in Moscow region;[12] and we have drawn, in addition, upon surveys conducted by the Public Opinion Fund and the Russian Centre for the Study of Public Opinion.

Official statements of the Russian position on a 'wider Europe' are, of course, not difficult to find. But they can give little impression of the extent to which positions of this kind are shared – or contested – between the government and Duma, or across the wider foreign policy community. Our interviews targeted key elite groups and we asked similar questions in each case – about Russia's 'identity', about its perceptions of the outside world, and about perceptions of the current and likely future expansion of the EU and NATO in particular. As well as oral testimony we made every effort to obtain in-house documents and statements of policy; and we sought, working at these various levels, to achieve a 'triangulation' of evidence that would be more reliable than any single source, and certainly more reliable than a series of casual discussions.

Struggling with exclusion

When dealing with Russian views and expectations of the external world one has to keep in mind that most of the population displays a deep distrust of – and lack of confidence in – the officials who act on their behalf on the world stage. In February 1999 (when Primakov was still Prime Minister), 49 per cent said they did not trust the government (66 per cent in June 1997 when Chernomyrdin was Prime

Minister; 62 per cent in August 1998 when Kirienko was Prime Minister) and 61 per cent said they did not trust the State Duma.[13] As far as President Yeltsin was concerned, during our interviews and focus group discussions we did not hear anybody say anything positive about him. During one of the focus group discussions the following exchange took place:

> 'I have been all over the world. Russian people are respected, we just don't have the right kind of leaders and so it has always been. And so now, too, he is not in charge, there are other rulers over him . . .'
> *Moderator:* 'It's the President who rules over us. And if I understand you correctly, there is someone else above him? God – or who?'
> 'He has the Mafia in mind.'
> 'The government is corrupted.'
> 'The President is a puppet.'

Several members of the elite sample were so filled with anger at the criminal nature of the current Russian executive that no matter what question we put to them, we soon heard them fulminating against their 'kleptocracy'.

Perhaps the strongest impression we gained both from the interviews and the focus group discussions was the high degree of realism displayed by our interviewees regarding Russia's current situation. With almost no exception, they had few illusions concerning the state of the Russian economy and its impact on the capabilities of the Russian state. They saw their state as a weak state. And their time-perspective for recovery ranged from five to twenty-five years.

Related to this realism, an overarching theme was their acute preoccupation with the fact that internationally Russia no longer counts. Some of the more perceptive members of the elite felt that the country had not yet emerged from the 'post-traumatic syndrome' that followed the collapse of the USSR. Whereas people did not have any 'imperial nostalgia', some claimed that they suffered greatly from the sense of *having been* a great power. The perception of Russia as a great power 'is a basic element of the self-perception of high bureaucrats', a former member of the Presidential Administration told us. The perception 'continues to exist' and if any political leader were to behave as if Russia was no longer a great power, there would be 'a deeply rooted emotional reaction'. But many of our interviewees felt themselves that their country was a great power in potential only. Only a few sounded confused, like the Communist Duma deputy whose office was decorated with the map and flag of the USSR. He claimed that 'Russia is a great power', but at the same time that it would 'sooner or later take its rightful place as a great power' and that 'Russians still have a Soviet mentality and are not used to occupying this weakened position'.

Most Russians are painfully aware that their country is no longer a great power, whatever the rhetoric of some of their leaders whom many see as corrupted anyway. They also know that this is closely related to the country's economic problems. In a January 1999 poll, 49 per cent did not expect the country to recover to such an extent that there would be 'a normal, stable life' within five to ten years, and 58 per cent did not expect it to regain great power status within that period. More important perhaps was the fact that when asked to choose between these two goals, almost three out of every four (73 per cent) felt that a normal, stable life was the more important goal. Only 18 per cent felt that the goal of regaining great power status was pre-eminent.[14]

Nevertheless, particularly 'after Kosovo', Russians feel an acute sense of abandonment; and they are struggling to find new grounds for recognition. In the focus groups we heard from ordinary people that since the USSR has collapsed and Russia's economy is in such dreadful state, 'they have come to listen less to Russia', 'the weight of Russia at the international level is much less', and 'we are no longer one of the poles'. But how about the neighbouring countries of the CIS? Relations with them are 'very bad' and 'nobody loves us'. In the Kosovo conflict the West 'didn't listen to Russia since in the world community Russia doesn't count any longer'. Because politicians have made a mess of the economy, the outside world 'has no respect for us, we are fools to them. We are alone'. And so the litany goes on and on and on.

Not surprisingly, the overwhelming majority of Russians are strongly opposed to the use of force abroad. In particular, they want no more Afghanistans. A week after NATO started bombing Yugoslavia, 79 per cent disapproved of campaigns to send Russian volunteers to help Yugoslavia and only 5 per cent confirmed that someone in their family might be willing to go and fight for Milosevic.[15] As we have seen, Russians do not care too much whether Russia is considered a big power. However, this does not mean that they do not mind the ruin of the Russian army. 'They will not respect our country as long as the army is in disorder', said Svetlana, a 33-year-old housewife. They recognize that only economic recovery together with genuine military reform will make a difference. And yet they do not want their country to be feared. In the words of Anton, a 21-year-old student: 'I don't want anybody to fear us and I would want us not to have to be afraid of anybody.'

NATO and NATO expansion

In May 1998, less than a year before Poland, Hungary and the Czech Republic were admitted to the NATO alliance, only 28 per cent of the Russian population expressed themselves against NATO expansion and 63 per cent were still undecided.[16] In February 1999, in a differently worded question on the 'probable' admission to NATO of former Soviet republics such as the Baltic countries and Ukraine, 42 per cent expressed themselves fairly (25 per cent) or strongly (17 per cent) against, and 45 per cent were indifferent or didn't know.[17] But then NATO intervened in Yugoslavia, bypassing the UN Security Council – and for many Russians that made a big difference. In late March 1999, 90 per cent of Russian adults felt that NATO had no right to start bombing Yugoslavia without the approval of the Security Council.[18] When asked who was more to blame for the conflict, Yugoslavia or NATO, six per cent named 'Yugoslavia', 13 per cent 'both parties equally' and 63 per cent 'NATO'.[19] By mid-May 1999, 64 per cent of the population (72 per cent of those aged between 36 and 50 years) felt that the admission of Poland, Hungary and the Czech Republic one month earlier had increased the military threat to Russia.[20]

Among the elite members that we interviewed, reactions to NATO expansion differed considerably, although all agreed that perceptions of NATO had been seriously affected by the combination of the bombing and the Washington summit at which the new members were welcomed and a new strategy document was adopted. The population, they said, felt that Russia had deliberately been ignored during the Kosovo conflict. They warned that the result will be costly for the West because of the enormous effect on Russians. It 'made them suddenly realize how weak they had become'. The relentless accumulation of frustrations has made Russians an angry people. They feel powerless and degraded. But only a few extremist politicians will turn this anger into aggressiveness.

At one extreme of the spectrum one finds academics or businessmen who state that NATO expansion is not a *real* threat to Russia and that, however strong the rhetoric of their military and politicians, there is very little that they can do: 'Until Russia defines itself, resolves its existential problem, it can't really answer the question of whether NATO expansion is dangerous or not', observed a well-known political scientist. Even a former KGB general, now employed by an oil company, was laconic. If the Baltic countries join NATO, he said, 'it will be bad in terms of political rhetoric, but in concrete terms it won't really matter to Russia'. Ukraine, however, was different. But why should Russia feel threatened if an 'insignificant country' like Hungary becomes a NATO member? After all, the key role in NATO, as he explained, is played by only a few states. 'I can't see what the threat of NATO expansion is as long as we create order in our own house.' Somewhat to our surprise, our interlocutor announced that he intended to run for the Communist Party in the December 1999 Duma elections.

At the other extreme we find officers of the military and security forces and communist or nationalist politicians who speak strong language, claiming for example that NATO expansion poses the threat of liquidation of Russians as a people: the 'liquidation of the Russian genotype'. The West, they believe, has taken advantage of Russian weakness; the bombing of Yugoslavia was 'a testing ground' for NATO's new strategic concept. The bombing, they say, hardly suggests that NATO is a peacekeeping organization; and it showed the Russians that it is not a defence organization. If it had not taken place, the expansion of NATO would have had less impact among the population. But now the 'sense of having been deceived', of 'being pushed to the periphery', is very strong. Some expect the 'moral discomfort' created by the NATO action to evaporate quickly, but many in the elite believe that the bombing has dealt a severe blow to those politicians and opinion leaders who were in favour of Russia 'going into Europe' or becoming more European.

For many Russians and for some in the elite the NATO bombs on Yugoslavia have brought old Soviet stereotypes back to their mind and have forced questions such as the likelihood and the consequences of further NATO expansion to the background. NATO, one respondent said, 'was created right after the war in 1947, when the western countries declared the Cold War against the USSR with the well-known speech by Churchill ... In response the Warsaw Pact was signed and the military balance lasted for many years.' NATO was seen as an 'aggressive bloc', 'a puppet in the hands of the American government', a 'gun that of necessity will fire' as indeed it had in Yugoslavia. Some of the participants in focus groups were even more bellicose than the elite and felt that Russia's leaders had not reacted in a sufficiently 'resolute way'. Since the Warsaw Pact has been dissolved, they could see no reason for NATO's continued existence. 'NATO is a military organization and must simply be dispersed', said Vladimir, a male pensioner with a higher education: 'In their statute they speak soft words but as the latest events have shown, their business is very bad. NATO is an instrument of America, no doubt about it.'

The campaign manager of one of the centre parties was one of several in the elite who expected Russian foreign policy to become tougher as a result of NATO's expansion and the bombing of Yugoslavia. He referred to 'the strange, ideological style of American foreign policy that smells of a gang of youngsters without responsibility'. After 'Kosovo' 'any normal country has to protect itself' from the US-dominated NATO threat. The intervention in Yugoslavia had been particularly shocking to the elite because it showed that the problems of a Slavic country in Europe could be dealt with without the participation of Russia. As a result, some felt, Russian military leaders now have to take into account the possibility of NATO interference in, for instance, the northern Caucasus.

The European Union and its enlargement

The basic question to be asked prior to that of EU enlargement is that of Russian identity. Do Russians see their country as European, Asian or perhaps Eurasian? Do they feel themselves to be European at all? We will not enter the long historical debate on Russia's place and destiny between Europe and Asia. Neither will we deal with the multitude of political theories, some of them bordering on the absurd, currently *en vogue* in Russia.[21] Suffice it to summarize the remarks of some of our interviewees who stressed that Russia, like the eagle in its coat of arms, is two-headed, looking both East and West; that it is a multicultural society with a high degree of intermarriage; that most of Russia's population lives in Europe whereas most of its land mass is in Asia; but that its entrée to the external world is Europe and its chief trading partners are Western, not Asian. We should add to this the simple geographical fact that although Russia has had a (short) common border with NATO member Norway for a long time, it is only since 1995 that it has had a (more than 1300 kilometres long) common border with the European Union.

When in early 1999 Russians were asked directly, 'Do you feel European? Do you feel your affiliation with the culture and history of the European community?', only 27 per cent answered in the affirmative. More than half (56 per cent) answered 'no' and 17 per cent did not know.[22] But when (in a different survey) presented with a choice, the answers were different. When asked whether they thought that in terms of traditions, culture and history Russia was closer to Europe or to Asia, 45 per cent of the respondents (53 per cent of respondents between the age of 18 and 35) opted for Europe, and only 16 per cent for Asia.[23] It is significant, however, that 38 per cent of respondents could not provide an answer to this question. The percentage of 'don't knows' was far lower (17 per cent) when asked whether 'Russia has characteristics of both Europe and Asia' or whether it was 'a special country, similar neither to Europe nor to Asia'. Now 60 per cent chose the second option and only 23 per cent saw their country as Eurasian. Five months later, when asked to choose between two different ways in which Russia should develop, 69 per cent felt that their country should follow 'its own, special course of development', whereas 23 per cent stated that the country should orient towards world trends of development.

The participants in our focus groups seemed to agree. They were asked specifically what they thought the outcome of a survey question would be. 'As you know, we do survey research', the (Russian) moderator said. 'We asked what kind of country is Russia, Asian or European, or does it have her own, special path of development. How do you think people replied?' The answer came quick: 'Mainly, of course, our own special path'; 'I agree'; 'Our own special path, Asiatic and European in the third place.' Others felt that Russia was some sort of complex synthesis between Europe and Asia, but that its European aspects were perhaps dominant. Alexander, 47 years old and unemployed, who had been foreman at a defence plant, testified to this in a personal way: 'I am conversant with eastern culture since I was born in Tashkent [in Uzbekistan]. My godparents were Armenian. Since my sixteenth birthday I have lived in Dolgoprudnyi [in Russia, near Moscow], but I always feel the influence of three cultures. And still we are more Europeans.'

What then makes Russia special – if not unique? Some of the characteristics suggested by our interviewees and respondents were its enormous distances; the dispersed nature of its population and the variety in local traditions (including various forms of political rule); the special character of its main religion, Orthodoxy; and the spiritual strength of its people (*dukhovnost'*) which is in their genes ('for Russians, spiritual interests were always of more importance than economic ones', an acting FSB colonel told us). Some referred to the mystical concept of *sobornost'* or 'community' that only Russians seem able to understand but that is always opposed to the detested individualism of western societies. A former employee of the Presidential Administration, now campaign manager for one of the centre parties, had a more sober view. He pointed to the widespread feeling during Soviet times that a new type of society was being built, a new civilization that was different from all other societies. This optimism led to a high degree of tolerance for their many negative experiences, such as during the Brezhnev period, when a deeply rooted and emotionally rich mythology had taken hold. During Gorbachev's *perestroika* a new myth engulfed the general public and the new elite: 'It is possible for us to realize a miracle.' The disillusion came in the early 1990s and 'right now', he felt, 'Russia is the most atomized society I have ever seen.'

If many Russians believe they are at least partly European, there are profound problems with this orientation because, seen from Russia, Europe is the West. Due to heavy borrowing by its corrupted leadership from what are perceived as western institutions, Russia is bankrupt. The western model for transition to a market economy has failed. This has resulted in a loss of international status and power to such extent that 'the West' – the USA, using Nato and the IMF – can easily expand its geopolitical position at the expense of Russia. The hopeful attempts of the early postcommunist years to have friendly relations with the West 'backfired' and led to a negative reaction in Russia itself, the FSB colonel told us: 'You no longer believe in us and we no longer believe in you.' Great numbers of Russians feel that they have become far too dependent on western countries (75 per cent) and that financial and economic cooperation with these countries does Russia more harm than good (60 per cent).[24] Related to this are survey results showing that three out of every four Russians feel that their country should not opt exclusively for strengthening ties with either European or Asian countries, but with both types of countries equally.[25]

It was therefore quite surprising that, with few exceptions, our interviewees and respondents had a very positive attitude towards the European Union, and its enlargement. This may well be related to the fact that they were ill informed about the EU, its institutions, procedures and policies. This was particularly – and somewhat shockingly – the case with a significant proportion of the elite members interviewed by us. A Communist Duma deputy, deputy chairman of one of its committees, displayed his ignorance by saying that 'we want to enter the EU but we have 120 nationalities and we can't live in a system with only one set of rules'. The FSB colonel had not the faintest idea what we meant by the EU's Common Foreign and Security Policy. When asked the same question, a recently retired colonel-general with 42 years of service started his answer with the words 'If there is to be a European Union, then . . .'

It may also be that their positive view of the EU is related to their dislike of NATO. With few exceptions, NATO (including its bombing of Yugoslavia) was strongly identified with the USA and it seemed to us that a high proportion of anti-NATO feeling was directed against the US.[26] Only a few were aware of the belligerent role played by the British government, or the dissenting voices from Germany and Greece. 'Europe' benefited from this anti-Americanism, and so did the EU.

This was illustrated graphically by a game played in one of the focus groups. The group was asked to order a number of cards with country names in any way they liked. After prolonged confusion and heated discussion, the criterion the group agreed for ordering the countries was whether they considered them Russia's friends or foes. Later, with the cards still on the table, a discussion ensued on Russian relations with the EU and one of the participants pointed out that 'we placed the countries that are members of the EU in the group of enemies. The USA is the enemy. But now we in Russia have the chance of helping our enemies. They are enemies but we will relate to them in a good way.' Many in the group felt that European countries were under severe pressure from the US. We heard that 'their euro now is completely crushed and of course their vitality will depend on their relations with the US. They want to create their own future but the USA won't let them.' And that 'the dollar is doing all it can to destroy the euro . . .' 'And for the same reason they bombed Yugoslavia.' A high official of a Duma committee said the same thing in different words: NATO expansion is a '*diktat*' to the Europeans. The US is a relatively young country that has a strong need to expand. But 'Europe is not their home. *We* have to live in Europe, together, you and us!'

Nevertheless, the positive view of EU enlargement displayed by common Russians and many in the elite should be put in perspective. All of them feel quite strongly that Russia cannot and must not ignore its Asian neighbours and other important powers in the world. They see Russia as a potentially significant power in several regions of Europe *and* Asia. They reject the 'unipolar' world of the Americans and hope for a multipolar world in which Russia has a strong voice. They also reject the thought that their country should have only one strategic partner. 'We have to have well developed, balanced relationships with all major countries, in a multipolar world.'

Conclusion

The demise of the Soviet empire has triggered a geopolitical reorganization of the Eurasian continent. As a result, in the words of one of the most westernized of the academics in Moscow to whom we spoke, 'Russians will have to learn to look at integration in a wholly new way: not integrating others in Russia but integrating Russia into bigger structures. If they cannot do that, Russia will indeed remain an outsider.' Some – but we need to stress: only some – of these structures are European, and the European Union is one of them. In its great majority, the Moscow elite has a positive attitude towards the EU and its enlargement, *provided* this process is not used to further marginalize Russia. Many accept that Russia will never be a member of the EU and that its enlargement to include central European and Baltic states will not necessarily harm Russian interests. But they are unanimous in pointing out that if European institutions want stability and prosperity for Europe, they should involve Russia in major decisions concerning the continent's future. Russian interests should not be wilfully ignored. 'I do understand that the West does not want a strong Russia', said a KGB general, now advisor to the Federation Council's Security and Defence Committee. 'But you should understand that neither is it in the West's interest to have a weak Russia.'

The NATO action in Yugoslavia has made the general population face the simple but uncomfortable truth that in the international arena Russia no longer plays a role of the same significance as before. NATO bombs destroyed the myth of make-believe partnership and Russian leaders speaking in terms of partnership with the West have lost credibility.[27] But as we have seen, there is a wide perception gap in Russia between NATO and Europe. 'Europe' and the EU are seen in a positive light. There is, therefore, considerable scope for an imaginative Common Foreign and Security Policy provided it is developed in an open dialogue with Russian leaders and, perhaps even more important, explained to the country's citizens.

Although the empirical base of this contribution is narrow, we found certain other constants that allow us to make one or two tentative policy recommendations. The interviews and focus group discussions left us with the impression that both NATO and the EU are failing in their public relations vis-à-vis the population of Russia. Most Russians have a biased view of the Kosovo conflict and members of the elite in Moscow felt that NATO could have done a far better job in terms of 'damage limitation' by trying to explain the complexity of the situation.

By not engaging in some straightforward and relatively cheap public relations aimed at the Russian population, NATO gave a signal that they really did not matter and harmed its own interests. There is room for improvement of the EU's public relations as well. Both the European Commission and EU member states have made significant investments in the Russian transition, but overall these are invisible to the population. There is ample room for improvement of information on the EU, its structures, aims, policies and its programmes in Russia in particular. The battered people of this country need to receive a strong signal from the European Commission saying simply that they matter to us. Only then will the word 'partnership' have any meaning.

Notes

1. Didier Bigo, 'Frontiers and Security in the European Union: The Illusion of Migration Control', in Malcolm Anderson & Eberhard Bort (eds), *The Frontiers of Europe*, London & Washington: Pinter, 1998, pp. 148–64 (149).
2. Didier Bigo, *op. cit.*, p. 161.
3. Anthony P. Cohen, 'Boundaries and boundary-consciousness: Politicising Cultural Identity', in Anderson & Bort (eds), pp. 22–35 (28).
4. Founding Act on Mutual Relations, Cooperation and Security between NATO and the Russian Federation, signed in Paris, 27 May 1997. See http://www.nato.int/docu/basictxt/fndact-a.htm.
5. The PCA with Russia was ratified by the Russian parliament in November 1996.
6. Common Strategy of the European Union on Russia. http://ue.eu.int/pesc/article.asp?lang-eng&id-99908199.
7. *Longman Dictionary of Contemporary English*, Harlow: Longman, p. 791. See also *Slovar' Russkogo Iazyka*, AN SSSR: Institut Russkogo Iazyka. Moscow: Russkii Iazyk, 1984, Vol. 3, p. 27.
8. Youri Borko, 'Russia and the EU relations in the 21st Century: Four Possible Scenarios', *The European Union Review*, Vol. 2, No. 3 (November 1997), pp. 91–113 (100).
9. Eberhard Bort, 'Grenzen und Grenzräume in Mitteleuropa', *WeltTrends* No. 22 (Spring 1999), pp. 75–94 (84).
10. Grant L213252007, ESRC 'One Europe or Several?' Programme: *The Outsiders: Russia, Ukraine, Belarus, Moldova and the New Europe*, 1 April 1999–31 March 2001. The full project involves nationwide opinion surveys, 16 focus groups (including 4 among military personnel), and approximately 140 elite interviews in the four countries concerned.
11. After the bombing of the Manezh shopping mall in Moscow (31 August), bombs went off in residential flats in Buinaksk, Dagestan, on 4 September, and again in Moscow, Guryanov street (9 September) and Kashirskoe Highway (13 September, the day that had been declared a day of mourning for the victims of previous attacks) and in Volgodonsk (Rostov oblast', 16 September).

12. One focus group was organised for us by VTsIOM in Moscow and included a 20-year old male student; a 24-year old woman doing external studies at a physics faculty; a 32-year old female secretary and teacher; a 34-year old male engineer; a 36-year old male electrotechnician; a 44-year old female artist; a 52-year old male radiotechnician and an almost retired female computer engineer. The focus group organised for us in Dolgoprudnyi by the Institute of Applied Politics consisted of a 21-year old male student; a 33-year old housewife with a psychology degree; a 33-year old female Russian language teacher now engaged in shuttle trade; a 47-year old male unemployed, former foreworker at a defence plant; a 53-year old chief accountant at a café; a 55-year old male welder; a 63-year old male pensioner with a degree in construction engineering and a 66-year old female pensioner who had also worked at the defence plant.
13. 'Komu doveriaiut rossiiane?' Survey (N = 1500) Fond 'Obshchestvennoe Mnenie', 13–14 February 1999, http:www.fom.ru/week/t1025_4.htm
14. Survey (N = 1500) 'Rossiia: chto nas zhdet i chto delat', 30–31 January 1999, Fond 'Obshchestvennoe Mnenie' at http://www.fom.ru/week/t1015_5.htm. These results broadly confirm earlier findings, see the analysis of a survey conducted by VTsIOM in May-June 1998: 'For Young Russians, 5 to 1, Prosperity More Important than Great Power Status', Washington DC: USIA Opinion Analysis M–130–98, 6 August 1998.
15. 'Vokrug sobytii v Iugoslavii', Survey (N = 1500), 3–4 April 1999, Fond 'Obshchestvennoe Mnenie' (FOM). See http://www.fom/ru/week/t1042_1.htm. 14 per cent approved of the sending of volunteers, 91 per cent said there was no one in their family willing to go.
16. Hans Peter Haarland and Hans-Joachim Niessen, *Transformationsbarometer Osteuropa 1998*. Frankfurt and New York: Campus Verlag, 1998, pp. 139–43. The percentage in favour was 9. Concerning the possible admission of the same three states to the EU the percentage 'undecided' was even higher: 66. The survey had an N of 2407 and took place between 17 and 31 May 1998.
17. Nationwide VTsIOM survey (N = 1600), 19–22 February, 1999, see http://www.RussianVotes.org/Mood_int_cur.htm. 13 per cent were fairly (10 per cent) or strongly (3 per cent) in favour of such expansion.
18. Nationwide VTsIOM survey (N = 1600), 27–30 March 1999, as reported by Richard B. Dobson, 'Why Russians Oppose NATO's Actions in Kosovo – And How Public Diplomacy Can Respond', Russia / NIS Opinion Alert L-15–99, Washington DC: USIA, 1 April 1999. In a survey organized by the Fond 'Obshchestvennoe Mnenie' on 27–28 March, one per cent answered that they didn't care; two per cent that they approved of the NATO bombing, and 92 per cent that they did not approve, see http://www.fom.ru/week/t1041_1.htm.
19. 'Vokrug sobytii v Iugoslavii', Survey (N = 1500), 3–4 April 1999, Fond 'Obshchestvennoe Mnenie' (FOM). See http://www.fom.ru/week/t1042_1.htm.
20. 'O novykh chlenakh NATO', Survey (N = 1500), 15–16 May 1999, Fond 'Obshchestvennoe Mnenie' (FOM). See http://www.fom.ru/week/t1048_7.htm. 17 per cent felt the threat had not increased, 20 per cent had difficulty answering the question.

21. For a summary of traditional views and their contemporary relevance, see Graham Smith, *The Post-Soviet States: Mapping the Politics of Transition*. London: Arnold Publishers, 1999, pp. 50–71.
22. VTsIOM survey (N = 1600), 19–22 February 1999, see http://www.RussiaVotes.org/Mood_int_cur.htm.
23. Survey (N = 1500) by Fond 'Obshchestvennoe Mnenie' (FOM), 23–24 January 1999. See http://www.fom.ru/week/t1011_1.htm. All survey data in this paragraph are taken from the FOM web-site.
24. Survey 'Russia and the West', 23–24 January 1999 by the Fond 'Obshchestvennoe Mnenie' as reported on http://www.fom.ru/week/t1011_3.htm.
25. 'S kem druzhit' Rossii?' Survey (N = 1500), 23–24 January 1999, Fond 'Obshchestvennoe Mnenie' (FOM). See http://www.fom.ru/week/t1011_2.htm.
26. In early April 1999, 57 per cent of the population stated that *before the bombing had started* they had had a positive attitude towards the US (28 per cent negative) and 72 per cent that they now had a negative attitude (14 per cent positive). 'Vokrug sobytii v Iugoslavii', Survey (N = 1500), 3–4 April 1999, Fond 'Obshchestvennoe Mnenie' (FOM). See http://www.fom.ru/week/t1042_1.htm.
27. This was illustrated by the words of the only dissenting voice among some 50 Russian politicians at a conference in Moscow. Boris Zamai, a lawyer from Belgorod, stated that 'We must stop thinking of ourselves as a great country. We must recognise that we helped Milosevic even as Stalin helped Hitler before the Nazis invaded us. It's no use shouting about NATO as if we could do anything about it; we have to understand and accept it.' See the report on a conference at the Moscow School of Political Studies in the *Financial Times*, 25 May 1999. One participant, advisor to the governor of Lipetsk, held that Western governments would act in the same way as president Milosevic if part of their country would try to secede: 'If Scotland tried to become independent from Great Britain, the English would bomb Edinburgh.' For a particularly outspoken view, see M. V. Il'in, 'Voina v Iugoslavii: ot zhertvoprinosheniia Serbii k samoubiistvu Zapada?', *Kosmopolis. Al'manakh 1999*. Moscow: Polis, 1999, pp. 184–7, written in April.

6
New Forms of International Migration: In Search of Which Europe?
Allan M. Williams

Introduction

International migration has provided one of the important preconditions for economic growth in post-1945 Europe. Yet a regulatory system based on the implicit assumption that migration would be temporary, legal and for work purposes has largely failed to address changes in the meanings of boundaries and citizenship in Europe and, moreover, in the very nature of international mobility. In the mid 1990s there were an estimated 15 million immigrants in Europe who are foreigners, without legal citizenship, in their countries of residence (Soysal, 1996). The majority do have permanent resident status which provides most of the same rights as national citizens in terms of social and welfare provision, and access to legal justice, but only limited electoral rights. However, across Europe, the pattern of national provision has produced a bricolage of territories with differentiated rights for different migrant groups.

European Union (EU) measures have provided limited harmonization of rights within the EU but in reality there are a number of different European spaces – defined by membership of the Schengen group, of the EU, or candidature for membership. Moreover, these are overlain on diverse national approaches to immigration, asylum, citizenship and trans-border mobility (Castles and Miller, 1993). In addition, there are substantial groups of illegal and temporary labour and consumption migrants who have no claims to the rights attached to even permanent residence, and face increasingly exclusive and non-integrationist national migration and settlement policies.

Despite the aspirations expressed in the Treaty on European Union of 1992 to construct a European citizenship, and in the Treaty of Amsterdam of 1997 to create 'an area of freedom, security and justice', the EU remains a highly fragmented migration space. Its constituent territories exhibit differential migration relationships with each other and with extra-EU territories, and operate through borders of varying degrees of permeability and closure. There are also differences among the increasingly diverse sets of migrants in their access to labour markets, and to the rights of residence and citizenship; these are gendered, racialized and dependent on both the countries of origin and of entry into the EU space. The mosaic of migration spaces, created by this social and territorial differentiation, has significant economic, distributional and political consequences for both the individual migrants and the destination countries and territories. For the migrants the key question is which (of the many) Europes they have accessed. For the EU and the member states, the key question is whether and how to reconcile the competing European models of borders, territorial definitions and social integration. How, if at all, can the different Europes be unified, or at least harmonized, so as to create the single space demanded by the concept of European citizenship? These issues are especially germane as the Union seeks to extend its membership further into the Mediterranean region and to central and eastern Europe, especially after the decision of the European Council in Helsinki in December 1999, which extended accession negotiations from 6 to 12 applicants, as well as adding Turkey to the list of active candidates.

This chapter seeks to explore three aspects of the European migration space: its fragmentation, the shifting location of the frontier of 'fortress Europe' and how that conflicts with the political and social construction of national borders, and the attempts to Europeanize this space.

A fragmented European migration space

For international migrants moving into or within Europe, the region represents a blurred map of disjointed spaces, of uneven and differentiated rights, punctuated by borders of variable porosity. The freedom of movement of labour provisions of the Treaty of Rome, later widened to freedom of movement of persons in the Treaty on European Union, has had a limited impact on this politicized landscape of migration rights, in terms of either imposing a second tier 'European mobility space', or of harmonizing the national systems of regulation. The 'eastern enlargement' negotiations will potentially create new barriers to mobility, and differentiated rights, in central and eastern Europe, even while it creates some new oppotunities. Even though the Helsinki agreement, which opened negotiations with five additional CEE countries (plus Malta), has diminished the potential for creating disruptive new barriers to mobility within the region, it has not eliminated this. If there are major time lags in the accession dates of the applicants, these could be sufficient to allow at least some temporary distortion of long-established forms of temporary and permanent trans-border population flows, based on economic and ethnic relationships (as, say, between Hungary and Romania). Moreover, the political re-definition of borders as a result of the enlargement will have a major impact on migration flows into the applicant countries, from the former Soviet Union or from parts of the former Yugoslavia.

The starting point for this analysis is an appreciation that the EU provisions for freedom of movement have been almost entirely constructed around the myth that international mobility is predominantly the preserve of permanent labour migrants who are citizens of member states. In other words, it is based on the notion of freedom of movement of workers within a single market, and implicitly this is of course a gendered construction. The pervading myth gives scant recognition to the realities of globalization, 'systemic turbulence' (Wallace, 1999), non-labour migration, and the increasing and diverse forms of clandestine and short-term movements. Consequently, there are a series of disjointed, and overlapping European spaces, where increasingly diverse international migrants experience variable entry barriers to individual territories and to what some call 'fortress Europe'. Similar differentiation also exists in their circulation across borders within the EU space, and to their access to national, let alone putative European, citizenship rights.

The EU has been constructed from member states with very different colonial histories, relationships with neighbouring states, and positions in the international divisions of labour (especially the contrast between net labour exporters and importers which was evident even among the original members). These differences have been rendered even more complex by the way that myths and caricatures have been created, or used by national policy makers, in the realm of migration. The initial approach of the then European Economic Community to this was informed by market-making concerns, which some described as a predominant neo-liberal agenda (Holland, 1980). This focused on negative measures to remove barriers to internal labour movement for citizens of member states, as a precondition for the creation of a functioning and larger market which would promote growth and economic balance. Moreover, there was an underlying assumption that integration would lead to substitution of trade for migration in the longer term (Straubhaar, 1988), if not in the shorter term. Migration was therefore largely reduced to the role of an equilibrating mechanism. In practice, the provisions of freedom of labour movement largely applied to non-professional workers. Yet, with the exception of Italy, the other founder member states were of limited importance as sources of unskilled labour. Moreover, over time international skilled labour migration – especially due to intra-company transfers (Findlay and Garrick, 1990) – has been integral to the globalizing economy, especially among the triad (US, EU, Japan) and particularly the world cities within this. The mutual recognition and harmonization of qualifications within the EU lagged behind this shift, so that professional and technical labour markets tended to remain nationally segmented. Their harmonization was given momentum only by the single European market programme, and constituted a belated (if, in practice, still partial) fulfilment of the market-driven vision of Europe. An increasingly powerful version of this neo-liberal perspective was also evident in the debate on economic and monetary union (EMU), in so far as internal labour mobility (in all its forms) is posited as being critical to the successful transition to a single currency.

The EU approach was, at best, truncated for it failed to recognize the significance of the concurrence of escalation, globalization and regionalization (Collinson, 1994). International migration can only be understood in a global perspective (Castles and Miller, 1993). Even in the 1950s and 1960s it was evident that extra-EU migrants provided most of the international labour which contributed to the 'surplus labour' conditions that Kindleberger (1967) held to be critical to the post-war boom in western Europe. Yet, while the freedom of movement of member state workers has been subject to increasing EU regulation, that of extra-EU workers has been almost entirely the preserve of national regulation. This has meant that 'fortress Europe' has presented different national legal and political gateways to workers from beyond its frontier. In consequence, the European space remained fragmented into national segments for extra-EU migrants. Entry into one of these national spaces also restricted their mobility (to varying degrees) between these bounded territories. The meaning of Europe for migrants, then, is dependent not only on citizenship, but on the nationality of their rights as permanent residents.

The lack of full citizenship also implies constraints in respect of electoral rights and access to welfare provision (Bauböck, 1994). Some of these are transferable within the EU for citizens, although they are constrained, but they are almost entirely nationally grounded for non-citizens. Migrants therefore are subject to the vagaries of different national models of citizenship qualification (Kofman and Sales, 1998), even though this is the gateway through which to access the collective rights of European citizenship. Therefore, for the migrants, the question of *which Europe* they have entered has fundamental political, social and economic consequences. The rights of European citizenship remain a lottery determined by national practices and interests territorially assigned by their original gateway into the EU space.

The disjuncture between extra- and intra-EU legal labour migration provides only one of the axes whereby the rights of residents and citizens within the Union are differentiated (Koser and Lutz, 1998). These are also differentiated in terms of the specific countries of origin, age and gender (Kofman and Sales, 1998). Men and women, children and adults all have different rights, which also vary depending on whether or not they come from countries from which visas are required for entry. There are also differences emanating from the legality, permanence, and labour/non-labour status of the migrants. Moreover, migration policy remains highly politicized and populated by myths about and caricatures of the migrants, many of which are explicitly or implicitly racialized. The remainder of this section focuses on four issues related to this.

First, *illegal immigration* by its nature is difficult to monitor and quantify, but there is broad agreement (Burgers and Engbersen, 1996) that clandestine international mobility has increased in recent years. The figure of 200–400 000 illegal migrants residing in the EU member states was suggested at the EU–Russia seminar on migration organized by the Finnish EU Council Presidency in July 1999; this illustrates both the scale of the phenomenon and its imprecise nature.[1] As will be seen in the next section, this is in part a consequence of the changing geopolitical configuration of Europe. It is also the outcome of the attempt to define a frontier for 'fortress Europe' from diverse national border constructions and practices, in the face of intense emigration pressures in the South, particularly in Africa and parts of Asia. Such migrants are excluded from most of the rights afforded to permanent residents, let alone citizens. In employment terms, they tend to be concentrated in sectors such as construction, and small firm industrial and service production which are dependent on relatively low cost and flexible labour.

This tendency is supported by the relative decline of Fordist production and the shift to more flexible forms of production, including small firms and the informal sector (Blotevogel and King, 1996). The status of such migrants is not, however, immutable, and there are opportunities afforded by periodic amnesties and other procedures, whereby they can apply for legal migrant status (Montanari and Cortese, 1993). Differences in national approaches to this inevitably politicized process only serve to fragment further the European migration space, and to highlight the importance of which of the many Europes they have entered.

Second, Europe's *borders are increasingly porous*, in terms of some forms of mobility, notably as regards clandestine migration. Even where barriers exist to legal labour immigration, there are alternative forms of transnational mobility. Whether in respect of tourism, shopping (Williams and Balaz, 2000; Williams and Shaw, 1998), or seasonal or daily pendular labour migration (King, 1998), there are many different routeways across borders that functionally link and divide territories within and without the EU. Progressive enlargements of the EU have redistributed rather than eliminated such movements, through the convergence of prices and wages (but not taxation) and changes in rights of residence and migration. The post–1989 shifts in central and eastern Europe have also increased the flows of temporary migrants, sometimes with spectacular economic effects for national economies such as Albania (Çuka *et al.*, 1996), and for border regions such as that between Germany and Poland (Krätke, 1998).

Whatever the economic effects for such countries, and especially for potentially dynamic border regions (such as Vienna–Bratislava), the socio-political outcome has been to fragment further the European mobility space. Daily and seasonal labour migrants are denied most of the rights of permanent residents, let alone citizens. Tourists and shoppers – despite an embryo EU consumer rights policy – are subject to the vagaries of national legislation, which rarely recognize the particular needs of international visitors. These types of movement also highlight another feature of recent migration trends – their multi-faceted nature. A combination of changing lifestyles, and reactions to barriers to legal labour migration and permanent residence, has meant a growth of multi-purpose international mobility. For example, a tourist trip may be combined with casual employment or petty trading. This highlights the inadequacy of existing regulatory frameworks for migration and mobility, and undermines the objectives ascribed to boundaries by states. It also adds to the fragmentation of Europe into different spaces for different types of migrants.

Third, there is increasing evidence that *consumption-led migration* is important. This encompasses both lifestyle migration and retirement migration (Buller and Hoggart, 1994). Both have grown in consequences of changes in life expectancy, effective retirement ages, lifetime flows of income, and the internationalization of tourism and labour markets (Williams *et al.*, 1997). For example, for most of the second half of the twentieth century, growing numbers of British older people have been retiring abroad for reasons of return, family reunification or amenity-seeking. By 1997 8 per cent of British pensioners received their state benefits abroad (Friedrich and Warnes, 1999). Research by Rodríguez *et al.* (1998) has shown that such retirement migration, in this case for amenity reasons, is generalized among northern Europeans. While many are permanent migrants, and acquire permanent residence status, others lead peripatetic lifestyles, which are extended across national borders and encompass two or more residences in different countries (King *et al.*, 1998). For various reasons, including taxation avoidance and evasion of taxes, as well as the barriers of cumbersome national administrative procedures, there is a high degree of under-registration among such migrants. More generally, this can be seen as a failure to create a single European space in terms of the practices that govern everyday life and residence. This has implications in terms of electoral rights (extended to all locally registered citizens of members states in respect of local and European Parliament elections) and access to health and welfare. This again contributes to fragmentation of the single European space that was implied by provisions of the Single European Act to facilitate the freedom of movement of persons.

Fourth, migration is also the mechanism by which, what Wallace (1999) terms, 'systemic turbulence in Europe' is transmitted between territories and across boundaries. This was most dramatically illustrated by the 1989 Hungarian decision to open its border with Austria, thereby allowing East Germans to move to West Germany, contributing to the chain of events that led to the transition in central and eastern Europe. More recent examples include the population movements triggered in the Balkans by the conflicts attending the break up of the former Yugoslavia, and the chaos in Albania. This is part of the global expansion of *refugee* movements in the 1980s and 1990s (Collinson, 1994). The number of *asylum*-seekers in Europe increased from 73 700 in 1983 to 693 700 in 1992, before declining to 283 400 in 1995 (Joly *et al.*, 1997). By 1999 numbers had increased to 437 400 excluding Italy (data not available) and including only the Baltic states among the territories of the former Soviet Union (UNHCR, 2000: 1). For refugees, as for labour migrants, their reception, rights and access to welfare support have depended on their initial point of entry to Europe, whether within or outside of the European Union. The EU attempt to harmonize national policies with respect to asylum-seekers and refugees has had relatively limited impact on this mosaic of national spaces. However, the meeting of the European Council accompanied by ministers of justice and home affairs, at Tampere in October 1999 signalled an intention to move to 'a single European asylum system', as heralded in the Treaty of Amsterdam.

Changing borders and frontiers

European integration has contributed to the reconfiguration of European boundaries in respect of migration, or at least to the overlapping sets of European spaces that have emerged in the course of deepening and widening. Thus boundary issues and migration have also shaped the enlargement process. There are two related issues. On the one hand, the granting of access to the European single space for the free movement of labour (and later persons) is implied for the new member states. On the other hand, this has increasingly been conditional on partial closure of access between these countries and those territories outside of this potential form of fortress Europe. These issues have been given added importance by the Schengen Agreement which implies a reduction, although not an elimination, of borders to internal mobility among the signatories. In reality, the reframing of relationships between the new members and non-member states is less absolute than is implied by the term fortress Europe. As has already been noted, European borders are relatively permeable because of the economic forces governing global migration, the recognition of special relationships with adjoining territories (for example, Norway and Iceland have association agreements with Schengen), and the realities of the various forms of legal and illegal migration.

The classic 'frontier' of the EU, in terms of an interface with a potential zone of large-scale immigration, was to the South. While Italy (or more precisely southern Italy in migration terms), was placed inside this boundary by the Treaty of Rome, the rest of southern Europe as well as adjoining regions of Africa and Asia were beyond the EU boundary. This had little impact on migration flows in the late 1950s and 1960s, with the growth of extra-EC migration outstripping that of intra-EC international migration. As Holland (1980: 58) argued, 'it was not the logic of economic integration as such but accumulation of capital and its demand for labour which attracted migrants from less to more developed countries'. Hence the zenith of Greek and Iberian migration to the EU was in the 1960s and the early 1970s, more than a decade before the southern enlargement of the Community. Iberian emigration was an issue in the southern enlargement negotiations leading the then European Community to impose a long transitional period for extending free movement of labour to Portugal and Spain. In practice this had relatively limited significance by the time of the accession of Spain and Portugal, for the migration frontier had shifted as net out-migration became net in-migration in these countries.

From the 1970s, and perhaps earlier in particular instances, the nature, meaning and the location of the southern frontier was reconstituted by new labour market dynamics (King and Donati, 1999). The demand for labour in Northern Europe had declined as their economies faced increased uncertainty and reduced growth, which contributed to more racialized and exclusionary national immigration policies for non-EU nationals. At the same time, economic growth and west European economic convergence led to reduced emigration from the new member states. Instead, they increasingly became targets for immigration from outside the Community. Countries such as Spain, Greece and Italy became net importers of people (as in a different context did Ireland, which had been one of the leading countries of emigration before the 1990s). To some extent, this reflected the increased closure of most northern European boundaries, the dynamism of the economies of the four southern member states, and the porousness of the long and open sea borders which constituted a 'vulnerable underbelly' to fortress Europe (King and Donati, 1999: 140). The extent of immigration is not known, given the scale of clandestine moves, but current stocks may be around 3.5 million. Slovenia has also effectively come inside the southern migration frontier leaving Albania, the remainder of the former-Yugoslavia and Turkey beyond, from among the adjacent Mediterranean states. Refugee flows from the Balkans have challenged the viability of the southern frontier. Hence we can observe the difficulties of constructing fortress Europe in the face of increasingly global patterns of migration and refugee flows, especially where there are language ties and socio-cultural networks that extend across the incorporated boundaries.

In contrast to the south, the boundaries between western and eastern Europe, although not constituting an absolute barrier, did represent a relatively effective eastern frontier for much of the post–1945 period.

After 1989, the boundary became increasingly permeable, with the relaxation of controls on the eastern side, and the hesitant willingness of the West not to close off the freedom of movement it had long advocated for the region. There were well-publicized fears in western Europe of a mass exodus for both economic and political reasons, the latter being linked to the revival of nationalism and xenophobia (Iglicka and Sword, 1998). The anticipated mass flows never materialized. Although they reached about 1.2 m in 1990 (Salt, 1993), by 1992 the peak had been passed (Papademetriou, 1994). The result has been that central and eastern Europe has become effectively a buffer zone, but a fragmented one, which faces further differentiation as the result of the multi-speed nature of EU enlargement negotiations. On the one hand the eastern borders of these states (with the former Soviet Union) are relatively porous, and their relative prosperity compared to the latter, has made them attractive to immigration from further east. In this case, they function as being within the eastern migration frontier. However, the western border remains partially closed, especially for migrants from further afield who are in transit through these countries. The western border is, however, semi-porous for the citizens of central and eastern Europe. Even if legal labour migration is still strictly controlled, there are sufficient opportunities as contract, seasonal or commuter labour migrants, or as illegal workers using tourist visas, to allow substantial flows into western Europe. Overall, however, central and eastern Europe has become a net destination rather than a sending region. For example, in Poland, between 1989 and 1997, there was an increase in the number of foreign arrivals from 5 to 90 million (Okolski, 1996), with many of the immigrants being from Ukraine and Byelorussia.

For the migrants from central and eastern Europe, as well as those from the former Soviet Union and elsewhere, the key question is to which Europe they have secured access. That question will assume even greater importance as the accession negotiations reach their conclusion. Membership of Schengen is not a condition of EU accession, but full application of the Schengen *acquis* is a condition of access to the Schengen Agreement. This means that there is a distinct possibility that the real limits to the European single mobility space will be redrawn in the near future, even assuming that a lengthy transition period is imposed on free movement of labour. Before the Helsinki European Council, there was a real probability that the negotiations with only some favoured applicants would result in the frontier of fortress Europe dissecting central and eastern Europe. The opening of membership discussions with five other east European candidates diminished this possibility. Nevertheless, the multi-speed nature of the negotiations mean that the frontier will shift over time and may, if only temporarily, impact on flows within the region. Not only will the EU enlargement process redefine the roles of different territories in the international chains of labour migration and refugee flows, but it could transect long established trans-border flows, such as those between friends and families across the Slovakia–Hungary border, the Hungary–Romania border, and between Czechs and Slovaks across what had once been an internal division within the former Czechoslovakia. In this case the process of European integration could serve to fragment, while appearing to unify the larger European migration space. Whether this will happen remains to be tested, and will depend on the aggregate outcome of the separate negotiations, which have now been set in train with all the central and eastern European countries, excepting parts of the Balkans. If some of the early new 'eastern' members do become party to the Schengen Agreement, this need not automatically imply a disruption to existing flows to and from neighbouring countries, but only if the Schengen Agreement could be made sufficiently flexible to incorporate associate eastern members. Whether the existing Schengen members would be willing and able to accept this, however, depends on who those neighbours are, and the estimated prospective flows of migration which would result, not to mention the ebb and flow of the domestic politics of immigration. Beyond this, there are important issues of freedom of movement, for example relating to the Roma peoples, which may well add another twist to the racialized nature of immigration policy and of borders.

The Europeanization of migration space: access to which Europe?

European integration has brought together a group of countries with contrasting approaches to international migration, seen in terms of both barriers to entry and policies for integration within their territories. Different colonial legacies and roles in the international division of labour, as well as varied relations with neighbouring countries, meant that the member states evolved different policies in terms of both border permeability and the integration of migrants, including access to citizenship rights. For example, the UK has freedom of movement provisions with the Republic of Ireland (including the extension of electoral rights to resident Irish citizens) since long before accession to the EU. It also did and does exercize preferential migrant status for its former colonies, although the meaning of this in terms of barriers to entry has been dictated by economic circumstances and domestic politics (Hudson and Williams, 1995: ch 6). Norway and Iceland have long established freedom of movement agreements with the other Nordic states, which are members of the EU.

Further differences are evident in social integration within the national territories. Within Europe, immigrants, especially from racial minorities, have been subject to four main types of social exclusion (White, 1999). These are, first, legal restraint whereby, for example, non-citizens are excluded from state bureaucracy jobs, and from the full rights of personal mobility to other European countries. Second, there are ideologies of 'othering', whereby various forms of discriminatory practices, and sometimes outright racism, are justified in terms usually of stereotyped myths. Most European countries provide examples of such 'othering' processes, but they have been given particular prominence in recent years by the growth in support for new right parties in Italy, Germany, Austria and France, among others. Third, there has been a failure to provide specific services for particular groups and, in the case of housing for example, this has contributed to racialized housing segregation. Only the Scandinavian countries have relatively inclusive welfare policies which largely recognize the needs of minority groups. Finally, racial characteristics often influence the labour market positions of individuals, and relegate them to the underclass in terms of labour mobility and exclusion from consumption. For example, King (1998) reports that the unemployment rates of foreigners have been about double those of the indigenous workforce in most major European economies. There are considerable differences in the experiences of different types of migrants in different states. In broad terms, Castles (1995) argues that there have been three main responses in the major destination countries, which he typifies as differential exclusion (Germany), assimilation (France), and pluralism (Netherlands). This commentary underlines the deeply rooted nature of territorial differences in the approaches to immigrants and the fact that citizenship does not automatically significantly reduce, let alone eliminate, disadvantage.

EU intervention in respect of the rights of international migrants has been limited, despite citizenship having become in recent years a central tenet of a strategy to build a sense of European identity. The Treaty on European Union stated that political union was to be a 'union amongst peoples' and not just a set of agreements among states, while the Treaty of Amsterdam emphasized the promotion of an 'area of justice, freedom and security'. In practice, however, EU provisions on freedom of movement still relate almost entirely to the rights of citizens of member states. The Schengen Agreement does provide for free circulation of third country nationals, for visits for up to three months, but does not provide full, free movement, which would imply establishment rights. Citizenship therefore remains an important gateway to the freedom of movement rights enshrined in this agreement. In summary, the Europeanization of immigration policies has mostly been imposed on, rather than substituted for, this bricolage of national arrangements. This applies to both the boundary and internal policies applied to migrants.

Moreover, EU social measures to assist immigrants have been limited. While the Treaty of Rome prohibited discrimination on the basis of nationality, this also applied only to citizens of the member states. Therefore, the emphasis mostly has been on negative measures and there have been only a few positive measures to assist integration or to reduce racism (Cesarini and Fulbrook, 1996). For example, there are no special provisions in the social chapter for the EU to tackle ethnic or racial issues, whether for citizens or non-citizens of member states. In consequence, there has been little Europeanization of human rights and citizenship policies. Waudrach and Hofinger (1997) examined the disparities among countries in their treatment of migrants – measured in terms of regulations governing residence, access to the labour market, family reunification, naturalization, and the rights of second generations, and concluded that there are still major differences in approaches to incorporation. Against this rather bleak assessment, however, these has been a string of cases in the European Court of Justice where plaintiffs used EU law to establish the rights of third country nationals.

The EU has been more active in seeking to harmonize policies at its external boundaries. Interest in an EU level response dates from the economic crisis of the 1970s and the shift to greater control in immigration policies (Collinson, 1994: 122). In practice, the main focus has been on refugees and asylum-seekers. This is consistent with EU overall priorities to strengthen controls at its external borders and increase security, rather than address issues of inclusion and rights. Indeed, it is this emphasis that has provoked critics to coin the phrase 'fortress Europe'. EU actions, such as the 1990 Dublin Convention, have essentially been based on intergovernmental cooperation. This was recognized in the commitment in the Treaty on European Union to harmonize asylum procedures on the basis that the issue was considered to be of 'common interest', and therefore to be determined by agreements between EU governments. This choice of method reflected the hesitations of some EU governments about handing over their national powers to full EU competence. The Treaty of Amsterdam, however, revealed an increasing willingness to develop a more harmonized EU regime.

The Tampere European Council was convened to put flesh on these bones. Monar (1999: 1) considers that the 'area of freedom, security and justice' has shown 'an extraordinary growth dynamic as a special regime of European governance'. This is evident in the fact that the member states proposed more than 200 legislative measures in respect of this policy arena during the preparation for the Tampere European Council. Perhaps even more significantly, the governance structures in respect of justice and home affairs are a highly flexible mixture of Community and intergovernmental structures (Monar, 1999). There are areas that are still strongly the preserves of intergovenmentalism, such as asylum and external border controls. But there are also areas of police and judicial cooperation which are now open to a greater role by the European Court of Justice, and to obligatory consultation with the European Parliament. Moreover, a host of new cooperative measures are emerging between member states and other bodies, which some commentators consider presage an important institutional shift.

The still largely intergovernmentalist approach to the highly politicized issue of refugees and asylum seeking means that there is not a uniform policy within the EU. This is problematic since there is a lack of effective international governance in this area. It is now recognized that the Geneva Convention, which defined refugees on the basis of 'fear of being persecuted for reasons of race, religion, nationality, membership of a particular social group or political opinion', is inadequate to meet the challenges of the large numbers of refugees displaced by wars and famine, whether in the Balkans or in Africa. One of the results of EU intervention has been to displace some of the pressures to just beyond its present borders. It reclassified many points of central and eastern Europe as 'safe countries', once the individual states had signed the Geneva Convention. At the same time individual member states, notably Germany, refused to accept refugees who had been in transit through the now 'safe' eastern buffer states (Collinson, 1996). Some progress has been made in respect of collective actions in the field of positive intervention in the countries of migration origin. The Barcelona Agreement 1995 and the Euro–Mediterranean partnership, in particular, has been developed partly to promote prosperity and stability outside of the EU, not only for security reasons but also to diffuse the pressures on emigration. The main means for achieving this has been to encourage various forms of cooperation, backed by the incentive of an EU funding programme. While the scale of the transfer of resources is limited, this does at least recognize the global framework within which international migration operates. The Tampere European Council also recognized the need to integrate foreign policy and immigration policy, and did result in some important advances in respect of creating common procedures and minimum guarantees for a common asylum system.

Conclusions

As one of the triad of global economic powers, the EU has long been a major destination of migration flows, and these have contributed to its economic growth, whether in the age of mass migration and Fordist production, or in the later shift to more flexible accumulation. Differences in national approaches and limited EU intervention have meant that EU-Europe has been reconstituted, however, as a set of overlapping and fragmented migration spaces. Not only does this contradict the goals of creating a single market, but it also means that the 'many Europes' have varied meanings for increasingly diverse groups of immigrants. At one extreme there are highly mobile professional and other skilled workers in internationally competitive labour markets, who constitute core workers, and have relatively privileged access to permanent resident status. At the other extreme are various forms of temporary and illegal workers who in economic terms form part of the underclass in European societies, without even the basic if limited citizenship rights to social provision and democratic participation that are ascribed to the indigenous members of that class. In between are a variety of other types of migrants, differentiated by their skills, their permanence, and whether or not they are citizens of EU member states. While the EU has generally not intervened directly in respect of the rights of non-EU citizens, EU enlargement has played an important role in defining the southern migration frontier of the Union (King, 1998). It is playing and will play a similarly important role in respect of asylum and the free movement of non-EU citizens in eastern Europe, as the eastern migration frontier is repositioned in the course of the eastern enlargement negotiations.

One of the keys to interpreting the approaches of both the EU and of individual states to international (non-EU) migration is the relationship between those policies that determine the permeability of external frontiers and those that affect internal mobility. While the EU is concerned with the creation of a single European migration space, it has not been able to extend this in any meaningful way to third country nationals. For example, the Schengen Implementation Convention was long delayed because of the resistance of member states concerned with balancing security and free movement. Even now, the rights of freedom of movement of persons are extended only to citizens of the EU, and the criteria of citizenship are determined by national governments rather than by the EU. For non-citizens, therefore, the EU remains a series of disjointed and fragmented territories, and the notion of European citizenship has little significance. Different approaches to incorporation serve further to underline this picture of nationally segmented spaces.

This version of EU-Europe in practice does not have a commonly defined set of national borders, nor is it actually an area without internal borders. The importance of borders lies not only in the obstacles that they present to mobility but also in the opportunities that they provide. Whether within or without the EU, there are differences in prices, taxation and labour market regulation which stimulate trans-border mobility, whether temporary or permanent, and whether of shoppers or workers. These not only facilitate inter-regional income transfers, but can be significant in determining where production is located and even for the competitiveness of individual regions. Boundaries are also given significance by the very process of enlargement. In the case of Turkey, there is little doubt that migration has been one of the latent, if not always articulated, reasons for that country's troubled attempt to open accession negotiations (Kadioglu, 1993). Now that the Helsinki European Council has accorded 'candidate status' to Turkey, there is increasing likelihood that such migration issues will have to be addressed, even if Helsinki has deferred 'accession negotiations' until such time as Turkey meets certain preconditions in areas such as human rights. Migration is also likely to figure large in the current round of negotiations with the central and eastern European applicants.

One important point to note here is that much of the public debate about migration policy is conducted in terms of stereotypes and caricatures. The real diversity among migrants, which has been emphasized in this chapter, is often brushed aside by single, stereotypical images. A related point is the time lag between shifts in migration and political recognition of these. Thus the South of Europe was seen as a potential source of mass migration to northern Europe, long after the former had become a macro-region of immigration. Similarly, much of the popular political debate about a possible 'flood' of immigration from eastern to western Europe, mirrors – at best – a short term rise in emigration in the difficult early transition years after 1989, which ignores the fact that this region has become one of net immigration. How that will change after the accession of one or more of these countries to the EU remains open to debate, but there is no historic precedent that EU accession will be followed by a sustained increase in emigration from the new member state.

Finally, it can be argued that any attempt to construct a European migration policy or a European migration space has to be seen in terms of globalization. Europe and the EU are key components of, rather than isolated from, the global migration system. This is evident in the case of refugee movements, which have increased sharply in the 1980s and 1990s, but with Europe being the destination of only a small part of these. Similarly, the implications of EU asylum and migration policies for central and eastern Europe can be understood only in the context of those countries' relationships with the former Soviet Union territories, and their roles as destinations for other migrants and refugees seeking to access the EU. The EU–Mediterranean partnership implicitly acknowledges such globalization, but the Union does not attach significant priority and resources to this so as to make a major impact on the position of the EU in respect of the global flux of international migration. However, it does serve to underline the view that migration has to be considered not only in terms of economic and demographic issues, but in terms of how the Union evolves, its priorities, and its political relationships with both the member states and with countries outside its boundaries.

Note

1. Estimates seem to be based on the rough assumption that the illegal migrants found are about 10 per cent of the total.

References

Bauböck, R. (1994) 'Changing the Boundaries of Citizenship: the Inclusion of Immigrants in Democratic Politics', in Bauböck, R. (ed.), *From Aliens to Citizens: Redefining the Status of Immigrants in Europe* (Aldershot: Avebury Press) 199–232.

Blotevogel, H. H. and King, R. (1996) 'European Economic Restructuring: Demographic Responses and Feedbacks', *European Urban and Regional Studies*, 3, 133–59.

Buller, H. and Hoggart, K. (1994) *International Counterurbanization: British Migrants in Rural France* (Aldershot: Avebury).
Burgers, J. and Engbersen, L. (1996) 'Globalisation, Migration and Undocumented Immigrants', *New Community*, 22 (4), 619–35.
Castles, S. (1995) 'How Nation States Respond to Immigration and Ethnic Diversity', *New Community*, 21, 293–308.
Castles, S. and Miller, M. J. (1993) *The Age of Migration* (Basingstoke: Macmillan – now Palgrave).
Cesarini, D. and Fulbrook, M. (1996) *Citizenship, Nationality and Migration in Europe* (London: Routledge).
Collinson, S. (1996) *Europe and International Migration* (London: Pinter Publishers, 2nd edn).
Çuka, E., Papapanagos, H., Polo, N. and Sanfey, P. (1996) *Labour Markets in Albania and other Transition Economies*, Studies in Economics, 96/17 (Department of Economics, University of Kent, Canterbury).
Findlay, A. M. and Garrick, L. (1990) 'Scottish Emigration in the 1990s: a Migration Channels Approach Towards the Study of Skilled International Migration', *Transactions of the Institute of British Geographers*, 15, 177–92.
Friedrich, K. and Warnes, A. M. (1999) 'Understanding Contrasts in Later Life Migration Patterns: Germany, Britain and the US', *Erdkunde*, 53, in press, 108–20.
Holland, S. (1980) *Uncommon Market* (London: Macmillan – now Palgrave).
Hudson, R. and Williams, A. M. (1995) *Divided Britain* (Chichester: Wiley).
Iglicka, K. and Sword, K. (1998) *The Challenge of East-West Migration for Poland* (London: Macmillan – now Palgrave).
Joly, D., Kelly, L. and Nettleton, C. (1997) 'Refugees in Europe: the Hostile New Agenda', *Minority Rights Group International Report 96/5* (London: Minority Rights Group).
Kadioglu, A. (1993) 'The Human Tie: International Labour Migration', in Balkir, C. and Williams, A. M. (eds), *Turkey and Europe* (London: Frances Pinter) 140–59.
Kindleberger, C. P. (1967) *Europe's Post-War Growth: the Role of Labour Supply* (Cambridge, MA: Harvard University Press).
King, R. (1998) 'Post-oil Crisis, Post Communism: New Geographies of International Migration', in Pinder, D. (ed.), *The New Europe: Economy, Society and Environment* (Chichester: Wiley) 281–304.
King, R. and Donati, M. (1999) 'The "Divided" Mediterranean: Re-defining European Relationships', in Hudson, R. and Williams, A. M. (eds), *Divided Europe: Society and Territory* (London: Sage) 132–162.
King, R., Warnes, A. and Williams, A. M. (1998) 'International Retirement Migration', *International Journal of Population Geography*, 4 (2), 91–112.
Kofman, E. and Sales, R. (1998) 'Gender Differences and Family Reunion in the European Union: Implications for Refugees', *Refuge*, 16 (4), 26–30.
Koser, K. and Lutz, H. (eds) (1998) *The New Migration in Europe* (London: Macmillan – now Palgrave).
Krätke, S. (1998) 'Problems of Cross-border Regional Integration: the Case of the German-Polish Border Area', *European Urban and Regional Studies*, 5 (3), 248–62.
Monar, J. (1999) *An Emerging Regime of European Governance for Freedom, Security and Justice*, ESRC One Europe or Several? Programme, Briefing Note 2/99.

Montanari, A. and Cortese, A. (1993) 'South to North migration in a Mediterranean Perspective', in King, R. (ed.), *Mass Migration in Europe: the Legacy and the Future* (London: Belhaven Press).

Okolski, M. (1996) 'Poland', in Frejka, T. (ed.), *International Migration in Central and Eastern Europe and the Commonwealth of Independent States* (New York: United Nations) 95–109.

Papademetriou, D. G. (1994) 'At a Crossroads; Europe and Migration', in Hamilton, K. A. (ed.), *Migration and the New Europe* (Washington DC: Center for Strategic and International Study) 12–36.

Rodríguez, V., Fenández-Mayoralas, G. and Rojo, F. (1998) 'European Retirees on the Costa del Sol: a Cross National Comparison', *International Journal of Population Geography*, 4, 183–200.

Salt, J. (1993) 'External International Migration', in Noin, D. and Woods, R. (eds), *The Changing Population of Europe* (Oxford: Blackwell) 185–97.

Soysal, N. Y. (1996) 'Changing Citizenship in Europe: Remarks on Postnational Membership and the National State', in Cesarini, D. and Fulbrook, M. (eds), *Citizenship, Nationality and Migration in Europe* (London: Routledge) 17–29.

Straubhaar, T. (1988) 'International Labour Migration within a Common Market: Some Aspects of EC Experience', *Journal of Common Market Studies*, 27, 45–61.

UNHCR (2000) *Asylum Application in Europe in 1999* (Geneva: United Nations High Commissioner for Refugees, Statistical Unit).

Wallace, H. (1999) 'Whose Europe is it anyway?' *European Journal of Political Research*, 35 (3), pp. 287–306.

Waudrach, H. and Hofinger, G. (1997) 'An Index to Measure the Legal Obstacles to the Integration of Migrants', *New Community*, 23 (2), 271–85.

White, P. (1999) 'Ethnicity, Racialisation and Citizenship as Divisive Elements in Europe', in Hudson, R. and Williams, A. M. (eds), *Divided Europe: Society and Territory* (London: Sage) 210–20.

Williams, A. M. and Balaz, V. (2000) *Tourism in Transition* (London: I. B. Tauris).

Williams, A. M. and Shaw, G. (eds) (1998) *Tourism and Economic Development: Experiences European* (Chichester: Wiley).

Williams, A. M., King, R. and Warnes, A. M. (1997) 'A Place in the Sun: International Retirement Migration from the UK to Southern Europe', *European Urban and Regional Studies*, 4 (2), 115–34.

7
Regional Trajectories and Uneven Development in the 'New Europe': Rethinking Territorial Success and Inequality

Adrian Smith, Al Rainnie and Michael Dunford[1]

Introduction: globalization, Europe and territorial inequality

At the start of the twenty-first century the 'new Europe' is characterized by significant and enduring territorial inequalities. Within Europe, much as in North America, the debate over such disparities revolves around two main issues. First, some researchers envisage the emergence of economies that are at the same time globalized and regionally integrated, and of a world in which sub-national regional economic life assumes increased significance in a global economy (Scott, 1998; Storper, 1998). Second, others offer a more sober analysis of contemporary trends, insisting that development is associated with a continued reproduction of inequality, and stressing the wide variation in the roles of global and local factors in shaping the trajectories of different regional economies (Dunford, 1994; Hudson and Williams, 1999).

This chapter assesses the dimensions of territorial inequalities in an increasingly integrated Europe, and examines how we might understand the mosaic of uneven development. In particular, the chapter engages critically with a debate on west European regional development, which focuses on 'successful' experiences of regional transformation – what Lovering (1999) has called 'the new regionalism'. We argue that this focus does not help us in explaining the divergence and differentiation of territorial development in Europe. We also argue that the focus upon the putative conditions of 'success' in 'successful' regions limits our understanding of regional economic performance in Europe.

We start with a discussion of the dimensions and trajectories of territorial disparities in the 'new Europe'. Then we examine the limits of much of the existing literature on the subject. We suggest, following Lovering (1999), that the 'new regionalist' orthodoxy fails to capture the variegated map of territorial inequality in Europe. Finally, we point to some possible ways of reconceptualizing regional dynamics in a more integrated Europe.

Globalization and regional transformations

One of the leading proponents of globalization, Kenichi Ohmae (1995), identifies three paramount tendencies in the global political economy that provide a starting point for us. The first is the growing and unstoppable dominance of transnational corporations (TNCs); the second is the increasing redundancy of the nation state; and the third is the emergence of regions as the major new sites for economic activity (cf. Scott, 1998). Globalization, it is argued, is being driven by the unimpeded flow across national borders of the 'four I's – industry, investment, individuals and information. Investment is no longer geographically constrained. Industry is far more global in orientation with the strategies of modern TNCs no longer shaped or conditioned by reasons of state. Location is driven by the desire for access to markets and/or resources, and subsidies have become irrelevant as location criteria. Information technology now makes it possible for a company to operate in various parts of the world without having to build up an entire business system in each country and facilitates cross-border participation and strategic alliances. Finally, individual consumers have become more global in orientation, with better access to information about lifestyles around the globe. For Ohmae, the implications of this analysis are startling. The nation state is seen as a meaningless territorial unit. In the now borderless economy, all meaningful operational autonomy is ceded to what Ohmae calls 'region states' (Ohmae, 1995). These emergent regions tend to have between five million and 20 million people. Furthermore, the powerlessness of the nation state is taken to herald the death of Keynesian style state intervention. Indeed some analysts have gone further, arguing that globalization represents the greatest ever threat to the social democratic agenda (Richards, 1997).

These claims have their echoes in Europe – one of Ohmae's emerging regional worlds of the global economy, itself made up of a mosaic of regional economies that others have baptized a 'Europe of the regions'.

Increasing integration and future enlargement of the European Union (EU) are seen as forces enhancing the position of Europe in the global economy. At the same time Europe is seen as comprising a series of territorial units of successful regional economies centred around areas such as the 'Third Italy' or Baden-Württemburg and economically strong, large metropolitan regions in the EU core (Dunford and Smith, 1998, 2000). Such sub-national regions have been seen either as Marshallian industrial districts, which owe their competitiveness and capacity for innovation to local clustering (Sabel, 1994; Sengenberger, 1993), or as diverse global-city regions, in which financial- and producer-service functions dominate. Clustering, it is argued, allows for savings to be made by joint procurement and use of resources and by pooling labour, financial and physical capital and infrastructure. At the same time, there are, it is argued, strong relations of cooperation and trust, which are vital to technological improvement. These districts or cities are also characterized by proactive regional strategies, facilitated by the emergence of post Fordist flexible technologies and associated forms of firm and work organization. Agglomeration therefore privileges the local over the national in the global economy in 'regional worlds of production' (Storper, 1998) or in 'networked learning regions' (Morgan, 1997). The result is a discursive rendering of sub-national regional success representing what Lovering (1999) has called a 'new regionalist' orthodoxy. The nation state in particular is seen to be receding in importance, as the local and regional levels emerge as the motors of the global economy.

At the start of the twenty-first century, however, the 'new Europe' is characterized by enormous and enduring territorial inequalities, and this focus upon 'success' overlooks instances of relative failure and overstates selected parts of individual regional economies. Just how wide are these inequalities? Using *per capita* income measured in purchasing-power-parities (PPP) for 1996 relative to the EU average, Luxembourg the wealthiest EU member state, was located at 168 per cent of the average.[2] Slovenia, the wealthiest central European state, was positioned at only 59 per cent of the EU average and Russia (prior to the collapse of the rouble in 1998) was positioned at only 23 per cent (see Dunford and Smith, 2000). The prospect of some countries from the former 'communist' world becoming EU members, therefore, raises concerns over the cohesiveness of this 'new Europe'. As Iain Begg (1996: 13) has argued, the addition of approximately 105 million people in the candidate countries from central and eastern Europe would increase the EU population by 28 per cent, while simultaneously adding only between 3.4 per cent and 8.5 per cent to EU GDP (depending upon whether one uses nominal exchange rates or PPP estimates). Consequently, average EU *per capita* GDP would be likely to drop by around 15 per cent. In other words, under current EU criteria, all of these candidate countries would be eligible for support from both the Cohesion Fund and the Structural Funds. This could cost something in the range of 42 billion euro. Such transfers would account for between 7 per cent of Slovenia's GDP and 51 per cent of Lithuania's (Grabbe and Hughes, quoted in Begg, 1996: 12).

The contemporary map of economic inequality in Europe reflects three important historical considerations. The first is that wide territorial inequalities are a product of the last 200 years. In 1820 the distance between the richest and poorest country in the world was of the order of three to one. This ratio stood at about 11 to one in 1913, 35 to one in 1950, 44 to one in 1973 and 72 to one in 1992 (UNDP, 1999: 38). The second is that Europe in particular has also been characterized by wide disparities. In the late nineteenth century there was a standard salient contrast between an industrialized west, on the one hand, and on the other hand, much of central and eastern Europe and Russia, where a version of capitalism was only just emerging in the 'first transition' (from late feudalism to emergent capitalist industrialization). At that stage territorial disparities in Europe (as in the world as a whole) were much lower than those found today: Russian *per capita* national product in 1870 stood at some 50 per cent of the European average and that of the Hungarian kingdom stood at 73 per cent (elaborated from Good, 1991: 228).[3] Significantly, however, as the economic historian Alexander Gerschenkron and others have taught us (Gerschenkron, 1962; Berend and Ránki, 1982; see also Dunford, 1998a), the European economy has included historically enduring forms of 'relative backwardness' in the East. Disparities were characterized by different forms of economic governance, which might be conceptualized as 'varieties of capitalism' (Hollingsworth, 1998). Forms of capitalist industrialization were found in large parts of western Europe, while the eastern part contained limited pockets of industrialization, alongside enduring 'late feudal' features and the dominance of agriculture (which in 1910 accounted for 80 per cent of the gainfully employed population in Russia and 64 per cent in Hungary). The third consideration is that the variegated territorial differences in the economy of the 'new Europe' are a major dimension of division across the continent as it enters the twenty-first century. The paradox of change since 1989 is that the transition to capitalism and the move towards economic and political integration between East and West have so far brought with them increasing economic divergence (Dunford and Smith, 2000). The various attempts to build and establish forms of capitalism and market economy in the former 'communist' world during the 'second transition' (since 1989) have had enormously uneven impacts at both national and subnational levels (Dunford, 1998b; Pickles and Smith, 1998; Smith, 1998).

Dimensions and dynamics of territorial trajectories in the 'New Europe'

Measuring disparities in territorial development in Europe is a complicated and problematic task. The various multilateral agencies (such as the World Bank, the European Bank for Reconstruction and Development, the United Nations Economic Commission for Europe and the EU) use estimates of economic development derived from national accounts collected by national statistical offices, increasingly on the basis of common principles. However, data of a consistent and comparable quality are difficult to obtain. They often do not capture the role of the informal or shadow economies, which can be of quite sizeable proportions (up to 40 per cent of Russian GDP for example) in both central and eastern Europe and EU countries (Altvater, 1998; Clarke, 1999; COM(98) 219 fin.). Consequently, any firm conclusions about relative wealth should be treated with some caution and the measures reported here should be regarded as orders of magnitude rather than precise estimates.

National economic disparities in Europe

Examination of national disparities in GDP per head (measured in PPP), relative to the EU average in 1996, indicates persistently wide disparities among the 15 EU member states (ranging from 66 per cent of the EU average in Greece to 168 per cent in Luxembourg). The countries of central and eastern Europe that have embarked on accession negotiations to the EU[4] lie well below even the poorest EU member states.[5]

Within the EU, four main clusters of countries are identifiable. Luxembourg performed strongest in terms of *per capita* income, as a relatively prosperous city that happens to also be a country. A second group comprises (in descending rank order) Belgium, Denmark, Austria, Germany, the Netherlands, France, Italy, and Sweden with *per capita* GDP ranging from just above average (101 per cent in the case of Sweden) to 114 per cent (Belgium). This core of strong national economies lies at the heart of EU-wealth generation. A third group lies just below the EU average; it includes Finland, the UK, and Ireland. Over the last ten years Ireland has significantly improved its GDP performance, though the incomes of Irish residents have increased much less quickly, since a substantial share of GDP is translated into profits repatriated by inward investors. There also has been a decline in the position of the UK. A final group which now comprises three countries are the poorer so-called 'cohesion countries' – Spain at 77 per cent, Portugal at 74 per cent, and Greece at 66 per cent of the average.

All the ten candidate countries from central and eastern Europe recorded *per capita* GDP levels in 1996 below 60 per cent of the EU average; that is, below the lowest level for any of the 15 member states. Slovenia, the wealthiest, stood at 59 per cent of the average and the Czech Republic at 54 per cent, while Romania stood at 23 per cent. Of those that had been part of the former Soviet Union, Estonia recorded a GDP *per capita* at 23 per cent of the EU average, while Latvia, the poorest, recorded a level of 18 per cent. Russia, not an applicant, recorded a score of 23 per cent in 1996, although its position is likely to have been significantly worsened as a result of the 1998 financial crisis and the further devaluation of the rouble.

Regional economic disparities in Europe

In addition to very significant territorial disparities between countries, there are also wide disparities in economic development *between* regions across the continent. These differences stand in the way of greater cohesion in a more integrated Europe. Strict comparisons between central and eastern Europe and the EU are not possible because of the different size of regional accounting units. Countries in central and eastern Europe are only beginning to implement a system of territorial organization which enables comparisons to be made across diverse national contexts (see, for example, recent GDP estimates for Slovak regions in comparison to the EU average (ŠÚSR, 2000). However, it is possible to identify the scale of disparities in 1995 by using PPP estimates of regional *per capita* GDP, relative to the EU average for the so-called 'NUTS III' regions,[6] in fifteen EU member states and for Hungary, Slovakia and Russia, the three other countries for which data are available (see Dunford and Smith, 2000).[7] Output per head in regions in these countries varied enormously from 353 per cent of the EU average in Frankfurt-am-Main to four per cent in the Ingush Republic in the North Caucasus of Russia. A large number of

Russian regions lie in the poorest income range and Slovakia has both poorer regions and greater internal disparities than Hungary. Within the EU, 19 per cent of the population lived in 'NUTS III' regions with a *per capita* GDP of less than 75 per cent of the EU average. In many of these areas unemployment levels are high, often the share of income from low-productivity agricultural sectors is large, and some have experienced high levels of industrial decline in mining, steel, textiles and shipbuilding.

In the three central and east European countries by far the majority of regions for which we have data fall below three-quarters of EU *per capita* GDP. No Hungarian region appears above 66 per cent of the average, not even the capital city region of Budapest. In Slovakia, the capital region of Bratislava[8] (144 per cent of the EU average) and the industrialized region of Košice in the east (78 per cent) lie above the 75 per cent threshold, but the distribution of regional *per capita* GDP is significantly more polarized than in Hungary. The relative strength of these richer Slovak regions is in part due to the concentration of comparatively high value-added industrial activity, with Bratislava and Košice alone accounting for 35 per cent of Slovak industrial output (Smith, 1998). Another factor contributing to the high *per capita* wealth of Bratislava and other city regions is the role of significant net in-commuting, such that large numbers of people who contribute to output do not reside in the area. As in most other countries of central and eastern Europe, there is also a large divide in terms of development between the capital city region and the rest of the country in Hungary and Slovakia (Smith, 1998). In Russia, no region lies above 75 per cent of the EU average *per capita* income. The two wealthiest regions, (Tyumen' in West Siberia [72 per cent of the EU average] and the Sakha Republic in the Russian Far East [42 per cent]) derive their status from major resource extraction industries – oil and gas in Tyumen' and diamonds in the Sakha Republic. Together these accounted for approximately 47 per cent of Russia's exports in 1995 (Bradshaw *et al.*, 1998).

At the opposite extreme, within the EU a significant number of German regions and two French regions were located above 200 per cent of the average EU *per capita* income. In both countries several regions had their *per capita* GDP scores inflated by the scale of net inward commuting: Frankfurt-am-Main, Munich, Darmstadt and Wolfsburg in Germany, and Paris and Hauts de Seine in France. More generally, a large share of the regions located at 125 per cent above the EU average were West German. Most were city economies clustered around an axis (the so-called 'blue banana') that extended from

Greater London through Belgium and the Netherlands along the Rhine and into Lombardy and Emilia Romagna in the north of Italy.

Dynamics over time

A clear development divide characterizes, then, the contemporary economic geography of an increasingly integrated Europe. How have these territorial disparities changed over time? Is there any evidence of a longer-run convergence of differentials in Europe?[9] The *Cohesion Report*, produced by the European Commission in 1996, argued that within the EU between the early 1980s and the 1990s national disparities narrowed significantly, while those between the constituent regions of the EU remained largely unchanged, and within each member state regional income disparities widened (European Commission, 1996).

Taking a more long-run view of national trends in income inequality between European countries there is evidence of a significant convergence of economic outcomes in the period immediately following World War II, in contrast to the 130 years from 1820 to 1950 when divergence predominated. During this latter period, rapid industrialization and growth in parts of western Europe were accompanied by sluggish growth in peripheral areas of western and eastern Europe (Dunford and Smith, 2000). Convergence, however, then increased until the mid-1970s, when the trend was reversed and divergence set in again. In 1989 to 1992 the divergence trend intensified in Europe, largely as a result of the economic collapse of countries in central and eastern Europe.

An important factor influencing convergence and divergence stems from differences in the models of economic growth in different parts of Europe: a Keynesian, or Fordist, development model in western Europe; and a model of state socialist industrialization in central and eastern Europe (Smith, 1998). The first countries to narrow the gap with western Europe were the Soviet Union in the 1930s and the state socialist countries of central and eastern Europe in the 1950s and 1960s. Extensive industrialization programmes put in place by governments in the former communist world produced a significant increase in economic growth in the early post-war period. By the late 1980s, however, growth had slowed down, if not ended, with sharp declines in output in the early 1990s. It was the associated profound shedding of economic capacity that explains the overall divergence that has occurred since 1989.

How are these disparities likely to change in the future? Calculations undertaken by researchers at the World Bank (Barbone and Zalduendo,

1997) suggest that the likelihood of convergence of economic performance in the near future in 'the new Europe' is doubtful. Analyses of the relative situation and of development tendencies in the two parts of Europe reinforce this conclusion. There are obvious and significant east–west technological gaps that will be difficult to close. More important, perhaps, is the evidence within central and eastern Europe of uneven development at the sub-national level. On the one hand, capital accumulation is increasingly centred in core areas, such as capital city regions and western border areas (Dunford and Smith, 1998; Pavlínek, 1998; Smith, 1998). On the other hand, capitalist development strategies and marketization are leading to the peripheralization of more marginal regions that are increasingly 'left behind' (Smith, 2000). While disparities in economic performance also characterized state socialism, forced industrialization did have some effect on reducing sub-national territorial disparities (even if it created rather unsustainable local economies, often dominated by relatively few, large enterprises) (Smith, 1997, 1998). Indeed, since 1989 we have witnessed the emergence of complex patterns of uneven development, both within and between countries in central and eastern Europe, and between them and the EU and former Communist countries. The recent positive growth in central Europe has been accompanied by continued decline in much of the former Soviet Union, as well as most of the former Yugoslavia, and by sharp fluctuations in economic fortunes in countries such as Bulgaria. Indeed, so marked are these differentials that they may well recreate the 'old' east–west division of labour and development divide that never fully disappeared in the post-war period.

Theoretical challenges: Beyond 'the new regionalism'

Much of the theoretical work on territorial development has focused not on uneven development, but on those places and regions that are considered 'successful' regions in the global economy. Lovering (1999) termed this the 'new regionalist' orthodoxy: a set of theoretical frameworks that concentrate upon success stories, rather than considering the political economy of divergent interests in 'successful' regions ('winners' *and* 'losers') and the broader mosaic of uneven development. We argue that the 'new regionalism' does not help to explain the divergence and differentiation of territorial development in Europe. Nor does it provide us with the policy tools from which to develop sensible scenarios for the 'emerging economies' of central and eastern

Europe. We argue, that the continual focus upon identifying the putative conditions of 'success' in only 'successful' regional economies limits our understanding of regional economic performance in Europe. Furthermore, such claims limit the scope for considering alternative scenarios.

Among the large body of research on regional development in Europe two main themes are identifiable: one dealing with the role of firms; and another dealing with the relationship between firms and regional institutions. The research on the *role of firms* in regional economic change has two main strands. The first has focused on the role of large, externally owned manufacturing plants in regional development (see, for example, Amin and Tomaney, 1995; Dicken *et al.*, 1994; Grabher, 1997; Turok, 1993; Young and Hood, 1995). Focusing largely upon inward investment projects, this research has attempted to identify the conditions under which foreign-owned plants become the basis for the creation of 'embedded' regional development in which an upgrading of domestic supply networks occurs. The major concern of this research has been to examine the ways in which branch plant 'outposts' can become 'performance' plants and to assess the relative importance of sectors being locked into, or excluded from, the international and European economy through inward investment.

A second strand of research has examined small and medium enterprises and endogenous development trajectories in industrial districts. Much of this work has concentrated upon explaining the seemingly enduring strength of localized agglomerations in an increasingly globalized and interconnected world (Storper, 1998), and the respective roles of particular sectoral structures in promoting regional growth. It has been argued that dense networks of flexibly specialized inter-firm cooperation found in industrial districts help to explain the enduring 'success' of local agglomeration economies (Asheim, 1996; Scott, 1988). However, a problem found in both of these bodies of work is the assumption that there is one best way (lean production, the learning firm, the learning region, and so on) for restructuring to occur. We argue that the continuous restructuring of economic practices under capitalist social relations means that a *variety of solutions* underpin the outcomes of regional and corporate organization and linkages.

A second, more recent, line of work has examined the governance of *relations between firms and regional institutions*. Storper (1998), for example, has suggested that dense local tissues of corporate and institutional interaction – not only those between firms through 'traded' supply networks – are important in explaining the 'success' of industrial agglomerations. These firm–institution relations have been identified as 'untraded interdependencies' – conventions and norms of interaction that foster collective and localized learning – and promote 'trust' between economic actors. This literature has focused upon the *governance* of regional economies by institutions and the role of learning across institutional formations in promoting innovation and the strategic upgrading of local economies (Maskell *et al.*, 1998; Morgan, 1997). This work argues that regional success is rooted in the way in which local resources and institutions are mobilized to enhance competitiveness, trust and innovation (see also Humphrey and Schmitz, 1998).

However, both Lovering (1999), in his critique of the Welsh experience of 'the new regionalism' and Phelps *et al.* (1998) in their treatment of the politics of inward investment, suggest that institutional interactions favour particular interests (such as multinational capital) over others. An additional criticism is that the 'social' dimensions of regional economic development, such as increasing income inequality and poverty are often ignored.

Furthermore, workers as conscious active beings are almost entirely absent from the analysis. Sadler and Thompson (1999) have emphasized that a shortcoming in explanations of regional uneven development has been the limited attention paid to the role of organized labour. Writers on industrial restructuring in central Europe have also stressed the importance of including labour at the heart of the analysis. Thirkell *et al.* (1994: 85) argue that analyses of patterns of transformation have tended to ignore the importance of labour relations; they stress the importance of trade unions as agents in strategy formulation, at both enterprise and national level, as well as their key role in interest representation. While not disagreeing, Hardy and Rainnie (1996) argue the point more theoretically in emphasizing not only the extraction of economic surplus, but also the realization of wealth in determining organizational development and change. Sadler and Thompson (1999), in their discussion of steel trade unions in the north-east of the UK, argue that organized workers have had three main roles in shaping a 'regional industrial culture'. First, they argue that unions in the region have played upon the social construction of work activities in the steel sector (in particular the hierarchical and seniority-dependent job pattern). This has meant that the main union has had a 'separatist attitude towards other unions organizing workers in this industry and more generally within the region' (Sadler and Thompson, 1999: 28). Second, they argue that trade unionists in this sector have developed deep affiliations between work and region and this creates cleavages between union branches operating in different places. This may affect the capacity of unions to organize across sectors and across territories, although the full implications of this are not discussed by Sadler and Thompson. Finally, the increasing fragmentation of tasks within steel plants has led to a fragmentation of union politics and worker representation. Workers have found it difficult to contest management strategies to increase productivity at the expense of worker conditions, a classic example of the value of a commodity being enhanced by reducing the price of labour inputs.

'New regionalist' accounts of regional performance confine themselves to putative 'success stories' of firms, sectors and regions. They fail to indicate the relative importance of the firms, sectors and regions within the wider processes of uneven development, which we observe in the variegated map of 'winners' and 'losers' in Europe. In this sense they fail to explain the mechanisms by which wealth is distributed across the territories of Europe or who gets access to that wealth. The reconfiguration of the regional economies of central and eastern Europe since 1989, against the background of the enlargement of the EU, raises important issues about the potential for *real* convergence of economic outcomes. Too much of the literature fails to explain the determinants of overall regional economic performance. It leads too easily to the implication that development programmes formulated in one time-space context can be transferred to other sites, without considering the specificity of regional trajectories underpinning the identified 'success' (Hudson, 1998).

Furthermore, the research on the role of firms in regional performance has tended to polarize debate on the relative merits of endogenous *vis-à-vis* exogenous factors in promoting development, rather than the relations between the two types of regional dynamics. This debate has largely ignored parallel work in economic sociology, that focuses upon the flows of value through commodity chains at various geographical scales and with variant structures of firm and regional governance (Gereffi, 1994, see also Smith *et al.*, 2000, 2002). Much of the analysis of value chains suggests that we should shift the focus away from the issue of whether multinational corporations benefit or limit the capacity for local development towards examining varieties of firm organization. These seem to have differing impacts on where firms are located and hence deserve more attention as a means of tracing the dynamics of a chain of value. In this reading, there is no one best way (flexibility, learning and so forth) contrary to the widespread assumption of much of the literature on regional development.

In addition, recent research on industrial 'learning' also inadequately specifies the links between *mechanisms of firm-level governance and change* and the *institutional contexts of regional development* (Hudson, 1999). Moreover, and perhaps paradoxically, the focus upon the specifically *regional* dimensions of economic dynamism and institutional governance tends to sideline the importance of *national* frameworks of economic governance in accounting for localized change (Gertler, 1997).

A key concern of the 'new regionalism' has been on how best to transfer 'success' from one environment to another. This immediately raises issues of central importance for dealing with the divergence of regional economies in the 'new Europe'. Many writers emphasize 'building the wealth of regions (not the individual firm), with upgrading of the economic, institutional, and social base as the prerequisite for entrepreneurial success' (Amin, 1999: 370; see also Scott, 1998; Storper, 1998). This can be achieved, it is argued, through a variety of mechanisms that might include the development of *clusters of interrelated industries*, with long roots in a local skill or capabilities base, so as to enhance international competitive advantage. Such clusters may be linked to the *construction of economies of association* by encouraging 'social dialogue and learning based on shared knowledge and information exchange', through inter-firm exchange and reciprocity (Amin, 1999: 370–1). Enhanced regional performance might also be achieved by *learning to learn and adapt* to changing external firm and sectoral environments, and thus becoming able to predict and shape future trajectories of growth, and to evolve in order to adapt. The *broadening and mobilizing of the local institutional base* enhances locally democratic and interactive associations between state and non-state actors to unlock local potentials. Finally, the *creation of socially inclusive entrepreneurship and employment* is also important as a means to nurture skills, expertise and capabilities, rather than solely to increase the overall volume of jobs.

Together, then, such claims represent the basis for constructing alternatives to market-dominated regional economies. This might promote the establishment of forms of what Amin and Thrift (1995: 150) have called 'regionally-based associative democracy', or a 'third way' between state and markets organized by large (often multinational) corporations.

The third way is an attempt to set up networks of intermediate institutions in between market and state that can act as a counter to such decisions and outcomes (arising from large corporations and dominant state institutions). The third way is also an attempt to build networks of institutions *democratically*, at local, national and international levels, so that they can be used to give a region 'voice'. The third way is an attempt to avoid simply reproducing local statism. Its emphasis is on forms of governance which integrally involve institutions in civil society, especially those without hegemonic power.

There is much to be welcomed in this alternative to the neo-liberal renderings of liberalized markets and regions in competition. However, a number of concerns remain. In particular, it draws on a specific interpretation of 'internationalization'; it makes some questionable assumptions about the role of labour; and it provides models that may not transfer well to central and eastern Europe.

One problem of 'new regionalism' is that it rests on a rather pluralist analysis of the state, and is tied to a particular view of the impact of 'internationalization' (Burnham, 1999). This internationalization involves both internal and external restructuring of the state, rather than its destruction, in contrast to the more extreme forms of globalization analysis. States have historically acted as buffers and bulwarks, protecting national economies from disruptive external forces in order to sustain domestic welfare and employment. Since the economic crises of the mid–1970s this priority shifted to one of adapting domestic economies to the perceived exigencies of the world economy. The structures of national governments have changed, as agencies that act as conduits for the world economy have become pre-eminent. A transnational process of consensus formation (through the Organization for Economic Cooperation and Development [OECD], the International Monetary Fund [IMF] and G7) transmits, it is argued, guidelines to pre-dominant state agencies, which in turn enact national policies. The state's role, from this internationalization perspective therefore becomes one of helping to adjust the domestic economy to the requirements of the world economy. The state is seen as a 'transmission belt' from the world to the domestic economy, it is 'internationalized' from the outside in. Analysis along these lines resembles much of the literature on new regionalism except that now the regional governments' role is limited to making its soft and hard infrastructure as attractive as possible to mobile international capital.

Burnham, however, argues that this form of analysis and its 'new regionalist' variant underplay the role of labour. Organized labour and the state are depicted as powerless, passively responding to the demands of the post-Fordist economy. The approach does not address the extent to which globalization may be authored by states and be regarded by state agents (both liberal and social-democratic) as one of the most efficient means of restructuring labour-capital relations in a time of economic crisis. Hudson (1998), for example, has warned against the uncritical embracing of a perspective (apparent in both the literature on internationalization and the new regionalism) based around localized learning and supply-side improvements. He argues that this has been suggested as a model for enhanced regional performance in central and eastern Europe, even though it has been derived from a small set of largely west European examples. As Hudson (1999: 10) indicates, learning in an internationalized economy and a more integrated Europe 'is by no means a universal panacea to the problems of socio-spatial inequality and in some respects is used as a cloak behind which some of the harsher realities of capitalism can be hidden. Addressing the problems of uneven development and inequality . . . poses very hard policy and political choices for those who seek to devise progressive development trajectories.'

In particular, Hudson argues, first, that the production of knowledge and learning may be less important facets of corporate success than aspects of corporate practice, such as rationalizing and increasing the production efficiency of existing commodities or devising new commodities for profitable production. Second, new forms of 'inclusive' work practices and management techniques, based around re-skilling and team work, may be less significant than an intensification of the labour process under contemporary capitalism. '[W]orkers are enmeshed within disempowering regimes of subordination, characterized by control, exploitation, and surveillance, accepting arrangements through which they discipline themselves and their fellow workers, while bound together through the rhetoric of team working' (Hudson, 1999: 7). There is strong evidence that this has been the case of new work practices implemented in many foreign investment projects throughout central and eastern Europe (Hardy, 1998; Pavlínek and Smith, 1998). Third, new work practices are increasingly concerned with no-union and one-union agreements, such that the basis for inclusion and negotiation of democratic work places is eroded further. Fourth, the proposed role for increased network relations between firms may be based less upon equal exchange and reciprocity than upon 'sharp asymmetries in power between companies, and . . . subtle coercion if companies wish to keep their customers or suppliers' (Hudson, 1999: 8). Finally, 'institutional thickness' and dense mosaics of state and non-state interaction may be no guarantee for *long-term* innovation, learning and competitiveness as institutional lock-in can also constrain change, a point discussed by Smith and Swain (1998) in relation to the experience of lock-in in central and eastern Europe.

To what extent then is there a potential for the implementation and development of such 'wealth of regions' policies in an increasingly interdependent European economy? We suggest that the scope is limited for three main reasons. First, there are limits to the extent to which inward direct investment, one of the major forces for regional economic restructuring in 'the new Europe', can provide the basis for the enhanced wealth of regions. The corporate strategies of multinational companies investing in central and eastern Europe are typically not conducive to the enhancing of regional economic performance. Strategies tend to capitalize on the low wage, low cost locational advantages of the region and upon gaining access to new markets (Hardy, 1998; Pavlínek and Smith, 1998). It therefore seems unlikely that the significant development divide between East and West in Europe will be overcome simply by enhancing the role of western corporations.

Second, regional capacities *within* central and eastern Europe have been starkly eroded as a result of two main processes. The first has been the deindustrialization of large parts of the region in the early 1990s (Smith, 1998; Dunford, 1998) and the second has been the continued adherence to neo-liberal policies and macroeconomic prudence under a regime of global governance (Gowan, 1995; Smith, 1997, 1998). The latter in particular has constrained the options that are open to policy makers in the region.

Third, the regional institutional structures of central and eastern Europe under state socialism could be characterized as 'thin'. This legacy remains an important impediment to enhanced regional performance, in both the state and non-state sectors. In the state sector there are few actors to build on, aside from those attached to the former hegemony of the Communist Party. In the non-state sector there were few firms (with limited subcontracting linkages between them), and a stress upon local autarky, although the case of Volkswagen-Škoda in the Czech Republic may be different (Pavlínek, 1998; Pavlínek and Smith, 1998). Outside the enterprize sphere, there is little basis for enhancing civic involvement and 'local voice', factors generally seen as important for growth in, for example, parts of Italy.

Overall, we argue that 'the new regionalism' literature largely fails to provide the conceptual tools necessary to understand the changing divisions of labour across space or the differentiation of regional economies in an increasingly integrated Europe. On the contrary, it is the changing functional and sectoral patterning of the geography of economic activities that is, we would argue, fundamental to understanding the performance of regional economies. This needs to be understood alongside the mechanisms of wealth creation and (re)distribution to give us a better handle on the variegated map of uneven development in Europe.

A focus on the geography of these activities is one way of thinking about inequalities in the creation and appropriation of value and the (unequal) flows of value between places that underpin the mosaic of regional inequality in Europe (Smith *et al.*, 2000, 2002). A key starting point rests on the role of the production and flow of value associated with different forms of economic activities in different locales. Gereffi (1994) argued that commodity, or (in our terms) value-chains, have three main dimensions. First, commodity chains have a specific input–output structure that links various nodes of production, distribution and consumption into a chain of economic activity through which value-added is produced. Second, commodity chains have a territoriality in the sense that the various activities, nodes and flows within a chain are geographically situated, with implications for levels and processes of development depending upon where a locale is within a chain. To the extent that Europe has since 1989 become a thoroughly internationalized 'space-economy', we need to understand the extension of value chains across European territory. Finally, commodity chains imply a structure of governance that Gereffi (1994: 97) defines as 'authority and power relationships that determine how financial, material, and human resources are allocated and flow within a chain'. This approach provides the basis for understanding the geographies of power and control across different sites (locations, territories) within chains of commodity and value-producing systems. For us it is more convincing than an approach based around forms of largely localized associationalism. This latter stresses the importance of developing democratically formed local systems of governance, but largely neglects issues of power and control within and across space (Allen *et al.*, 1998).

Conclusions

At the start of the twenty-first century, then, regional economies in Europe are faced with a momentous task. The collapse of state socialism revealed the enormous disparities between territorial economies within central and eastern Europe, as well as in comparison with the

EU, at both the national and sub-national scales. The implementation of transition policies has, in many ways, further eroded the economic capacities of these territories. Furthermore, within the EU, while there have been some notable successes, significant territorial disparities remain. Indeed, the evidence suggests that within EU countries the divide between rich and poor territories has been growing over the past decade. The challenges to analysts of territorial development take two main forms. First, we need frameworks that enable us to understand the enormously variegated map of uneven development in Europe. A crucial issue is whether or not we can rely upon models and frameworks based on the putative success stories of industrial districts and learning economies from western Europe, given that these are challenged within the west (Lovering, 1999). Second, we need to bring together approaches that more thoroughly deal with economic performance and the governance mechanisms that underpin different territorial outcomes. One such approach might derive from understanding how flows of value, across chains of economic activities located in different territories, affect territorial divisions of labour (Smith *et al.*, 2000; Gereffi, 1994). Governance is a crucial element, in that these flows of value are shaped by the mechanisms of organization within the chains: buyers or suppliers, capital or labour. A governance perspective raises immediately the question of differential power: who controls? and who wins and loses? (Allen *et al.*, 1998: 132–5). This, we would argue, should be the starting point for understanding the nature of territorial uneven development within 'the new Europe'.

Notes

1. This chapter is based on research for a project on 'Regional Economic Performance, Governance and Cohesion in an Enlarged Europe', funded under the Economic and Social Research Council's 'One Europe or Several?' Research Programme (grant no: L213 25 2028). We are grateful to our fellow collaborators on this project (Jane Hardy, Ray Hudson, David Sadler and Bill Haywood). A different version of part of this chapter appears in Dunford and Smith (2000).
2. Luxembourg is an economically successful city that happens also to be a country. Its position is somewhat at variance from the norm of larger territorial units.
3. The data for 1996 and 1870 are not strictly comparable, but used for illustrative purposes only. The 1870 data are in US dollar equivalents, based on a comparison with 16 European countries (Good, 1991). The data for 1996 are in PPP equivalent units and comparisons are made with the average of the 15 EU member states.

4. Ten central and eastern European states have applied to join the EU: Bulgaria, Czech Republic, Estonia, Hungary, Latvia, Lithuania, Poland, Romania, Slovakia and Slovenia. Five opened negotiations in 1999: Czech Republic, Estonia, Hungary, Poland and Slovenia. The Helsinki European Council in December 1999 agreed to open negotiations with the other five.
5. The data set used in this national level analysis is the World Bank's 'World Development Indicators'.
6. EU member states are divided territorially into five levels of aggregation, or NUTS (Nomenclature of Territorial Units for Statistics). NUTS II regions are called Basic Administrative Units and NUTS III regions are subdivisions of these Units. NUTS II data are used for Italy, though Valle d'Aosta is also a NUTS III area.
7. The regional divisions adopted for central and eastern European countries are not NUTS III equivalent. At present a system for regional statistical analysis in CEE countries is being implemented. The regions used here are: Slovakia – 38 districts; Hungary – 20 counties; Russia – 89 regions. The sources of data are national statistical offices and various other estimates, which are not standardized. Sources: Slovakia – estimates produced by Kárász et al., 1996; Hungary – Hungarian Central Statistical Office, 1996; Russia – Goskomstat Rossii, 1997.
8. The figure for Bratislava should be treated with some caution. The capital city region dominates the rest of the Slovak space economy (Smith, 1998), and the level of *per capita* GDP recorded places the city on roughly the same level as Greater London. This is due largely to the relatively small resident population of Bratislava as well as significant in-commuting.
9. Here we are concerned with convergence of outcomes that give rise to territorial inequalities measured in *per capita* GDP terms. Convergence can also be seen as a process involving *characteristics* of regions, firms or economies, not examined in any depth here. Convergence and divergence are not exclusive categories and can be found alongside each other at different spatial scales (Dunford and Smith, 2000).

References

Allen, J., Massey, D. and Cochrane, A. (1998) *Rethinking the Region* (London: Routledge).

Altvater, E. (1998) 'Theoretical Deliberations in Time and Space of Post-socialist Transformation', *Regional Studies*, 32 (7), pp. 591–605.

Amin, A. (1999) 'An Institutionalist Perspective on Regional Economic Development', *International Journal of Urban and Regional Research*, 23 (2), pp. 365–78.

Amin, A. and Tomaney, J. (1995) 'The Regional Development Potential of Inward Investment in the Less Favoured Regions of the European Community', in Amin, A. and Tomaney, J. (eds), *Behind the Myth of European Union: Prospects for Cohesion* (London: Routledge), pp. 201–20.

Amin, A. and Thrift, N. (1995) 'Institutional Issues for the European Regions: From Markets and Plans to Socioeconomics and Powers of Association', *Economy and Society*, 24 (1), pp. 41–66.

Asheim, B. (1996) 'Industrial Districts as "Learning Regions": a condition for prosperity?', *European Planning Studies*, 4 (4), pp. 379–400.
Barbone, L. and Zalduendo, J. (1997) 'EU Accession of Central and Eastern Europe: Bridging the Income Gap', *Policy Research Working Paper* No. 1721 (World Bank: Country Department II, Europe and Central Asia Division).
Begg, I. (1996) 'Inter-regional Transfers in a Widened Europe', *South Bank European Papers*, 5 (European Institute: South Bank University).
Berend, I. and Ránki, G. (1982) *The European Periphery and Industrialization 1780–1914* (Cambridge: Cambridge University Press).
Bradshaw, M., Stenning, A. and Sutherland, D. (1998) 'Economic Restructuring and Regional Change in Russia', in Pickles, J. and Smith, A. (eds), *Theorising Transition: The Political Economy of Post-Communist Transformations* (London: Routledge), pp. 147–71.
Burnham, P. (1999) 'The Politics of Economic Management', *New Political Economy*, 4 (1), pp. 37–54.
Clarke, S. (1999) 'Making Ends Meet in a Non-monetary Market Economy', *New Forms of Employment and Household Survival Strategies in Russia* (Coventry: ISITO/CCLS), pp. 111–48.
Dicken, P., Forsgren, M. and Malmberg, A. (1994) 'The Local Embeddedness of Transnational Corporations', in Amin, A. and Thrift, N. (eds), *Globalization, Institutions and Regional Development in Europe* (Oxford: Oxford University Press), pp. 23–45.
Dunford, M. (1994) 'Winners and Losers: the New Map of Economic Inequality in the European Union', *European Urban and Regional Studies*, 1 (2), pp. 95–114.
Dunford, M. (1998a) 'Differential Development, Institutions, Modes of Regulation and Comparative Transitions to Capitalism: Russia, the Commonwealth of Independent States and the former German Democratic Republic', in Pickles, J. and Smith, A. (eds), *Theorising Transition: the Political Economy of Post-Communist Transformations* (London: Routledge), pp. 76–111.
Dunford, M. (1998b) 'Economies in Space and Time: Economic Geographies of Development and Underdevelopment and Historial Geographies of Modernization', in Graham, B. (ed.), *Modern Europe* (London: Arnold), pp. 53–88.
Dunford, M. and Smith, A. (1998) 'Uneven Development in Europe', in Pinder, D. (ed.), *The New Europe: Economy, Society and Environment* (Chichester: Wiley), pp. 203–22.
Dunford, M. and Smith, A. (2000) 'Catching Up or Falling Behind? Economic Performance and Regional Trajectories in the New Europe', *Economic Geography*, 76 (2), pp. 169–95.
European Bank for Reconstruction and Development (EBRD) (1996) *Transition Report 1996* (London: EBRD).
European Commission (1996) *First Report on Economic and Social Cohesion 1996* (Luxembourg: European Commission).
Gereffi, G. (1994) 'The Organization of Buyer-driven Global Commodity Chains: How US Retailers Shape Overseas Production Networks', in Gereffi, G. and Korzeniewicz, M. (eds), *Commodity Chains and Global Capitalism* (Westport, CT: Praeger), pp. 95–122.
Gerschenkron, A. (1962) *Economic Backwardness in Historical Perspective* (Cambridge, MA: Harvard University Press).

Gertler, M. (1997) 'The Invention of Regional Culture', in Lee, R. and Wills, J. (eds), *Geographies of Economies* (London: Arnold), pp. 47–58.

Good, D. (1991) 'Austria-Hungary', in Sylla, R. and Toniolo, G. (eds), *Patterns of European Industrialization* (London: Routledge), pp. 218–47.

Gowan, P. (1995) 'Neo-liberal Theory and Practice for Eastern Europe', *New Left Review*, 213, pp. 3–60.

Grabher, G. (1997) 'Adaptation at the Cost of Adaptability? Restructuring the Eastern German Regional Economy', in Grabher, G. and Stark, D. (eds), *Restructuring Networks in Post-Socialism: Legacies, Linkages and Localities* (Oxford: Oxford University Press), pp. 107–34.

Hardy, J. (1998) 'Cathedrals in the Desert? Transnationals, Corporate Strategy and Locality in Wroclaw', *Regional Studies*, 32 (7), pp. 639–52.

Hardy, J. and Rainnie, A. (1996) *Restructuring Krakow: Desperately Seeking Capitalism* (London: Mansell).

Hollingsworth, J. R. (1998) 'New Perspectives on the Spatial Dimensions of Economic Coordination: Tensions Between Globalization and Social Systems of Production', *Review of International Political Economy*, 5 (3), pp. 482–507.

Hudson, R. (1998) 'What Makes Economically Successful Regions in Europe Successful? Implications for Transferring Success from West to East', *Sussex European Institute Working Papers in Contemporary European Studies*, 27 (Brighton: University of Sussex).

Hudson, R. (1999) ' "The Learning Economy, the Learning Firm and the Learning Region": a Sympathetic Critique of the Limits to Learning', *European Urban and Regional Studies*, 6 (1), pp. 59–72.

Hudson, R. and Williams, A. (eds) (1999) *Divided Europe: Society and Territory* (London: Sage).

Humphrey, J. and Schmitz, H. (1998) 'Trust and Inter-firm Relations in Developing and Transition Economies', *Journal of Development Studies*, 34 (4), pp. 32–61.

Kárász, P., Rencko, J., and Pauhofova, I. (1996) *Economic Potential of the Regions of Slovakia from the Viewpoint of their Development Possibilities* (Bratislava: Institute for Forecasting, Slovak Academy of Sciences).

Lovering, G. (1999) 'Theory Led by Policy: the Inadequacies of the "New Regionalism" (Illustrated from the case of Wales)', *International Journal of Urban and Regional Research*, 23 (2), pp. 379–95.

Maskell, P., Eskelinen, H., Hannibalsson, I., Malmberg, A. and Vatne, E. (1998) *Competitiveness, Localized Learning and Regional Development* (London: Routledge).

Morgan, K. (1997) 'The Learning Region: Institutions, Innovation and Regional Renewal', *Regional Studies*, 31 (5), pp. 491–503.

Ohmae, K. (1995) *The End of the Nation State: the Rise of Regional Economies* (New York: Free Press).

Pavlínek, P. (1998) 'Foreign Direct Investment in the Czech Republic', *Professional Geographer*, 50 (1), pp. 71–85.

Pavlínek, P. and Smith, A. (1998) 'Internationalisation and Embeddedness in East-Central European Transition: the Contrasting Geographies of Inward Investment in the Czech Republic and Slovakia', *Regional Studies*, 32 (7), pp. 619–38.

Phelps, N., Lovering, J. and Morgan, K. (1998) 'Tying the Firm to the Region or Tying the Region to the Firm? Early Observations on the Case of LG in South Wales', *European Urban and Regional Studies*, 5 (2), pp. 119–37.

Pickles, J. and Smith, A. (eds) (1998) *Theorising Transition: the Political Economy of Post-Communist Transformations* (London: Routledge).

Richards, H. (1997) 'Global Theatre', *Times Higher Education Supplement*, 7 February.

Sabel, C. (1994) 'Flexible Specialisations in the Reemergence of Regions', in Amin, A. (ed.), *Post Fordism – A Reader* (London: Blackwell).

Sadler, D. and Thompson, J. (1999) 'In Search of Regional Industrial Culture: the Role of Labour Organizations in Old Industrial Regions', paper presented to the 7th seminar of the Aegean 'Towards a Radical Cultural Agenda for European Cities and Regions', Paros, Greece, September.

Sengenberger, W. (1993) 'Local Development and Economic Competition', *International Labour Review*, 132 (3), pp. 313–29.

Scott, A. (1988) *New Industrial Spaces: Flexible Production and Regional Economic Development in the USA and Western Europe* (London: Pion).

Scott, A. (1998) *Regions and the World Economy* (Oxford: Oxford University Press).

Smith, A. (1997) 'Breaking the Old and Constructing the New? Geographies of Uneven Development in Central and Eastern Europe', in Lee, R. and Wills, J. (eds), *Geographies of Economies* (London: Arnold), pp. 331–344.

Smith, A. (1998) *Reconstructing the Regional Economy: Industrial Transformation and Regional Development in Slovakia* (Cheltenham: Edward Elgar).

Smith, A. (2000) 'Employment Restructuring and Household Survival in "Post-communist Transition": Rethinking Economic Practices in Eastern Europe', *Environment and Planning A*, 32, pp. 1759–80.

Smith, A. and Swain, A. (1998) 'Regulating and Institutionalising Capitalisms: the Micro-foundations of Transformation in Eastern and Central Europe', in Pickles, J. and Smith, A. (eds), *Theorising Transition: the Political Economy of Post-Communist Transformations* (London: Routledge), pp. 25–53.

Smith, A., Rainnie, A., Dunford, M., Hardy, J., Hudson, R. and Sadler, D. (2000) 'Where the Jobs Will Be in the United States of Europe: Networks of Value, Commodities and Regions in Europe after 1989', *ESRC 'One Europe or Several?' Working Paper*, No. 4/00 (Brighton: University of Sussex).

Smith, A., Rainnie, A., Dunford, M., Hardy, J., Hudson, R. and Sadler, D. (2002) 'Networks of Value, Commodities and Regions: Reworking Divisions of Labour in Macro-Regional Economics; *Progress in Human Geography*, 26 (1), forthcoming.

Statistický úrad Slovenskej republiky (2000) *Regionálny hrubý domáci produkt v roku 1996*, available at: http://www.statistics.sk/webdata/slov/infor/1296/hdp1996.htm [accessed 11 February 2000].

Storper, M. (1998) *The Regional World: Territorial Development in a Global Economy* (New York: Guilford).

Thirkell, J., Scase, R. and Vickerstaff, S. (eds) (1994) *Labour Relations and Political Change in Eastern Europe* (London: UCL Press).

Turok, I. (1993) 'Inward Investment and Local Linkages: How Deeply Embedded is "Silicon Glen"?', *Regional Studies*, 27 (5), pp. 401–17.

UNDP (1999) *Human Development Report 1999* (New York: Oxford University Press).
United Nations Economic Commission for Europe (UNECE) (1997) *Economic Survey of Europe in 1996–1997* (New York: United Nations).
World Bank (1996) *World Development Report 1996: From Plan to Market* (New York: Oxford University Press).
Young, S. and Hood, N. (1995) 'Attracting, Managing and Developing Inward Investment in the Single Market', in Amin, A. and Tomaney, J. (eds), *Behind the Myth of European Union: Prospects for Cohesion* (London: Routledge), pp. 282–304.

8
Enlargement and Regionalization: The Europeanization of Local and Regional Governance in CEE States

James Hughes, Gwendolyn Sasse and Claire Gordon

Introduction

In building any home location is key. Geography is widely regarded as the single most important reason why the post-communist countries of central and eastern Europe (CEECs) can realistically aspire to inclusion in a common European home that is democratic and prosperous (Przeworski, 1991: 190–1). This hypothesis may have sound structural foundations in that those transition states that are most proximate to the vibrant democratic market economies of central and western Europe are most likely to benefit from 'spillover' and contagion pressures for Europeanization. Moreover, some of the CEECs contiguous with the European Union (EU) share a pre-communist historical legacy of close relations with their EU neighbouring states dating from their interwar era of independent statehood. In the immediate period after the fall of commmunism there existed a widely held perception in many of the CEECs that post-communism equated with a 'return to Europe', and that swift European integration would follow. In the decade after the fall of communism, however, the concept of Europe-building has been stretched by the pull of two policy agendas: first, a process of *'deep integration'* among a historical core-group of EU states driven by a distilled notion of European exceptionalism; and, second, a process of eastward enlargement of EU membership driven by the diluted notion of a *'wider Europe'*. Thus far, the inherent tension between these alternative *grand projects* has been analysed, on the whole, as a macro-level problem between supranational, transnational and national institutions and elites (Wallace, 1999: 1–13).[1]

Generally, then, the existing studies of post-communist Europe-building tend to focus on 'high-level' governance issues and developments, and tend to overlook the fundamental sub-national arena of regional and local politics within and across states. One of the most important mechanisms by which the CEECs will benefit from EU membership is through regional and cohesion policies. The effective implementation of these policies requires local and regional governance systems that are compatible with EU practice and regulatory norms. If the deep integration of a wider Europe is to become a reality it must involve the penetration of the Europe-building project to 'low-level' governance and to sub-national elites in particular. While there is an immense research literature on regional and local governance in western Europe and the term 'Europe of the Regions' has penetrated EU rhetoric and institutions alike, much less has been written about this dimension in the CEECs. Most importantly, the link between Europeanization and regionalization has remained underexplored in the context of EU enlargement. Not only is there a dearth of research into the structure of regional and local governance in the CEECs, but we also know very little about the institutional capacity, practices and attitudes of the elites at this level.[2] EU enlargement is reconfiguring Europe at large, but one of the most hotly contested zones of engagement over jurisdictions and boundaries is how the pressures for Europeanization as a conditionality of enlargement 'from without', imposed by the European Commission, are operationalized in the candidate CEECs. Two divergent trends are evident: a Europeanized regionalization is being pursued 'from above' by national governments anxious to meet the EU conditionalities, while on the other hand, the Europeanization of regionalization has received a mixed reception 'from below' by local elites within the CEECs. It is this triadic engagement between the EU, the national and the sub-national level that is forging a radical transformation in regional and local governance in post-communist Europe.

Bifurcated models of regional governance

Studies of regional and local governance are often based on a path-dependent bifurcated model that divides Europe into western-democratic and eastern-post-communist domains. Consequently, top-down and bottom-up pressures for democratic change are generally understood to be bifurcated along a western–eastern cleavage. Post-communist reform of local and regional governance is viewed as a process of 'catching up with the West'. As Bennett (1993: 28) observed: 'The 1990s are seeing the overcoming of that democratic deficit by a rapid catching up in the East by borrowing concepts from the West and by developing entirely new concepts.' The West–East system cleavage may be characterized by two opposing models. The first is the asymmetric model that exists in the EU member states. Here the diversity of regional and local governance has evolved largely on the basis of country-specific historical path dependencies and the interaction of national and regional and local politics (Goldsmith and Klausen, 1997).[3] The second is the symmetric model that has originated as a supranational formula in the EU Commission as part of the conditionalities of the eastward enlargement process. This symmetric model aims to reconfigure regional and local governance in the new member states under the guise of the enlargement criterion for enhancing 'regional capacity'. Discussion of a conditional symmetric EU model of regionalization and its implications has been noticeably absent from analyses of eastward enlargement (Senior Nello and Smith, 1998).[4]

The distribution of power between central, regional and local authorities varies widely in western Europe. As a general rule, this distribution of power should be viewed organically, as it is subject to periodic negotiation between central and regional/local elites whose interests and strategies may coalesce or diverge over time. These elite negotiations are transacted through a complex institutional framework of networks, parties, bureaucracies, agencies, private sector companies and interest groups. Since the 1970s states in western Europe have undergone major rationalizing reforms of regional and local governance that have reduced the number of territorial authorities, in many cases endowing them with new responsibilities, and in some cases devolving new powers. This process was partly driven by rationalizing strategies for modernizing service provision, and partly by New Right ideology that favoured 'shrinking the state' through privatization and the use of private sector agencies. Recent studies suggest that the responsiveness of local and regional governance units to EU processes have been highly particularistic and can be categorized by a fourfold matrix of proactive, reactive, passive, and counteractive responses. Why one region in a particular country falls into one category or another is largely determined by two main factors: first, the EU-shaped priorities for regional development, and second, the attitudes of local or regional elites towards Europe (Goldsmith and Klausen, 1997: 239 *et seq*). This is, in essence, an interest-based explanation that views the upward redistribution of power from central states to the EU through deep integration as having created opportunities for regional and local elites to carve out new functional areas and responsibilities for themselves. The paradox of supranational integration, as with globalization, is that it revitalizes territorial politics and the politics of the *locale*.[5] Regionalization in western Europe, consequently, has been enhanced by processes at the national and supranational (EU) level. While the power of the nation-state is weakened or subordinated in specific areas, both the sub-national and the supranational level are steadily gaining in importance.

Despite the absence of uniformity in regional and local governance in western Europe the emergence of regions as significant political and economic actors has been contingent on domestic political traditions and developments (Bennett, 1993). These historic path dependencies make for a high degree of evolutionary diversity and are, arguably, an obstacle to uniform Europeanization of sub-national governance in the EU. There is, at the same time, a post-Maastricht trend for increased regionalization through the development of 'meso-governance' in the EU member states (Keating, 1993: 302–7). The gradual entrenchment of diversity is most evident in the strengthening of the EU institutional arrangements for regional and local governance, beginning with the Consultative Council of Regional and Local Authorities set up by the Commission in 1988 and reinforced in the Treaty of European Union at Maastricht and by the concept of 'subsidiarity' and the new Committee of the Regions (CoR). Although the regional and municipal governments represented on the CoR enjoy limited consultative rights within the EU hierarchy of institutions, the expectation is that over time this will change as regional government is strengthened (Loughlin, 1996: 147–8). Although EU regional policy is closely tied to the dispersion of structural funds, the implementation procedures for structural funds are not universalized; rather they vary according to the institutional arrangements for regional and local governance in each member state. Thus, the dispersement of regional funds may not necessarily connect regional elites with the EU, in particular when overseen by the national government.[6] Regional authorities that are most deeply embedded in EU regional policy-making are those from states that are federal or have strong regional government, such as Germany, Spain and Italy. The obstacles to a uniform EU model for regional and local governance in the historic core-member states are also evident from the fact that the funding criteria for EU regional funds in themselves are an obstacle to deep regionalization, since they are determined by measures of economic deprivation that tend to cross-cut regional administrative boundaries, and are increasingly urban-focused. On the other hand, EU policy aspirations in key activities such as transport and economic development (in particular via the Initiatives) are creating a dynamic toward a territorial functional specialization in policy implementation that is logically most effectively coordinated at the regional level.

A similar pattern of evolutionary diversity in regional and local governance was apparent in the CEECs in the immediate aftermath of the breakdown of communist regimes. While regional and local governance under communism was relatively uniformly structured, it was heavily depoliticized and strictly functionalist, with sub-national units acting as an organizational pillar of the one-party state and central planning. Two main contradictory trends were evident in the post-communist era: decentralization versus recentralization. The first trend was characterized by a decentralizing impetus in those states which experienced a fragmentation of state authority leading to a proliferation of local governance units (Hungary, Czech Republic, Slovenia). This trend was driven by a combination of five main factors: first, new local government self-financing regulations provided an incentive for fragmentation in local government that led to the proliferation of municipalities and communes; second, it was partly an opportunistic reaction by sub-national elites to the weakness of central states in the early phase of transition; third, the competition between central and local elites over distributive issues, in particular the rush into 'nomenklatura privatization' was reflected in institutional struggles between central and regional/local authorities; and fourth, this trend was partly driven by a democratizing counter-reaction to the overly centralized and functionalist 'command–administrative' communist system. This counter-reaction abolished or decreased the role of regional government, a level which had represented the direct link to the centre in the communist era. The fifth factor is the incentive structure provided by EU accession criteria, specifically the EU demand for regional 'administrative capacity' (see below). Significantly, in many states post-communism led to a revival of local identities with historically bounded sub-national government, as in the counties of Hungary. Elsewhere, functionalist criteria were abandoned in the organization and orientation of regional and local governance, as in the new regions of Poland, or diluted as in Slovenia.

The second trend involved a reconcentration of power to the centre, though the reasons for this varied. The reimposition of strong central governance was driven by authoritarian reactions by central elites to democratic transition (Slovakia), or was impelled by the need for strong central government in states where sovereignty was perceived to be threatened by territorialized internal minorities or an external power (as in the Baltic states). In some states it was motivated by a combination of authoritarian reaction and fear of territorialized internal minorities (as in Romania). Consequently, by 1993 when the Copenhagen European Council meeting transformed the eastward enlargement question into a major agenda for the EU, regional and local governance in the CEECs was not uniform but mirrored the asymmetric model of the EU, with a wide diversity of institutional forms and practices. The CEECs shared, however, a common starting-point: the two trends of decentralization and fragmentation of local government on the one hand and the reconcentration of central power on the other hand had temporarily deflated the importance of regional policy and regional governance.

Europeanization as conditionality

Despite the fact that enlargement has been a recurrent phenomenon in the history of the EU, it is a poorly conceptualized process and remains so four years after Schmitter noted that 'the discussion about deepening and widening is taking place in a theoretical vacuum' (Schmitter, 1996b: 14). The current wave of enlargement to the CEECs involves an even more complex set of issues compared with previous enlargements, primarily because of the simultaneity with post-communist political and economic transition and state-building. The literature on post-communist transition and democratization generally analyses these as national-level phenomena, as embodied by national institutional engineering and national elite pacts (O'Donnell *et al.*, 1986). Recently, while more attention has been paid to analysing the international dimension of transition, transition processes at the sub-national level continue to be thoroughly unexplored territory.[7] The evolution of Europeanization and regionalization as intrinsically linked processes during EU enlargement to the CEECs forms a convenient bridge allowing us a three dimensional analysis of the roles of the European Commission, state-level governments and the sub-national level.

Conditionality as an international pressure exerted on regime change has been analysed as a factor related to the institutional preferences of international institutional lenders (IMF, World Bank, EBRD) in the pursuit of neoliberal fiscal policy (Schmitter, 1996a). In the case of EU enlargement a qualitatively different kind of conditionality is being applied. When we examine how the EU has addressed the issue of regional and local governance during the enlargement process we find a steady consolidation of a preference for a particular kind of administrative uniformity in territorial organization. In effect, there is a new functionalist Brussels model for the reconfiguration of the territorial dimension of governance in post-communist states. The EU institutional preference is shaped not by fiscal ideology, however, but by administrative convenience for structural funding.

Enlargement eastwards to include the current candidates entails a territorial increase of 34 per cent, a population increase of 105 million, and the incorporation of new member states with diverse histories and cultures. It is also the first significant enlargement of the EU 'en bloc' and, not surprisingly, requires a more elaborate set of guidelines and criteria. To some extent this diversity of political traditions and state capacity has been recognized by the fact that from the outset the process of enlargement has been essentially one of bilateral negotiation between the European Commission and the central governments of aspiring members from the CEECs. The conditionalities imposed by the EU, however, are essentially uniform. While the process of eastward enlargement has been ongoing for seven years, it is only in the last two years that the EU has begun systematically to address the dimension of regional and local governance. When the EU first acknowledged that associated CEECs that 'so desire' could become members, at the Copenhagen European Council meeting in June 1993, it expressed the political and economic conditions for membership in vaguely worded and normative statements of intent. The so-called 'Copenhagen criteria' laid down three conditions for applicant states (the stability of democracy, the functioning of a market economy, and the capacity to integrate) and a fourth condition related to the EU's capacity to absorb new members. Although the details of how these conditions were to be met were not elaborated at the time, by implication it was understood that some objective criteria would be devised by which to evaluate applicants. The fourth condition gave the EU a pocket veto on accession of new members, since it would take the decision on whether it was ready to enlarge. Eastward enlargement, consequently, is inextricably tied to internal policy and institutional change within the EU itself.

Following Copenhagen, the EU pursued a 'pre-accession strategy' for enlargement which focused on bilateral arrangements with the national governments of applicant states (Andrews, 1998; Grabbe and Hughes, 1997).[8] The strategy had four key elements; the 'Europe

Agreements' on the liberalization of trade; the Phare programme of aid and technical assistance; the 'Single Market' Commission White Paper of June 1995 which suggested a pre-accession sequence for enlargement; and the 'Structured Dialogue' which was to provide a multilateral framework of ministerial meetings by which applicant state national elites could be acculturated into EU norms. The bilateral strategy for enlargement, however, was steadily reinforced both at the Essen European Council in December 1994 and the Madrid European Council in December 1995. What is striking about this cumulative bilateral strategy is that the process of enlargement is inherently viewed as one for negotiation between the EU and the *national* elites of the applicant states.

The paradox is that while the EU marginalized the participation of sub-national elites in the pre-accession strategy, among its main concerns over integration was the issue of how to best organize and involve regional and local governments. After all, the administrative capacity of these levels is seen as critical for the success of the whole enlargement project. At Essen, for example, issues of regional cooperation and infrastructural integration via trans-European networks were introduced into the pre-accession strategy, and regional development became one of the priorities of Phare. The regional dimension of enlargement also loomed over the Madrid European Council, as existing EU member states grappled with their own self-interests as to the implications of enlargement for the allocation of structural funds – the EU's key financial instrument for regional development. It was only at this stage, two and half years after the Copenhagen criteria were formulated, that the Commission was charged to prepare a detailed analysis of the impact of enlargement on the EU and draft 'opinions' evaluating each applicant country individually.

The resulting Commission report 'Agenda 2000 For a Stronger and Wider Europe', published in July 1997, adopted a 'reinforced pre-accession strategy', which side-lined the 'Structured Dialogue' and concentrated on bilateral accession negotiations and the applicant country-specific needs identified in the Commission's Opinions published contemporaneously. Hereafter, enlargement was viewed as a monogamous affair based on the 'Accession Partnerships' between the EU and applicant states. While emphasizing that the processes of 'deepening' and enlargement were complementary and feasible within the EU's resource ceiling, 'deepening' in this sense referred to the nebulous expectation that candidate states must have the capacity to integrate and that Phare aid would be so targeted to achieve this. Not surprisingly, the vision of enlargement that was promoted by the EU and the governments of applicant states was of a 'national' one, symbolized by the National Programme for the Adoption of the *Acquis* (NPAA) to be implemented in each country. At this stage, there was virtually no reference to regional or local dimensions in the evaluation of fulfilment of the Copenhagen criteria. The shift in focus from the national level as the unit of analysis was evident only in the Commission's opinions on the readiness of each applicant state, as only here, for the first time, was 'regional capacity' stated as a condition.

The Agenda 2000 and the Commission's Opinions provided the basis for the decisions at the Luxembourg European Council in December 1997 to proceed with enlargement by commencing accession negotiations with five of the CEECs (Czech Republic, Estonia, Hungary, Poland, Slovenia) and Cyprus. The basis for the negotiations with these 'in' states, which opened on 31 March 1998, is the condition that they must adopt the *acquis communautaire*. Their progress in this regard was to be monitored by the Commission in Regular Reports on each country. This condition is also the basis for the extension of the accession negotiations to a further five CEE states (Bulgaria, Latvia, Lithuania, Romania, Slovakia) and Malta agreed at the Helsinki European Council in December 1999. Essentially then, by making the adoption of the *acquis* the touchstone for enlargement to proceed, the EU has set the membership hurdle for the CEECs and other applicants at a height that existing EU member states have achieved mostly only after a long period of life within the EU. Only Austria, Finland and Sweden, advanced industrial countries, adopted most of the *acquis* in advance of accession to the EU.

Regionalization became a salient issue in most CEECs, only with the conditionalities imposed by the EU for accession, specifically the requirement to adopt chapter 21 (regional policy and coordination of structural instruments) of the *acquis*. With the exception of Hungary where reforms began in 1996 (see below), debates about regional reforms that had been dragging on for years were galvanized by the Commission's Opinions on accession from 1997 onwards, as the Commission identified 'regional administrative capacity' as a core requirement. An efficient system of public administration at regional and local levels is seen by the Commission as essential for both the implementation of the *acquis* and the dispersion of structural funds. The Commission's drive for Europeanization is, thus, awakening and empowering regional and local identities in the CEECs, some of which have been long dormant, while others are being newly imagined.

Regionalization and Europeanization in central and eastern Europe

In order to address the hypothesis of whether institutional choices for managing regionalization pressures have been shaped by historical path-dependencies or EU conditionality, it is necessary to review the emergence of patterns of local and regional government in central and eastern Europe. By focusing on selected cases from the core group of 'in' applicant states, our analysis highlights both the similarities, as well as evident differences, in the administrative reforms embarked upon by different states in response to the twin pressures of Europeanization and regionalization 'from without' and 'from within'. Our discussion centres on the reforms and reorganizations that have been introduced in response to the demands emanating from the Commission and broadly outlined in the Commission's 1997 Opinions, the 1998 Accession Partnerships, and the 1998 and 1999 Regular Reports.

Communist local government

The system of local government was relatively homogenous across eastern Europe under communism. While there was an extensive system of 'elected soviets' (councils) and attendant executive apparatuses at the local, district and regional levels, these organizational structures did not mask the reality of a highly centralized, Communist-Party dominated monism that undermined all semblance of local autonomy. While local councils were supposedly democratically elected, the elections were a sham as candidates tended to be vetted by Communist Party officials and in most cases electorates were offered no choice of candidates. Local councils and their executive apparatuses were subject to the dual oversight of superior bodies in the vertical administrative hierarchy and the Communist Party apparatus, which was organized in parallel vertical hierarchies. Local soviets had extremely limited resources at their disposal, and these were overwhelmingly centrally allocated and controlled. Given the lack of real autonomy, the absence of horizontal interaction across different levels of government, and the functional dominance of economic enterprises and their managers (usually subordinate to branches of central ministries) which often performed important service-provision roles locally (building roads, running schools and hospitals, providing welfare services and so forth), the structures of local government were in essence hollowed out and ritualistic (Illner, 1992).[9] These different functional roles made the dilemma of territorial versus sectoral control one of the perennial problems for the reform of local government under the communists. This is not to say that the system was characterized by *stasis*. During the communist era most CEE states attempted local government reform (for example, reforms in Poland in 1970s; in Hungary in the 1970s and 1980s). None of these reforms altered the highly centralized nature of the communist system of governance and the largely impotent structures of local government (Horváth, 1996: 27–8).[10]

Consequently, on coming to power the first generation of post-communist leaderships were faced with the legacy of extreme centralization, vertical top-down administrative hierarchies, weak horizontal networks, and a lack of capacity in terms of resources, efficiency and qualified personnel at the sub-national level. Such weaknesses were major constraints on local government reform. At the same time, in most countries there was an upswell of pressures in counteraction to years of central domination of the local level. In the heady momentum of democratization following the collapse of the communist regimes, the trend was for the extreme fragmentation of local government structures and ever smaller communities staking their claims to local 'self-government'. This 'bottom-up' decentralization occurred at the expense of the regional level, which was either abolished (as in Czech Republic and Slovakia), became an appendage of the central government (as in Poland, Bulgaria and Romania), or had marginal powers (as in Hungary) (Horváth, 1996: 22).

Post-communist local government

Newly installed democratic governments moved quickly to reform their systems of local government, the majority passing legislation in the early 1990s.[11] Laws on local self-government usually granted broad rights of autonomy to the local level. In contrast, the new national governments opted to delay decisions over the organization and functions of intermediary or meso-levels of government. The reasons varied but generally included: (i) a reluctance to decentralize further given the exigencies of political and economic transition including the limited resources at the disposal of central government; (ii) hostility towards the regional tier of government which had been influential and unpopular during the communist period due to the pivotal role of regional party secretaries in the communist system of rule and economic planning; (iii) a lack of consensus about how to organize the meso-tiers; (iv) an unwillingness among newly elected national ruling elites to decentralize and relinquish newly acquired powers to what were often seen as regional and local governments controlled by old communist elites; and (v) an unwillingness among the newly empowered local elites to relinquish powers. The immense rent-seeking opportunities inherent in administrative power during transition provided a sub-text for this struggle over reform.

Electoral sequencing also had a damaging effect on centre–regional–local relations and the potential for institutional reform. In many cases the different sequencing of national and local elections, combined with a natural political cycle, led to situations where there was almost permanent confrontation between ideologically opposed central and local governments. Such territorialized political conflicts have been an obstacle to decentralization, and indeed, in some cases resulted in recentralization (Regulska, 1997). The ebb and flow of transition politics has generally contributed to a 'democratic deficit' at the intermediary meso-level of governance (Bennett, 1997).

Nonetheless, the early reforms resulted in a firm legal basis for the jurisdictional separation of central and local governments, with a system of self-governing units at the lowest level enjoying considerable autonomy, and central governments exercising a strategic role of supervising the legality of local government activities and controlling the funding arrangements (Hesse, 1998). In the absence of provisions for the intermediary tier, central governments ran the administration at the county level and above. An exception to this rule was Hungary, where after 1989 a prefect-like system of Commissioners of the Republic oversaw local government operations and the activities of local branches of state administration in seven regions and the capital. This short-lived institution was abolished in amendments to the Law on Self-Government in 1994 (Kovács, 1999: 65–7).

Contrary to the processes of rationalization and reduction in the number of local authority units that have characterized the development of local government in western Europe in recent decades, the trend in most of the CEECs has been for greater fragmentation. In Hungary the number of municipalities virtually doubled between 1991 and 1998 from 1607 to 3154 (Kovács, 1999: 55). In the Czech Republic the number of municipalities soared by over 50 per cent after 1989 reaching a total of 6196 by 1993 (Bennett, 1993: 10).[12] The extremely small size of many of these local self-government units makes for a high degree of dysfunctionality as they lack a sufficient tax base to fund service-provision and that has greatly complicated resource allocation by the central governments. The problems arising from the dysfunctional fragmentary nature of local government has been a disincentive for further decentralization, if not offering a rationale for recentralization tendencies at the national level. Attempts to amalgamate or promote cooperation among local government units have had minimal success. Legislation in Hungary, for example, to regularize the procedures for amalgamations both on a voluntary and compulsory basis has not been enforced (Davey, 1995: 69–70).

Country cases

Poland

The accession to power of the Mazowiecki government in August 1989 (the first non-communist government in any of the CEECs) and the subsequent implementation of Balcerowicz's radical neoliberal variant of 'shock therapy', led to a reconcentration of power to the centre. The 1990 Local Government Act transformed Poland from a three-tier system (regional, district and local) into a two-tier system with strong central government and local self-government limited to about 2500 local authorities responsible for all public activities that were not assigned by law to other public institutions (Regulski, 1999). The 49 provinces remained as institutional appendages of the central government, as did the 287 district offices of state administration that retained responsibility for the most important services. Reform of the meso level of governance became highly politicized. A Task Force for Regional Policy was established by the Mazowiecki government in 1989 (including politicians and experts) to draw up a territorial redivision. The interminable political wrangling, compounded by the instability of governments in the mid–1990s, meant that reform was continually postponed. While some new responsibilities were decentralized to the local level following the 1990 reform, the capacity of municipal governments to act was constrained by their weak fiscal position during the years of economic depression. One consequence of the impoverishment of local government was that there was a return to some of the operational practices of the communist era. In particular, there was a resurgence in the power of sectoral hierarchies at the meso-level as regional administrative branches of particular economic ministries were established in some areas.

Hungary

Hungary was one of the first post-communist countries to implement a democratizing reform of local government. The 1990 Local Government Act established a two-tier, non-hierarchical system of self-government at both the county and local levels, with each level of government enjoying its own separate mandate and jurisdiction. The stipulation in the constitution that any enfranchized citizen of a village, town or county is entitled to local self-government resulted in the mushrooming of local government units (to some 3200 local self-governments). At the county level 19 self-government units with elected councils were formed with a four-year mandate. Local authorities have extensive powers over local affairs and these are protected by the Constitutional Court. Approximately 66 per cent of their resources are derived from central budget transfers and the rest is locally raised. In addition, provision was made for a network of state administrative offices, independent of the county and municipal governments and responsible directly to central administrative authorities, ministries or the central government. The state administrative offices operating at the county level manage administrative matters that fall outside the authority of local self-governments in several areas, including land registration, tax administration and public health. The control function inherent in this institution is indicated by the fact that they are entirely financed by the central state budget through the Ministry of the Interior.

A third feature of the Hungarian system was that Commissioners of the Republic were appointed by the President for seven 'regions'. In effect, these regions were created on the basis of the communist era planning regions for the country and the capital. Their main responsibilities involved prefect-like supervision of the legality of operations of local governments and the coordination of the activities of the local officials of the state administrative authorities. The Commissioners of the Republic were abolished by an amendment of the Local Self- Government Act in 1994 and replaced by a system of public administration offices but with essentially the same functions. Thus under Hungary's two-tier system there was a high degree of jurisdictional autonomy between central and local affairs and also between the two tiers of local government.

Estonia

One of the central elements of Gorbachev's perestroika was the revitalization of 'socialist self-government' at local level. The democratization of local government proceeded slowly at first, but accelerated as Estonia moved toward independence in 1989–91. By 1993 Estonia had a two-tier system of local self-government, comprising local self-government units at both the municipal level and the county level. Contrary to the majority of the CEECs, where the trend has been for more decentralization, Estonia rationalized its system of local self-government into a one-tier vertical and highly centralized structure. The first centralizing reform was adopted in 1993 when the elected intermediary tier of local self-government was replaced by an appointed stratum of state administrative officials at the county level.

The single tier system of local self-government includes 45 urban and 209 rural municipalities. Local authorities enjoy considerable autonomy, are responsible for administering public services and have their own budget, although they remain fiscally dependent on the centre since 65 per cent of local government resources come from a share of state incomes taxes and grants. Locally raised funds represent around 10 per cent of the budget, mainly from the land tax, which local authorities fix and receive directly. County level governance is an administrative appendage of the central government. The 15 county governments are responsible for organizing and coordinating the work of national institutions at the local level and for implementing national policies in accordance with the law and instructions of government and ministers. The county governor is appointed for a five-year term by the national government in consultation with local government representatives. The county governor is also charged with supervising the legality of legislation adopted by local government units within their respective jurisdictions. The work of the governors is directly financed from the state budget. Certain ministries also have single representatives or separate institutions at the county level. Consequently, there is no regional self-government in Estonia and little evidence of elite support for meso government or the existence of regional identities.[13] There is, however, an ongoing discussion about a further rationalization and reduction in the number of both counties and local governments. A reform of their functions and financing is seen as essential to create the more powerful regional and local administrative capacity demanded by the EU. It is likely, however, that this will be attempted without fundamentally altering the political determinants of the current system.

Slovenia

Despite the institutional legacy of Yugoslavian federalism, and its close geographical proximity to EU and west European states that have highly decentralized systems of local governance (Austria, Italy and Switzerland), Slovenia exhibited no contagion effects to engage in post-communist reform of its local government system. As in Estonia, the system remained highly centralized. Governance structures outside the centre consisted of a state-directed fused system in which municipalities typically performed both state administrative and local government functions. A constitutional right for referenda on the formation of communes led to a multiplication of local governments and a high degree of fragmentation in local politics. When reform of local government was introduced in 1994 it maintained this highly centralized system. The country was divided into seven municipalities and 65 large local government units that were composed of 194 communes. No allowance was made for regional territorial governance. Instead the central ministries implemented policy through their local offices, which were organized on a vertical basis, much like the former Yugoslav (and Soviet) line ministerial structure. Every ministry had a counterpart at the local level in the form of departments in each local government unit. There was, however, no horizontal coordination between the territorial offices of the different ministries.

Czech Republic

While proposals for regionalization have been extensively discussed in the the Czech Republic, it remains a highly centralized state. One argument is that the trauma of the break-up of Czechoslovakia has made central elites reluctant to devolve power, fearing a further disintegration. The post-communist Czech constitution envisaged a bicameral parliament where elected regional assemblies ('higher territorial self-governing bodies') would elect the senate (Horváth, 1996: 32). There is no consensus, however, over how many regions there should be or what boundaries they should have. The main variants include a retention from the communist era of the nine districts of the Czech part of former Czechoslovakia plus one new one for Moravia, or, alternatively, 17 new regions based on urban centres. Another proposal suggests that the country be regionalized and federalized into 13 districts based on 'historic' districts of Bohemia and Moravia. Local administration consists of both state organs (state district branches of the central administration) and local municipalities, independently administered via an elected assembly. Local governments may also be given secondary 'commissioned' responsibilities, where the central government may allocate specific tasks, and issue binding ordinances on them. The most powerful institutions in local governance were the 76 District Offices (including three major cities) of general state administration, together with the local branches of sectoral ministries. The Act on District Offices was one of the first acts passed in the immediate post-communist era in 1990. It reflected a profound ideological schism and lack of trust between local elites and central elites. The District Offices are headed by nominees of the central government and act as a check on the indirectly elected district assemblies (composed of delegates of the local self-governments). These assemblies enjoyed the critical function of distributing budgetary transfers from the centre. This system was, in essence, a return to the bipartite administrative model of the Austro-Hungarian Empire (Galligan and Smilor, 1999: 50).

Proto-regional government in central and eastern Europe

Despite the fundamental shared characteristics of local government arrangements across central and eastern Europe in the immediate post-communist period, the conditionalities of accession as defined by Agenda 2000 and the Opinions are forcing changes to strengthen regional and local 'administrative capacity'. The imperative of finding appropriate organizational forms to meet the requirements for EU regional and cohesion policies has been a catalyst for reform of local and regional government in the CEECs. The Commission views regional governance units as the foundation of the European Union's structural policy and is imposing this model on the accession states. Concurrently, elites in the candidate CEECs recognize the benefits of this model, for as Illner observed: 'Specialists and policy-makers alike have highlighted the importance of designing the regional level of government to be compatible with the regions of western Europe, to have the ability to associate and compete with them in transnational structures of inter-regional cooperation, and to participate in European regional programmes' (Illner, 1992: 16).[14] The institutional design of new meso-levels of governance in the CEECs can, therefore, be understood as a development influenced by three key factors, including: historical and geographic determinants; conditionalities from Brussels; and the specific trajectory and political context of transition in each country.

Over time, institutions mould their own loyalties and identities. In designing a viable structure of meso-level governance some governments have built on pre-existing regional identities. Where such identities are weak or non-existent, this route is much more problematic. In terms of local and meso-level governmental arrangements, policy-makers have looked both to their pre–1945 past as well as to the systems of local government in western Europe and the model promoted by the EU. States that were formerly part of the Austro-Hungarian Empire, such as the Czech and Slovak Republics and

Hungary, had the experience of a system of state administrative and self-governing territorial administration dating from the mid-nineteenth century and enduring until 1945. Conversely, Poland, which was divided until 1918 between the three neighbouring powers (Germany, Austro-Hungary and Russia) and then had an authoritarian regime under Pilsudski, lacks a tradition of pre-communist local self-government. Consequently, Poland opted to follow the Austrian and German systems of territorial administration as the model for its 1999 reform, though without adopting full-blown federalism (Illner, 1992: 15). The most significant trend, however, is for policy-makers in the CEECs to revive communist era economic planning regions in response to pressures emanating from the European Commission to establish regional administrative capacity at the spatial level above the county and local level. The accession conditionalities have forced most candidate states to undertake appropriate reform of the regional level of government.

The Brussels model aims to institutionalize administrative capacity at the regional or meso-level in preparation for the implementation of structural and cohesion policy. The prescriptive element of this model is generally vaguely stated in the Commission's Opinions. The 1997 Opinion on Estonia, for example, merely states that the 'main administrative requirements in this area are the existence of appropriate and effective administrative bodies, and in particular a high degree of competence and integrity in the administration of Community funds' (Commission Report, 1997: 102). Similarly, the Commission's Regular Report on Hungary published in November 1998 stated: 'Hungary has not adequately addressed the short-term Accession Partnership priority relating to reinforcement of institutional and administrative capacity in regional development ... Concrete implementation of regional policy objectives and the accompanying structures and institutions is still weak' (Commission Report, 1998: 33). The most perennial weaknesses, however, as recognized by the Commission's Regular Reports for 1999, are the under-funding and lack of trained personnel at the regional level. The identification of this gap will, inevitably, lead to a new bonanza for the 'technical' assistance industry in the EU.[15]

Nonetheless, the process of adapting to the implementation of the *acquis* has served as a catalyst for the reform of regional public administration in the candidate CEECs.[16] In general, the candidate countries have been encouraged: (i) to make further reforms to develop administrative capacity at all governmental levels; (ii) to make greater financial and human resources available at both the regional and local level to facilitate political and budgetary decentralization; (iii) to improve financial control systems at both the local and regional government level; and (iv) to increase coordination between administrative bodies at every level of government. Although the Commission has not overtly recommended that the candidates should structure their regions according to the average size of NUTS-II regions, the Regular Reports have commended those states which have made reforms in this direction. The newly recreated Polish vojvodships, for example, correspond to NUTS-II level regions, and Hungary's seven planning and administrative regions created under the 1996 Law on Regional Development and Physical Planning are similar to NUTS-II regions (see below). Furthermore, some observers have noted how Eurostat has positively advocated the systematic use of NUTS-II regionalized categories in its interactions with the statistical offices of the candidate countries – an example of standardization promoting integration (Hoich and Larisova, 1999).

Previous EU enlargement processes – the accession of Ireland, Greece, Spain and Portugal – widened regional disparities across the community considerably, increased the significance of structural funds and gave rise to the NUTS system as a means to collate and evaluate data and analyse regional development (Keating, 1993: 301). Joining the NUTS system is a condition of the pre-accession stages, as it represents the EU's established channel for the CEECs to become part of the EU regional, cohesion and accession funds. The NUTS system consists of five different levels; in particular the NUTS II level has an impact on regional development (NUTS I plays only a supplementary role in cohesion). NUTS II categories are the main instrument for the formulation and implementation of regional policy in the EU. They provide not only the statistical information and analysis for regional development planning and programmes, but are also the *administrative* level at which structural funds and other regional and cohesion funds are managed (Horváth, 1998: 56). The existing NUTS II regions in the EU were drawn up largely on the basis of designations arrived at by individual member states and subsequently approved *pro forma* by Brussels (Horváth, 1998: 63–4). The reverse appears to be the case for CEECs, as Brussels has deeply involved itself in the designation process.

Regionalization trends in the EU suggest that the size and economic potential of the currently existing local and regional governance units in the CEECs may be too small to make them the basis for an efficient and decentralized regional policy (Horváth, 1998). Consequently, additional reforms are needed if EU conditionalities are to be met and if the CEECs are to compete with each other and the existing EU members for regional and cohesion funds. The response of the CEECs in terms of the institutional design of systems of local and meso-level governance can be broadly categorized into two main types: (i) *democratizing reforms* specifically designed to promote an efficient regional development policy, and improve administrative efficiency, service delivery and the implementation of policy at the meso level; and (ii) *administrative reforms* aimed more generally at preparing for EU membership, including developing the necessary administrative capacity to access, process and administer structural and other regional development and cohesion funds (for example, PHARE, IPSA and Sapard). Some candidate states are pursuing purely administrative reforms, for example, by creating systems of regional development agencies. Though these new structures are still in their nascence, they clearly have no political institutional component and their interactions with existing county and local government structures have yet to be developed. However, it is not inconceivable that such institutional structures could be the foundation for an elected regional government. In fact, the trend of EU enlargement policy suggests to some researchers that: 'The Commission's remarks on regional administration indicate that its preference appears to be democratically elected regional self-governments which possess substantial financial and legal autonomy' (Brusis, 1999).

Country cases

Poland

Whereas other candidate states have followed a Brussels model for administrative regionalization, the first, and so far only, democratizing reform of both regional and local governance in a CEEC has been realized in Poland. To some extent a political regionalization was easier for Poland on account of its spatial size and prior history of regional government. What is noteworthy, however, is that the discussions and planning for this democratized regionalization predates EU enlargement conditionalities for regionalization. Thus, the Polish reform that was enacted by the January 1999 law on local government should be seen as an inherently endogenous development. The law introduced a three-tier system, with about 2500 self-government authorities operating at the local level, 308 rural and 65 urban districts (*powiats*), and 16 regional authorities (*vojvode*). All three levels have an elected council to supervise administration in their jurisdiction (Regulski, 1999).[17] The vojvodships also perform state administrative tasks, mainly of a supervisory and inspectory nature. The funding base for the new institutions of local and regional governance was also considerably improved as a result of the reform. For local authorities 70 per cent of revenues are derived from the central budget via tax-sharing and transfers, and 30 per cent are raised locally. Districts and vojvodships are funded overwhelmingly from the national budget. The main responsibilities of the meso-level vojvodships include: (i) promotion of economic development; (ii) public services of a regional character; (iii) environmental protection; and (iv) development of regional infrastructure. These emphases on 'regional administrative capacity' illustrate precisely the kind of conditionality which the EU imposes, driven by the model of its own structural funds. Poland has also established a system of regional development agencies under the overarching mantle of the Polish Agency for Regional Development. While the vojvodships correspond to NUTS-II regions, their design was influenced as much by historical and other endogenous Polish factors as by European. This reform is an example of a CEEC responding both to regionalization pressures 'from without' and 'from below', as there was intense pressures from regional elites for regionalization to enhance regional economic development programmes (Horváth, 1999: 29).[18]

Hungary

The most active EU involvement in regionalization in a candidate CEEC has occurred in Hungary. Yet while there has been substantial progress on the creation of administrative structures, there has been little or no progress in creating a democratized regional governance level. Unlike in Poland, the EU's Hungarian model was heavily administrative in character and was central to the policy-learning process for the EU in addressing regionalization in the candidate CEECs as a whole. Inevitably, the scale of Brussels' involvement has given rise to local level claims of EU 'colonization' at worse and the feelings of a 'forced marriage' at best. Brussels has guided Hungarian regional policy through PHARE programmes, since 1992 and was closely involved in the drafting of the Act on Regional Policy and Physical planning (XXI/1996), which made provision for a system of Regional Development Councils (RDC). PHARE also assisted with the formation of a National Regional Development Concept (1998). When Hungary delimited its scheme of seven NUTS II regions they were derived from the previous communist era planning regions that had been retained as the commissioners' regions in the immediate post-communist period.

In theory the RDCs were established at the voluntary initiative of groups of counties under the auspices of the National Council for

Regional Development. The administrative organization remains largely skeletal, with few employees and limited financial resources. The voluntary element of the structure was not entirely fictitious, since as of autumn 1999 five regional development councils had actually been set up to cover virtualy the whole country. Though the Commission's Opinions clearly welcomed the establishment of the seven administrative and planning regions and the system of RDCs, Hungary was still criticized for the administration of its regional policy via the Ministry of Agriculture and Regional Development in the central government. Nevertheless, the Commission Opinion on Hungary of July 1997 acknowledged that it was the first country in central and eastern Europe to adopt a legal framework conforming to EU structural policy requirements and the *acquis*, although problems remain in terms of institutionalization and implementation (Horváth, 1998: 49). In recognition of the progress on enhancing regional administrative capacity the EU, in July 1999, simplified and devolved power over PHARE and other programmes operating in Hungary. Thereafter, evaluation of applications and decisions on funding were supposed to be taken by the RDCs subject to the approval of a National Office and the EU Delegation. Decentralization was needed to cope with the massive increase in applications. For example, between 1988 and 1996 there were 57 PHARE projects for Hungary, but in 1998 in the RDC of South Transdanubia alone there were 40 projects approved.[19] Apart from the EU funding, the RDCs have a weak resource base and, as unelected quango-like agencies, are generally considered to be politically ineffectual (Kovács, 1999). There is, clearly, a major problem of non-identification in Hungarian society with the meso-level, since the focal point for local territorial political identity are the centuries-old counties. By the 1999 Regular Report Hungary was attracting sharp criticism for failing to address sufficiently the short-term Accession Partnership priority for regional capacity. By failing to assign adequate human and financial resources to strengthen regional and local government bodies and advance the goal of 'political and budgetary decentralization', Hungary was viewed as slipping in its progress toward accession.[20]

Estonia

An outline plan for restructuring the county government system into new regional units which would correspond to NUTS-II regions, and thus create an appropriate institutional instrument for the management of EU structural funds, has been widely discussed in Estonia over the past two years (Janikson, 1999). As yet there is no political consensus on this issue.[21] Estonia has no history of regional-level government and our elite-level survey suggests that there was considerable ambivalence towards the idea of adjusting administrative boundaries in Estonia in order to comply with EU-funding criteria (see below). The strong culture for centralization and local control in Estonia is evident from the continued subordination of the Department of Local Government and Regional Development to the Ministry of the Interior. Like Hungary, Estonia is pursuing an administrative solution to the regionalization conditionalities of accession, though in a much less systematic manner. Fundamentally, regional development in Estonia is viewed by its national level elites as a national level policy issue. Consequently, the Estonian Regional Development Agency was set up in May 1997 as a national level agency to coordinate and provide technical support to regional development programmes and local Business Support Networks. A National Regional Policy Council was established to act as a forum for representatives from all the ministries as well as county and local self-governments and to foster inter-institutional cooperation. It is little more than a talking shop, however, and effective inter-ministerial and central–local coordination remains very weak. Accordingly, the Commission's 1997 Opinion declared Estonia's regional policy as weak and its institutional basis very limited. This evaluation changed little in the 1998 Regular Report and the 1999 Regular Report. One of the major stumbling blocks for progress in Estonia is that no decisions have yet been taken on how structural funds will be distributed and whether the country will be one NUTS II region or several. These non-decisions are reflected in the fact that, so far, Estonia has not introduced a specific law on regional policy.

Slovenia

Slovenia has been one of the slowest of the candidates to address regionalization conditionalities. A Law on the Promotion of Regional Development passed in July 1999 established a system of twelve unelected functional planning regions but without any accompanying governance structures. As an administrative reform for rationalizing the distribution of regional funding it was positively received by the Commission in Brussels which issued its by now formulaic approval: 'The law is based on the same principles as the EU Structural Funds and establishes a general administrative framework for the implementation of a regional structural policy'.[22] As with the other candidate CEECs, the Commission's criticisms concentrated on demanding more funding and additional staff for the regional level.

Following the EU model of good practice, the law also makes provision for the establishment of a system of regional development agencies under a National Regional Development Agency and a Council for Structural Policy. As in Estonia, regional development is viewed by the Slovenian central government as its prerogative, though in Slovenia it is the responsibility of the Ministry of Economic Relations and Development.

Czech Republic

After years of delay the Czech system of local and regional governance was reformed according to European conditionalities by a new law of October 1997, which came into force on 1 January 2000. The law approved the establishment of 'Higher Territorial Self-Governing Units' and provided for a two-tier system of self-government with the local self-governments as the basic level (approximately 6590 in number) and 14 territorial self-governments (*kraj*) at the regional or meso-level. While the institutions of the meso-level have been formed, their competences have thus far not been stipulated by law. According to the Constitution, the regional self-governments must not subtract competences from local self-governments, but are to be empowered by responsibilities devolved from the central government level. The Ministry of Regional Development has drafted a list of competences which should be transferred to the counties, but so far it has not been actioned. It is not clear how the new reform will affect the powers of the centrally appointed district offices, which have been so powerful in post-communist local governance in the Czech Republic. To conform with EU conditionalities a national concept for regional policy was developed (termed 'Principles of Regional Policy'), and eight statistical regions corresponding to NUTS II regions were created in October 1998 by government decree. The legal framework for a regional development policy, however, in the form of a Regional Development Act, has been delayed by political wrangling. Nevertheless, the Commission's Regular Report on the Czech Republic for 1999 acknowledged the advances that had been made on developing the 'necessary' institutional structures for implementing regional and cohesion policies.[23]

Local elites and Europeanization

Institutions are the epicentre where structure and agency converge. The institutional framework shapes the perceptions and actions of the elites functioning within the institutional space. At the same time, the institutions are defined and changed by the actors at all levels of governance. In addition to the institutional change, resulting from pressures of Europeanization and regionalization from 'without' and from 'within' outlined above, elite perceptions help to gauge how deep the wider Europe already is. This important building block of the integration process is consistently neglected by the Commission in its Opinions and bilateral reports. The focus on compliance with accession criteria as a state-level phenomenon, with conditionalities externally defined and turned into national policy by the central governments of the applicant states, is a shallow understanding of the enlargement process.

Though there is no area of local or regional government that is not affected by European regulation or conditionality, our research suggests that there is relatively little engagement with and knowledge about the European Union among local elites in CEE accession states. This poverty of awareness affects both the regional and local prerequisites for EU membership, and the potential benefits from the funding of regional development programmes.[24] The lack of familiarity with EU institutions and policies stands in sharp contrast to the often detailed knowledge of the local and regional elites about local government practices and administration in west European countries. This experience and exposure is the result of frequent visits, work practices and participation in different Europe-wide networks involving local elites. This may be a sign of the beginnings of a horizontal deepening of the integration process. Knowledge of democratized regional and local governance structures and practices in EU member states, however, is qualitatively at odds with the kind of administrative regional and local governance structures and practices entailed in the Brussels model of regionalization.

Our research reveals that local elites in the CEECs are highly receptive to changes that will accommodate accession, even such radical proposals as the reform of local administrative boundaries (see Figure 8.1). Despite the fact that the regional cities of our surveys all stand to benefit considerably from EU structural funds for regional cohesion, this was not considered one of the key factors in local elites' understanding of what the EU stands for (see Figure 8.2). These are counterintuitive responses since we would expect local elites in CEE countries to instrumentalize the economic advantages inherent in EU membership. The benefits of the EU most often identified by local elites are those seen in terms of national-level

170 *Enlargement and Regionalization*

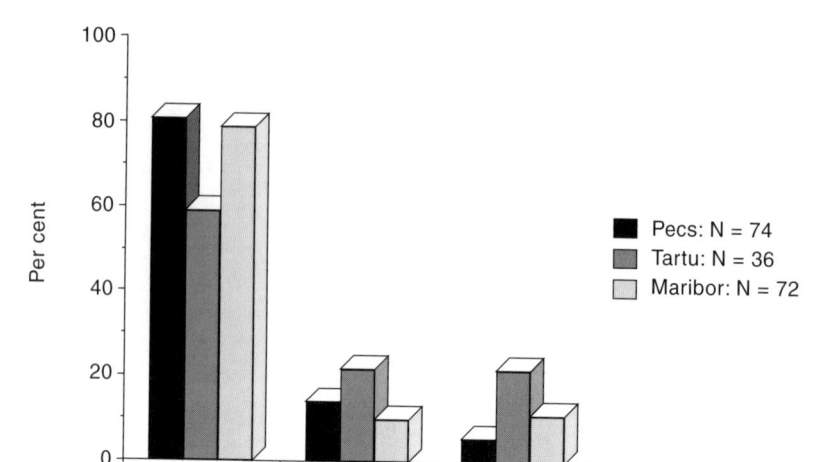

Figure 8.1 Attitudes to regionalization in compliance with EU-funding criteria

■ Pecs: N = 74
■ Tartu: N = 36
□ Maribor: N = 72

Respondents were asked: 'Do you agree or disagree with the proposition that local administrative boundaries in Hungary should be redrawn, if necessary, to comply with EU funding criteria?

referents (economic cohesion, free trade). Subsidiarity, one of the EU's key principles for integration and regional policy, and structural funds, the EU's main mechanism of regional development, rank low down among local elites' perceptions of the EU.

Our survey data suggests that social and economic issues linked to the transition process remain the dominant concerns of local elites, with EU accession barely getting a mention[26] (see Figure 8.3). Most significantly, local elites tend to have poor or limited knowledge of EU programmes, even when operating in their own areas (see Figure 8.4). The general perception among local elites is that the potential benefits of the EU are greater for the national rather than the local level (see Figure 8.5).

These preliminary results clearly demonstrate a 'regional gap' in the enlargement process. Accession to the EU is widely perceived of as a national project by and for national governments and national elites. This is hardly a project for realizing 'deep integration'.

Figure 8.2 The meaning of European Union

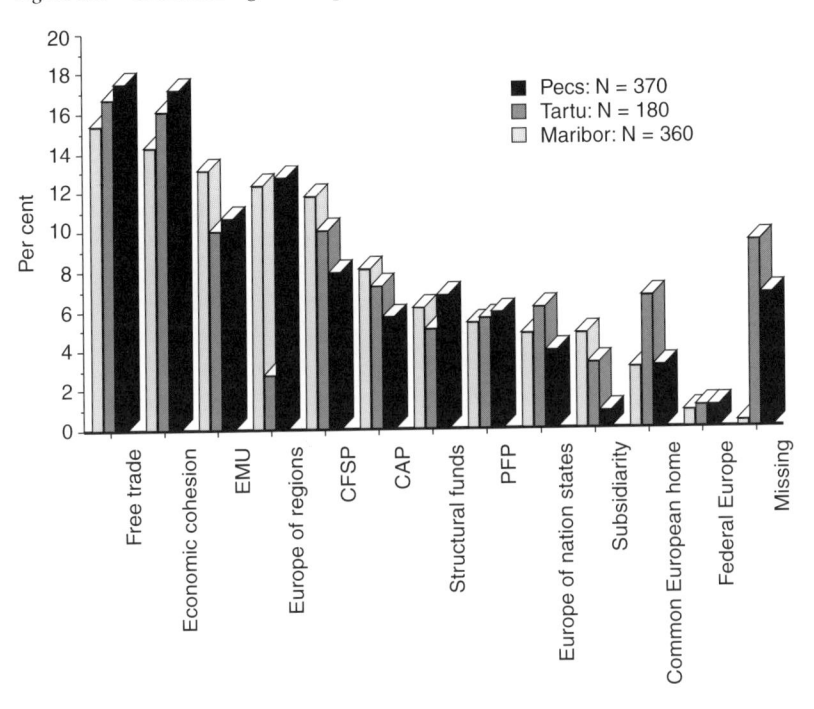

The maximum possible score is 20 per cent. Respondents were asked: Which five of the following phrases best sums up the European Union for you?

Figure 8.3 Key issues facing your city

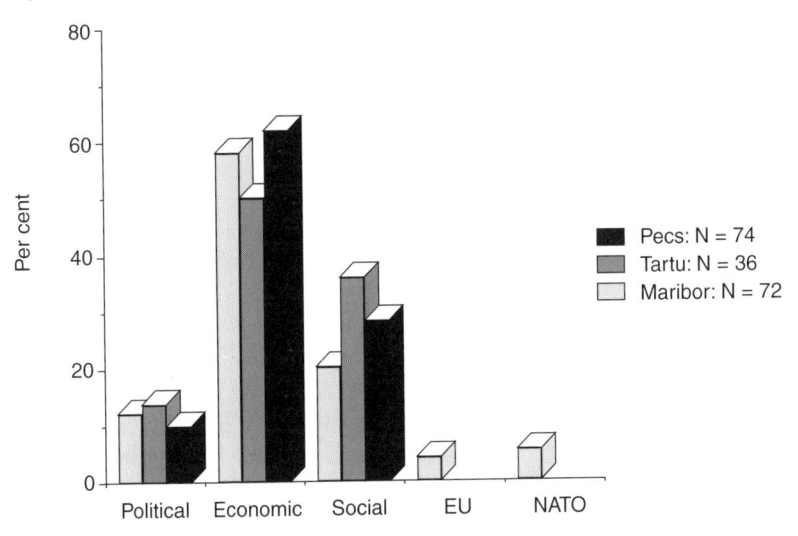

Respondents were asked: What, in your opinion, are the most important issues facing your city and country at this time?

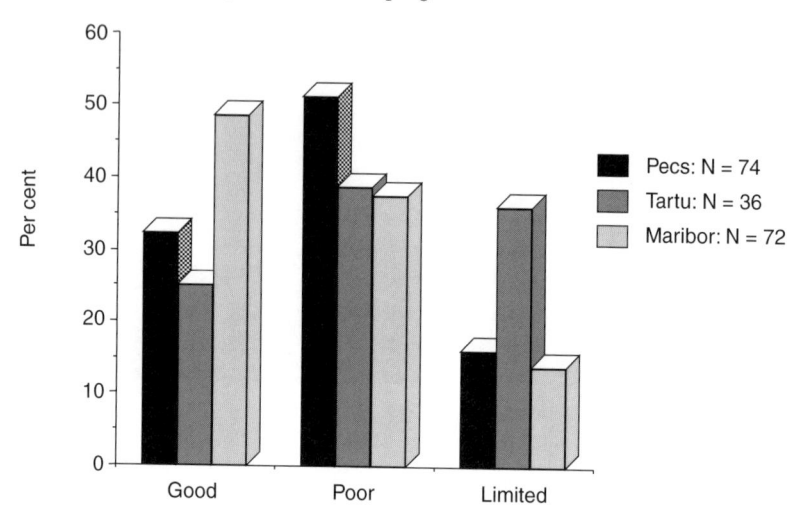

Figure 8.4 Knowledge of EU-funded programmes

Respondents were asked: Can you name (up to) three (or more) current EU funded (wholly or partly) projects in your city?

Answers were coded 'good' if respondents were able to name projects and the source of funding; 'poor' if respondents were unable to name any projects or sources of funding; 'limited' if respondents showed knowledge of projects, but were unable to identify the source of funding.

Conclusion

For most of the post-communist era local and regional governance in the CEECs has been characterized by a high degree of fragmentation, by the absence of a politically empowered regional level and by a tendency for recentralization at the national level. Similarly, for much of the period since the Copenhagen European Council of 1993 the process of EU enlargement has been conducted as a bilateral 'state-level' negotiation, between the Commission and national governments of the candidate CEECs. The voice of local and regional actors has been barely audible and, for the most part, ignored. Even when regionalization began to be deliberated as part of the fulfilment of chapter 21 of the *acquis*, the process remained in essence a bilateral exchange between central governments and the Commission. From 1997 a

Brussels model of regionalization promoted an administrative, as opposed to democratic, solution for achieving a consistent regional policy and the institutional incentives necessary to enhance administrative capacity at the local and meso level. Consequently, unelected Regional Development Councils and overlapping NUTS II regions have sprung up in the CEECs in response to the conditionalities imposed by Brussels for accession.

The compliance of CEE states with EU conditionality followed three variants: they complied in copy book fashion, as with the administrative regionalization of Hungary; or exceeded the demands, as with the democratizing regionalization of Poland; or, pursued regionalization as an administrative task for the central government, as in the smaller countries of Estonia and Slovenia, where regionalization has become a policy paradox. It remains to be seen whether these regional institutions will eventually take on a more political role and become effective regional governments. In this respect we should not downplay the strong contagion effect that is likely to come from the Polish variant of democratized regional government. The Brussels model is a stark contrast with the way in which regionalization has developed in western Europe, where it evolved in tandem with regionalist mobilizations 'from below' and 'from within', acting as an anvil against which the drive for EU integration hammered the nation-state. Enlargement to CEECs is witnessing a different type of regionalization. Here it is induced 'from without', through EU conditionalities, and the required regional reform is implemented 'from above' by national governments. In contrast to western Europe, regional institutions are being created in most CEECs prior to, if not in the absence of, regionalist mobilizations.

Our research demonstrates that seven years after Copenhagen, local elites are disengaged from the enlargement process. It is not altogether surprising, therefore, that the Commission's Regular Reports of 1999 record a lack of sub-national implementation and enforcement of EU rules and policies which have formally been agreed to in bilateral negotiations with national governments. This gap between 'state-level' compliance with EU accession conditionalities, and their weak implementation at the local level is likely to persist until the divergence between national and regional level perceptions and engagement with enlargement is addressed. The wider Europe will not become deeper until there is a substantive democratizing regional reform and active promotion of intergovernmental linkages across all four levels of governance: the European, national, regional and local.

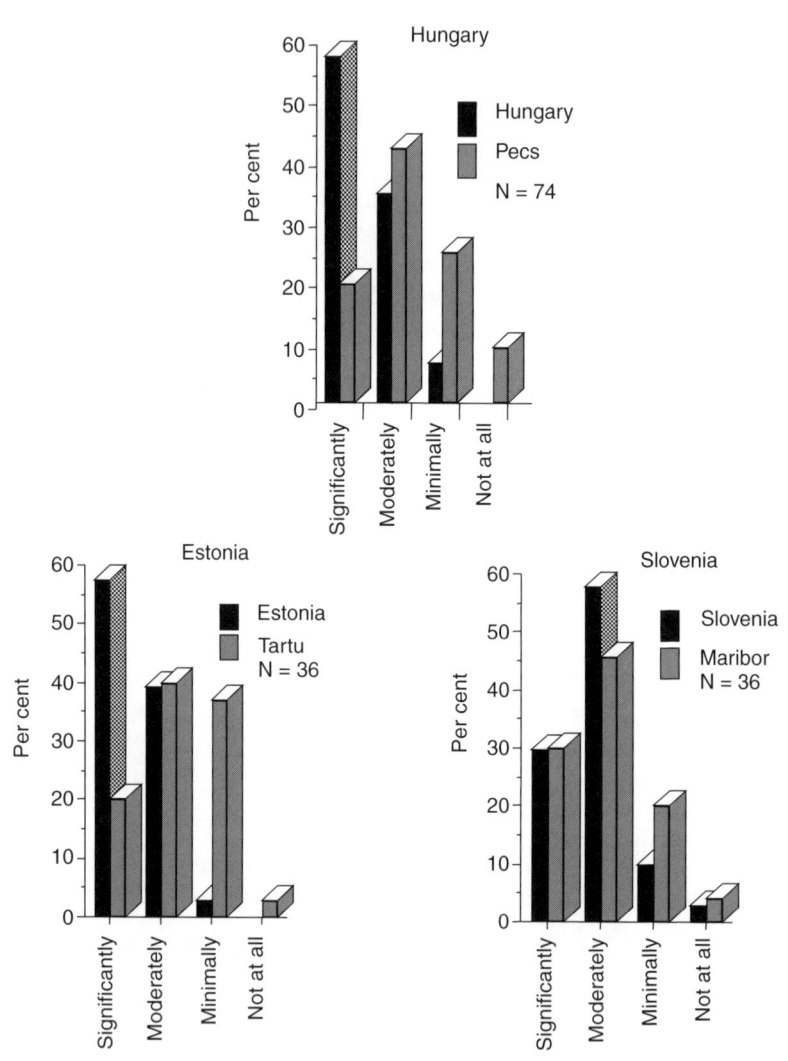

Figure 8.5 Perceptions of the benefits of EU membership

Respondents were asked: How much do you think your country benefits from its relationship with the EU? And, How much do you think EU enlargement has benefited your city? (Answers were coded according to a four point scale of 'significantly', 'moderately', 'minimally', and 'not at all'.)

Notes

1. For Wallace, the functional, territorial and affiliational dimensions of deep integration are essentially 'cross-country' in nature, while the territorial dimension hinges solely on border and security issues (Wallace, 1999). The common understanding of 'region' in this context, whether in western or eastern Europe, is one derived from an international relations construct of 'region' as a geographical group of states that understands the regional dimension of politics to involve relations between states. This perspective is also taken by Senior Nello and Smith (1998: 24).
2. The authors' research project under the *One Europe or Several Programme?* aims to focus precisely on these areas of weakness by employing large-scale elite surveys and interviews (n = 100) in important regional cities in six states of central and eastern Europe. We are investigating the attitudes of sub-national elites to the European Union and to reform of regional and local government. One of our aims also is to create a taxonomy of local and regional government systems in central and eastern Europe and measure the impact of EU enlargement on the evolution of these systems. ESRC Project L213252030 'Elites and Institutions in Regional and Local Governance in Eastern Europe'.
3. For analyses of the impact of European integration on local government in western Europe see Goldsmith and Klausen, 1997.
4. In contrast, the importance of conditionality as a sub-context for the exercise of international influence on regime change is recognized by Schmitter and others (Schmitter, 1996a: 26–54).
5. The revitalization of the *locale* is a constant referent in the work of Anthony Giddens on globalization.
6. In some states structural funds are controlled by central finance ministries (as in UK, Ireland and France). For a criticism of the 'fairy-tale character' of the structural funds which are often treated as a reimbursement for national spending rather than a genuine instrument of regional development policy, see Keating (1993: 299–300).
7. For analyses of the international dimension of transition see Whitehead (1996).
8. See also http://europa.eu.int/comm/enlargement
9. For a discussion of the influence of economic structures in local and regional governance in Eastern Europe, see Illner (1999).
10. For further details of reforms, see Brusis (1999).
11. For details on the administrative reforms see Galligan and Smilov (1999).
12. See Bennett (1993: 10) for a table on number and size of local government units in post-socialist countries in 1993.
13. In interviews conducted in September to December 1999 with 36 members of the local elite in Tartu, Estonia's second city, none of our respondents identified themselves with the county, which is seen as an administrative construct.
14. See Illner (1999: 16). See also Horváth (1999b).
15. Information taken from the 1999 Regular Reports on the CEECs.

16. Regional reforms and adjustments are also under consideration in the 'pre-in' candidate countries but they are at the preliminary stage of negotiations over the *acquis*.
17. For further details on responsibilities of local and district government, see Regulski (1999).
18. Interestingly, in Poland the first proposals for regional administrative reform came from the vojvodship level when Poznan vojvodship launched an economic development programme. This kind of regional mobilization was exceptional.
19. Interview with Katalin Kovacs, Managing Director, South Transdnaubian Regional Development Agency, July 1999.
20. Regular Report on Hungary for 1999.
21. The Commission's Regular Report on Estonia for October 1999 noted that for the time being a specific law on regional policy is 'not anticipated'.
22. Regular Report on Estonia, October 1999.
23. Regular Report on Czech Republic, October 1999.
24. This section is based on 182 elite interviews conducted in 1999–2000 in three regional cities in three candidate CEECs: 74 in Hungary (Pécs), 72 in Slovenia (Maribor) and 36 in Estonia (Tartu).

References

Agenda 2000 (com [97]2000, July 15, 1997).
Andrews, C. (1998) 'EU Enlargement: The Political Process', *House of Commons Library Research Paper*, 98/55.
Bennett, R. J. (1993) 'European Local Government Systems', in Bennett, R. (ed.), *Local Government in the New Europe* (London: Belhaven).
Bennett, R. J. (1997) *Local Government in Post-Socialist Cities*, Discussion Papers 2, Local Government and Public Sector Reform Initiative (Prague: Open Society: Institute).
Brusis, M. (1999) 'Recreating the Regional in Central and Eastern Europe: An Analysis of Administrative Reforms in Six Countries', online at http://www.euintegration.net
Commission Report (1997) European Commission, Opinion on Estonia's Application for Membership of the EU (July).
Commission Report (1998) European Commission, Regular Report from the Commission on Hungary's progress towards Accession (November).
Davey, K. (1995) 'Local Government in Hungary', in Coulson, A. (ed.), *Local Government in Eastern Europe* (Cheltenham: Edward Elgar).
Galligan, D. J. and Smilov, D. M. (1999) *Administrative Law in Central and Eastern Europe* (Budapest: CEU Press).
Goldsmith, M. and Klausen, K. (1997) (eds) *European Integration and Local Government* (Cheltenham: Edward Elgar).
Grabbe, H. and Hughes, K. (1997) 'Redefining the European Union: Eastward Enlargement', *RIIA Briefing paper*, 36.
Hesse, J. J. (1998) 'Rebuilding the State: Administrative Reform in Central and Eastern Europe', in Hesse, J. J. (ed.), *Preparing Public Administrations for the European Administrative Space*, Sigma Paper, 23 (Paris: OECD).

Hoich, J. and Larisova, K. (May, 1999) 'Reform der offentlichen verwaltung und bildung der regionalen selbsterwaltung in der tschechischen republik im kontext des EU-beitritts', online at http://www.euintegration.net
Horváth, G. (1996) *Transition and Regionalism in East-Central Europe*, Occasional Papers 7 (Tübingen: Europäisches Zentrum für Föderalismus-Forschung).
Horváth, G. (1998) *Regional and Cohesion Policy in Hungary*, Discussion Paper 23 (Pécs: Centre for Regional Studies of the Hungarian Academy of Sciences).
Horváth, G. (1999a) 'Changing Hungarian Regional Policy and Accession to the European Union', *European Urban and Regional Studies*, 6 (2), pp. 166–77.
Horváth, G. (1999b) 'Regional Effects of the Transition in Central and Eastern Europe', in Hajdú, Z. (ed.), *Regional Processes and Spatial Structures in Hungary in the 1990s* (Pécs: Centre for Regional Studies).
Illner, M. (1992) 'Municipalities and Industrial Paternalism in a Real Socialist Society', in Dostal, P., Illner, M., Kara, J. and Barlow, M. (eds), *Changing Territorial Administration in Czechoslovakia* (Amsterdam: University of Amsterdam, Charles University and Czechoslovak Academy of Sciences).
Illner, M. (1999) 'Territorial Decentralization: An Obstacle to Democratic Reform in Central and Eastern Europe', in Kimball, J. (ed.), *The Transfer of Power: Decentralization in Central and Eastern Europe* (Budapest: Open Society Institute).
Janikson, K. (1999) 'Creation and Reform of Intermediate Administrative Bodies in Estonia', May 1999, online at http://www.euintegration.net.
Keating, M. (1993) 'The Continental Meso: Regions in the European Community', in Sharpe, L. (ed.), *The Rise of Meso Government in Europe* (London: Sage).
Kovács, I. P. (1999) 'Regional Development and Local Government in Hungary', in Hajdú, Z. (ed.), *Regional Processes and Spatial Structures in Hungary in the 1990s* (Pécs: Centre for Regional Studies).
Loughlin, S. (1996) 'Europe of the Regions and the Federalization of Europe', *Publius: The Journal of Federalism*, 26 (4), pp. 141–62.
O'Donnell, G., Schmitter, P. and Whitehead, L. (1986) (eds), *Transitions from Authoritarian Rule: Tentative Conclusions about Uncertain Democracies* (Baltimore: Johns Hopkins University Press).
Opinions (com [97] 2001–2010, July 15, 1997).
Przeworski, A. (1991) *Democracy and the Market: Political and Economic Reforms in Eastern Europe and Latin America* (Cambridge: Cambridge University Press).
Regulski, J. (1997) 'Decentralization or (Re)centralization: Struggle for Political Power in Poland', *Environment and Planning: Government and Policy*, 15 (2), pp. 187–207.
Regulski, J. (1999) 'Building Democracy in Poland: The State Reform of 1998', *Discussion Paper No. 9* (Budapest: Local Government and Public Sector Reform Initiative, Open Society Institute).
Schmitter, P. (1996a) 'The Influence of the International Context upon the Choice of National Institutions and Policies in Neo-Democracies', in Whitehead, L. (ed.), *The International Dimensions of Democratization, Europe and the Americas* (Oxford: Oxford University Press).

Schmitter, P. (1996b) 'Examining the Present Euro-Polity with the Help of Past Theories', in Marks, G. *et al.* (eds), *Governance in the European Union* (London: Sage).

Senior Nello, S. and Smith, K. (1998) *The European Union and Central and Eastern Europe: the Implications of Enlargement in Stages* (Aldershot: Ashgate).

Wallace, H. (1999) 'Whose Europe is it Anyway? The 1998 Stein Rokkan Lecture', *European Journal of Political Research*, 35(3), pp. 287–306.

Whitehead, L. (ed.) (1996) *The International Dimensions of Democratization, Europe and the Americas* (Oxford: Oxford University Press).

9
Germany's Power in Europe
Charlie Jeffery and William E. Paterson[1]

Introduction

If, as Helen Wallace (1999: 287) suggests, 'many in the academic community are groping for an understanding' of post-1989 pan-Europe, then the same applies in an extreme form to post-1989 Germany. The problem is less one, though, of being 'locked into the paradigms' of the 'old Europe', because the 'old' (West) Germany never conformed very much to these in the first place. West Germany was something of an extreme case in its sheer enthusiasm for multilateral integrationist projects, along all three constituent dimensions of Wallace's 'deep' integration. Fundamental concerns about security in an initial postwar atmosphere understandably ill-disposed to Germany and the Germans were rapidly overlain and reformulated by the ideological divides – including Germany's own national division – of the cold war to embed a clear *territorial* dimension in West German integrationism. This was captured in the evocation by Simon Bulmer and William Paterson of West Germany as Swift's Gulliver during his captivity in Lilliput: divided from the German Democratic Republic (GDR) by the iron curtain, and integrated tightly into the structures of European integration and North Atlantic Treaty Organization (NATO), this was a European colossus tethered tightly – but unlike Gulliver, willingly – to its smaller and weaker counterparts (Bulmer and Paterson, 1989). West German integrationism had much more to it, though, than its own and others' security concerns. West Germany became (usually in tandem with France) a persistent demandeur for multilateral solutions in a *functional* integration process in the European Community (EC), which radiated out across ever-wider policy portfolios. And the whole integrationist momentum was underpinned in the *affiliational* dimension by a deep-seated elite consensus (itself resting on a supportive, 'permissive' public opinion) that multilateral cooperation was not just a valuable means to peace, security and prosperity in Germany and Europe, but had also become an end in itself, a guiding value of West German politics.

In the pervasiveness of its commitment to multilateral integration along these territorial, functional and affiliational dimensions, it was perhaps West Germany that was the 'outlier' of west European politics, rather than those states which were 'not fully engaged' in postwar institutions of multilateral cooperation (Wallace, 1991). West Germany was a state 'ostentatiously modest' (Hodge, 1992: 224) in the way that it pursued foreign policy goals through multilateralist channels, its 'reflex' (Paterson, 1993: 10) was to avoid overt positions of leadership. New terminologies had to be deployed to capture its idiosyncracy: this was a 'civilian power',[2] a 'trading state' (Rosecrance, 1986) relying on its economic weight – 'the combined resources of a predominantly private market economy' (Kaiser, 1992: 204) – rather than 'power politics' in engaging with its European partners. Especially puzzling for those schooled in realist traditions of rationalism, this was a state that had come to define its external goals in terms of *shared European* rather than *specifically national* interests.

This was the case at least before the collapse of communism, the opening of the iron curtain and the unification of Germany in 1989–90. The gropings of the academic community since have largely been about how to understand *united* Germany's role, what its interests are, how its power is deployed, in an emerging *pan-Europe*. For all sorts of reasons an effective understanding of this role has remained vital for the rest of Europe. The intensity of West Germany's Euro-engagement was such that it had taken up a position at the heart of pretty much every significant transnational network in Europe, not least the then EC, in which it had been at the centre of successive waves of both 'deepening' and 'widening'. Would this be sustained or, perhaps more to the point, sustain*able* given the multiplication of both the internal and external demands levied on the German state after 1990? Was there a will and a capacity to replicate and redeploy the energies committed in western Europe to multilateral cooperation in the wider Europe which communism's collapse had opened up – a wider Europe which, after all, starts on Germany's eastern doorstep? Or was West Germany's multilateralism an aberration, an 'abnormal', instrumental solution based in the geopolitical realities of the cold war, now due for the scrapheap as the united Germany evolved into a 'normal' power motivated by its own self-interest rather than a specious and contingent Europeanism?

This chapter aims to review some of the major themes that have emerged as academic analysis in Britain, Germany and the USA has grappled with these and similar questions. It does so with an eye to nuancing the way we deploy some of our familiar intellectual paradigms, in particular the ways we might think about power in European international relations. It begins with a brief review of some of the initial reactions to the question of how German unification was expected to lead to a substantial reformulation – a 'normalization' – of the means and ends of German foreign policy. There then follows a fuller discussion of some of the more nuanced understandings of 'Germany-in-Europe' that have evolved since. This discussion is based on a differentiated understanding of how German power is manifested through different 'faces' and is inspired in particular by the work of Simon Bulmer (1997 and Bulmer *et al.*, 2000). We propose in the conclusion that only through such a differentiated understanding can we get to grips with the nature and scope of Germany's power in Europe.

After 1989: the German puzzle persists

Many of the earliest works on new Germany/new Europe – some already published in 1990 – were imbued with a broadly realist frame of reference focused on the impact of unification in restoring German sovereignty. In this view West Germany had projected Europeanized rather than national interests because, tied by its western allies (and erstwhile enemies) into multilateral structures of European integration and transatlantic security, it had *no other choice* in the circumstances of the cold war. West Germany was an externally 'semi-sovereign' state, which lacked the capacity to pursue specific national interests. Seen from this perspective, the collapse of the GDR and the gathering momentum for unification were understood as an impending release from semi-sovereignty. The effect of this would be to reinstate Germany as 'the natural hegemon of any European political system' and – as a result – to pose 'awkward problems of adjustment for its neighbours' (Wallace, 1991: 169–70). Among the adjustment strategies mooted were the following, listed roughly in chronological order:

- keep Germany divided (so some of the views in the UK, Italy and France in response to the fall of the Berlin Wall) (Beyme, 1990: 83; Spence, 1991: 5–8);

- neutralize united Germany or, at the very least, prevent united German membership in NATO (the view of the short-lived reform-communist government in the GDR and, initially, until Stavropol, the USSR) (Beyme, 1990: 258);
- contain German power by tethering it yet more tightly to existing multilateral frameworks, especially the EC but also, as Soviet concerns moved on, NATO (the adapted view in France and the USSR as the dynamic of unification unfolded; this was also the view of Poland and other reform governments in East Central Europe, and of the European Commission) (Kielinger, 1990: 262; Pond, 1990: 78) Spence 1991: 8; Wallace, 1991: 173);
- only the USA looked forward – despite the alarmist promptings of some US academics (Mearsheimer, 1990) – to a united Germany as an equal sovereign partner, within NATO, throughout (Pond, 1992: 114).

The outcome, clear in outline by the end of 1990, was a mix of the two final points – restored sovereignty amid deepened multilateralism (via the EC's Intergovernmental Conferences on economic and monetary union (EMU) and political union which culminated at Maastricht) and refashioned security cooperation (including self-imposed strategic limitation within NATO, and flanked fleetingly with the idea that the Conference on Security and Cooperation in Europe (CSCE) might take on a stronger security role) (Pond, 1992: 82). The implicit identification of unification as the release of the inevitable hegemon from cold war external semi-sovereignty continued however even as the initial dust kicked up by the sheer speed of events cleared. Despite reaffirmed commitments to multilateral cooperation, there was still, for some commentators, a sense of 'Gulliver' becoming unbound by the restoration of sovereignty and destined to display (paradigmatically realist and/or threatening/malign) 'normality' in international relations. There are a number of variations on this theme, set out below in a descending scale of presumed German malignancy:

First, there was the 'Chequers seminar view'[3] of German 'normality' as reflective of an irredeemably flawed national character: 'There are things that people of your generation and mine ought never to forget. We've been through the war and we know perfectly well what the Germans are like, and what dictators can do, and how national character doesn't basically change'.[4] Unsurprisingly, this view failed to find much of an airing in serious academic debate.

Second, there were references to a possible reversion to Bismarckian '*Schaukelpolitik*' ('see-saw policy'), referring to the old intra-European balance of power in which Germany balanced (or, more sinisterly, played off) East versus West. In the post-unity context this would have been manifested in some kind of downgrading of attachments to western institutions (including the possibility of leaving the EC) (Cerny, 1993: 91–2; Treverton, 1993: 74–5) and the development of a free hand and a new (or renewed) sphere of influence in the East, not least given the post-communist weakness of the old Soviet/Russian rival for preeminence in the East. Empirical evidence for this was limited beyond the interpretation of Germany's 'bouncing' the EU into recognizing Croatia/Slovenia as an example of a new assertiveness in the East and a retreat from multilateralism in the West (Treverton, 1993: 75). Moreover, despite some talk of 'Stavrapallo' in summer 1990, the weakness of the Soviet Union/Russia foreclosed even the theoretical option of reviving the historical tradition of *Schaukelpolitik*.

Third was a conception of a German introspection resulting from post-unification economic weakness. The concern was voiced by a range of authors that the economic problems of integrating the former GDR would be either greater or longer term than initially imagined and would stimulate protectionist tendencies, which would qualify the inherently multilateralist character of the West German free trading tradition. This would have inevitable implications for European integration as the EC approached the completion of the 1992 single market (Arnold, 1991: 467–8). In a related vein, there was a concern that Germany would renounce its paymaster role for the EC because of the cost burdens of unity (Garton Ash, 1994: 68), and that the social dislocation produced by post-unity economic adaptation in East and West would revive the far right, with the implication that nationalist pressures on foreign policy would result (Geipel, 1993: 37–9; Treverton, 1993: 74).

An additional spin on this kind of argument was provided by the externalities of *Bundesbank* interest rate policy which helped to cause the European exchange-rate mechanism crisis of 1992. This reflected the primacy of the Bundesbank's specifically national brief (to use anti-inflationary interest rate policy to damp down the post-unity boom) over external/multilateral responsibilities arising from the international role of the Deutschmark (DM) (the 'export', via high interest rates, of deflation): Germany, in other words, was becoming insular and introverted, pursuing its narrow concerns with disregard to those of its partners:

> Throughout the postwar period, a politically stable and economically prosperous Germany has been a strong supporter of European

integration and of a liberal global economic order. Germany may become politically less stable and economically considerably weaker in the future. This will translate into a less reliable external position with less room for manoeuvre (Arnold, 1991: 470).

Fourth was what might be termed a 'soft realist' view of 'Gulliver unbound' – a 'return to European normality' (Arnold, 1991: 462) – derived from the removal of cold war constraints and the net increase in German power resources following unity: 'In time ... the deep underlying changes in the country's internal and external position must affect Germany's foreign policy' (Garton Ash, 1994: 66). 'As a normal state of its size and wealth it must make its voice heard and its presence felt' (Arnold, 1991: 462) even in terms of military power: 'If Germany were not, in the longer term, to seek enhancement of this dimension of its power ... it would be behaving differently from most large states in history' (Garton Ash, 1994: 68).

Finally, there was John Mearsheimer's (1990) bizarre, 'hard realist' conception of post-cold war normality as that of a nuclear-armed Germany outside of NATO in a Europe without the USA. Interestingly, Mearsheimer did not see – as most Germans and most Europeans certainly would – a nuclear-armed Germany outside NATO as a worrying thing, but, more or less, as a 'normal' thing. This merely confirms how his ideal-type realism lacked any evident contextualization in or by the real world of European politics.[5] Nevertheless the themes he raised had some echoes in the US at least, where some concerns were expressed in near-policy circles about the renewability – or, possibly, the redundancy – of NATO in the post-cold war era and an attendant 'renationalization' of European security, including the possibility of a nuclear Germany (Arnold, 1991; Pond, 1992).

The above did not prove to be interpretations with a long shelf-life. It rapidly emerged, as the EC became the European Union (EU):

(a) that Kohl did not share the same 'national character' as Hitler;
(b) that Germany was committed via the EU and other multilateral fora, to an East *and* a West strategy, widening western structures to encompass the East, while deepening them at their western core (including, via economic and monetary union [EMU], an abdication of the Bundesbank's 'unilateral' power to shape the DM currency area);
(c) that, notwithstanding the problems of post-communist reconstruction in the former GDR, Germany, in the context of the 1992

single market programme and the modalities of integrating the decrepit ex-GDR economy into the EU, remained committed to free trade and did not renounce its commitments as the largest EU net contributor;[6]
(d) that instances of 'normal' pursuit of national interests were isolated and ambiguous rather than harbingers of deep change;[7] and
(e) that Germany remained wholly committed to NATO, and – shaped by a 'post-military' society reluctant to accept an autonomous security role – was engaged in a close partnership with the USA in redefining NATO's *collective* security mission for the post-cold war era (not least through the presence of the former German Defence Minister, Manfred Wörner, as NATO Secretary General).

In other words, Germany was still puzzling – at least for those who expected unification to release Germany to conform to a realist paradigm. A rather larger part of the literature however, foresaw continued multilateralist commitment as the enduring hallmark of united Germany's foreign policy. Significantly, though, accounts of this continued multilateralism also came in a growing number of variants, proposing different – though not necessarily competing – explanations of why forms of multilateralism have been chosen and of what implications they have for understanding Germany's role, and the disposition of its power, in Europe. In part, these accounts also display undercurrents of the 'normalization' debates touched on above. They collectively point to a reality of German power in Europe which is both rather more differentiated and rather more *encompassing* than that which we might 'normally' assume. A useful framework for capturing this differentiation has been provided by Simon Bulmer, for whom in recent years the distinction of different 'faces' of German power has been a persistent theme (Bulmer, 1997, Bulmer *et al.*, 1998, 2000). Developing on the work of Guzzini (1993), he distinguishes four 'faces' of power:

- *Deliberate*, or realist power, is a familiar conception which would see German power 'as a function of the forceful articulation of interests, combined with valuable power resources for articulating leverage' (Bulmer, 1997: 73). Needless to say, this conception underlay much of the early post-unity analysis discussed above: released from semi-sovereignty and, simply, bigger, united Germany would be in a position both to articulate its interests more forcefully and to mobilize greater power resources in doing so.

- The notion of *institutional* power is rather more subtle – a notion of 'soft' power (Katzenstein, 1997b: 3–4; Nye, 1990) – which suggests that Germany's particular domestic institutional configurations, political, legal and economic, might present it with inherent advantages in pursuing its external goals.
- *Unintentional* power is precisely that: power which 'arises from the unintended consequences of domestic economic and political power', which is 'dispositional rather than the product of deliberate action'. A classic example was discussed above: the unintentional, but for other states extremely unwelcome 'export' of deflation by the Bundesbank in 1992 as it went about its rightful business of managing the German domestic economy.
- *Systemic empowerment*, the 'dyadic', 'reverse image' of the other faces, assumes that 'German power is not just the product of forces emanating *from* Germany' (whether deliberate, unintentional or institutional), but may also be generated by particular features of the international system(s) with which Germany interacts.

This multifaceted conception of power provides a vital navigational aid through the following discussion of alternative understandings of the multilateralist puzzle Germany continues to present. Though Bulmer has used it elsewhere specifically to analyse German EU politics, we deploy it below also in relation to other forms of transnational interaction running in parallel with EU integration, and to questions of security politics.

Multilateralism between domestic politics and transnational governance

A number of interpretations of Germany-in-Europe see the perpetuation of multilateralist commitments (in the EU in particular) into the post-cold war era as a function of domestic politics. Of these, work on *institutional pluralism* has the longest pedigree. This is the internal dimension of the (West) German semi-sovereignty identified by Peter Katzenstein (1987) and explored in its significance for European integration policy by Bulmer and Paterson (1987).[8] The assumption was that European policy-making was an externalized reflection of the institutionally complex domestic policy process which Katzenstein in particular had illuminated. Works written in this vein did not argue, though, that West Germany was multilateralist because of internal semi-sovereignty/institutional pluralism, but rather that *it was not* a realist state because of internal semi-sovereignty/institutional pluralism. West Germany was not a state internally structured in a way consistent with realism's assumptions: the constraints of coalition politics, federalism, departmental sectorization, the role of 'parapublic' institutions – the Bundesbank at their forefront – and (in some fields at last) strong, centralized forms of interest representation undermined the realist assumption of a coherent state representing a clearly defined national interest.

This image of Germany as a polycephalic European policy actor was routinely projected forward into post-unification analysis, with honourable mentions in despatches going to the *Länder* and the Bundesbank in particular, but also, on occasion, to the combination of sectorized, uncoordinated house policies in federal government departments (facilitated by a relatively weak foreign ministry), the Constitutional Court, coalition politics and the private sector (Garton Ash, 1994: 71; Goldberger, 1993: 290–3; Kaiser, 1992: 205; Wallace, 1991: 171). Accounts of the *significance* of all this for the German role in Europe have varied. One view was that it served to perpetuate internal constraints on the 'Gulliver' whose external constraints had been cast off with the restoration of sovereignty (Jeffery, 1995): put simply, not much was likely to change in Germany's multilateralist heritage with so many actors vying for a European role: 'In such a system, incrementalism is the name of the game. Sudden, far-reaching policy changes, whether domestic or foreign, are most difficult to bring about' (Cerny, 1993: 93–4). Others have identified sectoral incoherence as the name of the German EU policy game: as individual federal ministries merrily pursue often incompatible 'house' priorities, the prospect of a clear and purposive German grand strategy to which all relevant policy actors subscribe is minimal. There has, for example, long been recognition of the incompatibility of the opposed institutional rationales in EU politics of the Agriculture Ministry and the Finance Ministry (Bulmer and Paterson, 1987); more recently, these clashing rationales prevented the Kohl government – committed simultaneously to serving the interests of the farming constituency while also reducing the German net contribution to the EU budget – from developing any kind of rational position in the Agenda 2000 debates in 1997–98 (Jeffery and Handl, 1999). The pursuit of separate departmental agendas similarly undermined attempts to generate a coherent negotiating stance during the 1996–97 IGC as particular ministries opposed proposals to extend qualified majority voting in their fields, notwithstanding the federal government's formal 'collective' position in favour of extending QMV (Bulmer *et al.*, 2000).

There is a sense, though, in which institutional pluralism, and even the policy incoherence it can end up producing, may actually empower the federal government in European negotiations. This is a position represented in particular by Bulmer and Paterson, turning their earlier conclusions (1989) about the *constraining* impact of institutional pluralism on their head. The suggestion is that, on occasion, it has been quite plausible for the federal government to claim that on a given issue it is bound to a particular position because a key domestic policy actor has a veto power (Bulmer, 1997: 68; Bulmer and Paterson, 1996: 20–1). This has been most prominently the case in the process of constructing EMU. Initially less than keen on the idea of abolishing the source of its power – the DM – the Bundesbank responded by arguing that the institutional structure of EMU, not to mention the location of the European Central Bank, should be modelled on itself. Subsequent modifications had a similar origin, most notably the Stability Pact designed to ensure that a Bundesbank-style anti-inflation policy could be sustained after the initial dash for the EMU convergence criteria. These were not, of course, positions unwelcome to the federal government. Given: a) that they were supported directly by the German Constitutional Court and indirectly in a sceptical public opinion, and b) that the Bundesbank model was the subject of admiration elsewhere in the EU, they created the opportunity for the federal government to ensure an enduring German imprint on the organization of EMU (Bulmer *et al.*, 2000).

The role of the Bundesbank in shoring up the wider German position on EMU is an example of what we have called elsewhere institutional export (Bulmer *et al.*, 2000) and what Bulmer termed institutional power: the supply of institutional models from the domestic arena which then set the parameters for policy-making at the European level. Though clearly the most prominent, EMU is not an isolated example, either at the 'constitutive' level of EU politics or in the day-to-day routine of EU policy-making. For example, the German *Länder* left their mark on the constitutive level in the treaty amendments they – both with and without the support of the federal government – secured in the Maastricht negotiations and, in the case of subsidiarity, at Amsterdam in 1997. This institutional capacity extends too into the private sector, with German firms playing a defining role in standard-setting in the European single market programme. More fundamentally, the landmark judgment of the German Constitutional Court on the constitutionality of the Maastricht Treaty confirmed that Germany can continue to participate in the EU integration process only if the treaty foundations of the Union remain compatible with German domestic constitutional principles. In these ways, directly and indirectly, internal structures have externalized on to Germany's external partners. The pattern is consolidated by Germany's traditional role as an integration deepener. As a long-standing demandeur for multilateral solutions, it has naturally left much more of an imprint than, say, the UK, in shaping how things are done. It is because of this that Germany has a 'growing ability to set the rules of product regulation, trade, and monetary relations inside the EC and often on a larger scale' (Geipel, 1993: 25).

The net result is the extensive congruence Bulmer has noted between the German and the EU systems of governance, with both displaying comparable constitutional foundations, operational norms and conventions and, in large part, policy goals (Bulmer, 1997: 61–72). It completes a virtuous circle of two of the 'faces' of power which Bulmer identifies: the institutional power which Germany has exerted by 'shaping institutional development in such a way as to mobilize a bias in the character of EU governance' (Bulmer, 1997: 74); and the 'systemic empowerment' of Germany by the familiarities with the 'biased' structure of EU governance which results. As Jeff Anderson and John Goodman (1993: 61) put it: 'Institutions are rarely neutral; rather they are shaped by the interests and resources of member states, and consistently privilege some, particularly the more powerful, over others'. Germany has clearly done much to shape a system which, through institutional congruence, then feeds back such 'privilege'.

This is so far a fairly familiar argument (Bulmer, *et al.*, 2000).[9] However, the notion of systemic empowerment raises a number of further questions. First, as regards the extent that systemic empowerment occurs because Germany 'exports' institutions, do we adduce from this a pattern of intention, a purposeful instrumentalization by German actors of the virtuous circle which privileges them over others? Is there, in other words, a disguised pattern of deliberate power being exercised? The ill-coordinated institutional pluralism discussed above might make such a conclusion seem implausible; notions of an 'instinct' or a 'reflex' to seek multilateral solutions offer an alternative explanation, and are addressed in the next section. Second, if systemic empowerment can occur as a result of the 'export' of German institutional patterns, does this not imply that it can occur also because others '*import*' German institutional patterns into the 'system'? This is a possibility raised (though using different terminology) by Andrei Markovits and Simon Reich (1991). Though at the time this was received critically,[10] its conception of an emergent German 'hegemony' bears revisiting in the context of ideas of systemic empowerment.

The 'hegemony' Markovits and Reich evoke is understood in a 'consensual', 'Gramscian' sense, not a coercive, realist one, and proposes that the EU and the (extending) European market order provide a structure for German economic and cultural domination. To summarize (and simplify) their argument: the (West) Germans developed after World War II a *'Modell Deutschland'* of stable and successful democracy and a powerful, export-led market economy. The German model was so impressive that it 'won Europe's hearts and minds' (Markovits and Reich, 1997: 11), attaining 'hegemony'; that is, others aspired to emulate it 'as a suitable model for their own economic development'. The result, though, under the EU's free trading conditions, was of asymmetrical benefit to Germany, which persistently ran a trade surplus with (and financed by) all its major EU trading partners: German 'prosperity was built on an economic domination of these [trading partner] countries' (Goldberger, 1993; Markovits and Reich, 1994). Why, then, would these partners acquiesce in their own economic subordination? First, because of the unchallenged 'hegemony of the principle of unadulterated free trade' (Markovits and Reich, 1991: 12); and, second, because a pluralist democratic Germany was viewed as a benign and legitimate partner. According to Markovits and Reich (1991: 14) 'German economic penetration has not been seen as part of an imperialist policy of an authoritarian state as was the case in earlier epochs of Germany's relations with its European neighbours.' In other words this was an *unintended, non-purposive* domination constructed on the basis of shared beliefs in the merits of free trade in Europe and trust in and admiration of Germany. A form of systemic empowerment of Germany was thus created by the beliefs and decisions *of others*.

Importantly, Markovits and Reich went on to argue that this systemic bias was also being replicated, even more intensively, in central and eastern Europe as the states looked to *Modell Deutschland* as a blueprint for economic prosperity and a model of democratic governance. This argument provides a useful perspective on the issue which, perhaps more than any other, raises questions about the nature of German power in post-cold war Europe: how Germany deals with the opening up of the former communist states directly to its East. The question of how that power is deployed is inevitably nuanced by (negative) historical memory[11] ranging from the arrogances of *Schaukelpolitik* to the atrocities of physical devastation and genocide.

Markovits and Reich provide an unexpected answer: central and eastern Europe will seek to emulate Germany by importing the structures of its success. The process they foresaw was not one of the 'export' of German models, but their 'import', not the purposive projection of German power, but the magnetic attractions of the German model. The net result may well be the same – a form of systemic empowerment or 'hegemony' engendered by Germany being able to interact with familiar, even replicated structures of governance throughout its 'regional milieu'.[12] But the route there, and the implications for a full understanding of Germany's goals and roles in 'post-1989 Europe', are quite different.

Markovits and Reich find a growing number of echoes in the literature. Timothy Garton Ash writes of Germany's 'social power', 'the overall attractiveness of a particular society, culture and way of life' (Garton Ash, 1994: 68–9). Others have written about the emergence of institutional patterns in central and eastern Europe – corporate and banking systems, central banking structures, electoral systems, legal and constitutional structures – directly or indirectly drawn from German models (Pond, 1992: 126; Katzenstein, 1997a: 25). The essential point is that Germany is, in these depictions, largely a *passive* force, a model to be emulated, a resource to be drawn on; 'East Central Europe's *Drang nach Westen* is much more relevant to Europe's future than older visions of a German *Drang nach Osten*' (Hamilton, 1991: 129). Or, to put it more coarsely, as in the old Czech joke: 'the only thing worse than being dominated by the German economy is not being dominated by it' (Livingston, 1992: 168).

The process by which institutional forms become emulated naturally also has an 'export' side in which German actors make an *active* contribution to shaping central and eastern Europe in the course of their engagement with it. Examples include: the deployment of foreign aid and assistance (Davis and Dombrowski, 1997); the promotion of the German language through the institutions of 'foreign cultural policy' (Wood, 1999); the activities of the (party)-political foundations (Pond, 1992: 126); and the mass of activities undertaken or sponsored by German state actors in the attempt to put the groundwork of an enlarged EU in place (the German Interior Ministry and its counterparts in some of the *Länder*, notably Bavaria, have, for example, supported the modernization of the Polish and Czech border policing infrastructure) (Jeffery, 1999: 56–7); cross-border cooperation schemes between the eastern German *Länder* and their counterparts across the Polish and Czech borders are removing barriers to integration and generating grass roots 'social capital' to flesh out the formal integration process (Jeffery and Collins, 1998: 99–100); and countless know-how and personnel exchanges underway at all levels of public administration – the *Land* of Berlin alone can claim some 240 agencies involved in advice, consultancy, education and training in the central and eastern European states.[13]

Then there is the private sector – its role in providing meshing between societies and acting as conduits for the export (or import) of institutions is curiously unresearched for a country often characterized as a 'trading state'.[14] Few commentators suggest that the private sector is a power resource which can be purposefully deployed in central and eastern Europe (Livingston, 1992: 165).[15] 'Private firms generally do not see their investment decisions as instruments of their government's foreign policy. They invest because of perceived needs and opportunities, which the low wage structures and untapped markets of eastern Europe present to nearby Germany' (Geipel, 1993: 24). German investment in, and trade with, central and eastern Europe, while undeniably massive, is therefore fundamentally unmarshalled, the results of a cacophony of unconnected boardroom decisions 'of countless independent economic actors, many not even German, but foreign or internationally controlled' (Kaiser, 1992: 204). The impact, though, in facilitating the reproduction of German ways of doing things is, we suspect, considerable.[16]

Disentangling agency and causality in processes of institutional reproduction – whether export or emulation, effected through private or public sector channels – would require its own research programme.[17] For the purposes of this chapter it suffices to say that such processes are a manifestation of the new, 'de-bordered' 'transnational governance' that Markus Jachtenfuchs, Beate Kohler-Koch, Thomas Risse and others have identified (Jachtenfuchs and Kohler-Koch, 1996; Risse-Kappen, 1997; Wessels, 1999). Their net effect is extremely significant. In an entirely uncoordinated way, myriad aspects of Germany's institutional and regulatory structures are being implanted into central and eastern Europe, in parallel to, but separate from, the formal processes of EU enlargement. German norms are thus being 'preemptively' diffused in central and eastern Europe *beyond the reach of* the EU's current multilateral framework. Germany's 'near-abroad' is being institutionally shaped without the involvement of Germany's existing partners in multilateral cooperation; the implication is that this stands to 'pay back' asymmetrically in Germany's favour once enlargement is realized. The effect is potentially of tremendous significance for German power and systemic empowerment in the post-enlargement EU. As Christoph Jessen, head of the department in the German Foreign Office responsible for the Agenda 2000 negotiations, put it:

> Germany . . . profits . . . from the extension of the familiar environment in which common norms, *most of which have been decisively shaped by Germany*, come to be applied. Any adaptation costs arising from this fall to member states which are less strongly able to shape these norms. *In this way benefits accrue to Germany which are numerically scarcely verifiable but nevertheless considerable* (Jessen, 1999: 168) (emphasis added).

From 'reflexive' multilateralism to 'delayed normalization'?

We return at this point to the more 'orthodox' form of systemic empowerment discussed earlier – the virtuous circle of institutional export and systemic bias *within* the EU – and to the question we raised earlier. Is this a virtuous circle, deliberately set in motion by German actors, or a 'reflexive' commitment to multilateralism? This is a question nicely framed in Jeff Anderson and John Goodman's distinction between 'reflexive' and 'instrumental' multilateralism (1993: 60). The latter implies a rational (and therefore contingent) calculation of cost and benefit in multilateralist engagement. Garton Ash writes, for example, of Germany's 'attritional' capacity and skill in using multilateral structures as a means of realizing specific, German national interests *'in Europe's name'*:[18] 'Germany has excelled at the patient, discreet pursuit of national goals through multilateral institutions and negotiations, whether in the European Community, NATO or the Helsinki process' (Garton Ash, 1994: 71). The notion of a multilateralist 'reflex' implies, by contrast, an enduring commitment to multilateralism not explicable solely by rational calculation:

> Over the course of forty years, West Germany's reliance on a web of international institutions to achieve its foreign policy goals, born of an instrumental choice among painfully few alternatives, became so complete as to cause these institutions to be embedded in the very definition of state interests and strategies. In effect, this is what we mean when we describe Germany's institutional commitments in the post–1989 period as reflexive; they have become ingrained, even assumed (Anderson and Goodman, 1993: 60).

In their exhaustive trawl through early (1989–91) post-unity foreign policy discourse Anderson and Goodman find no evidence that the 'ingrained, even assumed' German commitment to these institutions was at all reappraised after unification. Indeed, if anything the German response was to rely even more on these institutions as the best framework for adapting to the new post-1990 European environment, even if in some cases – for example EMU (Anderson and Goodman, 1993: 52–4) – this defied rational calculation (in the realist sense of maximizing power resources). The explanation therefore has to be a 'non-rational', 'reflexive' one.

This is all plausible as far as it goes, but the explication of this 'non-rational' drive remains opaque. Hints are dropped: a 'reflex' is, in the dictionary definition, 'an automatic response to a stimulus that does not reach the level of consciousness'. What is presumably meant is an immovable (or at the very least slowly moving) frame of reference, a 'core belief' (Anderson and Goodman, 1993: 54) 'the dream' (1993: 56), a normative assumption that European integration is right and good that has become so engrained it has entered the 'genetic code' of German policy-makers (Goetz, 1996: 24). Shaped by a post-national European identity, the Germans have 'internalized positive interdependence and the negative risks of solo operation' (Pond, 1992: 114, 116). Bearing 'special burdens of self-doubt' Germany displays 'a great deal of idealistic commitment to the process of European integration' (Garton Ash, 1994: 71, 78). All this points to the immaterial, the affective, the weight of 'collective memory' (Markovits and Reich, 1997: xiii), the *ideational* in shaping German European engagement. What has been lacking, however, is a clear conception about how such ideational factors are reproduced, how they change (Germany has not always had a post-national identity!) and, most importantly, how these and politics intersect.

The quest to pinpoint the role of the ideational in foreign policy-making has been the signal feature of the social constructivist 'turn' in international relations.[19] The enduring German puzzle has rapidly become one of constructivism's key testing grounds, with a range of leading figures – Peter Katzenstein (1996), Thomas Banchoff (1997, 1999), Gunther Hellmann (1996, 1999), Thomas Risse (1997) and his colleagues (Risse *et al.*, 1999) – deploying broadly constructivist methods, in particular forms of discourse analysis, to find new ways of understanding that puzzle and the place of ideas in helping to solve it. These attempts to capture the processes of social construction of German European policy have not, however, evaded the wider constructivist problem of identifying relations of causality between the 'ideational' and 'material' worlds (Kowert and Legro, 1996: 491). In particular, constructivists have been unable to point to clear examples where significant material interests have been conceded despite German rhetoric of sacrifice. This was a criticism set out strongly by Patricia Davis in a paper casting doubt on the capacity of 'ideational variables' in Germany actually to affect material policy outcomes (Davis, 1998). There is a danger, here, of trying in the interests of a specious parsimony to construct an over-simplistic theoretical frame. Few would actually claim that ideational variables *make* outcomes; rather they set certain limits – what Arthur Hoffmann and Vanda Knowles have called 'the parameters of the possible' (Hoffmann and Knowles, 1999) – within which policy actors make decisions on outcomes, *including* the deliberate deployment of material power resources to secure specific objectives. Peter Katzenstein makes precisely this point in discussing German reflexive multilateralism:

> This is not to argue that German policy reflected idealistic motives in the 1980s or 1990s. It did not. It reflected German interests. But those interests, pursued through power and bargaining, were fundamentally shaped by the institutional context of Europe and the *Europeanization of the identity* of the German state that had taken place in the preceding decades (Katzenstein, 1997b: 14–15) (emphasis added).

Relating German policy 'in the 1980s or 1990s' to identitive factors traceable to the 'preceding decades' raises a much more interesting question of causality. How – and in particular how quickly – do *changes* in ideational variables such as identity recalibrate the 'parameters of the possible' for decision-making? Katzenstein takes the long view: an 'instrumental calculation' for the European option by Adenauer in the 1950s had become for Helmut Kohl, 'Adenauer's "grandson" ... an unquestioned assumption of policy' in the 1980s (Katzenstein, 1997b: 14). Others also identify similarly long-term patterns in the embedding of the collective assumptions which shape contemporary policy. Markovits and Reich (1997: 34–42) point to 'critical memory junctures' extending back to 1945. For Banchoff (1999: 176–9) there is the emergence 'only gradually' – and as the product of, at times, polarized debate such as on Ostpolitik in the 1970s – of a 'dominant postwar narrative' on foreign policy. For Berger (1997: 42) the 'lessons of the past' in security policy will remain a powerful influence 'for some time to come'.

Though the general message of such accounts is that the ideational legacy has proved robust enough to transcend unification, it is worth re-posing the question of *how quickly* change in the (re)-definition of the 'parameters of the possible' might occur in the context of post-unity. Given the fundamental reshaping and the intensification of the internal and external demands on the German state since 1989–90, might we not expect the ideational bases which have sustained reflexive multilateralism over decades to be subject to shorter-term dynamics of change?

This question is nuanced by three factors indicative, a decade on from unification, of a growing potential for significant change in defining what is possible and what is not:

- First, the change of government in 1998 – after 16 years of Helmut Kohl as Chancellor – raises the question of *generational* change. German multilateralism may have been safe in Kohl's hands, but what about his successors? 'It is far from certain that the Euro-idealism of the middle and younger generations in Germany is as widespread or deep as that of the immediate postwar generation' (Garton Ash, 1994: 74). Could the effects of a generational change of leadership to the Schröder-Fischer '68ers', and the attendant dimming of historical memory of war and the austere conditions of reconstruction, redefine the parameters of what is possible in Germany?
- Second, the relocation of Germany's seat of government from Bonn to Berlin, effected during 1999, creates a different perspective from which to view Germany's role and interests in Europe. Berlin is rather closer to central and eastern Europe than the old West European core of European multilateralism, and more like London or Paris in its metropolitan *grandeur* than Bonn. As Bulmer and Paterson (1996: 19) put it: 'one might expect some kind of "culture-change" – albeit difficult to quantify – in the norms, values and identities expressed in the Foreign Office's new location, when compared with the present tranquil outlook onto the Rhine'.
- Third, in 1999 German forces went to war above Kosovo. The decision to participate in war over Kosovo broke an extraordinary range of historically rooted and contemporary taboos about the use of military power (Jeffery and Handl, 1999). It added up, without doubt, to the most significant departure in German foreign policy since rearmament in 1955 and – given German reactions just eight years earlier to the prospect of participation in the Gulf War of 1991 – a quite fundamental redefinition of what fell within the realms of possibility in German foreign policy.[20]

This combination of generational renewal, the shift from the Bonn to the Berlin Republic, and the reconsideration of the use of military force opens up the possibility that the reflexive multilateralism of old might now be losing its historically grounded power. As a result Germany might undergo a form of 'delayed normalization'. Such, at least, is the subject matter of the debate on the nature and extent of Germany's 'normalization' which has simmered away during the 1990s. This debate is, in a sense, a delayed replay of some of the 'soft realist' expectations of German foreign policy presented in the discourse of unification. Although the German 'supertanker' (Nonnenmacher, 1993) may have taken a long time to change direction, the collective mindset of German policy-making has now (at last) begun to change, escaping some of the limits hitherto imposed by historical memory and 'post-national' identity. Germany as a result is becoming more 'normal', beginning to 'punch' its 'size and wealth' and to 'make its voice heard and its presence felt' (Arnold, 1991: 462). This more 'normal' Germany is beginning, in other words, more systematically to deploy what Bulmer called deliberate, or realist power.

What, then, is 'normal'? Few have deployed the term with much in the way of conceptual underpinning. Philip Gordon provides a partial exception by at least providing a definition. For him, the 'normalization' of German foreign policy consists in 'the gradual attenuation of the particular restrictions that have influenced and constrained Germany's international actions since World War II' and in consequence the development of an 'international behaviour – in terms of both style and substance – . . . more like that of other large western states' (Gordon, 1994: 225). On closer scrutiny, this really means getting more like France or the UK (Hellmann, 1999a: 847). While some might doubt that these provide especially useful templates of 'normality', the comparison does help a little in identifying the kind of 'style and substance' of international behaviour which we might expect a more 'normal' Germany to exhibit. For Gordon (1994: 228) this would be a Germany 'more self-assured, less military averse, more global, and more assertive than in the past'; for Gunther Hellmann (1999a: 847) (more polemically) it would mean the return of *the* (singular) national interest as a routine category of thought and action, a preparedness to use the *ultima ratio* of military force as an instrument of policy, and a more instrumental conception of what alliances are for, and what they can do for Germany.

This debate has been nuanced by the contributions of a group of highly distinguished, conservative political scientists and historians, including Arnulf Baring, Christian Hacke, Hans-Peter Schwarz and Michael Stürmer, who have issued powerful *Plädoyers* for a more 'normal' Germany. Their pleas for normalization rest on a belief that the 'genetically' embedded European policy ideas that held sway before 1990 are no longer adequate to the task of serving the interests of either Germany or its neighbours, according to the first view. In the turbulent post-cold war era, what is needed is a rational and clinical definition of what Germany's interests are and how they should be pursued – for Schwarz a 'responsible power politics' (Schwarz, 1985: 173) – rather than an amorphous Europeanism which fails to draw clear boundaries between the national and the European. Without a more conscious articulation and balancing of *national* interests within frameworks of European interaction, Germany runs the risk of putting at risk its own security, welfare and democracy (Hacke, 1996: 8); or – in a more indignant form of the same argument – the legacy of pre–1989 reflexive multilateralism. Another view suggests that German Europeanism reflects the 'moral megalomania' of a left-wing (West) German intelligentsia. This drew a 'perverse pride' from the history of 'German evil' in the twentieth century and had made taboo the expression of 'solid bourgeois values' which Germany now urgently needed – 'national unity, historical consciousness, and the identification of national interests' – to help define and understand its role and needs in Europe (Hacke, 1998: 3).

It needs to be stressed that this group of *eminences* does not seek in any way to renounce German commitments to European multilateralism, but rather to put the reasoning behind them on a more rational, nationally focused footing – indeed, much like Britain and France would. Schwarz (1994: 90) wrote in an apparently envious way of the 'hard-hearted, penny-pinching' way in which 'England' sought to protect its own interests under Margaret Thatcher 'and as France has done for a long time'. And Stürmer (1994: 41) wrote approvingly of a speech which the then UK Foreign Minister, Douglas Hurd, made in 1993 on Britain's national interests, suggesting that every generation needs anew to consider what resources and means it can deploy in meeting the nation's own requirements and others' expectations; 'what applies for England after the cold war applies no less for Germany'. There is a certain irony here. Schwarz, Stürmer *et al.* seek in effect to 'nationalize' German foreign policy by pleading for policy to be defined in terms of specifically national interests and, indirectly, for the reinvigoration of the nation as focal point of identity. However, German history offers no easily usable models of a nationally oriented foreign policy; indeed the only period of German history to offer an enduringly positive impression of German foreign policy is that of post-1949 multilateralism. Hence the British and French examples have to be mobilized in (indirect) service of the German 'nationalization' project.

This irony serves to confirm a persistent subtext in the 'normalization' debate: it is a debate on whether 'German European policy is becoming more British' (Hort, 1997) (or French), as Schwarz *et al.* think it should, and Gordon and Hellmann suggest it might. What concrete evidence is there of Germany 'growing out' of its reflexive multilateral instincts and moving towards a more self-conscious and instrumental articulation of its national interest(s) and a more assertive deployment of material power resources in pursuing them? Can we observe German power being deployed more *deliberately* ten years on from unification? The following explores this question under two themes: first, EU politics; and then Kosovo, by some way the most vivid example of an apparent, new, Germany 'normality'.

'Normalization' I: Germany and the EU

In EU politics, Schwarz's references to 'hard-hearted penny-pinching' provide a useful starting point. Germany has traditionally played a selfless (soft-hearted?) and very generous paymaster role in EU integration, in particular in financing the 'side-payments' which have kept the integration momentum going through successive enlargements. Can this selflessness endure beyond the 1990s, given: domestic fiscal tightness rooted in the legacies of unification and the rigours of EMU; and high external demands in supporting post-communist transformation in central and eastern Europe and beyond; new security responsibilities – like fighting wars; and, not least, the inevitable cost burdens of EU eastern enlargement. This is a difficult circle to square, and Schwarz (1994: 90) has the solution: 'Germany can no longer indulge in a kind of generous checkbook diplomacy within the EC for the sake of advancing political integration'.

Germany's policy-makers have come to a similar conclusion concerning the *Nettozahlerdebatte* – net contributor debate – about Germany's disproportionate contribution to the EU budget. This has emerged since the mid-1990s to become as much part of the terminology of German politics as the budgetary issue was under Mrs Thatcher in the UK in the early 1980s. The main catalyst was the debate surrounding the Agenda 2000 package of policy and budget reforms, designed to prepare the ground for eastern enlargement. This brought home just how much EU eastern enlargement could cost, and how much of the tab Germany's partners expected it to pick up. Agenda 2000 led even Helmut Kohl over the last 12 months of his Chancellorship to pursue a specifically national concern – the 'correction of budgetary imbalances' (Lippert, 1998: 44) – ahead of his archetypal pro-integration reflex. Or, as his Finance Minister Theo Waigel put it: 'eastern enlargement should not cost one *pfennig* more to the German tax payer' (Tewes, 1998: 129). Upon assuming the Chancellorship in September 1998, Gerhard Schröder pressed a similar line, but now nuanced explicitly by notions of the generational change his accession to office represented, and open aspirations to UK/French-style 'normality':

> My generation and those following *are Europeans because we want to be not because we have to be*. That makes us freer in dealing with others . . . I am convinced that our European partners want to have a self-confident German partner which is more calculable than a German partner with an inferiority complex. *Germany standing up for its national interests will be just as natural as France or Britain standing up for theirs*' (*Financial Times*, 10/11/98: 6) (emphasis added).

Schröder's intention to 'stand up for' national interests, liberated from the constraints of German history, spawned a rather more forthright tone in the net contributor debate than had been typical under Kohl, a much more vigorous language of national interest versus Europrofligacy. The problem was that 'the Germans pay more than half the contributions which are *frittered away* in Europe' (Langguth, 1999: 55) (emphasis added). It set the scene for the new government's contribution to the ongoing Agenda 2000 debate. In particular it was argued that, as enlargement approached, others would have to forego privileges to relieve the pressure on the German net contribution: Britain its rebate; Spain the Cohesion Fund; and France some of its benefits from the common agricultural policy. In the end, of course, a reform package was stitched together which left most elements of the budget reform question fudged or deferred (Jeffery and Handl, 1999). Nonetheless this episode suggested a change of approach under Schröder, one focused on making more open and 'rational' calculations of cost and benefit in EU policy, and defining policy choices on that basis. The shift away from a more reflexive EU policy was inadvertently underscored by the transfer by Schröder of coordinating responsibilities in EU affairs from the Economics to the Finance Ministry. This brings a different institutional rationale into play. Whereas the Economics Ministry has an institutional commitment to the positive-sum game of free trade, the Finance Ministry is, naturally enough, money-focused and privileges a narrow, even zero-sum, conception of German priorities. The contrast is significant, with Finance Ministry officials envisaging a more 'streamlined', 'cost-conscious' and 'realistic' approach to EU policy-making as a result.[21]

The net effect might be termed a new, 'yes, but . . .' politics of European integration: an unchallenged basic commitment to the integration project; but now hedged with conditions to soften its implications for Germany. This of course approximates to Anderson and Goodman's conception of 'instrumental', rational multilateralism and indicates a more *deliberate* deployment of German power resources. Further examples would include the growing insistence that the German language should be treated on an equal basis to English and French in the operation of the EU and – returning to the issue of eastern enlargement – the appointment of Günther Verheugen as EU Commissioner for enlargement questions. The latter was a departure in two ways: first, Verheugen is, unlike many of his German predecessors in the Commission, a politician of stature; and second, Schröder expressly insisted, against the will of the President of the Commission, Romano Prodi, that Verheugen be appointed to run a policy brief of specific, *national* concern in Germany (Paterson and Jeffery, 1999: 22).

A note of caution needs to be entered at this point: the above examples do not add up to a *grand strategy* of wielding deliberate power in a new instrumental multilateralism. They are fairly isolated examples where Schröder has had an obvious platform – EU summits, the German EU Presidency – to rehearse his point that his is a new Germany unhampered by redundant historical constraints. But if we look beyond this 'platform' politics into policy detail, even a more assertive leader like Schröder runs up against the perennial barriers of Germany's institutional pluralism. It remains extremely difficult to cajole even the various departments of the federal government into a single policy line, let alone the Bundesbank, the *Länder*, and so on. This is a key theme in Jeff Anderson's recent work (1997; 1999) which examines German EU policy across a range of policy sectors. Anderson finds the same kind of differentiation in how the relevant actors define and pursue 'German' priorities as existed pre-unity. What is new, compared to the pre-unity era, is a growing emphasis on distributional questions – Germany getting its fair share – which he traces back to problems of domestic politics, not least the continued indigestion caused by the integration of the former eastern *Länder*. Getting a fair share requires 'a more assertive and self-regarding exercise of German influence', 'a more visible, assertive projection of power' (Anderson, 1997: 106, 82). In this context, Schröder's cost–benefit rhetoric may well have an effect in justifying and reinforcing a more hard-nosed and instrumental approach to EU policy issues among Germany's EU policy actors. But what it does not and cannot do is manufacture coherence across Germany's fragmented, highly sectorized government structures. We are currently observing a classic example in the EU eastern enlargement process, which has shifted, with the commencement of the detailed accession negotiations in March 1998 'into the phase of bureaucratic politics' (Lippert, 1998: 38). Here we can see particular ministries, particular *Länder*, particular private sector interests manoeuvring to defend their 'possessions' (Lippert, 1998: 38). In areas such as environmental standards, border controls and, in particular, free movement of labour, German negotiators are setting out tough positions and will pursue them vigorously – to coin a phrase – 'in Germany's name'. What they will not be doing is acting in concert in the context of a single, overarching German strategy.

This should not necessarily lead to a negative conclusion about institutional pluralism run wild. While the various actors will work hard to defend their particular institutional 'possessions', none of them is likely to question the desirability of enlargement in principle, and most of them have taken active steps to facilitate enlargement. This recalls the point made earlier about the role of German actors in building the transnational networks that are providing much of the underpinning for the enlarged EU, not least through the diffusion of German institutional patterns. In other words, and returning to Bulmer's 'faces' of power; Germany's fragmented institutional structures have begun increasingly to deploy (an equally fragmented) deliberate power, *while also, at the same time* engaging intensively in the transnational networking which feeds into the virtuous circle of institutional power and systemic empowerment discussed earlier.

If, then, we can observe a process of 'normalization' in EU politics, then it is a rather odd and complex form of normality, ranging institutionally plural deliberate power alongside intense engagement in transnational cooperation.

'Normalization' II: Kosovo

Kosovo provides an equally multi-faceted picture. If the templates for a German 'normality' are the UK and France, then an obvious yardstick for the 'level' of normality achieved is the use of military force, about which the UK and France have traditionally displayed no scruples. By contrast, Germany has been influentially characterized by Hans Maull (1992: 271-3) as a 'civilian power' – a power in which military force is an absolute last resort, which seeks a legally codified system of international relations, which has a cooperative and consensus-oriented approach to international politics, and which seeks to diffuse the democracy, prosperity and security it enjoys to other states. This notion of 'civilian power' in effect describes the reflexive multilateralism of the old West Germany: its commitment to building – and widening – institutions of multilateral cooperation; and its renunciation of power politics for the 'softer' methods of the 'trading state'.

Viewed against this background, post-unity Germany's attitude to the use of military force has become a litmus test of the 'normalization' debate (Hellmann, 1997: 24), with the implicit assumption that civilian power is 'abnormal' and a preparedness to use military force 'normal', even if, given Germany's recent history, deeply controversial. In a capricious coincidence of timing it fell to Gerhard Schröder's red-green government, large parts of which were steeped in post-1968 pacifism, to resolve these questions of normality and history in the 1999 Kosovo war.

The German decision in the night of 23–24 March 1999 to contribute to the air war over Kosovo was highly remarkable. First, German military forces *fought* for the first time since the collapse of the Third Reich in 1945. Second, they did so *offensively and 'out of area'*, decisively overturning a postwar military doctrine focused on defensive action within NATO territory. Third, they did so in a theatre where the *burden of historical memory* suggested German troops would and could never be involved again. Fourth, in joining a NATO action *lacking an explicit UN mandate*, they did so without clear sanction in international law, and in fairly open contravention of the terms of the red-green coalition agreement of October 1998.[22]

The decision to break such a range of historically rooted and contemporary taboos had three main sources.[23] The first, and overriding reason for participation was *Allianztreue*, 'alliance loyalty'. The concern to demonstrate loyalty was in part due to the need to confirm the new government's credibility; not unexpectedly the red-green coalition was viewed as containing foreign policy 'apprentices', with a dubiously pacifist past to live down (*Die Zeit*, 1999: 18). *Allianztreue* was an unequivocal way of doing so. It was also a logical corollary of Germany's postwar multilateralist heritage; membership in multilateral institutions brings with it obligations to partners which have to be observed. As Schröder put it in February 1999:

Germany cannot and does not want to follow a unique path. We reached our [national] adulthood ... in alliance. We want to remain just like that. We are therefore ready today, without any ifs and buts, to take over responsibility as a 'normal' ally – whether in the EU or in NATO (Hellmann, 1999a: 841).

A second impulse behind German participation was the moral imperative of preventing human suffering. From the German perspective, in particular as articulated by Defence Minister Rudolf Scharping (1999a) and Foreign Minister Joschka Fischer, military intervention had a humanitarian justification: to stop the atrocities being committed against the Kosovars. In a general sense this response was one conditioned by a postwar German identity rooted in the rejection of nazism. It had received a particular nuance, though, in a decade punctuated by the ethnically driven wars of the former Yugoslavia. Images of genocide on Germany's doorstep moved many on the formerly pacifist (red and green) German left to revise their views on military force, most prominently Joschka Fischer in the aftermath of the massacre in Srebrenica, Bosnia, in 1996. For many the old refrain of 'never again war' had become relativized by the need to ensure there was 'never again Auschwitz'.

The third main impulse behind intervention had more pragmatic roots, also in the wars of Yugoslav succession: war in south-east Europe generated massive flows of refugees, many of which ended up seeking asylum in Germany. Throughout the 1990s the area of 'foreigners policy' had been controversial in Germany, feeding social tensions which parties of the far right were periodically able to capitalize on. The Kosovo crisis threatened to do the same. In the words of Defence Minister Scharping (1999b: 218) 'do we deal with force, murder and expulsion by tackling these problems at their source? Or do we watch passively and wait until their consequences come home to us?'

While this combination of multilateral obligation, humanitarianism, and concern to prevent mass migration was enough to bring about the commitment to wage war, it did not subdue the more instinctive commitment to pursue a 'political way' to peace. In this respect it was – in the German government's own words – 'a stroke of luck'[24] that Germany held the Presidencies of both the EU and the G7/8 during the Kosovo crisis. The former provided the opportunity for constant liaison among the main European members of NATO and for developing ideas on the post-conflict reconstruction of Kosovo and the wider stabilization of south-eastern Europe. The latter provided a forum in which to build a European bridge over the divide which separated the USA and Russia on Kosovo (and which had to be resolved in order to restore the policing of the Kosovo crisis to international law and the UN).

Out of this emerged an extraordinarily dense web of diplomatic interaction, from which the German Government, in particular Joschka Fischer, patched together a framework of agreements and missions which made possible the cessation of the war on 3 June 1999. These included:

- the 'Fischer Peace Plan' presented to the EU Foreign Ministers on 12 April 1999, which formed the basis of the 'general principles' on the political solution to the Kosovo crisis agreed by the G7 and Russia on 6 May;
- the 'Stability Pact for Southeast Europe' aired at the NATO Summit on 25 April, fleshed out by the European Commission and at the Franco-German Summit at the end of May, and agreed as an EU-led project in June; and
- the Ahtisaari/Talbott/Chernomyrdin (EU/US/Russian) mission which negotiated the final terms of the peace deal accepted by the Yugoslav Parliament on 3 June, and which provided the basis for the 'return' to the UN.

Quite remarkably, the nature of Germany's participation in the Kosovan war did much to resolve the tension highlighted above: that German 'civilian power' was 'abnormal', yet that German military power was, for historical reasons, problematic. First, there was manifestly no 'realist' geopolitical strategy behind the decision to send Germany into war. The strong moral thrust behind the decision to intervene reflected a central feature of the 'civilian power' model, which itself was anchored in the rejection of Germany's own 'realist' excesses in the past: actively to embed and protect the rule of law in international society. Intervention in the cause of human rights certainly falls under Hans Maull's (1992: 274) remit of 'civilianization', and the notion of civilian power does not exclude – as a last resort – the 'military implementation of international norms and decisions'.[25]

Equally reassuring for those whose concerns about 'normalization' were shaped by former abuses of German military power, the Germany which went to war in 1999 was one which did so in full recognition of its multilateral obligations, and with extraordinary commitment to the principle of multilateral action. This went some way beyond any merely formal demonstration of *Allianztreue*. Despite deep domestic sensitivities about embarking on military action, the German commitment to the NATO bombing campaign was unswerving. The imagination and perseverance which were invested in drawing together a multilateral political framework for the resolution of the conflict (and, indeed, the post-conflict reconstruction effort) in the EU, NATO, G7/8 and the UN were remarkable.

Perhaps even more significant over the long term will be the efforts – separate from, but intimately interlinked with, the Kosovo crisis – made during the German EU Presidency in the first half of 1999 to strengthen the EU's foreign and security policy capacity. This was something which had long been an aim of German policy, and which was ritually reiterated in the red-green coalition agreement. However, the deepening Kosovo crisis provided a catalyst to move beyond ritual declarations to concrete achievements, not least because it revealed the continued dependence of EU-Europe on the USA in managing European conflicts (Marx, 1999).[26] The strengthening of the EU's common foreign and security policy (CFSP) capability thus emerged as one of the main objectives of the German Presidency. And it bore considerable fruit:

- The Western European Union (effectively the West European arm of NATO, of which German also held the Presidency in the first half of 1999) Summit in Bremen in May 1999 paved the way for the functions of the WEU to be integrated into the EU by the end of 2000;
- Javier Solana (the then Secretary General of NATO) was appointed High Representative ('Mr GASP' in German) of the EU in the field of CFSP at the EU Cologne Summit on 3 June 1999;
- The Cologne Summit also approved a German Presidency 'Report on the Strengthening of Common European Security and Defence Policy' which proposed *inter alia*: regular meetings of foreign and defence ministers in the General Affairs Council on foreign and security matters; the establishment of a 'political and security' standing committee advised by an EU 'Military Committee' of military representatives; and the establishment of an EU Military Staff supported by a situation centre (1999).[27]

Though it remains to be seen how quickly or effectively these measures will develop (not least given the membership of a number of neutrals in the EU), they do establish a new infrastructure and potential for collective, intra-European crisis management. In other words, the German government's essentially *reflexive* response to the accelerated normalization process the Kosovo crisis imposed on it was to strengthen the multilateral framework within which future European crisis management would take place. This strategy of *multilateralization* places Germany's 'normalization' as a military power into a reassuringly familiar context. It suggests that the accumulated postwar weight of 'the ideational' still has the power to direct German policy, even in radically changed circumstances, into well-trodden and predictable paths.

Conclusion

Günther Hellmann (1999a: 837) remarked that 'the most prominent feature of German foreign policy after 1990 has been the continuity in the rhetoric of continuity' expressed by German policy-makers. The implication is, of course, that under the surface discourse all sorts of subterranean change has been under way. And, of course, it has. Germany has had to come to terms with vastly changed material conditions, internal and external, which have opened up new and difficult questions and generated in places new kinds of response. Some of these – the adoption of a tougher, *national* line in EU negotiations, breaking taboos on using military force – indicate, in line with the 'normalization' debate, that post-unity Germany has indeed become rather more like the UK and France than it used to be. Its many foreign policy actors have (had to) become more conscious of its material power resources, and have become less reticent in deploying them for what Jeff Anderson calls 'self-regarding' ends. In other words, Germany indisputably uses deliberate power; confirming some of the expectations raised in the early post-unity period, it now conforms to realist paradigms much more than it used to.

But this is by no means the end of the story of German power, and to stop the story there would be both to misunderstand and – crucially – to *underestimate* Germany's power in the new pan-Europe. Indeed, Germany still does not score especially highly on most measures of deployment of *deliberate* power; it still punches some way below its real(-ist) political weight. Where it does score heavily in comparison with, say, the UK and France is on the other faces of power Simon Bulmer has applied to the German case. Germany's sheer economic strength and importance generates power *unintentionally*, not least in lending structure to Europe's international economic system; David Marsh's (1993) description of the Bundesbank as 'The Bank that Rules Europe' evokes this rather well – as both those ejected from the exchange-rate-mechanism in 1992, and the millions in eastern Europe using the Deutschmark (DM) as a parallel currency will equally testify. In a sense, the Bundesbank will continue to 'rule Europe' even after the

DM has gone because of its success in shaping the rules of EMU. This testifies to Germany's *institutional* power, which, driven on by a reflexive commitment to multilateral solutions, has left a distinctly German mark on the way the EU does its business. And even though it seems likely that some of this reflexiveness will ebb away as the historical experience which created it becomes more remote, it still has sufficient power to shape the 'parameters of the possible' – as the attempt to multilateralize the use of force in Europe during and after Kosovo confirms.

Institutional power is also reflected in the central role of German institutions in the new transnational networks fanning out across central and eastern Europe and beyond. These networks provide channels both for the 'export' of German institutional patterns, and for meeting the demand in central and eastern Europe and beyond for access to the secrets of Germany's success as they embark on their *Drang nach Westen*. The intensity of this transnational exchange – whether 'exported' or 'imported' – again leaves a distinctly German mark on the way central and eastern Europe and future waves of applicant states reshape the way they do their business as they prepare for EU accession. No other EU member state, with the partial exception of Austria, has this advantage; it adds to the ways in which the 'system' empowers Germany, in which Germany's engagement with its regional milieu in Europe engenders a systemic bias loaded in its favour. It is because Germany continues to engage deliberately, unintentionally, institutionally and, above all, intensively with the states and the multilateral institutions of its regional milieu that its power in Europe has become so unusually encompassing and comprehensive.

Notes

1. This chapter sets out some of the themes and ideas which are guiding the ESRC research project on 'Germany and the Reshaping of Europe' based at the Institute for German Studies at the University of Birmingham, and funded under the 'One Europe or Several?' Research Programme, award number L213252002. Many thanks are due to the *Centrum für Angewandte Politikforschung* for providing both inspiration and a superb working environment for writing this contribution. Many thanks too to Vladimir Handl for the flow of excellent ideas he contributed.
2. The term coined by Maull (1992) after unity – but evocative in particular of pre-unity West Germany.
3. As convened by Margaret Thatcher in 1990. Its minute, composed by Mrs Thatcher's personal foreign policy adviser, Charles Powell, was leaked

to great public embarrassment. It was later published in full in James and Stone (1992: 233–9).
4. Mrs Thatcher in conversation with George Urban (who was at the Chequers meeting), quoted in 'The Alf Garnett View of History', *The Independent*, 7 October 1996.
5. See Katzenstein of (1997b): 14. Characteristically, the views Mearsheimer expressed found no echo in serious German or European debates; see Wessels (1999: 392).
6. The question whether commitments to free trade and being paymaster could persist nevertheless later reappeared some years later as the implications of eastern enlargement for the German economy become more concrete. See further below in the final section of this chapter.
7. See the re-evaluation of the Croatia/Slovenia controversy in Conversi (1998).
8. Their subsequent 'Gulliver' analogy was also predicated on the growth of internal constraints on the exercise of external power.
9. It is developed most fully in Bulmer, *et al.* (2000) including case studies on the 1996–97 IGC, EMU and eastern enlargement, chapters 4–6.
10. Largely because the Gramscian assumptions underlying it were not spelt out, leaving the authors open to unwarranted accusations of 'realism' (bracketed alongside Mearsheimer) and anti-Germanism. See Goldberger (1993) and Markovits and Reich (1994).
11. An important theme in Markovits' and Reich's subsequent book (1997).
12. So the term used in Bulmer *et al.* (1998) Germany's European Diplomacy, following Arnolf Wolfer' usage in his *Discord and Collaboration* (1962: 72–5).
13. As collated in the internal paper, *Zusammenarbeit des Landes Berlin mit Mittel-und Osteuropa*, Senatskanzlei E 11, Bonn, 13 January 1999.
14. See Michael Staack's (1998) otherwise insightful article on the German trading state, which neglects to talk at all about firms – the agents of trade.
15. Though Livingston (1992) provides an exception: 'Germany's corporatist approach enables it . . . to marshal its economic power and . . . to deploy it for political purposes abroad'.
16. This suspicion is being explored in research conducted by Julie Pellegrin in our ESRC 'One Europe or Several' project on 'Germany and the Reshaping of Europe'.
17. 'Policy transfer' is the central theme of the ESRC Research Programme 'Future Governance' directed by Ed Page.
18. So the title of Garton Ash's *In Europe's Name. Germany and the Divided Continent* (1993).
19. For overviews of this 'turn', see Adler (1997); Checkel (1998).
20. The shifting terrain of ideas on the use of military force from Kuwait to Kosovo is masterfully dissected in Hellmann (1999b).
21. Confidential interviews conducted by Charlie Jeffery in Bonn, June 1999.
22. Which stated that: 'The participation of German forces in measures to preserve world peace and international security is bound by observance of international law and of German constitutional law. The new Federal Government will commit itself actively to preserving the monopoly of force of the United Nations and the role of the General Secretary of the United Nations.'

23. We are grateful on the following points to Adrian Hyde-Price (1999).
24. Vorläufige Bilanz der deutschen Präsidentschaft vom 22.06.1999, http://www.bundesregierung.de/03/0302/99072/index.html. (1999).
25. Maull does, though, regard military intervention as 'the most dramatic' and exceptional form of collective sanction.
26. See also *Frankfurter Rundschau*, 17 November 1998.
27. This source is an unpublished official document, written by the German Foreign Ministry (1999: 33).

References

Adler, E. (1997) 'Seizing the Middle Ground: Constructivism in World Politics', *European Journal of International Relations*, 3 (3), pp. 314–63.
Anderson, J. J. (1997) 'Hard Interests, Soft Power, and Germany's Changing Role in Europe', in Katzenstein, P. (ed.), *Tamed Power. Germany in Europe* (Ithaca: Cornell University Press), pp. 80–107.
Anderson, J. J. (1999) *German Unification and the Union of Europe* (Cambridge: Cambridge University Press).
Anderson, J. J. and Goodman, J. B. (1993) 'Mars or Minerva? A United Germany in a Post-cold war Europe', in Keohane, R. O., Nye, J. S. and Hoffmann, S. (eds), *After the Cold War: International Institutions and State Strategies in Europe, 1989–1991* (Cambridge: Harvard University Press), pp. 23–62.
Arnold, E. (1991) 'German Foreign Policy and Unification', *International Affairs*, 67 (3), pp. 453–71.
Banchoff, T. (1997) 'German Policy Towards the European Union: The Effects of Historical Memory', *German Politics*, 6 (1), pp. 60–76.
Banchoff, T. (1999) *The German Problem Transformed. Institutions, Politics and Foreign Policy, 1945–1995* (Ann Arbor: University of Michigan Press).
Berger, T. (1997) 'The Past in the Present: Historical Memory and German National Security Policy', *German Politics*, 6 (1), pp. 39–59.
Beyme, K. von (1990) 'Transition to Democracy or Anschluss? The Two Germanies and Europe', *Government and Opposition*, 25 (2), pp. 70–90.
Bulmer, S. (1997) 'Shaping the Rules. The Constitutive Politics of the European Union and German Power', in Katzenstein, P. (ed.), *Tamed Power. Germany in Europe* (Ithaca: Cornell University Press), pp. 49–79.
Bulmer, S. and Paterson, W. E. (1987) *The Federal Republic of Germany and the European Community* (London: Allen & Unwin).
Bulmer, S. and Paterson, W. E. (1989) 'West Germany's Role in Europe: "Man Mountain" or "Semi-Gulliver"?', *Journal of Common Market Studies*, 28 (2), pp. 95–117.
Bulmer, S. and Paterson, W. E. (1996) 'Germany in the European Union: Gentle Giant or Emergent Leader?', *International Affairs*, 72 (1), pp. 9–32.
Bulmer, S., Jeffery, C. and Paterson, W. E. (1998) 'Deutschlands Europäische Diplomatie: Die Entwicklung des regionalen Milieus', in Weidenfeld, W. (ed.), *Deutsche Europapolitik. Optionen wirksamer Interessenvertretung* (Bonn: Europa Union Verlag), pp. 11–102.
Bulmer, S., Jeffery, C. and Paterson, W. E. (2000) *Germany's European Diplomacy. Shaping the Regional Milieu* (Manchester: Manchester University Press).

Cerny, K. H. (1993) 'The Future Role of a United Germany in the European Community', in Geipel, G. L. (ed.), *Germany in a New Era* (Indianapolis: Hudson Institute), pp 90–110.
Checkel, J. T. (1998) 'The Constructivist Turn in International Relations Theory', *World Politics*, 50 (2), pp. 324–8.
Conversi, D. (1998) 'German-bashing and the Break-Up of Yugoslavia', *The Donald W. Treadgold Papers in Russian, East European and Central Asian Studies*, 16.
Davis, P. (1998) 'National Interests Revisited. The German Case', *German Politics and Society*, 16 (1), pp. 32–111.
Davis, P. and Dombrowski, P. (1997) 'Appetite of the Wolf: German Foreign Assistance for Central and Eastern Europe', *German Politics*, 6 (1), pp. 1–22.
Garton Ash, T. (1993) *In Europe's Name: Germany and the Divided Continent* (London: Jonathan Cape).
Garton Ash, T. (1994) 'Germany's Choice', *Foreign Affairs*, 73 (4), pp. 65–81.
Geipel, G. L. (1993) 'The Nature and Limits of German Power', in Geipel, G. L. (ed.), *Germany in a New Era* (Indianapolis: Hudson Institute), pp. 19–48.
Goetz, K. H. (1996) 'Integration Policy in a Europeanised State', *Journal of European Public Policy*, 3 (1), pp. 23–44.
Goldberger, B. (1993) 'Why Europe Should not Fear the Germans', *German Politics*, 2 (2), pp. 238–310.
Gordon, P. H. (1994) 'The Normalization of German Foreign Policy', *Orbis*, 38 (2), pp. 225–43.
Guzzini, S. (1993) 'Structural Power: The Limits of Neo-Realist Analysis', *International Organization*, 47 (2), pp. 443–78.
Hacke, C., (1996) 'Nationales Interesse als Handlungsmaxime für die Außenpolitik Deutschlands', in Kaiser, K. and Krause, J. (eds), *Deutschlands neue Außenpolitik, Band 3: Interessen und Strategien* (Munich: Oldenbourg), pp. 3–14.
Hacke, C. (1998) 'Die nationalen Interessen der Bundesrepublik Deutschland an der Schwelle zum 21, Jahrhundert', *Außenpolitik*, 49 (4), pp. 1–21.
Hamilton, D. (1991) 'A More European Germany, a More German Europe', *Journal of International Affairs*, 45 (1), pp. 127–56.
Hellmann, G. (1996) 'Goodbye Bismarck? The Foreign Policy of Contemporary Germany', *Mershon International Studies Review*, 40, pp. 1–39.
Hellmann, G. (1997) 'Jenseits von "Normalisierung" und "Militarisierung": Zur Standortdebatte über die neue deutsche Europapolitik', *Aus Politik und Zeitgeschichte*, No. B1–2/97, pp. 24–33.
Hellmann, G. (1999a) 'Nationale Normalität als Zukunft. Zur Außenpolitik der Berliner Republik', *Blätter für deutsche und internationale Politik*, 44 (7), pp. 837–47.
Hellmann, G. (1999b) 'Weltpolitik and Self-Containment? Germany's Global Ambitions', *University of Birmingham Discussion Papers in German Studies*, No. IGS99/10.
Hodge, C. C. (1992) 'The Federal Republic and the Future of Europe', *German Politics*, 1 (2), pp. 222–38.
Hoffmann, A. and Knowles, V. (1999) 'Germany and the Reshaping of Europe. Identifying Interests – the Role of Discourse Analysis', *One Europe or Several? The Birmingham Discussion Papers*, No. ESRC-IGS 99/9.
Hort, P. (1997) 'Die deutsche Europapolitik wird "britischer" ', *Frankfurter Allgemeine Zeitung*, 30/10/97.

Hyde-Price, A. (1999) 'Berlin Republic Takes to Arms', *The World Today*, 55, June, pp. 13–15.
Jachtenfuchs, M. and Kohler-Koch, B. (eds) (1996) *Europäische Integration* (Opladen: Westdeutscher Verlag).
James, H. and Stone, M. (eds) (1992) *When the Wall Came Down. Reactions to German Unification* (London: Routledge).
Jeffery, C. (1995) 'A Giant with Feet of Clay? United Germany in the European Union', *Institute for German Studies Discussion Papers in German Studies*, No. IGS95/6.
Jeffery, C. (1999) 'Niemieckie landy a normalizacja' dyskusji o rozszerzeniu UE', in *Wspolnota Sprzecznych Interesow?* (Warsaw: Friedrich-Ebert-Stiftung).
Jeffery, C. and Collins, S. (1998) 'The German Länder and EU Enlargement: Between Apple Pie and Issue Linkage', *German Politics*, 7 (2), pp. 86.
Jeffery, C. and Handl, V. (1999) 'Germany and Europe after Kohl: Between Social Democracy and Normalisation?', *One Europe or Several? The Birmingham Discussion Papers*, No. ESRC-IGS 99/11.
Jessen, C. (1999) 'Agenda 2000: Das Reformpaket von Berlin, ein Erfolg für Gesamteuropa', *Integration*, 22 (3), pp. 167–75.
Kaiser, K. (1992) 'Germany's Unification', *Foreign Affairs*, 70 (1), pp. 179–205.
Katzenstein, P. (1987) *Policy and Politics in West Germany: The Growth of a Semi-Sovereign State* (Philadelphia: Temple University Press).
Katzenstein, P. J. (ed.) (1996) *The Culture of National Security: Norms and Identity in World Politics* (New York: Columbia University Press).
Katzenstein, P. J. (1997a) 'Germany and Mitteleuropa', in Katzenstein, P. (ed.), *Mitteleuropa. Between Europe and Germany* (Oxford: Berghahn), pp. 1–38.
Katzenstein, P. J. (1997b) 'United Germany in an Integrating Europe', in Katzenstein, P. J. (ed.), *Tamed Power. Germany in Europe* (Ithaca: Cornell University Press), pp. 1–43.
Kielinger, T. (1990) 'Waking Up in the new Europe – with a Headache', *International Affairs*, 66 (2), pp. 247–64.
Kowert, P. and Legro, J. (1996) 'Norms, Identity and their Limits', in Katzenstein, P. J. (ed.), *The Culture of National Security: Norms and Identity in World Politics* (New York: Columbia University Press).
Langguth, G. (1999) 'Ein sozialistisches Europa? Ist die These "vom Ende des sozialdemokratischen Jahrhunderts" widerlegt?', *Politische Studien*, 50 (2).
Lippert, B. (1998) 'Die Erweiterungspolitik der Europäischen Union', in Weidenfeld, W. and Wessels, W. (eds), *Jahrbuch der Europäischen Integration 1997/98* (Bonn: Europa Union Verlag), pp. 37–50.
Livingston, R. G. (1992) 'United Germany: Bigger and Better', *Foreign Policy*, 87, Summer, pp. 157–74.
Markovits, A. S. and Reich, S. (1991) 'Should Europe Fear the Germans?', *German Politics and Society*, 23, Summer.
Markovits, A. S. and Reich, S. (1994) 'A Rejoinder to Goldberger', *German Politics*, 3 (1), pp. 129–30.
Markovits, A. S. and Reich, S. (1997) *The German Predicament. Memory and Power in the New Europe* (Ithaca: Cornell University Press).
Marsh, D. (1993) *The Bundesbank: The Bank that Rules Europe* (London: Mandarin).

Marx, B. (1999) 'Lücken zur Halbzeit. Das informelle EU-Außenministertreffen offenbarte die Defizite der deutschen Ratspräsidentschaft', *Deutsche Welle*, Analysen 15.
Maull, H. W. (1992) 'Zivilmacht Bunderepublik Deutschland. Vierzehn Thesen für eine neue deutsche Außenpolitik', *Europa-Archiv*, 47 (10), pp. 269–78.
Mearsheimer, J. (1990) 'Back to the Future. Instability in Europe After the Cold War', *International Security*, 15 (1), pp. 141–92.
Nonnenmacher, G. (1993) 'Germany', in Weidenfeld, W. and Janning, J. (eds), *Europe in Change* (Gütersloh: Bertelsmann Foundation).
Nye, J. (1990) *Bound to Lead: The Changing Nature of American Power* (New York: Basic Books).
Paterson, W. E. (1993) 'Muβ Europa Angst vor Deutschland haben?', in Hrbek, R. (ed.), *Der Vertrag von Maastricht in der wissenschaftlichen Kontroverse* (Baden-Baden: Nomos).
Paterson, W. E. and Jeffery, C. (1999) 'Deutschland, Frankreich – und Großbritannien? Eine britische Sicht deutscher Europapolitik', *Internationale Politik*, 54 (12), pp. 19–27.
Pond, E. (1990) *After the Wall: American Policy Toward Germany* (Washington, DC: Twentieth Century Fund).
Pond, E. (1992) 'Germany in the New Europe', *Foreign Affairs*, 70, Spring, pp. 114–30.
Risse, T. (1997) 'Between the Euro and the Deutsche Mark', *Center for German and European Studies, Georgetown, Working Papers*.
Risse, T. *et al.*, (1999) 'To Euro or not to Euro? The EMU and Identity Politics in the European Union', *European Journal of International Relations*, 5 (2), pp. 147–88.
Risse-Kappen, T. (1997) (ed.) *Bringing Transnational Relations Back In* (Cambridge: Cambridge University Press).
Rosecrance, R. (1986) *The Rise of the Trading State. Commerce and Conquest in the Modern World* (New York: Basic Books).
Scharping, R. (1999) 'Der Stein auf unserer Seele. Deutschland und der gerechte Krieg', *Frankfurter Allgemeine Zeitung*, 3 May.
Schwarz, H. P. (1985) *Die gezähmten Deutschen. Von ders Machtversessenheit zur Machtvergessenheit* (Stuttgart: Deutsche Verlags Anstalt).
Schwarz, H. P. (1994) 'Germany's National and European Interests', *Daedalus*, XX, Spring, pp. 81–108.
Spence, D. (1991) 'Enlargement Without Accession: The EC's Response to German Unification', *RIIA Discussion Papers*, No. 36.
Staack, M. (1998) 'Großmacht oder Handelsstaat?', *Aus Politik und Zeitgeschichte*, No. B12/98, 14–24.
Stürmer, M. (1994) 'Deutsche Interessen', in Kaiser, K. and Maull, H. W. (eds), *Deutschlands neue Außenpolitik Band 1* (Munich: Oldenbourg), pp. 34–62.
Tewes, H. (1998) 'Between Deepening and Widening: Role Conflict in Germany's Enlargement Policy', *West European Politics*, 21 (2), pp. 117–33.
Treverton, G. F. (1993) 'Force and Legacies Shaping a New Germany', in Geipel, G. L. (ed.), *Germany in a New Era* (Indianapolis: Hudson Institute), pp. 61–80.
Wallace, H. (1999), 'Whose Europe is it Anyway? The 1998 Stein Rokkan Lecture', *European Journal of Political Research*, 35, pp. 287–306.

Wallace, W. (1991) 'Germany at the Centre of Europe', in Kolinsky, E. (ed.), *The Federal Republic of Germany: the End of an Era* (Oxford: Berg), pp. 167–73.

Wessels, W. (1999) 'Zentralmacht, Zivilmacht oder Ohnmacht? Zur deutschen Außen- und Europapolitik nach 1989', in Weilemann, P. R. *et al.* (eds), *Macht und Zeitkritik. Festschrift für Hans-Peter Schwarz zum 65. Geburtstag* (Paderborn: Ferdinand Schoningh), pp. 334–406.

Wolfers, A. (1962) *Discord and Collaboration* (Baltimore: Johns Hopkins University Press).

Wood, S. (1999) 'Culture, Commerce and Foreign Policy', *German Politics and Society*, 17 (2), pp. 55–80.

10
Rethinking European Security

Lawrence Freedman

The meaning of security

Over four decades, until 1989, the question of European security generated a substantial, although often repetitive, literature. The upheavals of that year, in which the cold war effectively came to an end, appeared to render the bulk of this literature obsolescent, not only in its detail, but also the theoretical and policy assumptions upon which it rested. Attempts to develop a new framework, appropriate to the new conditions, became caught up with debates over whether these conditions were amenable to interpretation through long-established concepts or rather required a reappraisal of the very meaning of security in the post-cold-war world.

In this debate the more traditional approaches tend to get caricatured as dominated by realist preoccupations with the state and military power, to the exclusion of domestic and transnational considerations, and as paying scant regard to peaceful means of exerting influence and resolving disputes. Not only the end of the cold war, but also those other great trends of the late twentieth century, such as globalization and the information revolution, are now taken to demand a much broader perspective. Questions of military strategy, doctrine, training, organization and operations appear beside the point. The problems of contemporary insecurity and their prospective solutions are judged to lie elsewhere – or, to the extent that these still have a military dimension, this is the fault of those who legitimize armed force as an acceptable instrument of policy. This view has fitted a drive among some sections of the international relations community to cut states down to size as dubious mental constructs rather than the building blocks of the international system, in the process thus extending the concept of security. By focusing less on what makes states secure and more on what makes individuals and particular groups secure, a case can be made for a new agenda dominated by concerns over human rights, world poverty and the environment.

This debate has become particularly polarized in the United States where security studies have been a battleground for competing schools of thought, with neo-realism in one corner and liberal institutionalists in the other.[1] One of the unfortunate consequences is that realism, which referred initially to an approach to political analysis that prided itself on coming to terms with the world as it is rather than as idealists would like it to be, has become something of a dogma, claiming that key international events can largely be explained by the structurally defined means through which states must safeguard their security. This has encouraged expectations of a gloomy continuity in international affairs rather than any bright new dawn. When applied to Europe this approach has tended to dismiss the claims of the European Union (EU) to be causing a qualitative change in the character of the regional system; it could even to look to the German acquisition of nuclear weapons as the natural consequence of this system's inner logic (Mearsheimer, 1991).

More appropriate to an understanding of European security may be a non-dogmatic realism. Temperamentally this simply means looking hard at Europe as we find it, and not assuming a natural projection to something altogether more coherent, peaceful, harmonious and fraternal. It does not, however, mean discounting all positive developments, or the significance of non-state actors, or the impact of social, economic, cultural and local political factors on state behaviour, or ignoring the role of values, or the epistemological issues raised by presumptions of objectivity. The strength of realism during the middle decades of the last century was that it was tuned in to the categories adopted by the practitioners of international politics. If those practitioners have now picked up on issues of identity, norms and globalization, then there is no excuse for realists to dismiss them as passing fads: their very adoption has made them part of international reality.

Security studies, however, cease to be useful if expected to deal with all events and developments that generate anxiety. Politicians may dramatize the more troublesome social problems by calling for 'wars' against them (on drugs, cancer and so on) and suggest that strong 'generalship' is needed for them to be defeated. Yet while it is understandable that governments wish to mobilize all national resources to address the more intractable social problems, the war analogy can be extremely misleading. In the case of drugs, for example, it may have some relevance to confrontations with third world drug cartels, but less so to attempts to make sense of patterns of consumption. Equally the notions of 'economic security' can encourage a confrontational approach to trade policy and 'environmental security', a search for explanations based on hostile actions rather than natural causes or everyday economic activity. Even more difficult is a term such as 'internal security'. This might once have referred to the ability of states to deny armed groups, whether criminal or political, the ability to challenge their authority, but it is now being extended to take in anything to do with the control of borders, including economic migration or the smuggling of contraband.

The constant and steady focus of security studies should be on questions of the state and the control of organized violence. The characters and competences of states may have been subject to many changes, but an enduring feature remains the aspiration to define and to dominate the means of legitimate violence within territorial borders. The traditional issue for security studies was the threat posed to this aspiration by other states. But challenges arising from within state borders – from secessionists or revolutionaries or elitist conspirators – are not at all novel. More recent are concerns about the ability of diverse groups, such as drug cartels and gangsters, religious sects and minority political movements, to put together their own terrorist cells or private armies and even to gain access to the most destructive forms of weapons.

The problem of European security, as opposed to the security problems of individual European states, concerns the possible impact of conflicts within and among European states on the regional equilibrium and of the region-wide measures that might be taken to prevent, resolve and contain these conflicts or mitigate their effects. During the cold war the problem of European security became one of sustaining an apparently stable relationship between two great alliances – the Warsaw Pact, led by the Soviet Union, and the North Atlantic Treaty Organization (NATO) led by the United States. A fair charge that might be laid against the security studies community during the cold war decades might be that insufficient attention was paid to the political, social and economic dimensions of East–West conflict. During the 1990s regional affairs became much more fluid and the need to appreciate a broad range of phenomena became even more apparent. Strong rates of economic growth and forms of interdependence may well reduce tensions between states and create a stake in peaceful coexistence. Environmental disasters can undermine the credibility of the state apparatus, so that it becomes vulnerable to other types of challenges. Changes in family structures and social mores may affect attitudes to violence, and so on. An awareness of these issues is essential to any attempt to make sense of the changing state system. Security studies therefore embrace an unavoidably wide context, but need to compensate with a very sharp focus.[2]

In, out and down during the cold war

One of the neatest characterizations of the European security problem, at least from a west European perspective, came when NATO was described as being designed: to keep the Russians out, the Americans in, and the Germans down.

In formal terms 'keeping the Russians out' dominated security studies, and was reflected in the cold-war doctrine of containment. This argued that the Soviet Union would be deterred from further aggression in Europe by the thought of having to take on the United States. Hence, it required efforts to prevent a retreat into isolationism so as to 'keep the Americans in'. For their part the allies needed to do enough in defence terms to demonstrate that they deserved American support, although not so much that they could manage without the United States. This raised the question of the role West Germany could play as a front line state. Moscow's sour view of this process was aggravated by the West German government's refusal to reconcile itself to a separate East German state. It was only when this was more widely accepted at the end of the 1960s that a temporary solution was deemed to have been found to the German problem.

With *détente*, the principle of containment was mitigated by respect for peaceful coexistence. A hot war, with the associated risk of a nuclear catastrophe, required that both sides refrain from interfering in each others' internal affairs. Mutual ideological restraint was far more difficult than military restraint, where the risks were not that difficult to calculate. The Soviet leadership comprised the guardians of a revolutionary ideology to which they continued to pay lip service, including anticipating the downfall of capitalism as a result of its internal contradictions. Communist parties in the West were devoted to hastening this process, although eventually their ardour was cooled by the evident futility of the endeavour and electoral considerations. The liberal ideology of the West encouraged the active promotion of 'human rights' in the East, through such mechanisms as the 1975 Final Act of the Helsinki Conference on Security and Cooperation in Europe.

Nonetheless, the consensus was that the West was in no position to push the Soviet Union to dismantle its political system and any attempt to do so would be a provocation and thus counter-productive.

Substantial analytical resources were devoted to measuring and evaluating the military balance between the two alliances, and to debating the extent to which the presence of large nuclear arsenals provided a formidable disincentive to any attempt to change the status quo through aggressive means. In practice, however, the key to European security was to be found in the contrasting sources of alliance cohesion. The Warsaw Pact brought together repressive, one-party states with command economies. The Soviet management style was coercive. NATO relied much more on consent and therefore appeared less disciplined than the Pact, and extremely dependent upon the commitment of the United States to the security of like-minded liberal-capitalist states an ocean away. Within each alliance, the main impact of military developments tended to be on the underlying political relationships – as signals of commitments or as attempts to shift risks to others. In the end the confrontation was resolved through the evident failure of state socialism as a governing ideology.

Security in post-communist Europe

With the end of the cold war, 'keeping the Russians out' no longer seemed an issue, in which case 'keeping the Americans in' was perhaps less important. There was good reason to suppose that the American role would become increasingly marginal, as a result of its own preferences for a quieter life after the exertions of the cold war as well as the collapse of the Soviet threat. As a result of unification there was no longer a prospect of 'keeping the Germans down'. This particular issue became phrased instead (not least by the Germans themselves) in terms of calming fears of an ascendant Germany by demonstrating that it was safely embedded in a complex institutional network. Because of a 'European Germany' there was, it was said, no need to fear a 'German Europe' (Janning, 1996). The mechanisms of European economic and political integration were used, often quite explicitly, as the central plank of security policy, with another war among the European great powers held up as one possible danger of failure. Integration would restrict Germany's ability to throw its weight around. In practice Germany's own inhibitions and post-unification economic difficulties would have sufficed as constraints, while the integration project turned out to be as demanding as it was radical.

By the early 1990s, however, Europe's security problem was less the risk of reversion to bad old ways by the west European states and more how the political vacuum created by the collapse of communist power in central and eastern Europe was to be filled.[3] This was an area where past turbulence, as well as competition by external powers for influence, had triggered European conflicts. Even during the cold war years it had been pacified by the Soviet Union only with difficulty, and Moscow had notably failed in the Balkans: Yugoslavia never joined the Warsaw Pact and Albania withdrew. Even before the Berlin Wall came down there were worrying signs of Hungarian–Romanian, Bulgarian–Turkish and, most ominously, inner-Yugoslavian conflicts developing.

The development of a more fluid political system meant that not only did the definition of security become contentious, but so did the definition of Europe. Previously every country in Europe could be categorized as being part of NATO, Warsaw Pact or the 'neutral and non-aligned' group. In international institutions due regard was paid to the balance between these three groups. Now the Warsaw Pact no longer existed and neutrality and non-alignment had lost much of their meaning. The essential division became between those within one or both of the two key western institutions – NATO and the EU – and those without. While for security purposes, as in the Organization for Security and Cooperation in Europe (OSCE), 'Europe' could include all of the former Soviet Union, including central Asia, in practice many of the 'without' states have been left in something of a limbo, with neither alliance or strong supranational organizations to fall back upon.

There was some hope at the start of the 1990s that the new Europe might be held together by ideological glue. Because the West had subverted the East simply by its comparative economic success and the personal freedom it permitted, the leading political tendencies in post-communist Europe leaned towards the West, even in Russia. There was a brief period of optimism that the power of virtuous example would lead Europe as a whole towards the ways of liberal democracy and free markets. Economic recovery would be almost spontaneously generated through declarations in favour of capitalism, while the adoption of democracy would by itself turn the most bellicose societies into model international citizens and calm their internal tensions.[4] Unfortunately, it soon became apparent that a tough nationalism and democracy were by no means incompatible, especially when politicians were uncertain of what they could offer on the economic front. Transition from socialism to capitalism was an unavoidably painful process. In the case of Russia, unleashing market forces, without a proper legal and regulatory process, produced impoverishment for many and enrichment of gangsters and well-placed apparatchiks.

Western Europe and the United States became unclear about the extent to which post-communist Europe constituted a security problem for them. There were no significant trade or raw material dependencies. Some parts were prone to political tumult and occasional violence, but did that matter if there was little risk of this spreading westwards? Worries about influxes of asylum seekers do not necessarily justify regular intervention in local squabbles. Yet it was hard to ignore trouble to the East. Media images of civil wars pricked consciences and it appeared imprudent and unrealistic to ignore upheavals close to home, even when their direct effects were hard to measure.

This ambivalent attitude produced interventions that were spasmodic and reactive (Freedman, 1994). Given the expectations of large-scale subsidy that would have been aroused, and the excess of variables in the situation, it may well have been sensible in 1990 not to have a grand plan for post-communist Europe. Nonetheless the absence of a coherent strategy, and only a tentative contribution to the reconstruction of post-communist Europe, had serious consequences, most notably in terms of the inadvertent acquisition of the Balkans (other than Serbia) as a NATO protectorate and poor relations with Russia.

At the outset the West approached post-communist Europe on the basis of conditionality. This suggested that economic support would be given to countries that met the highest standards in their political behaviour, both internally and externally. The difficulties with this formula were that politically deserving cases could not always cope efficiently with support designed to modernize (rather than merely subsidize) their economies, while undeserving cases could threaten regional chaos unless given some support. Moreover there were limits on the economic largesse available, especially when it came to offering market access in highly sensitive areas such as agriculture and textiles. Inevitably countries adjacent to the EU had a higher priority, as they had the best economic prospects and became important as a buffer between the advantaged and disadvantaged parts of the continent. In 1999 the Czech Republic, Hungary and Poland were able to mark their membership of the western club by joining NATO.

NATO and the EU as security providers

The curiosity here was that these countries joined the West through membership of a formal alliance rather than an economic community.

The explanation for this was that membership of NATO involved fewer economic hurdles than the EU and had the great merit of providing a close link with the US. The alliance could also lay claim to be a club based on shared values. Nonetheless, as an organization geared to integrating armed forces and providing collective defence, its enlargement gave a high salience to traditional security concerns, even though none of the 'first wave' new members faced severe threats. This served to highlight the awkward positions of those excluded. Russia responded by taking this as a snub and a challenge, thereby granting an even higher salience to issues of military security. It saw justification in the fact that, rather than turn to more pacific pursuits with the end of the cold war, NATO became even more activist. First it provided an unofficial framework for joint operations against Iraq in 1991. Then it provided command arrangements for Bosnia. Lastly, in 1999, it actually went to war against Yugoslavia, on behalf of persecuted Kosovar Albanians. In all of these cases there were political difficulties, but the overall impression was of a powerful alliance able to act decisively and with reasonable efficiency when necessary.

The EU's claims as a security provider have proved to be much harder to establish. The starting point was different. Rather than a formal military alliance, the EU could be considered a 'security community'. This is a looser concept, depending on the quality of integration and interdependence among the respective societies rather than explicit security guarantees. It involves a degree of mutual solidarity based on shared values and an awareness that an attack on one would directly affect all, even where there is not always the firmness of an alliance obligation to come to the aid of a partner under threat.

The creeping enlargement of a security community, with the growth of a general interdependence, might have been preferable to the sharp drawing of lines by an alliance, which inevitably confines some countries to an uncomfortable non-alignment. Progress in this direction, however, was limited by the EU's caution in addressing the security concerns of wider Europe through its own enlargement when so many other practical issues of economic and legal structure had to be addressed, but also because it did not want to put at risk its own 'deepening process' by too much 'widening'.[5] Yet in other respects the performance of the EU was disappointing. One of the potential strengths of the EU supposedly lay in its ability to bring to bear substantial economic and political strength on a variety of international problems. Here the experience of the 1990s was unimpressive. It devoted considerable resources to post-communist Europe, but failed to develop a coherent strategy. It was bypassed in the Middle East, and inhibited in policy towards North Africa and the Balkans, not least by the particular interests of France and Greece respectively. After painful incoherence was exhibited during the Gulf crisis of 1990–91, there was great determination to realize Europe's potential by taking on crises in its own neighbourhood. The developing civil war in Yugoslavia in the summer of 1991 led to the notorious proclamation that Europe's hour had come and that no American help was required. The palpable failure that followed, meant that the Yugoslavia problem was handed over to the UN and NATO; this cast further doubt on the EU's ability to serve as a regional security provider (Gow, 1997).

This weak performance can be explained by the increased complexity and fluidity of the international system since the end of the cold war. It is hard for all political entities, even the United States, to design appropriate policies. Moreover, the very structure of modern democratic states inhibits the development of intergovernmental efforts, especially within such a tortuous institutional framework as the EU (Zielonka, 1998). Furthermore, the EU could not compete with NATO in terms of the projection of military force, and this limited its role in crisis management. This particular limitation was exasperating to those who assumed that the logic of the European project was to create an entity with the full attributes of a state, including its own armed forces. This objective was more to do with internal development than power projection and, to many critics, missed the point of European weakness. Even assuming that the EU could inject greater coherence and activism into its common foreign policy, questions would still be asked about the inability of such a rich collection of nations to muster substantial military strength.

There are again particular explanations: a reluctance to use conscripts in roles other than the defence of the homeland (a restraint that France, in particular, worked to overcome during the late 1990s); Germany's unavoidable inhibitions when it came to sending the Bundeswehr where the Werhmacht had been before; and the cumulative effects of years of cuts in defence budgets, which had been accelerated by the end of the cold war and the evaporation of the Soviet threat. There were other structural problems: the resources available were too much used to sustain national defence industries; and front-line forces were duplicated across countries at the expense of such critical areas as logistics, notably strategic lift, and intelligence. In these areas Europe has remained well behind the United States.

European security and defence initiative

The issue of how to develop a European defence entity brings together two distinct agendas, which are not necessarily compatible. The first is the possibility of the EU turning itself into a military alliance capable of displacing NATO as the main security provider in western Europe, with the risks of duplication of effort and alienating the Americans. The second is the ability of EU states to contribute more to collective defence, by building up the 'European pillar' in NATO to match 'the American pillar' (Howorth and Menon, 1997).

The initial institutional response in Europe during the 1990s was to strengthen the Western European Union (WEU), an organization that always had a clearly subordinate role to NATO, though it could trace its origins back to pre-NATO days. The WEU acquired its own planning cell and some capacity to pull European forces together for contingencies that were unlikely to draw in the United States. This did nothing to redress the basic problem of the limited military clout of the EU countries, nor to help the EU do a better job of relating its internal policies to its external environment. Towards the end of the decade, with the strengthening of the machinery for a common foreign and security policy and the adoption at the Helsinki European Council of December 1999 of a plan for a European defence entity, some effort was made to take the issue further forward.

The two sponsors of this defence initiative, Britain and France, represented contrasting approaches to alliance with the United States. Britain, and most other European states, had always seen high risks in loosening this alliance. Talk of getting the Americans out played to isolationist American sentiment in Washington, where there was always a strong lobby for cutting back on the commitment on Europe. Claims that Europeans could defend themselves unaided would provide just the excuse for the Americans to give three cheers and withdraw to safety on the other side of the Atlantic. The French had portrayed the Americans as unreliable allies, exacting an excessive political price, and insisted that Europeans could look after themselves unaided. The French case had been undermined by suspicion of their motives – that they were unwilling to pool sovereignty and sought instead to supplant the Americans as leaders of western Europe.

Once there was no Warsaw Pact to worry about the old case for an independent European defence capability was revived. Events soon refuted it again. If anything the post cold-war position was worse. Questions about involvement in actual military operations arose – first in the Gulf and then in the Balkans. Both turned out to be embarrassing for proponents of an independent and assertive Europe. The stunning experience of Desert Storm in the Gulf demonstrated just how far ahead the American capabilities were in the whole infrastructure of war, as well as precision weapons. It was, however, the wars of Yugoslavia's dissolution that had the most substantial long-term effect on European strategic thinking.

The Bosnian and then the Kosovan wars indicated the crucial difference made by American aircraft, up to three quarters of the total available, and also in logistics and intelligence. The UN force in Bosnia from 1992 to 1995 was largely a European enterprise. It proved an operational nightmare, culminating in Dutch peacekeepers finding themselves in an invidious position, as Srebrenica was overrun and Moslems were massacred. Much good work was done by Europeans in easing distress and containing the conflict, but the UN units were too small and too weak to impose themselves on the warring parties, and were vulnerable to retaliation. The lesson drawn was that any future land operations had to include some protection and backed by serious air power. The trouble was that the Americans, while quite willing to supply air power, were remarkably reluctant to commit ground forces. If Washington remained unresponsive to European aspirations the handicap appeared fatal: nothing much could be done. If the Americans were to respond, then as the main providers they would naturally expect to take political leadership in defining goals and choosing a strategy. In the event the American reluctance to put their forces too much into harm's way, or into situations which may involve prolonged and complicated commitments, was inescapable, and handicapped NATO's crisis diplomacy and military campaign over Kosovo.

Part of the thinking behind the Franco–British initiative was therefore that important military options were lost if Europe could not provide the necessary ground forces, especially when they might still require American logistical support to get them into position and sustain them. While it might have been unrealistic to take on the combined might of the Warsaw Pact, European countries by themselves should not have been at a loss when faced with Serbia. The core Franco–British proposal was for a dedicated European rapid reaction force designed to meet the gap. EU member states should be 'able, by 2003, to deploy within 60 days and sustain for at least one year military forces of up to 50,000–60,000 persons capable of the full range of Petersberg tasks' (Presidency Conclusions, 1999). In response to criticisms that this aimed to realize the discredited dream of NATO being replaced by the

EU, European governments pointed to American arguments that Europeans must make a more credible contribution, if Congress was to accept that the allies deserve support. The inherent modesty of the proposed new forces was far from a truly independent capability, and any operation would still be highly dependent upon the NATO command structure, and probably American logistics and intelligence. It would be hard for Europeans to act against American wishes.

The political logic underlying this is that, whatever Europeans do, there is a growing presumption in the United States that it can engage in international affairs on its own terms, irrespective of the views of allies and without any respect for multilateral organizations. The fascination with the potential of a 'National Missile Defense' system, ostensibly to deal with rogue nuclear states, confirmed in Europe a tendency to address American vulnerabilities, even with a highly dubious project, at the expense of international obligations, in this case the 1972 ABM Treaty. While American policy-makers insist that this tendency has been exaggerated by Europeans overplaying the peculiarities of American domestic politics, it seems only prudent for Europeans to prepare to take more responsibility for their own security.

The problem of Russia

There are limits to how far the transfer of responsibility can go, especially when the issue of Russia still dominates European security thinking, albeit in a quite different guise from that of the cold war years. Even with the post-Soviet contraction this is just too large a country, and too distinct in its strategic culture and preoccupations, to be accommodated in a straight forward way into European security structures. During the cold war the concern was Soviet strength, but long before the Berlin wall came down, progressive ideological and economic weakness, and the associated political stagnation, increasingly figured in western security calculations. Now concerns about Russian weakness, including the possibility of its considerable residual nuclear capability falling into incompetent or malevolent hands, tend to take over from concerns about strength, although the reassertion of Russian power remains a continual preoccupation of those around its periphery. In this NATO governments agree entirely with Moscow that the Russian state must reassert itself, if it is to collect taxes, confront corruption and gangsterism and avoid further fragmentation. Where they have differed is about the means necessary to achieve these tasks. For western policy there has been a dilemma over whether priority should be given to economic reform, the promotion of human rights, or stability and order (Baranovsky, 1997; Kaiser and Arbatov, 1999). The response to the Putin Presidency illustrated the dilemma. On the one hand there was relief that Russia now had a healthy, and sober, leader prepared to push forward with market reforms. On the other hand there was unease that the price for this was human rights abuses and repression in Chechnya.

A major source of difficulty is that Russia still considers itself a great power and wishes to be treated as such. The West has played along with this by turning the Group of Seven leading industrial nations into the Group of Eight, when non-economic matters are discussed, and establishing a NATO–Russia Cooperation Council. The difficulty is that when policies are left unaltered after consultations, the irritation to the Russians can be worse than if no consultation had taken place at all. As could be seen with Kosovo, Russian support is now more a bonus for the West than a necessary condition for action, and there is no inclination to pay a high price. The most difficult issues for the future will arise where Russia considers its core security concerns to be at stake, such as further enlargement of NATO, especially into the Baltics. Here there is a strong security argument for their inclusion in NATO, but precisely for that reason a requirement to honour security guarantees might arise – and therefore direct confrontation with Russia at a geographically unfavourable location could not be precluded. Aspirant NATO members, including the Baltic states, have made common cause in requesting a shared enlargement, to avoid being picked off one against the other. The pressure on NATO has been further aggravated by evidence that the EU may be unable to adhere to its own strict timetable on enlargement because of difficulties in reforming its decision-making procedures and fears for the integrity of the integrative project if there are more members who prefer to move slowly. The problems of adjustment to NATO membership are not trivial, but if these are used to excuse delay, the aspirants will claim that Moscow is being appeased. The question of how far Russia can be pushed on this matter may well prove to be one of the trickiest European security issues of the coming years.

Conclusion

It is widely assumed to the point of unanimity that there is no longer a serious risk of war among the former great powers that now inhabit the EU. It would take a series of unexpected and miserable events for this assumption to be shaken. One event that would unsettle all political relationships would be a major down turn in the global economy. If monetary union became unsustainable, or extreme nationalism gained a serious grip in some western European countries (perhaps as a reaction against globalization), then it is possible to imagine this leading to real political strain among EU countries. Even then, however, it remains hard to envisage that this would lead to military confrontation, for few harbour the expansionist urges that led to wars in the past.

The core issues of European security revolve rather around the question of what those within the zone of stability are prepared to do for those without. European security has become the product of the interaction between a reasonably stable set of EU countries, supported by North America, and a neighbourhood that is much more volatile. Through the expansion of EU or NATO membership, the zone of stability might be expanded, but each new border becomes more difficult, as each successive candidate on the other side appears to have a shakier economy and weaker polity, or a reduced commitment to liberal democracy and market economics. Benign economic trends, the norm for almost a decade, can ease the tensions of political transition, but the corollary would also be true, should the global economy falter. It may be, as in East Asia following the 1997 economic collapse, that most countries can adjust to harsh conditions without a descent into authoritarianism or anarchy, but some may well get caught. So the gloomiest scenarios for Europe's future involve the EU struggling to cope with a demanding integration programme internally against a background of a deteriorating international economy. Not only would the internal cohesion become fragile, but there would be a need to act to stabilize parts of the neighbourhood at a time when the Union still lacked the capacity to act decisively.

The simplistic equation would therefore appear to be as follows. Western Europe cannot ignore, nor escape, instability in proximate areas, including North Africa as well as post-communist Europe. To the extent that it is able to calm that instability through the imaginative and innovative use of economic programmes, diplomatic initiatives and institutional embraces, then the impact will be limited and incidents of violence will be manageable and contained. To the extent that it fails and the instability gets worse, then situations are more likely to develop that can be calmed only through large-scale military interventions, with their own risks of escalation and the probability of being followed by long-term military and economic commitments. This is what has happened in the Balkans. One consequence of such an adverse trend would be to reinforce European dependence on the United States. The conclusion, for those who wish to reduce this dependency (or believe that the United States will become less dependable), is to recognize the importance of a vigorous foreign policy geared to the spread of stability, well before any more of the simmering neighbourhood tensions reaching boiling point.

Notes

1. The standard texts in the international relations debate are Keohane (1989) and Waltz (1979). A recent addition is Wendt (1999).
2. I discuss my approach in Freedman (1998).
3. For some early post-cold war assessment see Buzan *et al.* (1990); Hyde-Price (1991); Ullman (1990).
4. On the proposition that greater democracy leads to more peace see Fendius Elman (1997).
5. For a sharp critique see Garton Ash (1998).

References

Baranovsky, V. (ed.) (1997) *Russia and Europe: The Emerging Security Agenda* (Oxford: SIPRI/OUP).
Buzan, B., Kelstrup, M., Lemaitre, P., Tromer, E. and Wæver, O. (1990) *The European Security Order Recast: Scenarios for the Post-Cold War Era* (London: Pinter).
European Council Presidency Conclusions (1999) *Common European Policy on Security and Defence* (Helsinki).
Fendius Elman, M. (ed.) (1997) *Paths to Peace: Is Democracy the Answer?* (Cambridge, MA: MIT Press).
Freedman, L. (1994) (ed.) *Military Intervention in European Conflicts* (Oxford: Blackwell).
Freedman, L. (1998) 'International Security: Changing Targets', *Foreign Policy*, 110.
Garton Ash, T. (1998) 'Europe's Endangered Liberal Order', *Foreign Affairs*, pp. 51–65.
Gow, J. (1997) *Triumph of the Lack of Will: International Diplomacy and the Yugoslav War* (London: Hurst).
Howorth, J. and Menon, A. (eds) (1997) *The European Union and National Defence Policy* (London and New York).
Hyde-Price, A. (1991) *European Security Beyond the Cold War: Four Scenarios for the Year 2010* (London: Sage Publications/RIIA).
Janning, J. (1996) 'A German Europe – A European Germany? On the debate over Germany's foreign policy', *International Affairs*, 72 (1), pp. 33–42.
Kaiser, K. and Arbatov, A. (eds) (1999) *Russia and Europe* (New York: Institute for East West Studies).

Keohane, R. (1989) *International Institutions and State Power* (Boulder, Co: Westview).

Mearsheimer, J. (1991) 'Back to the Future: instability in Europe after the Cold War', *International Security*, 12 (1), pp. 5–56.

Ullman, R. (1990) *Securing Europe* (New York: Adamantine Press).

Waltz, K. (1979) *Theory of International Politics* (New York: McGraw Hill).

Wendt, A. (1999) *Social Theory of International Politics* (Cambridge: Cambridge University Press).

Zielonka, J. (1998) *Explaining Euro-Paralysis: Why Europe is Unable to Act in International Politics* (London: Macmillan – now Palgrave).

Part III
The Affiliational Dimension

11
Imagining the Union: a Case of Banal Europeanism?
Laura Cram[1]

'all communities larger than primordial villages of face-to-face contact (and perhaps even these) are imagined' (Anderson, [1983] 1991:1).

Introduction: imagining the union

In recent years there has been a revived interest among students of the European Union (EU) in the work of the early integration theorists such as Karl Deutsch and Ernst Haas. Scholars have, for example, begun to recognize the importance of transactions in the creation and maintenance of the governance regime within the EU (Sandholtz and Stone Sweet, 1998) which were so central to the work of Deutsch. Meanwhile, a focus on the learning of 'integrative habits' as a result of prior cooperation, emphasized by the functionalists (Mitrany, 1943),[2] the communication school (Deutsch, 1953, 1957, 1966) and neo-functionalist scholars (Haas, 1958), has once again begun to come to the fore. An extensive literature, drawing upon new institutionalist approaches, examining the role of institutions, institutionalization, lock-in, path dependency and the question of preference formation (Armstrong and Bulmer, 1998; Pierson, 1996), has, for example, emerged.

Meanwhile, the term Europeanization has increasingly become a part of the vocabulary of scholars studying the impact of European integration. A number of studies focus on the Europeanization of different member states (Cole and Drake, 2000; Mény *et al.*, 1996; Rometsch and Wessels, 1996), policy areas (Mazey, 1998) or actors (Lavdas, 1997). Yet, there are few systematic studies of how *societal actors* within member states have adapted in response to European integration or of how this adaptation has impacted upon the individual or collective values and identities of citizens of the EU and ultimately upon the process of European integration. The extent to which a re-evaluation of the preferences of societal actors in EU member states does or does not take place, as transactions within the territory of the EU become increasingly institutionalized and as intra-EU communication channels and patterns become ever more complex, remains a key question.

The importance of the societal dimension of European integration has long been recognized. As Jean Monnet said, when establishing the European Coal and Steel Community in 1951, 'we are uniting people, not forming coalitions of states' (Duchêne, 1994: 363). Indeed, it has been argued that Monnet 'was interested less in perfected constitutional blue-prints than in shaping human patterns of response to induce a change of process' (Duchêne, 1994: 367). For political scientists too, the extent to which the preferences of individuals involved in interactions at the EU level may be 'redefined in terms of regional rather than a purely national orientation' (Haas, 1958: 45) has long been viewed as a crucial question for the study of European integration. Still, the question of 'how – if at all – cohesion is obtained' (Haas, 1958: 4) remains unanswered.

The process of 'social learning' and the 're-evaluation of preferences' were central concerns for Deutsch and later Haas. Yet, this particular aspect of their work is one which even some of their sympathizers have specifically sought to avoid. Sandholtz and Stone Sweet (1998: 5), for example, state that they 'acknowledge the insights of two of the founders of integration theory, Karl Deutsch and Ernst Haas' and believe that 'on crucial questions they got it right'. However, they choose to 'set aside Deutsch's concern with the formation of communities and identities *per se*, and the issue of whether or not identity formation precedes state-building' (Sandholtz and Stone Sweet, 1998: 5). Deutsch ([1953]1996: 174) did not, of course, view this as a monolinear process, but rather saw the two processes of identity formation and state-building as mutually reinforcing: 'experience and complementarity may then continue to reproduce each other, like the proverbial chicken and egg, in a syndrome of ethnic learning'. Similarly, in borrowing from Haas, Sandholtz and Stone Sweet (1998: 6) nevertheless 'leave as an open question the extent to which the loyalties and identities of actors will shift from the national to the European level'.[3]

Although there has been a recent rise in social constructivist approaches to the study of the EU (see, for example, Christiansen,

Jørgenson and Wiener (eds) [1999]) which claim that ideas and identities are important in the construction of the EU, there is, as yet, little empirical evidence to back up these claims. Once again, broader debates in international relations have been mirrored in the study of the EU. Yet, as many have acknowledged, the EU is not simply an area of contestation between states, but a functioning polity or system of governance. In this context, it is surprising that there have been so few scholarly attempts to explore systematically the various perceptions or 'imaginings' (cf Anderson, [1983]1991) of the Union which prevail amongst the European people(s), let alone how these have or have not changed and their implications for the process of integration or for the potential for disintegration.

Perhaps most surprising of all is how little systematic use has been made of the literatures on nationalism and national identity in the EU context.[4] Clearly, the EU presents a challenge to traditional notions of nationalism: 'primarily a political principle, which holds that the political and national unit should be congruent' (Gellner, 1983: 131). Indeed, the study of the EU can be problematic in a world in which the ideology of nationalism has become so all pervasive that 'the world of nations has come to seem the natural world – as if there could not possibly be a world without nations' (Billig, 1995: 37). However, as Sbragia (1992: 267) has argued, one important aspect of the study of the EU is that it may 'stimulate scholars of politics within unitary states and federations to rethink what they have so far taken as givens'. Moreover, although the EU is a unique entity, 'analysis is more likely to suffer from studying it in isolation from other systems than from using the comparative method in less than ideal circumstances' (Sbragia, 1992: 268). Viewed from this perspective, the fact that the EU is not a typical national state does not preclude the use of theories of nationalism and national identity to further our analysis of this unique construct.

This chapter deliberately avoids the major debates as to whether the EU can be called a state or whether a European nation is in the making.[5] The focus is rather on the impact which the governance regime at the EU level has already had upon the perceptions of the various European peoples and what this may mean for the process of European integration. For this purpose it is argued that there are many insights to be gained by reassessing the contribution to the study of the EU made by Deutsch, and more generally by studying the extensive literature on nationalism and national identity.

Territory, function and affiliation in deep integration: insights from nationalism

Perhaps nowhere are the three concepts, *territory, function* and *affiliation*, which Wallace (see Chapter 1) argues are central to an understanding of the emergence of deep integration in western Europe, more evident than in the literatures on nationalism and national identity. In this chapter, the issue of territory is not discussed in any great detail, although the territorial dimension of the EU and of its various member states and applicant members is an underlying theme in any discussion of the societal dimension of European integration. Crucially, however, neither is the discussion in this chapter simply limited to the affiliational aspects of the integration process. Rather, it is argued, that insights from the study of nationalism illustrate a *key link between function and affiliation*. Thus, the extent to which a sense of attachment to the EU develops is contingent upon the satisfaction of its citizens with developments in the functional dimension.

This argument is nothing new. Renan (1990: 19) famously wrote in 1882 that the very existence of a nation 'is a daily plebiscite'. Nationalism, in this view, is less a romanticized notion of emotional attachment to a homeland or culture than a choice, or act of will, even a calculated decision concerning the costs and benefits of affiliation. In their discussion of the contingent nature of functional nationalism, Deutsch *et al.* (1957: 87) made precisely this point:

> The issue of political integration (thus) arose primarily when people demanded greater capabilities, greater performance, greater responsiveness, and more adequate services of some kind from the governments of the political units by which they had been governed before. *Integration or amalgamation were first considered as possible means to further these ends, rather than as ends in themselves* (emphasis added).

From this perspective then, the initial decision about whether to support integration, or to maintain the status quo or to push for devolved powers, is taken in response to a more or less rational calculation concerning the costs and benefits of integration or devolution. However, the actions of the self-interested may also have lasting consequences: 'in trying to gain and exercise power for its own ends, the efforts of nationalists may transform a people into a nationality'

(Deutsch, [1953]1966: 104). This point is also made by Breuilly (1982: 65) in relation to the process of unification nationalism[6] in nineteenth-century Europe: 'Nationalism was more important as a product than as a cause of national unification'.

As Edelman ([1967]1985: 195) has argued, 'the study of the construction of meaning must focus upon the interpretations of the subjects more than upon the observation of objects'. Deutsch *et al.*'s (1957: 85) thesis on the contingent nature of national identity is that 'political habits of loyalty to a particular unit could be more easily shifted to a political unit of another size, either larger or smaller, if this seemed to offer a more promising framework within which this attractive way of life could be developed'. This deserves further exploration and testing from this perspective. To what extent, for example, must the new attractive way of life be based on an objective reality and to what extent can symbols and myths be manipulated to encourage a shift in expectations and activities towards the new political centre or to encourage particular 'imaginings' of the Union?

Deutsch ([1953]1966: 170), for example, argued that communications and symbols were central to an understanding of the emergence of a 'national consciousness'. Thus, 'a person, an organization, or a social group – such as a people – can do more than merely steer some of its behaviour by balancing its current experiences with its recalled traditions. It can achieve *consciousness* by attaching secondary symbols – that is symbols about symbols – to certain items in its current intake of outside information, and to certain items recalled from memory' (ibid). Viewed from this perspective, how the various perceptions or imaginings of the EU by the European people(s), and of their place within it, are derived may be crucial for the process of European integration and for the development of deep integration or otherwise.

Of course, this focus on ideas, identities and symbols should not be prioritized to the exclusion of the issue of power. On the contrary, the tools of nationalism are potent ones: 'So long as competitive institutions continue to prevail, nationalism can mobilize more people and organize them more firmly than can many competing types of organization. The potential rewards of nationalism then grow in proportion to the potential resources of wealth and power to which members of a particular people have, or can gain, access on preferred terms' (Deutsch, 1953: 184). As Deutsch (ibid.) argued, 'all this is sound power politics'. Thus, a key question for students of the EU is: whose 'imaginings' of the Union prevail and why?

From 'background' space to 'homeland' space

Perhaps one of the most common criticisms of Deutsch's approach to the study of the EU is the patent lack of any strong sense of 'Europeanness' on the part of EU citizens. However, in this chapter it is suggested that Billig's (1995: 43–6) distinction between 'banal' nationalism and 'hot' nationalism might facilitate a better understanding of Deutsch's use of the terms 'people', 'community' and 'nationality'. Billig (1995: 44) notes that the term 'nationalism' is frequently reserved by scholars to refer to 'outbreaks of "hot" nationalist passion, which arise in times of social disruption and which are reflected in extreme social movements'. What is often neglected, he argues, is the day-to-day reinforcement of national consciousness which is so crucial to the maintenance of national regimes: 'All over the world, nations display their flags, day after day. Unlike the flags on the great days, these flags are largely unwaved, unsaluted, unnoticed. Indeed, it seems strange to suppose that occasional events, bracketed off from ordinary life, are sufficient to sustain a continuingly remembered national identity. It would seem more likely that identity is part of a more banal way of life in the nation-state' (Billig, 1995: 46).

Students of the EU looking for evidence of the growth of 'hot' nationalism, and who go in search of fervent Europeans are likely to be disappointed (or relieved that their expectations have been confirmed so effortlessly). Here it is suggested that the sense of community, which Deutsch *et al.* saw as crucial for the maintenance of an integrated regime, was much closer to Billig's notion of 'banal' nationalism than to the 'hot' nationalism usually evoked by scholars of nationalism and national identity. For example, the 'sense of community', which Deutsch *et al.* saw as a prerequisite for integration, did not imply a wholesale shift to a 'sense of Europeanness' or even the pre-eminence of a European identity. Rather it needed simply the existence of a shared belief that 'common social problems can and must be resolved by processes of "peaceful change"', that is, 'the resolution of social problems, normally by institutionalized procedures, without resort to large scale physical force' (Deutsch *et al.*, 1957: 5). Meanwhile, Deutsch's ([1953]1966: 97) functional definition of nationality consisted 'in the ability to communicate more effectively, and over a wider range of subjects, with members of one large group than with outsiders'. Three factors in particular, he argued, provided the primary basis for an alignment of preferences to occur:

- complementarity of communication habits;
- complementarity of acquired social and economic preferences which involve mobility of goods or persons; and
- the need for security and success in a changing environment (Deutsch [1953]1966: 101).[7]

By misrepresenting the input made by Deutsch and others, it has been relatively easy for scholars, to ignore this major contribution to the study of European integration. Clearly, no great sense of Europeanness is even yet apparent in the EU.[8] However, how function and affiliation interact within a given territory is much more nuanced than this approach suggests. The EU is more than simply an international organization, and more than just a set of institutions. The EU is also a space or place within which reside a European people or peoples. Indeed, the remit of the EU executive is to act in the European interest: presumably the interest of the European people(s). Hence it is less interesting to ask whether some elusive 'sense of Europeanness' has emerged than to establish to what extent the new arrangement has become the accepted status quo. To what extent, for example, has the EU come to be viewed by its inhabitants as less of a 'background' space and more of a 'homeland' space (cf. Billig, 1995: 43)? This is something which could, usefully, be measured and tested by students of the EU.

Forgetting to remember: the normalization/domestication of the EU

As well as identifying the need for the daily reproduction of nationalism, Renan (1990: 11) also emphasized the importance of the collective forgetting of inconvenient pasts for the maintenance of contemporary national identities. Currently, the notion that EU citizens could form a nation seems inconceivable. However, processes of collective forgetting, in which disparate histories (even warfare) are glossed over, are not uncommon in the creation of nations. As Anderson (1991: 201) reminds us: 'A vast pedagogical industry works ceaselessly to oblige young Americans to remember/forget the hostilities of 1861–65 as a great "civil" war between "brothers" rather than between – as they briefly were – two sovereign nation-states'. In similar vein, Billig (1995: 38) argues that 'the nation which celebrates its antiquity, forgets its historical recency'. Of course, part of the *raison d'être* of the EU was to create lasting habits of peaceful cooperation between previously warring nations and to tie Germany irrevocably into a union with its European neighbours. In many respects, the collective forgetting of these relatively recent past hostilities has been highly successful. To some extent, this collective forgetting takes place through the normalisation or domestication of previously unfamiliar practices. Thus, as patterns of behaviour shift, what at first appeared 'new' gradually becomes unremarkable.

Billig (1995: 42), building on Bourdieu's concept of the *habitus*, calls the process of collective forgetting *enhabitation* and argues that this constitutes a key aspect of nationalism: 'Patterns of social life become habitual or routine, and in so doing embody the past. One might describe this process of routine-formation as *enhabitation*: thoughts, reactions and symbols become turned into routine habits and, thus, they become *enhabited*. The result is that the past is enhabited in the present in a dialectic of forgotten remembrance' (Billig, 1995: 42). This argument strikes a clear chord with Deutsch's arguments concerning the process of social learning through which shifts in identification might be reinforced: 'And, as with all learning processes, they need not merely use this new information for the guidance of their behaviour in the light of the preferences, memories and goals which they have had thus far, but they may also use them to *learn*, that is, to modify this very inner structure of their preferences, goals and patterns of behaviour' (Deutsch, [1953]1966: 117). Indeed, the notion of enhabitation is highly reminiscent of the learning of 'integrative habits' as a result of prior cooperation, emphasized by Mitrany (1943), Deutsch (1953, 1957, 1966) and Haas (1958). It is precisely these routines and habits which, by acting as daily reminders of belonging, Billig argues (1995: 43), 'serve to turn background space into homeland space'.

At a basic level, that a degree of *banal Europeanism* already exists within the EU seems undeniable. As EU politicians have increasingly high profiles at, for example, international summits or in trade negotiations, this has begun to become unremarkable. National media coverage is frequently taken up with issues relating to the EU, often expressing neither opposition or support, but simply reporting relevant information. To some extent, news about the EU has become 'home' news (cf. Billig, 1982: 175). In addition, EU-level media sources, such as the *European Voice*, an Economist publication, have begun to reinforce a sense of the existence of the EU as an entity that needs significant political coverage. Similarly, many national daily newspapers now employ a Europe correspondent. This, in turn, it can be argued, may facilitate the emergence of the 'complementarity of communication habits' (Deutsch, [1953]1966: 101). Meanwhile, the daily presence of 'unwaved flags' constantly reinforces the dual membership of citizens who belong to any given member state of the EU.[9] As individuals stop noticing the presence of the EU flag among other national flags, find their EU driving licences and passports unremarkable, stop noticing signs indicating the support of EU funding, stop thinking about going through the EU nationals' channel at customs, or say in relation to, for example, working hours, 'isn't there an EU ruling on that?', then it could be argued that membership of the EU has increasingly become the norm. In Billig's terms then, the EU has become *enhabited* in so far as individuals 'forget to remember' that the current situation is not how things always were.

Clearly, anecdotal evidence is not enough. A detailed mapping exercise is required. Billig (1982: 175), for example, suggests: 'Taxonomies of flaggings could be constructed to list the different genres and their customary rhetorical strategies; and the extent of flaggings in different domains, and in different nations, could be calculated. Above all, the lives of citizens in established nations need to be profiled, in order to document the nature and number of flaggings which the average person might encounter in the course of a typical day'. This is very much in tune with Deutsch's suggested mapping of communication patterns and how they are experienced by individuals. Crucially, Deutsch also stressed the importance of mapping the extent to which secondary symbols, carrying implicit messages about nationhood, have become attached to these daily events and patterns of communication. 'How wide is the range of interests and the volume of communications and experiences among the members of a people? To what share of these have national symbols become attached? How often are those national symbols then found in circulation? What persons, things and institutions are devoted to producing these secondary symbols, and *how important is that portion of the primary communications to which they have become attached*?' (Deutsch, [1953]1966: 172–3).

The elusive project: waiting for push to become shove

Of course it is difficult to assess whether or not Deutsch's view of the contingent nature of national identity is accurate until a serious conflict emerges. However, as has been argued above, it is certainly possible to establish indicators that would help to establish how individuals might react should the 'double process of habit-breaking', which Deutsch *et al.* (1957: 85) saw as a facilitating integration, take place within a member state of the EU. Thus, should 'the emergence of a distinctive way of life' take place, with a concomitant change in previous habits of behaviour, and be faced with an external challenge, detailed attitudinal studies should provide some indication of how individuals would respond. However, even if so stark a situation were never to occur in the EU, the insights of Deutsch *et al.* and the wider theories of nationalism and national identity are still of central importance to the study of the EU.

First, it appears that some degree of banal Europeanism has already begun to emerge within the EU. Thus, a key question for students of the EU follows: how has this been allowed to happen by existing elites at the national level? Deutsch ([1953]1966: 104) argued that 'whatever the instruments of power, they are used to strengthen and elaborate those social channels of communication, the preferences of behaviour, the political (and sometimes economic) alignments which, all together make up the social fabric of nationality'. Similarly, examining the effectiveness of social movements at the national level, Banaszak (1996: 35) has argued that 'one value common to most status quo philosophies is the positive worth placed on the use of existing channels when participating in politics and the condemnation given to attempts to challenge status quo institutions'. As regards the competition with 'hot' nationalisms, there seems little contest. Within the EU, being Scottish, English, French, German or Greek takes preference over being European. However, this does not mean that banal Europeanism has not become embedded. Hence how this latter varient is, or is not, transmitted among the European people(s), and the role that societal actors play in European integration, may have long-term implications for national elites and for the processes of European integration which have not yet been fully realized.

Second, there is little doubt that in many respects the EU already serves, for its member states, the same function which national states have been said to perform for their people: 'In a competitive economy or culture, nationality is an implied claim to privilege. It emphasizes group preference and group peculiarities, and so tends to keep out all outside competitors. It promises opportunity, for it promises to eliminate or lessen linguistic, racial, class or caste barriers to the social rise of individuals within it. And it promises security, for it promises to reduce the probability of outside competition for all sorts of opportunities, from business deals to marriages and jobs' (Deutsch,[1953]1966: 102). Perhaps nowhere is this clearer than in discussions over the enlargement of the EU to central and eastern Europe. The work of Deutsch and the many students of nationalism and national identity may also provide valuable insights into the process of integration beyond western Europe.

Conclusion: a case of banal Europeanism?

Haas (1970: 607) wrote of Deutsch's 1954 work on regional integration: 'Deutsch raised all the major questions and introduced many of the concepts that still preoccupy and guide the research effort'. In this chapter it has been argued that the insights developed by Deutsch, and more generally by scholars of nationalism and national identity, have been under utilized in contemporary studies of the EU. While, at first glance, there is little evidence of 'hot' Europeanism, many unwaved flags exist as daily reminders of the presence of the EU as a 'homeland' within which member states are nestled and the implications of this need to be explored. The extent to which a sense of belonging to the EU could be said to have become *enhabited* within the daily practices of EU citizens, or the extent to which a sense of *banal Europeanism* can be said to exist, may be a crucial element in the study of European integration. Moreover, it has been argued that closer attention must be paid to the societal aspect of European integration and to the implications for the process of European integration of the various 'imaginings' of the Union held by the various European people(s).

To pursue the research agenda that would confirm this, considerable empirical data are required. There is a need for a detailed mapping of indicators, of unwaved flags and their significance and of secondary symbols, for example. Similarly, large scale, theoretically informed attitudinal surveys, conducted on an EU-wide basis, are required. Such detailed empirical data would provide a starting point for more nuanced in-depth research, which could seek to establish the mechanisms through which Europeanism, hot or banal, is (or fails to be) transmitted. In short, scholars need not become preoccupied with the question of whether or not the EU is, or will ever be, a national state in order to utilize the insights and approaches developed by students of nationalism and national identity. Perhaps now is the moment to develop a more nuanced political sociology of the European Union which acknowledges that the EU is more than simply a system of governance which can be viewed in isolation from its broader societal dimension.

Notes

1. Many thanks to James Mitchell for his conversations and advice throughout the drafting of this chapter. It draws on work for a project on The Europeanization of State Society Relation for the ESRC 'One Europe or Several?' Programme, award number L213252023.
2. Of course, Mitrany ([1943]1966: 46) specifically opposed the creation of a territorially based institution in Europe arguing that 'the problems which now divide the national states would almost all crop up again in any territorial realignment; their dimensions would be different, but not their evil nature'.
3. Indeed, further they state that 'There is substantial room for supranational governance without an ultimate shift in identification' (Sandholtz and Stone Sweet, 1998: 5). This point Haas would undoubtedly agree with as he specifically argued that any shift in loyalties, in response to the activities of the new centre, need not be absolute or permanent: 'multiple loyalties' may continue to exist (Haas, 1958: 15).
4. But see Mitchell and McAleavey (2002)
5. There is, however, a powerful argument from scholars of nationalism that states generally precede nations (Keating, 1988), that national states frequently emerge from multiple centres (Breuilly, 1982) and that nationalism does not simply emerge but is actively created: 'It is nationalism which engerders nations, and not the other way round' Gellner (1983: 55)
6. Unification nationalism, involving the 'unification of a number of nominally sovereign states' (Breuilly, 1982: 65–89) (as occurred, for example, in Germany and Italy), is particularly appropriate as a model for examining the EU. Although these studies of states and nations refer to an earlier, predemocratic era, there is still much to learn from students of these phenomena.
7. Similarly, Haas' focus on shifting loyalties is often misconstrued. For Haas (1958: 15–16), it was more likely to be the convergence of a very disparate set of interests which would drive the process of integration and result in the establishment of a new political community, than any mass conversion to the doctrine of 'Europeanism'. Ultimately, a self-interested shift in loyalty, or in the focus of political activities, by the political elite would, he argued, increase the dynamic towards the development of the new political community, whether it resulted from positive or from negative long-term expectations of the integration process (Haas, 1958: 297).
8. It should be noted noted that any sense of Europeanness would have been expected to develop only over a period of several generations through 'a historical process of social learning in which individuals, usually over several generations, learn to become a people' (Deutsch, [1953]1966: 174). In any case, lack of a sense of Europeanness is not in any sense unique to the EU. Indeed, Weber (1977: 486) has argued that the transformation of 'peasants into Frenchmen' emerged only through the expansion of universal education, military service and improved communications.
9. Even the very term member state could be viewed as an unwaved flag – unremarkable, but a constant reminder of membership/belonging to the EU.

References

Anderson, B. ([1983]1991) *Imagined Communities* (London: Verso).
Armstrong, K. and Bulmer, S. (1998) *The Governance of the Single European Market* (Manchester: Manchester University Press).
Banaszak, L. (1996) *Why Movements Succeed or Fail* (Princeton, NJ: Princeton University Press).
Billig, M. (1995) *Banal Nationalism* (London: Sage).
Breuilly, J. (1982) *Nationalism and the State* (Manchester: Manchester University Press).
Christiansen, T., Jørgensen, K. and Wiener, A. (1999) (eds) 'The Social Construction of Europe', special issue, *Journal of European Public Policy*, 6 (4).
Cole, A. and Drake, H. (2000) 'The Europeanization of the French Polity: Continuity, Change and Adaption', *Journal of European Public Policy*, 7 (1), pp. 22–43.
Deutsch, K. ([1953]1966) *Nationalism and Social Communication* (Cambridge MA: MIT Press).
Deutsch, K. (1953) 'The Growth of Nations: Some Recurrent Patterns of Political and Social Integration', *World Politics*, 5 (1), pp. 5–62.
Deutsch, K. (1954) *Political Community at the International Level: Problems of Definition and Management* (Garden City: Doubleday & Co).
Deutsch, K. et al. (1957) *Political Community and the North Atlantic Area* (Greenwood: New York).
Duchêne, F. (1994) *Jean Monnet: The First Statesman of Interdependence* (London: W. W. Norton & Co.).
Edelman, M. ([1967]1985) *The Symbolic Uses of Politics* (New York: Greenwood).
Gellner, E. (1983) *Nations and Nationalism* (Oxford: Blackwell).
Haas, E. (1958) *The Uniting of Europe: Political, Social and Economic Forces, 1950–1957* (Stanford: Stanford University Press).
Haas, E. (1970) 'The Study of Regional Integration: Reflections on the Joys and Agonies of Pre-theorising', *International Organisation*, 24 (4), pp. 607–46.
Keating, M. (1988) *State and Regional Nationalism. Territorial Politics and the European State* (London: Harvester-Wheatsheaf).
Lavdas, K. (1997) *The Europeanisation of Greece* (London: Macmillan – now Palgrave).
Mazey, S. (1998) 'The European Union and Women's Rights: From Europeanization of National Agendas to the Nationalization of a European Agenda', *Journal of European Public Policy*, 5 (1), pp. 131–52.
Mény, Y., Muller, P. and Quermonne, J. L. (1996) *Adjusting to Europe* (London: Routledge).
Mitchell, J. and McAleavy, P. (2002) *Regionalism and Regional Policy in the European Union* (London: Palgrave).
Mitrany, D. ([1943]1966) *A Working Peace System* (Chicago: Quadrangle).
Pierson, Paul, (1996) 'The Path to European Integration: a Historical Institutionalist Analysis, *Comparative Political Studies*, 29 (2), pp. 123–63.
Renan, E. (1990) 'What is a Nation?' in Bhabha, H. K. (ed.), *Nation and Narration)* (London: Routledge).

Rometsch, D. and Wessels, W. (1996) (eds) *The European Union and Member States: Towards Institutional Fusion* (Manchester: Manchester University Press).

Sandholtz, W. and Stone Sweet, A. (1998) *European Integration and Supranational Governance* (Oxford: Oxford University Press).

Sbragia, A. (1992) 'Thinking About the European Future: Uses of Comparison', *Euro-Politics* (Washington: Brookings Institute), pp. 257–91.

Weber, E. (1977) *Peasants into Frenchmen: The Modernisation of Rural France* (London: Chatto & Windus).

12
European Identity and National Identity in Central and Eastern Europe

Judy Batt[1]

Identity in the politics of democratic transformation

The politics of identity has been a central feature of the transformation of post-communist states in central and eastern Europe. The meaning of the revolutions of 1989 was readily understood in this region as the culmination of two centuries of struggle for 'national self-determination' against imperial rule in various guises – the Habsburg, Ottoman, Prussian and Tsarist Russian empires, then the Nazi 'Third Reich' and Soviet 'socialist internationalism'. At the same time, there re-emerged the characteristic tendency of previous struggles for 'national self-determination' to elide the idea of 'freedom', as a set of political rights for individuals, defended and promoted by a state accountable to the people, with the right of the people as a collective entity – a nation – to express their particular ethnic identity as a homogenous cultural community in possession of a state of 'its own'. While national identities in western Europe are by no means devoid of an ethnic component, conditions in central and eastern Europe have reproduced the tendency to emphasize pre-political criteria of 'belonging' as the primary condition for the enjoyment of rights. This is what the Hungarian historian Istvan Bibo (1946) identified as a certain 'political hysteria':

> This means that nations living in this region lacked what was naturally, clearly precisely and concretely present in the everyday life and community consciousness of nations in western Europe: A *reality in their own national and state framework*, a capital city, a *harmony* between economy and politics, a unified social *elite* and so forth. In eastern Europe a national framework was something that

had to be *created, repaired, fought for, and constantly protected*, not only against the power factors existing in the dynastic state, but also from the *indifference exhibited by a certain proportion of the country's own inhabitants*, as well as from the wavering state of national consciousness.

This situation contributed to the development of a trait most characteristic of the unbalanced central and east European political attitude: *an existential fear for one's community*. Each nation in the region has been living under the (sometimes more or less civilized, at other times intolerably oppressive) pressure of foreign and rootless state powers. Wars about historical and ethnic borders soon accustomed peoples to *being at each other's throats* as well, and given a chance they used on each other the methods they learned from the emperors, czars and sultans. They have all come to learn what it means to see their histories, hallowed places endangered, lost or in the hands of hostile foreign powers, and to see all or some of their people dominated or oppressed by foreigners. In this region, it is not necessary to exterminate or forcibly deport a nation's inhabitants in order to evoke a sense of danger; it is enough to forcefully and violently *cast doubts upon its very existence* (Bibo, 1946: 38–40).

The historical propensity to resort to the politics of identity is reawakened in the contemporary period by the extraordinary demands of reconstituting the state out of the post-communist debris. Questions of identity have been propelled to the fore by the very nature of 'democratic transition' itself. Democratic self-government presupposes the existence of a consensual community with shared understandings not only of *what* the state is for and *how* it is to function, but also of *whom* the state is for, who belongs to the community to which it is to be held accountable. The rules of democracy do not by themselves provide answers to the questions of who belongs to the political community, nor where its territorial borders should be drawn. In this region where national identities have had to be painfully constructed and fought for, and territorial borders have been chronically insecure and frequently changing, democratization rapidly exposed the fact that the existence of political communities could not be taken for granted. All three multinational communist federal states (Czechoslovakia, Yugoslavia, and the Soviet Union) disintegrated between 1989 and 1992, leading to the formation of a set of new states based on the demand for 'national self-determination'. Throughout the post-communist region, the place of national and ethnic minorities within the political community, and the question of their rights as cultural communities, continue to be a matter of contestation.

In important respects it makes sense to approach all the states of post-communist Europe as *new* states, given the nature of their histories and the contemporary challenges they face (Hare, *et al.* 1999, ch 1). It is therefore not inappropriate to compare the dynamic of their politics with that of other new states formed in the 1950s and 1960s in post-colonial Asia and Africa. The work of Clifford Geertz, one of the leading political anthropologists working in the latter field, provides illuminating insights into the nature of the basic political challenge facing new states:

> It consists in defining, or trying to define, a collective subject to whom the actions of the state can be internally connected, in creating, or trying to create, an experiential 'we' from whose will the activities of government seem spontaneously to flow (1993: 240).

The process of collective political self-definition, Geertz argues, brings to the fore tensions and ambiguities that had been submerged in the struggle for national liberation against the colonial oppressor. 'The day after' national independence is achieved, a new set of questions moves on to the political agenda: what purposes the state is to serve, what its internal constitution is to be, and how it is to relate to the rest of the world. Answers to these questions rest on certain assumptions about the nature of the political community the state represents, and yet at this point it becomes clear that the unity of the 'people' in whose name independence was achieved can no longer be taken for granted. The search for answers reveals divergent understandings of the nature of the political community, fracturing the preceeding consensus on goals and values.

In Geertz's view, the basic dynamic of politics in new states can broadly be understood in terms of the interaction between two partly competing, partly complementary, and in any case 'intimately related' motives. The first motive is to promote and express the 'indigenous way of life': 'to look to local mores, established institutions, and the unities of common experience – to "tradition", "culture", "national character", or even "race" – for the roots of a new identity' (Geertz, 1993: 240). The second motive is to align with what he calls the 'spirit of the age': 'it is a demand for progress, for a rising standard of living, more effective political order, greater social justice, and beyond that of "playing a part in the larger arena of world politics", of "exercising influence among the nations" ' (Geertz, 1993: 258).

It is important to note that Geertz does not reduce the issue to an 'either/or' choice between expressing 'primordial' ethnic identity and developing a 'modern', rational and universalistic form of 'civic' political consciousness. On the contrary:

> The two motives are . . . most intimately related, because citizenship in a truly modern state has more and more become the most broadly negotiable claim to personal significance, and because what Mazzini called the demand to exist and have a name is to such a great extent fired by a humiliating sense of exclusion from the important centres of power in world society. But they are not the same thing. They stem from different sources and respond to different pressures. It is, in fact, the tension between them that is one of the central driving forces in the national evolution of the new states; as it is, at the same time, one of the greatest obstacles to such evolution (Geertz, 1993: 258).

Translated into the political idiom of present-day post-communist central and east Europe, the assertion of the 'indigenous way of life' is most evident in the agenda of ethnic nationalism, reviving the long tradition in the region which defines national identity primarily in terms of pre-political, cultural and linguistic markers. The goal of political mobilization is the ethnic nation's acquisition of a state of 'its own'. By contrast, in the contemporary central and east European context, aligning with the 'spirit of the age' implies adapting to the pressures of globalization, but above all, 'returning to Europe'. The latter concept is multifaceted: it operates at the psychological level of asserting the essentially 'European' character of the national identity; at the level of domestic politics, it means establishing the social, political and economic frameworks for a way of life similar to those enjoyed in western European countries; at the international level, it means acquiring the benefits associated with membership of the European Union (EU) and the North Atlantic Treaty Organization (NATO).

The importance of being 'European'

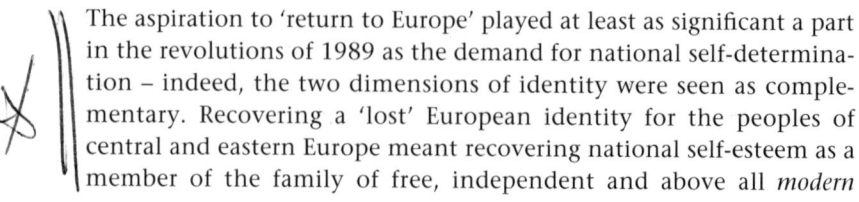

The aspiration to 'return to Europe' played at least as significant a part in the revolutions of 1989 as the demand for national self-determination – indeed, the two dimensions of identity were seen as complementary. Recovering a 'lost' European identity for the peoples of central and eastern Europe meant recovering national self-esteem as a member of the family of free, independent and above all *modern*

European states. Bringing the state into line with 'European norms' of democracy, the market economy, the rule of law and the protection of human and minority rights has become a prerequisite for admission to the EU and NATO, which most central and east European states have identified as their top priority in foreign policy, the basis for guaranteeing their future security and prosperity. The idea of 'returning to Europe' thus inextricably linked the internal and the external dimensions of change, and simultaneously expressed both psychological motives of identification with 'Europe' and more pragmatic expectations of security guarantees and economic benefits to be gained from membership. The potential tensions between the aspiration to national independence and the demands of joining an ever more tightly integrated Europe were readily passed over in a peripheral region anxious to escape from a history of external domination and internal instability. At the outset, the broad terms of the political and economic conditionality set by the EU and NATO seemed in line with what the people of the new democracies wanted for themselves as 'normal' Europeans.

The importance of the idea of 'Europe' to the intellectuals of central and eastern Europe is often hard to convey to west Europeans today, especially to the younger generations who did not live through World War II, and whose political imagination is far from fired with excitement by the 'real existing Europe' of the EU today. Its institutions are seen as remote from everyday life, staffed by arrogant technocrats and pampered, even corrupt elites, operating according to obscure, impossibly complex and bureaucratic procedures. The central Europeans' idealization of Europe in 1989, however, reflects not only their lack of contact with the Europe of the EU, but also their underlying sense of the precariousness of their geopolitical predicament and the fragility of their new political and economic institutions. In many respects, World War II only ended in this region in 1989, and the powerful political motives that underlay the original conception of the mission of the European Community – overcoming historic national rivalries and animosities and building a framework for enduring peace and prosperity – may now be more keenly appreciated in the central and eastern parts of the continent than in the West.

Western Europeans' weak attachment to the idea of Europe was first lamented by Milan Kundera (1984) in his seminal article on the 'Tragedy of Central Europe'. For Kundera, 'Europe' represents the paramount value of security in diversity for the variegated national cultures of the continent which together comprise a distinct civilization:

> Central Europe longed to be a condensed version of Europe itself in all its cultural variety, a small arch-European Europe, a reduced model of Europe made up of nations conceived according to one rule: the greatest variety within the smallest space (Kundera, 1984: 33)

Kundera's article nicely captures that peculiarly intense, characteristically central European commitment to the preservation of distinct cultural identities in the face of the ever-present threat of 'extinction' posed by an *'other'* civilization: the 'east', namely Russia: 'uniform, standardizing, centralizing, determined to transform every nation of its empire . . . into a single Russian people' (Kundera, 1984: 33). As he argues, for central Europeans, national identity is inseparable from European identity: 'The moment Hungary is no longer European – that is, no longer western – it is driven from its own destiny, beyond its own history: it loses the essence of its identity' (Kundera, 1984: 33). Being on the periphery, the small nations of central Europe are more acutely conscious of this danger than the larger, more secure nations of the West. For west Europeans, the threatening 'other' that propelled them towards cooperation with each other and integration was primarily their own past of mutual destruction. While the Cold War reinforced the incentive to integrate against the communist threat, much of the practical responsibility for averting this threat was left to the US-dominated NATO. The result, Kundera found, was complacency and lack of urgency in the commitment to common 'European' values and identity, and the dismaying tendency to 'forget' about half of itself – central Europe, the 'captured West' – by accepting the bipolar division of Europe. And yet it was here that 'European' values and identity were most deeply cherished and heroically defended against all odds.

A powerfully emotive moral argument emerges from Kundera's article. In defining the mission of 'central Europe' in terms of guarding and revitalizing the European idea against the Russian threat, he is also implicitly making a demand that the West recognize the debt it owes – a debt which would be called in after 1989. This notion was later reflected in the widespread expectation that, since the West had to some extent colluded in the division of Europe, it would therefore accept responsibility for picking up the pieces after the communist order collapsed. In Poland, where the idea of 'central Europe' was less enthusiastically embraced by the opposition intelligentsia than in the smaller countries of the former Habsburg territories, the sense of western indebtedness to the east was stronger and more explicit, and summed up in the understanding of 'Yalta' – the moment of betrayal of Poland. But this sense predates Yalta: it was already present in Polish literature of the nineteenth and turn of the twentieth centuries, from which emerges:

> . . . an image of Poland – the Martyr and Saviour of Nations, the country which suffered in order to purify and save Europe. Poland died (that is, lost political sovereignty) but would be reborn thanks to her spiritual and moral virtue. Her suffering would redeem other nations. (Mach, 1997: 36)

This pattern of discourse about Poland's relations with Europe led to a 'combination of the inferiority complex of a poor relative and the heroic image of a former protector, underestimated and forgotten by the rich and happy western Europeans who neglected the fact that Poles fought against communists for the values which were the essence of European identity' (Mach, 1997: 41).

The ambivalence of Polish intellectuals to the idea of 'central Europe' reflects not only the stronger conviction of Poland's historical and geopolitical importance to Europe, coupled with a more full-blooded romantic messianism, but also a lingering sense of Poland's other 'national mission' to the east, towards its neighbours which were once part of the Polish–Lithuanian Commonwealth, the 'Golden Age' in the Polish national myth. Thus the 'Europe' to which Poland would seek to return after 1989 was likely to have a different shape, not only from that envisaged by its western neighbours, but also from that of a committed 'central European' like Kundera. Citing the Czech Frantisek Palacky, who memorably proclaimed in 1848 that 'if Austria did not exist, we would have to invent it', Kundera suggests that the small nations of central Europe are existentially wedded to the idea of multinational federation. 'Returning to Europe', from this perspective, seems to imply 'reinventing Austria'.

Emerging tensions

The 1989 revolutions were a moment of truth for these notions of 'returning to Europe'. The slogan captured the mass popular imagination, which injected a new practical and substantive content into it. Nostalgic wistfulness and grandiose visions were overlaid by quite concrete expectations of rapidly acquiring the 'European way of life', in terms of welfare and consumer prosperity – expectations that were bound to be, at least in the medium term, disappointed. At the same time, the response of the west Europeans was sobering, if not dismaying. For central Europeans, it was self-evident that 'returning to Europe' meant rapidly becoming full members of the 'European club', in terms of joining every 'European' organization. Some proved more accessible than others: while Council of Europe membership was relatively quickly gained, the two key organizations, NATO and the EU, were much more resistant to the idea of enlargement. These organizations' efforts to persuade the central Europeans that membership was not necessary, either to guarantee their future prosperity and security, or to prove their 'European' identity and equal worth, were doomed to failure, and not only on account of the specific 'central European' mindset which made membership a self-evident necessity. They lacked credibility in themselves: the 'EFTA model' was not convincing when the EFTAns themselves were now seeking EU membership; neutrality was losing its meaning once bipolarity imploded; and anyway, central Europe was *not* like Norway or Switzerland.

However, as time has passed since 1989, and especially as the real implications of EU and NATO membership have had to be confronted, the relationship between the 'national' and the 'European' components of identity has become more problematic. The 'day after' the revolution, as Geertz predicted, euphoric unity gave way to contestation and uncertainty. This is, first, because of the ambivalent nature of nationalism, especially in its complex relationship with the 'European idea'; and, second, because the 'European idea' itself, ever elusive and subject to multiple contested interpretations, has entered a new phase of self-redefinition with the breakdown of the cold war division of Europe. These ambiguities offer scope for different groups to seize upon different interpretations of 'nation' and 'Europe' to justify their competing claims to the distribution of powers, rights and resources within the state, and to protest at the burdens thrust upon them by the goal of 'returning to Europe'.

The resurgence of nationalism in the new democracies often presented a collectivistic and authoritarian face, at odds with the idealized notion of a 'European' identity, centred on the values of toleration, respect for diversity and the rights of the individual, cherished by the central European intelligentsia. While some laid the blame for this 'un-European' phenomenon on the continuing manipulative influence of ex-communists seeking to cling on to power, Adam Michnik acknowledged it had deep roots in central European societies, and had become the main political cleavage structuring post-communist politics:

> The greatest threat to democracy today is no longer communism, either as a political movement or as an ideology. The threat grows instead from a combination of chauvinism, xenophobia, populism, and authoritarianism, all of them connected with the sense of frustration typical of great social upheavals . . . The most important conflict in Polish culture today is being fought between those who see Poland as part of Europe and those characterized by the Polish sociologist Jerzy Szacki as 'natiocentric' . . . these two approaches today divide the Polish intelligentsia; they cut across all political lines and can be found among adherents of the *ancien regime* as well as within Solidarity and the Catholic Church (Michnik, 1990: 7).

Democratization after 1989 undermined the moral hegemony of the central European dissident intelligentsia in the articulation of authentic collective identities with the advent of competition for the mass vote. Free elections exposed the tenuousness of the links between the intellectual elite and the people in whose name they had hitherto assumed the right to speak. Everywhere in the region, parties led by the heroes of the intelligentsia's struggle against communism were reduced to a minor role in the new parliaments. In the Polish case, the fragility of the intellectual–worker alliance that Solidarity had represented rapidly became clear in 1990 and 1991. As Michnik recognized, the power of the working class revolt against communism had been due to populism, appropriating the egalitarian discourse of communism and using it most effectively against the corrupt and discredited communist elite. But the consequences of this style of politics for the future democracy had to be faced:

> We also have to tell ourselves finally that the revolt against communism in Poland – and what a successful revolt – was the revolt of the crowd . . . The language of the crowd is the language of populist discourse. Today, it would seem that we are witnessing a reversion to this language of the crowd, in other words, to modes of conduct acquired during the period of resistance to communism; modes of conduct that used to be rational within the framework of a non-rational system because they offered the only means of delegitimizing the system. Today, these same modes of conduct are delegitimizing parliamentary democracy and opening the door to authoritarianism. We have reached democracy without the political culture appropriate to democratic order (Michnik, 1991: 181–2).

Michnik's response to this challenge was to reaffirm the 'civilizing mission' of the intelligentsia: 'it is our duty as inheritors of European culture to fight against those attitudes – in the name of all those values of Judaeo-Christian culture that were defended for centuries at the cost of great sacrifices' (Michnik, 1990: 7). If the intelligentsia saw the problem primarily in terms of a struggle for values and culture, for most central Europeans, the primary concern was the struggle for everyday survival in the throes of economic transformation. Most opinion polls show that everyday concerns such as incomes, the standard of living, employment prospects and law and order feature more prominently on central European citizens' list of priorities than issues of identity and culture, whether national or European.

But the struggle to be 'European' has been disillusioning for the intelligentsia too, especially in Poland, where the assumption of Poland's *right* to EU and NATO membership has been dealt blows, first by western prevarications and then by the conditions imposed. '[A]s heroes who have been protecting Europe for centuries, Poles believe that they warrant better treatment than they are actually receiving, that they deserve a certain reward for what they did and are doing' (Mach, 1997: 41). This shows up in acute resentment at perceived EU high-handedness, inflexibility, and double standards in accession negotiations; and at the damage done by the imposition of the Schengen regime to Poland's relations with its eastern neighbours – regarded as a matter of vital national strategic interest right across the political spectrum. The encounter with 'actually existing Europe' has been bruising for key groups of the elite, as well as for the mass (especially for impoverished Polish farmers), and the ground is prepared for the emergence of a sizeable 'Eurosceptic' movement. For the first time in October 1999, support for EU membership in Poland fell below 50 per cent.

In Czechoslovakia, the main challenge to the dissident intelligentsia's vision of the new order came from Slovak nationalism. The initial response of leading former Chartists like Vaclav Havel, Jiri Dienstbier and Petr Pithart was to fall back on the contrast between 'civic' and 'ethnic' nationalism, the former being 'modern', individualistic, open and tolerant, the latter being backward-looking, parochial, collectivistic and authoritarian. The 'return to Europe' clearly demanded the evolution of the 'civic' form of national identity, in line with the perceived 'norm' of western democracies and the imperatives of the age to multinational cooperation and supranational integration. The separatist implications of Slovak national self-assertion were seen as a challenge not only to the existence of Czechoslovakia as a federal state, but also to both nations' reintegration into European structures. As such, it threatened to undermine their claims to a 'European' identity.

This argument was bitterly resented by Slovaks, who saw in it the revival of the Czech habit of patronizing and denigrating Slovak identity. The idea of a common 'Czechoslovak' identity had always been more congenial to the numerically and culturally dominant Czechs than to the Slovaks. The Czechs themselves had recognized the futility of pursuing this idea some years ago, and, after the collapse of communism, were prepared to negotiate a reform of the federation. But the difficulties of reaching agreement on the reallocation of powers between the two national republics and the federation undermined confidence in the viability of coexistence in a common state: where agreement could not be reached on the *means* of coexistence, the credibility of both sides' professed commitment to the common *end* was undermined. In this context, mutual stereotypes were invoked to explain the problem: the Czechs mistrusted Slovak 'separatism', associated in their memory with Nazi occupation during World War II, at which time the Slovaks had for the first time acquired a state of their own. For Czechs, this state confirmed their worst suspicions of Slovak nationalism, being an authoritarian puppet-state dependent on Nazi support. Yet for most Slovaks, for all its shortcomings, the wartime republic had boosted their self-confidence as a nation capable of self-government.

The implicit charge of 'un-European' tendencies levelled against Slovak national assertiveness was countered by the Slovaks who reaffirmed their aspiration to 'return to Europe' – but on their own terms, with their 'own star on the European flag', occupying their own seat at the table of European nation-states, as the prominent Slovak Chartist and human rights lawyer, and briefly Prime Minister of Slovakia, Jan Carnogursky put it. After all, what was 'Europe' but a 'family' of sovereign nations, among which the Slovaks were merely claiming their rightful, equal place? It could convincingly be argued that the idea of a purely 'civic' political community of individuals, without reference to common culture and history, had much more to do with the American tradition than the European one. European integration had not led to – nor had it aimed at – the obliteration of nations, but provided a framework for their coexistence on equal terms. As such, it might prove a more satisfactory home for the Slovaks than Czechoslovakia had been, and it remained for the Czechs to demonstrate why a common Czechoslovak state was necessary for the Slovaks' 'return to Europe'.

This line of argument provoked the Czechs into a reappraisal of whether *they* needed Czechoslovakia either: the misty romantic notion of Czech–Slovak brotherhood having dissipated in the acrimonious constitutional wrangling, a more sober and calculating pragmatism came to the fore in the person of Vaclav Klaus. If the Czechs' original reasons for constructing Czechoslovakia after World War I had centred on the need for strategic reinforcement against the German threat – now neutralized in an integrated European Union – their current and future economic interests lay in detaching themselves from the burden of subsidizing the weaker Slovak economy, and pressing ahead with the radical economic transformation that the Slovaks were resisting. Thus for the Czechs too, the 'return to Europe' might most rapidly and effectively be accomplished as a separate nation.

The question of Slovakia's place in Europe remained, however, unresolved after independence, and was the source of much soul-searching *angst* on the part of Slovakia's democratic intellectuals. It became inextricably linked with the internal state-building process as the party system crystalized into two camps. The parties in the governing coalitions under Vladimir Meciar increasingly came to represent a certain style of politics: personalized, authoritarian rule exercised through leader-dominated parties organized on the basis of corrupt patron–client relationships, legitimated by a populist form of nationalism rooted in the assertion of ethnic identity. According to the political scientist Sona Szomolanyi, this was a deviation from the 'European standard' pattern of party politics which other central European countries were following. 'Standard' European-style parties, based on the familiar left–right spectrum (social democracy, liberalism, Christian democracy) were evident only in the opposition (Szomolanyi, 1995). The 1997 decisions of the EU and NATO not to include Slovakia in the 'first wave' of eastward enlargement tended to confirm this analysis on the practical level. Nevertheless, it embodies a peculiarly selective vision of 'Europe': far from departing from the 'European norm', Meciar's Movement for a Democratic Slovakia could be compared with Europe's less attractive 'post-modern' faces, Jorg Haider's Freedom Party and Silvio Berlusconi's *Forza Italia*.

In Hungary, intellectuals of that distinctive 'central European', cosmopolitan stamp have found it no easier to come to terms with the potent force of national identity in political life. In the pursuit of 'modernity' by means of prioritizing NATO and EU accession, the party formed by the intellectuals of the communist-era 'democratic opposition' found themselves joining forces with the former communists, rebranded as 'social democrats of the European type' in the Hungarian Socialist Party. The nationalist end of the political spectrum, however, has for the most part been equally infatuated with an idea of 'Europe' – a distinctive reading of Europe, of *nations*, but not of *nation-states*. Nationally minded Hungarians have a special difficulty with the idea of Hungary as a nation-state, because it does not encompass the whole Hungarian nation. They are thus peculiarly – for nationalists – attracted by the ideas of a 'Europe without borders' and a 'Europe of the regions'. These visions offer the prospect of transcending the division between Hungarians living in the 'motherland' and the Hungarian minorities 'beyond the borders', validate the Hungarian demand for the minority territorial autonomy, and suggestively hint at the impermanence of the Slovak, Romanian, Ukrainian and Serbian nation-states all round Hungary where the minorities live. To show the way, the Hungarian government in 1993 introduced one of Europe's most radical and far-reaching laws for the national and ethnic minorities living on its own territory, including the right to territorial self-governments. It has continued to press in European and international fora for wider recognition and acceptance of this as a model for the future. From the point of view of Hungary's neighbours, this looks like a wolf in sheep's clothing – old-fashioned revisionism deceptively dressed up in 'post-modern', impeccably 'European' garb. From the point of view of Hungary's largest ethnic minority, the Roma, the minorities law misses the point: their needs centre mainly on social inclusion, education and housing, rather than the (poorly funded) institutionalization of difference.

There is no doubt that the Hungarians have expended considerable effort and imagination in attempting to reconcile the demands of their national identity with those of 'returning to Europe', and in diverting deep-rooted revisionist instincts into less dangerous (and even potentially productive) channels. Nevertheless, a stable balance has not yet been struck. While Hungary's success in the race for EU accession has been a matter of obvious pride, it came at the price of preparing to implement Schengen-style border controls which undermine its commitment to free access for the minorities in neighbouring countries. While NATO membership was greeted as the culmination of Hungary's manifest destiny by most members of the political elite, Hungarian society had taken some persuading to approve it in a referendum. The rather fragile popular legitimacy of this aspect of 'returning to Europe' was dealt a bad blow when, within 12 days of joining NATO, Hungary found itself drawn in to supporting the aerial bombardment of Serbia, which included targets in Vojvodina, territory inhabited by the Hungarian minority. The nationalist assumption that a single, unified Hungarian national identity transcending Hungary's borders exists and must be at the centre of the Hungarian state's purposes thus faces new challenges.

Divergence and convergence

The idea of 'returning to Europe', first launched by central European intellectuals in the early 1980s, made an inextricable and mutually supportive linkage between national identity and European identity for the peoples of this region. It was a powerful, deeply resonating argument. But the real prospect of 'returning to Europe' has exposed its inherent tensions in the post-1989 context, and has provoked a fresh round of debate about national identities, how they relate to the new democratic institutions and to the emergent European polity.

The post-1989 trend towards diversity and the salience of national identity in political debate in central and eastern Europe coincided with the inauguration of a new phase of closer integration in western Europe, proclaimed in the Maastricht Treaty's commitments to monetary union, complemented by political union. Many commentators in the 1990s worried that this further confirmed the fundamental divergence of the historical paths of the two parts of the continent, making the central European aspiration to 'return to Europe' seem hopelessly quixotic. But ratification of Maastricht provoked fierce political debates in many EU member states. In the course of these it became clear that national identities and nation-statehood are still capable of evoking a deep popular response in west European politics. The relationship between the 'national' and the 'European' components of identity remains contentious even in some of the founder members of the Union. Moreover, the gulf that Maastricht exposed between a distant vision of 'Europe', promoted and managed by a narrow elite of cultural intellectuals, technocrats and politicians, and the real aspirations, concerns and fears of west European societies was paralleled in central Europe at the same time. Here governments and intellectuals began to face up to the task of embedding their visions of 'Europe' in the political culture and practices of post-communist societies. The much-bruited 'democratic deficit' of European institutions was discovered also to afflict the government of states across the continent.

Meanwhile, national identities both East and West are turning out to be more fluid and more contested than often assumed. National identity is by no means the dominant concern of most people in central and eastern Europe, where everyday material concerns regularly top the list of priority issues in public opinion polls. Attachment to the nation as the primary focus of loyalty is, somewhat surprisingly, found to be a minority sentiment: when asked to chose with which they identified most closely, only 31 per cent of those polled by the *New Democracies Barometer* placed their nation-state first. One might speculate that the intelligentsia constitute a disproportionate share of these. Nineteen per cent identified most closely with 'Europe', and 20 per cent combined their national identity with a sub-state regional or local identity. A rather striking 21 per cent identified only with the sub-state region or locality in which they lived (see Rose and Haerpfer, 1998a: 23). The perception of national minorities as a 'threat' diminished steadily throughout the 1990s, so that by 1998, only 25 per cent continued to see them in this way (see Rose and Haerpfer, 1998b: 41).

This suggests not divergence, but convergence between west and central Europe on terrain that is new and uncertain for both. New pressures are making themselves felt on national identities across the continent. Societies are increasingly open to cross-cultural contact as a result of international travel, labour mobility, and the globalization of mass communications. The effect has not been supranational cultural convergence so much as fragmentation, undermining the grip of state-promoted national cultural homogeneity from below. The appeal of the 'grand narrative' of nationalism seems to hold declining appeal in both parts of the continent. 'European' identity remains elusive, and yet the search to pin it down seems more urgent than ever as the EU confronts the challenge of enlargement: how an increasingly diverse range of national cultures can be managed without compromising the coherence of the Union, its capacity to sustain the momentum of integration, and its ability to meet its growing role at the centre of the new European order. While 'central European' idealism has taken a battering in the past decade, and the emergence of Eurosceptic movements seems inevitable, the underlying rationale of the 'central European' vision of 'Europe' as their best hope for overcoming their unhappy histories of marginalization and oppression by dominant Great Powers, socio-economic stagnation, recurrent national tensions and political instability has not lost its forcefulness (Amato and Batt, 1999). To that extent, the central Europeans can be expected to make a major contribution to the debate, by revitalizing the sense of purpose of European institutions that are ripe for radical reform, and still groping their way towards a redefinition of their roles in the new European order.

Note

1. Thanks to Martin Kovats, Brigid Fowler and Kataryna Wolczuk for helpful comments on the draft of this chapter. It draws on work for a project on ' "Fuzzy Statehood" and European Integration in Central and Eastern Europe' for the ESRC 'One Europe or Several?' Programme, award number L213252001.

References

Amato, G. and Batt, J. (1999) *The Long-Term Implications of EU Enlargement: The Nature of the New Border* (Florence: Robert Schumann Centre, European University Institute/Forward Studies Unit, European Commission).

Bibo, I. (1946) 'The Distress of the East European Small States', in Nagy, K. (ed.), *Democracy, Revolution and Self-Determination: Selected Writings* (Boulder: Social Science Monographs, 1991), pp. 13–87.

Hare, P., Batt, J., and Estrin, S. (eds) (1999) *Reconstituting the Market: The Political Economy of Microeconomic Transformation* (Amsterdam: Harwood Academic).

Geertz, C. (1993) *The Interpretation of Cultures* (London: Fontana Press).

Kundera, M. (1984) 'The Tragedy of Central Europe', *New York Review of Books*, 26 April, pp. 33–8.

Mach, Z., (1997) 'Heritage, Dream and Anxiety: The European Identity of Poles' in Mach and Niedzwiedzki (eds) *European Enlargement and Identity* (Krakow: Universitas).

Michnik, A. (1990) 'The Two Faces of Europe', *New York Review of Books*, 19 July, 7.

Michnik, A. (1991) 'Three Kinds of Fundamentalism', trans in Michnik, A., *Letters from Freedom* (Berkeley, Los Angeles, and London: University of California Press, 1998), pp. 178–83.

Rose, R. and Haerpfer, C. (1998a) *New Democracies Barometer V: A 12-Nation Survey* (Glasgow: Centre for the Study of Public Policy, University of Strathclyde).

Rose, R. and Haerpfer, C. (1998b) *Trends in Democracies and Markets: New Democracies Barometer 1991–1998* (Glasgow: Centre for the Study of Public Policy, University of Strathclyde).

Szomolanyi, S. (1995) 'Does Slovakia Deviate from the Central European Variant of Transition?', in Szomolanyi, S. and Meseznikov, G. (eds), *Slovakia: Parliamentary Elections 1994* (Bratislava: Slovak Political Science Association/Friedrich Ebert Foundation), pp. 8–39.

13
EU Citizenship and Pan-Europeanism
Elizabeth Meehan[1]

Introduction

In her invitation to the contributors to this book, Helen Wallace (1999) suggested that we might explore the themes of integration outlined in her Stein Rokkan memorial lecture of 1998. In that lecture, she suggested that, while there could be no definitive claim about where the eastern boundary of Europe lay, pan-Europe is what we have with the blurring of the east–west distinction following the end of the cold war. Thus, 'pan-Europeanism' in the title of this chapter refers to the spatial arena, and differences within that space, within which EU citizenship is, or after enlargement may be, practised.

The themes of integration explored in Helen Wallace's lecture include not only east–west issues but also different outlooks among west European states towards the functional, territorial and affiliational purposes of the 'deep' integration, of the European Union (EU). The primary aim of this chapter is to explore the affiliational purpose of 'deep' integration but it should also be noted that questions about EU citizenship 'spill-over' into its other two purposes. Indeed, the question of citizenship could be a key area for exploring her two general questions. These are: whether the 'deep' integration model is sustainable in the West; and whether central and eastern Europe can link into the three categories of purpose sufficiently to make 'deep' integration in pan-Europe feasible. It is not the intention of this chapter to answer these questions, but rather to indicate areas where further research, such as that within the 'One Europe or Several?' programme, might begin to provide answers.

In its Marshallian conception, citizenship is not only about formal political rights but also about material well-being and 'belonging', both of which enhance peoples' ability to use their rights and to participate in politics. Thus the first two parts of this chapter explore features relating to well-being and 'belonging'. Here, the question is raised as to whether the existence of economic and cultural differences, within western Europe and between East and West, rule out a sufficiently common basis for a 'deep' sense of pan-European citizenship. The chapter then indicates some policy questions arising from differences within the West and between East and West. Such differences, compounded by diverse political traditions and national identities, are often taken to imply that a 'deep' sense of European citizenship could never emerge. However, there is an argument that supranational citizenship is, in principle, more capable than national citizenship of being inclusive. In conclusion, the chapter considers whether this might be achievable in practice in an enlarged EU.

Differences in the material bases for participation

Socio-economic inequalities are irrelevant to a libertarian conception of citizenship; indeed, compensating for them would be detrimental to the rights of other citizens. This view is strongest in the United States of America (USA), though there are traces of it in the United Kingdom (UK), not only as a result of the advent of Thatcherism, but also deriving from a traditional preference for negative liberties over positive rights. Nevertheless, there has been a social and Christian democratic consensus in western Europe, both north and south and including the UK, that economic and social progress are linked. Its social and Christian roots may differ, as do British and continental theorizing about industrial citizenship (Streeck, 1997: 1–24), but the practical implications for society and state in all west European traditions are similar – workers' rights and state intervention to promote social cohesion. In this respect, the prospects for a common material basis for European social citizenship may be fragile, though such a judgement would have to be tempered by the coexistence of different assessments of cohesion in the West and rapid changes that are taking place in the East.

Economic indicators

Dunford and Hudson (1996) summarize economic and cultural differences in EU states and regions and among its neighbours, some of which are potential member states. Based on 1991 figures for GDP *per capita*, their report shows a strong correlation between wealth and EU membership and, discounting Norway and Switzerland, relative poverty among prospective or possible members. Among EU members, there were also significant internal differences.

In the EU, they suggest (1996: 5–12), there was a 'core of advanced city regions and major international cities most of which lie along a vital axis that extends from Greater London through the Rhinelands to Northern Italy with its centre of gravity in the western half of Germany'. The core was pulling southeast to Stuttgart, Munich, Zurich, Milan, Turin and Bologna because of faster growth there than in the major cities of the north-west, such as London and Paris. There was also a 'cluster of stronger economies' in southern Germany, Switzerland, and Northern Italy and in the 'global cities of London and Paris', with high *per capita* GDP relative to other regions of the continent and regions within those particular countries (Dunford and Hudson, 1996: 19). Conversely, more than 20 per cent of regions in EU countries fell below 75 per cent of the average *per capita* GDP.

More recent work, based on later GDP data, reinforces these findings of disparities among regions within member states and across the EU and demonstrates the complexity of inter-regional and inter-state differences. Dunford and Smith (1998: 8, 11, 12) report a renewed increase since the 1970s in disparities across the EU in regional development and income inequalities. Different member states are developing along different trajectories internally and in comparison with each other; only the Netherlands and Greece escape the trend of increased internal differentiation (Dunford and Smith, 1998: 52). Against this, Tsoukalis (1998: 19) suggests that the impact of the structural funds is 'mildly encouraging' in that, since the late 1980s, there are some signs of inter-regional convergence within the EU.

As regards East–West differences, Dunford and Hudson (1996: 7–10) identified a 'sharp development divide' between current and prospective EU members, although Rosati draws attention to some important changes: Poland (the first to regain its pre-transition GDP), the Czech Republic, Slovenia, and Hungary have 'stabilize[d] their economies . . . and embarked on a steady growth path' – at faster rates than the EU average (Rosati, 1998: 5–6). Moreover, other indices, such as Personal Purchasing Standards and the UN's Human Development Index [HDI], also suggest a narrowing gap between some of the applicant countries and the poorest EU states. For more detail see Chapter 7.

Education

Economic differences within and between countries are accompanied by differential access to education. Though there is little difference among EU member states or between them and prospective members, in levels of adult literacy and only slightly more in terms of school enrolment,[2] there are differences within the EU over access to further education and training. For example, in the late 1980s less than 40 per cent of young people in Portugal were in apprenticeships, training or non-university education and more than 85 per cent in Germany, the Netherlands and Denmark. In the UK and countries where 'a large number of regions are classified as lagging (Portugal, Greece, Ireland, Italy and Spain) the maximum participation rate was 60 per cent (Dunford and Hudson, 1996: 28).

Employment

Although social rights are central to a Marshallian conception of citizenship, there remains a sense that poor citizens are second-class citizens (Lister, 1990). Leonard 1998: 58) reminds us that 'Europe remains the only area of the world where even the unemployed can maintain a decent standard of living'. Nonetheless, if unemployment *can* be taken as an indicator of poverty, not only in terms of income, but also in the sense of access to those facilities and networks which form the basis of cooperative action (Women and Citizenship Research Group, 1995), the foundations of European citizenship may be fragile. For example, in Southern Italy and Spain there are areas where, in the mid 1990s, unemployment was in excess of 20 per cent.[3] This compared with less than 5 per cent in southern Germany, Luxembourg, parts of northern Italy and Portugal. In many parts of the EU, there is a problem of youth unemployment, more sharply experienced in some places than others. In the UK – even with its relatively stronger anti-discrimination legislation – unemployment falls disproportionately on members of ethnic minority communities, who also experience poor health, a strong sense of alienation from the educational system and discrimination in the criminal justice system (Meehan, 1999).

Implications of the socio-economic indicators of unequal citizenship

Rosati's (1998) purpose is to demonstrate that there is a strategic interest for the EU in assisting, not only those states in central and eastern Europe closer to membership, but also the others. How far this is achievable is open to question. Begg (1998: 11–12) suggests that the ability of the EU to extend the structural funds after enlargement, will be hindered by the persistence of serious disparities within and between the existing member states of the EU. These disparities may already limit the sense of solidarity within the current EU; yet to divert assistance from its poor regions to new member states would test the basis for East–West solidarity. Dunford and Hudson (1996: 27–8) link differences within and between current member states to the weakening of national policies of territorial equalization and the erosion of welfare states. This, they suggest, is intensifying social and spatial segregation and polarizing differences in lifestyles within and between cities and regions. EU funding to beneficiary regions affects interpersonal income inequalities only indirectly. EU member governments remain unwilling to tackle them through the 'Europeanization' of social protection (Begg, 1998: 5; Tsoukalis, 1998: 18, 29).

Closa (1996: 8–9), arguing from theories of citizenship, rather than socio-economic geography, identifies similar problems. He suggests that the processes of integration, though motivated by the idea that prosperity depends on collaboration and EU-wide cohesion, make it more difficult for states to tackle domestic inequalities unilaterally. The erosion of the welfare state at the national level coexists with obstacles to its recreation at the EU level. This is not only because the EU lacks the relevant policy powers, but also because of differences in national cultures and the weakness of transnational common identity. Closa (1996: 10) argues that, as a result, the EU has 'become an additional arena for defending privileged *national* forms of citizenship' (his emphasis).

Cultural differences – language and politics

Cultural differences remain a strong feature in Europe, both across and within states. Linguistic heterogeneity, as well as political variety, has implications for communication and cooperative development.

Language and social or cultural commonality

Within many European countries, both of EU members and potential members, more than one indigenous language is spoken. This can give rise to political tension in some EU member states: for example, Belgium, Finland, Denmark, Spain, Austria and, to some extent, Ireland and the UK (Northern Ireland and Wales). Many of the candidate countries have linguistic variety; for example, Hungary, Romania, Cyprus, Estonia, Latvia, Czech Republic, Slovakia and Slovenia. Countries with colonial histories have to accommodate non-European languages as a consequence of immigration. Linguistic heterogeneity persists despite the efforts of nation-building and modernization both to suppress indigenous minority languages and to make migrants assimilate. Knudsen (1995) argues that governments should accept that such attempts to suppress do not work and can be counter-productive.

A symbol of resistance to attempted suppression can be seen in (post-independence) Ireland. Articles 8.1 and 8.2 of the Constitution define 'Irish as the national language' and, therefore, 'the first official language', though it is now spoken by a minority of the population; 'the English language', now spoken by the majority, 'is recognized as a second language'. The modern conception of a more inclusive citizenship practice entails recognition of the value of diversity. This implies it is part of peoples' rights to be able to use, and be educated in, a minority language, as well as that of the majority. There are public policies for this purpose in, for example, Austria, Italy and Slovenia. Some policy-makers expect the linguistic rights of Italian speakers in Slovenia and Slovenian speakers in Italy – for example, in Trieste – to be facilitated when Slovenia joins Italy as an EU member.

The multiplicity of languages is often seen as an important barrier to the sense of commonality, required for European social citizenship. It might be thought that recognizing the legitimacy of multi-lingualism within states would compound the problem of trans-national empathy and commonality. Knudsen (1995), however, contests this by observing that people find their first second language the most difficult to learn, but that, having done so, it is easier for them to learn yet another.

However, it is clear that few Europeans (and not only the British!) have taken steps to speak the language of their neighbouring countries. Though, as noted, some states have policies of bilingualism which mean that minorities in border regions can speak the languages of both countries, a recent survey suggests that only about half of all EU citizens can speak another language well enough to hold a conversation in it (Leonard, 1998: 53). Young people are slightly less monolingual than the population as a whole. Even so, lack of confidence in a second language inhibits young people's mobility, at a time when an increasing number of firms look for such a skill among their employees. That only half the people of Europe can hold a conversation in the language of a neighbour may skew the benefits of a common labour market more towards the well-educated than to unskilled workers with poor linguistic abilities. It is hard to imagine a common democratic public space in which all voices can be heard without vast expenditure on multiple translation services by civil society organizations and political institutions. To achieve this for oral communications is one challenge, but an even greater one for written language, which is more difficult to master (Knudsen, 1995: 50).

However, lack of fluency in other languages need not rule out senses of commonality among people who see themselves as rooted in specific identities. Howe (1995: 27–46), for example, suggests that a common language is not the only source of empathy among peoples. Indeed, half of EU citizens have, or expect to have, a European component in their sense of identity (in addition to their nationality). They feel European in general without positively identifying with the EU. Moreover, this double identification is strongest among Poles and Czechs whose states are not yet members of the EU (Leonard, 1998: 19–20).[4] It also seems that most people may be tolerant of diversity – especially young people, only three per cent of whom 'feel uneasy with people from another nationality, culture or religion' and 5 per cent 'uneasy with people of different races'. Holiday travel, student exchanges and intermingling arising from migration appear to have increased peoples' interest in trying out each other's food, listening to each other's music, enjoying the skills of each other's footballers and so forth.

But, as with language, the growth of transnational contact may also be socially divisive. There is some evidence of class bias, hinted at above, in trans-European solidarity. Business and professional classes across Europe are more likely than people in other social categories to support the EU and to believe their countries to have benefited from membership (Leonard, 1998: 25–8). Indeed, 'ordinary people' may attribute their economic insecurity to the EU. Reactions to increased asylum-seeking are stark reminders of how easily pleasure in diversity can give way to xenophobia when people who are 'different' can be made scapegoats for the kinds of material inequalities discussed above. Solidarity, even among the better-off, may be strained by EU enlargement. The growing 'restlessness' in current EU richer states about resource transfers to the poorer ones is accompanied by only 'lukewarm support for enlargement – partly because of higher costs and fears of losing regional aid' (Leonard, 1998: 57).

Political culture, institutions and civil society

Differences in culture in its political sense also exist across and within countries, both of which are relevant to the creation of democratic European citizenship. It is not a simple question of whether member states favour '*l'Europe des patries*' or 'ever closer union' at the level of 'high politics'. Nor is there a clear 'north–south divide' in attitudes to European integration. In general, two 'northern' states, the UK and

France sometimes seem to be similar in preferring intergovernmental approaches, compared to other founding states and the 'south'. At the time of the recent enlargement to take in Austria, Finland and Sweden, there were concerns from some southern member states that 'the centre of gravity' of European ideas and policies would take a sceptical northern turn.

However, as regards the various aspects of citizenship, the range of opinion does not coincide with any clear geographical generalization. With respect to freedom of movement of persons, Denmark was on its own in insisting that such matters must remain a matter for national decision-making. Its neighbours, along with the 'core' and 'southern' states accepted in the Treaty of Amsterdam of 1997 the 'communitarization' of the Schengen agreements. The UK placed itself between them and Denmark and other EU members by accepting the inclusion of Schengen in the Treaty on condition that it could be exempt (a policy that Ireland chose to follow for different reasons). Though there is no disagreement that workers' and social rights may have some place on the European agenda, different understandings of industrial citizenship have impeded agreement on the appropriate scope of common legislation. Primarily, this has arisen not from a 'north–south divide', but as a result of a conflict of ideas between the UK and Germany (Meehan, 2000).

Another factor stems from the different constitutional understandings of the proper relationship between the centres of member states and their component parts, which can affect the capacities of sub-state regions to cooperate with other regions in trans-state alliances and with the central institutions of the EU. It is often said that regions in centralized states are at a disadvantage because they do not have the powers, administrative infrastructures and economic freedom to benefit from EU regional initiatives compared to countries where regions are constitutionally recognized. Indeed, having emerged from highly centralized state structures, the prospective members are said to be at a disadvantage in their limited 'institutional capacity to deliver regional development' via EU structural funds (Begg, 1998: 18). But, although there is a broad correlation between vigorous regional political structures and a capacity to succeed in terms of economic development, Dunford and Hudson (1996: chapters 5–6) show that this does not always work. They suggest, for example, that the relative independence of Saarland has not contributed notably to its success as a European region and that, in contrast, Abruzzo's achievements owe less to its constitutional status than to the way its political leaders work together to manage relations with Rome. In the component parts of the UK, centralization *has* been seen as an impediment to the achievement of regional interests through European channels. Northern Irish leaders, otherwise divided by sectarianism, work together, as in Abruzzo (although not through London), to place Northern Irish interests more to the forefront in the EU. In Scotland, members of the new Parliament are determined to have direct relations with EU institutions, as well as operating through those of the UK.

Other features of civil society differ in ways which may also affect the ability of citizens to influence European debates and, in turn, provoke different experiences of the impact of EU legislation. The German experience of co-determination at the workplace has been a manifestation of the shared idea of trade unions and government that social partnership was critical to economic prosperity. Their agreement that the national interest lay in the EU produced a powerful voice for the 'Europeanization' of the German social model. Resistance from other member states, notably the UK, has driven something of a wedge between German unions and the government's articulation of the national interest, and isolated them from other European unions. Streeck (1997) goes so far as to suggest that their domestic industrial partnership is at risk.

As O'Donnell argues elsewhere in this volume, it seems possible that the Irish model of social partnership could become an alternative basis for a European model. Other variants might, however, emerge. For example, the strength of French chambers of commerce and industry (in effect public institutions with considerable resources) means that they were and remain important actors as in the success of Rhone-Alpes (Dunford and Hudson, 1996: chapter 4), perhaps providing a capacity that counteracts the legislative weakness of French regions compared to the German *Länder*. As Closa (1996) argues, those civil society associations that are already strong within individual countries are likely to be able to compound their pre-existing national advantages at the EU level. Women's organizations in the UK (Bretherton and Sperling: 1996: 487–508), vary in their European engagement according to their domestic 'presence'. On the other hand, it has been shown that positive action can counteract the disadvantages of marginalized women in EU activities (Cockburn, 1991).

This suggests that similar steps would be necessary to encourage societal involvement in the candidate countries. It is not only the public institutional infrastructure that is weak as a result of totalitarianism but also the pattern of civil associations. Recognition of this has already led to a considerable effort by the EU Phare Programme to encourage the development of non-governmental organizations.

Implications of diversity for EU policy

All of these factors of diversity bear on the question of how the incipient values of European commonality might emerge and gain strength. We need to be clear about how to avoid jeopardizing them, especially given the member states' increasingly expressed ambitions in EU texts to ensure that 'Europe' is, indeed, 'brought closer to its peoples'.

Incipient values of commonality

Despite the disparities noted in the previous sections, it seems that there is already a degree of neighbourliness in the sense of interest in one another's difference. But, while Europe has always been, and remains, what Leonard (1998: 50–1) calls a 'travelling continent', the EU has not had as much success as one might have expected in building upon peoples' willingness to migrate or to see borders as porous. In addition to the language question, there are other barriers such as the high cost of air travel within Europe, compared to other parts of the world (notably the US) and poor progress on trans-European public transport networks.

Willingness to be mobile and to accept the permeability of frontiers should not, however, be taken to imply the promotion of homogeneity. Peoples' neighbourly interest in one another lie in their mutual awareness of the different things for which different parts of Europe are known (Leonard, 1998: 58). Rightly or wrongly, 'ordinary people' often believe that the integration project is about standardization. Although this has economic and practical advantages, it is also widely believed to jeopardize those things that people value in connection with national or local identities, their own or those of others. Issues relating to food are particularly emblematic in this regard, especially if standardization threatens favoured local products such as Cox's orange pippin apples or Bresse chickens. Dunford and Hudson (1996) note that the intentions of economic policy-makers and institutions of economic policy-making are often similar but differ in detail. Such differences have to be treated sensitively, as Knudsen (1995: 48–9) stresses in her example of letter boxes and postal systems. She suggests that it is not that Danish people believe that it is only the Danes that can organize a system of postal collection, but that they would be upset if the traditional colours and design of Danish letter boxes had to be changed.

Mrs Thatcher sometimes compared the EU with the USA to characterize her fears of deepening federation. A successful federation had to be built on social and political homogeneity; since this did not exist, the European project was doomed to failure. Alternatively, homogeneity would have to be compelled into existence by a central European 'state', the antithesis of the freedoms upon which the EU was based. This stark analysis rests on something of a misunderstanding about American federalism. In the ideas of the eighteenth century advocates of the US Constitution, social diversity and political pluralism were the *sine qua non* of their understanding of republican federalism. Thus, it would seem that, whether one's vision of Europe is that of *l'Europe des patries* or an 'ever closer union', diversity is equally important to both. The prerequisite for European democratic citizenship and neighbourliness, then, is not unlike the new language of citizenship within states – constructing a régime which simultaneously meets common interests and accommodates differences.

Practical policy needs

The demands of 'unity in diversity' have immediate policy implications, some of which may need to acknowledge difference and others of which reflect the need for some uniformity. For example, the mutual recognition of qualifications preserves diversity, while promoting more universal mobility, whereas cheap and easily usable public transport networks imply a degree of standardization.

There is, perhaps, also a need for member state governments to reconsider how well the overall package of EU policies reflects peoples' differing needs and aspirations. Recent presidencies of the Council of the EU have emphasized the need 'to bring Europe closer to its peoples'. Indeed, recent presidential agendas have reflected the concerns of public opinion: the quality of life, jobs, crime and the environment. But there is a risk of a continued mismatch between citizens' concerns and the goals of policy-makers. A member of the Irish negotiating team at Amsterdam (McDonagh, 1998: 80–1) qualified his claim that governments were paying more attention to citizens by suggesting that their responsiveness might be more presentational than substantive. For it to be substantive, a number of topics would need to be addressed, of which only a few can be illustrated here.

For example, a response to urban and environmental issues might imply a more radical reform of the common agricultural policy than has been achieved so far (Leonard, 1998: 54–5). There might need to be an adaption of cohesion policy to cater for differences. As Begg (1998:

15) points out, cohesion problems vary between: 'the decline of large manufacturing centres on the Franco–Belgian border, the inner city . . . in the UK, . . . bleak suburban developments in France, [and] . . . congestion and environmental degradation in Southern European cities'. Elsewhere in the EU the main problems remain rural. Thus, he suggests that support should be targeted on deprivation wherever it occurs and 'not on regions *per se*'. Moreover, if something of the social and Christian democratic consensus is to be maintained, attention must be paid to the uneasy, even contradictory, relationship between competition policy, which precludes national intervention, and regional policy (even if redefined as 'deprivation policy'), which implies calls for socio-economic intervention.

Social cohesion is also complicated by enlargement, not only from the economic point of view. The emergent concept of liberty in the applicant states seems to be more like that of the US; the negative one of 'freedom from' restraint, not the 'freedom to'. This is in contrast to that implicit in Christian and social democracy, the thinking which still influences the EU model by linking social inclusion and economic progress. This invites the question of whether the applicant states might be set fundamentally on a course that, in a new way, would continue to distinguish them from western Europe. On the other hand, a libertarian approach to freedom may be a reaction against anything 'tainted' with 'social' ideas, as being too similar to communism. For example, a transnational meeting in the early 1990s of the European socialist feminist movement was confronted by calls from east European women that the name should be changed. It may also be an indication of the constrained economic conditions in the new democracies which may rule out, at least for the time being, state intervention in the social sphere. If the answer lies in circumstance rather than fundamental philosophy, outlooks may become more common as situations improve. In the meantime, however, both this more libertarian conception of freedom in the applicant states and the resource implications of extending the existing Community *acquis* raise questions about the ideological commitment and material capacity of potential new members to conform with either the conceptual or the practical standards of solidarity in the EU.

As far as formal rights are concerned, migrants and would-be migrants need governments to face up to the complications arising from the decision to introduce the status of citizen of the EU while, leaving rules about nationality to member states. One way of proceeding would be to accept multiple and dual nationality; another would be to accept lawful residence, regardless of nationality, as a qualification for the exercise of rights (Closa, 1996: 7). It can be argued that there is some evidence of 'spill-over' from EU citizenship on to state-based nationality laws in attempts to reform nationality laws in Germany. Wiener (1998) suggests that, while nationality of a member state is still a pre-condition for European citizenship rights, a new paradigm exists in embryo in which citizenship might be more strongly rooted in the place of residence than in nationality. The relationship between lawful residence, whether as a national or an immigrant in a member state, and rights in the EU as a whole needs to be addressed more systematically. The basis for doing so is now present in the Amsterdam Treaty.

Civil society, national ties and supranational bonds

If rights are to be more than symbolic and result in real redistribution of power or influence, much depends on the ability of civil society 'to seize the day'. Closa (1998a,b) sees more potential, in principle, in supranational than national arenas for democratic citizenship. In practice, he suggests, however, that European civil society may be too fragile to transform EU citizenship into an arena for democratic self-determination from what he calls an enhanced set of private rights to make the most of new market opportunities (or be sheltered a little from its threats).

Closa's argument about the potential superiority of supranational citizenship rests on a critique of the case that a shared national identity is a pre-condition for citizenship. For, by insisting that citizenship can be built only on such bonds, such theories propose that a democratic practice be based on a commonality that was formed under pre-democratic conditions. In contrast, a site of democratic citizenship is one in which people live together under a set of principled bonds, such as those identified by Robert Dahl (1986) as voting equality, effective participation, enlightened understanding, control of agendas and inclusiveness. In drawing this contrast, Closa suggests that supranational citizenship is less likely than national citizenship to be exclusive and discriminatory because, being unable to draw on comparable nonprincipled bonds, its success must depend on democratic and human rights norms.[5]

Dahl, of course, is a citizen of the USA, where democratic norms and ties (albeit defective by today's standards) preceded strong national bonding in an overarching American sense. In contrast, Britishness was forged by elites, prior to democracy, so as to make bonds between peoples who had been enemies of one another. It worked for some centuries in the context of different sub-state national identities, while principled bonds were grafted on to the pre-democratic unifications. Now, however, there are claims in Scotland and, to some extent, Wales, which support Closa's case; that is, that, from a democratic basis, a new union of principled norms might be negotiated, either via the supranational level – the EU – or, at least, in its context.

The idea that a multi-state supranational union may be preferable to unification with a single neighbour arises from experience among the component peoples of the UK in trying to make what Closa calls their private EU rights have public consequences. That is, people whose material interests are enhanced by learning to use EU partnership and subsidiarity opportunities are trying to redefine their relationship to the domestic state in a European context, to bring about new forms of mobilization and interaction, and to influence agendas. But, again in line with Closa's theoretical case, unification into the British state left pre-British civil society institutions intact, especially in Scotland and Northern Ireland. Hence, there is a basis from which either to improve the principled bonds of the British state or to negotiate new ones in a different arena.

Closa (1998b) is guarded about whether there is a strong enough civil society in the EU as a whole to transcend the defects of national citizenship in order to bring about the benefits of a régime based on principled bonds. This would require a willingness on the part of states themselves to agree to cease seeking to maintain the impression that anxieties about national identities are well attended to in EU provisions. The changes which he suggests are necessary include: the avoidance of derogations and exemptions which 'offer shelter to communitarian understandings of the relationship between individuals and the state premised on nationality'; 'the full constitutionalization of a European political status'; greater opportunities for direct citizenship participation in EU affairs; stronger commonality and reciprocity of rights in different member states; and willingness by states to respond to 'spill-over' pressures from EU citizenship status on to varying nationality laws, including greater willingness to acknowledge dual or multi-nationality.

If Closa is right about the weakness of European civil society in combating a privatized, liberal or libertarian conception of citizenship, then enlargement may reinforce the challenge. Prospective member states will be expected to meet the pre-conditions of membership:

respect for liberty, democracy and human rights. As noted, however, the emergent concept of liberty in the applicant states seems to be more libertarian than that which Closa sees in the EU. Moreover, the construction of the new states in central and eastern Europe is closely related to highly developed senses of national identity. Indeed, it seems to be felt that this is the proper basis for the organization of collective life.

Despite the last point, the main issue in respect of enlargement should not be seen as about the addition of more nationalities *per se* into the EU with complex collections of pre-democratic identifications. Rather, it is that new mismatches among sets of principled bonds may inhibit the transformation of EU citizenship along the lines aspired to by Closa. If this is so, there is a heavy burden on those in the political realm to democratize the European public space so that the various associations of people can come face to face with their different interests and agendas (Tassin: 1992). Through a process of dialogue, they would need to try to achieve outcomes that are, if not wholly satisfactory to all, at least reasonable for the time being. Indeed, Kuper (1998: 285–94) persuasively argues that a project to 'constitutionalize' the EU along liberal lines as a means of removing its 'democratic deficits' is doomed to failure unless it is accompanied by the more republican political project of fostering an active European citizenry.

Notes

1. I am grateful to the Council of Europe for permission to include in this chapter sections of my report for its project on 'European Studies for Democratic Citizenship'. I should also like to thank Stefanka Hristoskova of the Higher Education and Research Section of the Council of Europe for her leadership of the project's Working Party and Expert Group and her encouragement of my work for it.
2. It should be noted, however, that school participation rates are far from constant (OECD, Education at a Glance 2000, Chapter A, http://www.oecd.org/els/educ/eag98/eag98_3a.htm). Indeed, since 1995, drop-out rates have become such a problem in Bulgaria that the Ministry of Education and Science, in partnership with a Danish–Irish Consortium (Democratic Development) and funded under the PHARE programme, has established a project, 'A School for Everyone' (http://wwwgo2school.bg/go2school/main.htm). 1995 figures used by Rosati (1998: 7).
3. These and following figures are from Dunford and Hudson (1996: 23–4, 29–33).
4. For subsequent figures, see Leonard (1998: 60–1).
5. Weiler (1997), too, calls for supranational democratic norms but in combination with measures to reassure people about state-based competences.

References

Begg, I. (1998) 'Structural Fund Reform in the Light of Enlargement', Sussex European Institute, SEI Working Paper, 25, Falmer.

Bretherton, C. and Sperling, L. (1996) 'Women's Networks and the European Union: Towards an Inclusive Approach', *Journal of Common Market Studies*, 34 (4), pp. 487–508.

Closa, C. (1996) 'A New Social Contract? EU Citizenship as the Institutional Basis of a New Social Contract: Some Sceptical Remarks', Florence, Robert Schuman Centre, European University Institute, EUI Working Papers RSC, 96/48.

Closa, C. (1998a) 'Some Foundations for the Normative Discussion on Supranational Citizenship and Democracy', in Preuss, U. K. and Requejo, F. (eds), *European Citizenship, Multiculturalism, and the State* (Schriftenreihe des Zentrums fur Europaische Rechspolitik. Baden-Baden: Nomos Verlagsgesellschaft), pp. 105–24.

Closa, C. (1998b) 'Supranational Citizenship and Democracy: Normative and Empirical Dimensions', in Torre, M. (ed.), *European Citizenship: An International Challenge* (Kluwer Law International).

Cockburn, C. (1991) *Getting Involved in Europe: The Experience of Three Innovatory Workshops for Women Trade Unionists* (Brussels: European Trade Union Confederation).

Dahl, R. A. (1986) *Democracy, Liberty and Equality* (Oslo: Norwegian University Press).

Dunford, M. and Hudson, R. (1996) *Successful European Regions: Northern Ireland Learning from Others* (Belfast: Northern Ireland Economic Council).

Dunford, M. and Smith, A. (1998) 'Trajectories of Change in Europe's Regions: Cohesion, Divergence and Regional Performance', Sussex University European Institute, SEI Working Paper, 26.

Howe, P. (1995) 'A Community of Europeans: The Requisite Underpinnings', *Journal of Common Market Studies*, 33(1), pp. 27–46.

Knudsen, A. (1995) 'European Cultures – A Possible Future', in Lukanovic, S. N. (ed.), *Overlapping Cultures and Plural Identities* (Ljubljana: Slovenia National Commission for UNESCO and Institute for Ethnic Studies).

Kuper, R. (1998) 'The Making of a Constitution for Europe', *Contemporary Politics*, 4(3), pp. 285–94.

Leonard, M. (1998) *Rediscovering Europe* (London: Demos).

Lister, R. (1990) *The Exclusive Society: Citizenship and the Poor* (London: The Child Poverty Action Group).

McDonagh, B. (1998) *Original Sin in a Brave New World: An Account of the Negotiation* (Dublin: Institute of European Affairs).

Meehan, E. (1999) 'Citizenship and Identity', in Holiday, I., Gamble, A. and Parry, G. (eds), *Fundamentals in British Politics* (Basingstoke: Macmillan – now Palgrave).

Meehan, E. (2000) 'EU Social Policy: British and German Approaches to Industrial Citizenship', in Larres, K. and Meehan, E. (eds), *Uneasy Partners: British–German Relations and European Integration since 1945* (Oxford: Oxford University Press).

Rosati, D. (1998) *Economic Disparities in Central and Eastern Europe and the Impact of Enlargement* (Geneva: United Nations Economic Commission for Europe and the Central European Initiative).

Streeck, W. (1997) 'Citizenship under Regime Competition: The Case of the European Works Councils', *European Integration on-line Papers* (EIoP) 1 (005), http://eiop.or.at/eiop/texte/1997-005a.htm, pp. 1–24.

Tassin, E. (1992) 'Europe: a Political Community', in Mouffe, C. (ed.), *Dimensions of Radical Democracy: Pluralism, Citizenship, Community* (London: Verso Press).

Tsoukalis, L. (1998) 'The European Agenda: Issues of Globalization, Equity and Legitimacy', *Jean Monnet Papers*, 49, Florence: The Robert Schuman Centre at the European University Institute.

Wallace, H. (1999) 'Whose Europe is it Anyway? The 1998 Stein Rokkan Lecture', *European Journal of Political Research*, 35(3), pp. 287–306.

Weiler, J. H. H (1997) 'To be a European Citizen – Eros and Civilization', *Journal of European Public Policy*, 4 (4), pp. 495–519.

Wiener, A. (1998) *'European' Citizenship Practice: Building Institutions of a Non-State* (Boulder, CO: Westview Press).

Women and Citizenship Research Group (1995) *Women and Citizenship: Power, Participation and Choice* (Belfast: Equal Opportunities Commission for Northern Ireland).

14
Immigrants, Cosmopolitans and the Idea of Europe

Ash Amin[1]

Introduction

Non-white residents and citizens of the European Union (EU) have no role to play in the 'Idea of Europe', which remains an ideal of unity drawing on a Christian-Enlightenment heritage to bridge the diversity of European national cultures. The Idea has become a rallying call for European integrationists, who promise the preservation of national cultural specificity and autonomy. But, if asked in whose image integration and preservation, the answer returns, consistently, to a 'Europeanness' defined by native Christian-Enlightenment traditions. And yet, the member states – virtually all of them – have become a veritable mixture of people and cultures from around the world. This is the result of postwar immigration from ex-colonies and the active recruitment of 'guest workers', and, more recently, the arrival of asylum-seekers and economic migrants from many Middle Eastern, Asian and African countries.

In this setting, the Idea of Europe seems strikingly exclusionary, backward looking, and irrelevant – a poor motif for the future. Is it of any appeal to the growing population of developing country immigrants who rightly wish to preserve their diaspora cultures? Why should they be fired by its ideal? As Yasmin Alibhai-Brown (1998: 38) summarizes in reference to Muslims:

> While European leaders worry endlessly about coins, bureaucrats and flags . . . the diverse Muslim communities of the EU . . . do not yet see themselves as part of the project in any meaningful sense and many of those in the wider community remain unconvinced that this group can ever be incorporated into their ideal vision of

the Union. Even in the most egalitarian states . . . Islam is seen as the massive blot on the landscape of the future.

Indeed, looking beyond the immigrants, what real purchase does the Idea of Europe have for the increasing number of culturally hybrid social groups and generations, who, through travel, consumption, mixture, social mobility, and so on, display complex geographies of identification – local, national, European and global? And what does it do for the millions of Europeans anxious to preserve their ethnic and regional identities and cultural heritage in fear of 'external dilution', however defined?

I wish in this chapter to dissent from this Idea of Europe on grounds of both its distance from really felt popular sentiment for national, regional or ethnic cultural preservation, as well as the opposite reason, namely that the Idea is not transnational or cosmopolitan enough. The second half of the chapter develops an alternative, seeking endorsement for the European project through meaningful provision of basics at the level of Europe, such as enhanced universal welfare rights. The first part of the chapter outlines the gap between contemporary ideas of Europe and debates – especially on racism and multiculturalism – related to the changing ethnic and cultural composition of European nations.

The Idea of Europe

The Idea of Europe has a long and varied history, with much written on the topic (see, for example, Delanty, 1995; Heater, 1992; Heffernan, 1998). The Idea of Europe builds on a long tradition stretching back to the late middle ages, involving a common European identity based on reason, Christianity and democracy. It is invoked in the name of peace within an oft violent continent, unity against a common enemy (Ottomans, Islam, Empire, Communism, Americanism) and difference from the 'other' – societies with different moral beliefs and cultural practices. Heikki Mikkeli (1998: 230) summarizes:

> Europe has, at different points of its history, been equated with civilization, Christianity, democracy, freedom, white skin, the temperate zone and the Occident. Correspondingly, its opposites have been identified as barbarism, paganism, despotism, slavery, coloured skins, the tropics and the Orient.

Somewhat ironically, the architects of European unity in the 1950s saw the horrors of the Holocaust and two world wars as a violation of – not in any way connected with – the ideals of action through reason, justice enshrined in Roman law and order, human rights, liberal democracy, and a humanism grounded in Christian charity. European federation would reinforce this tradition, so the script rolled from prominent French, Italian and German integrationists. The integrationists – then and now – looked primarily to Catholicism, with its history of crusade and points of collision with Islam, as the bedrock of European Christianity.

A lighter version of the script continues to inform the European project, now less driven by the imperative of internal peace (was it eclipsed during the Bosnian and Kosovan crises because this was the 'other' Europe of Muslims, communists, Albanians, unreason and dogma?). The Idea of Europe now is mobilized for reasons connected with Europe's standing in world affairs, of a primarily economic and politico-cultural. The economic case is straightforward: economic intenatural will offer the scale economies and market opportunities for Europe Ltd to compete against giant US and Japanese corporations in major world markets. The politico-cultural case relates to Europe's civilizational mission, as encapsulated in the aspirations of two great Europeanists, Jean Monnet and Jacques Delors. For Monnet in 1962:

> unity in Europe does not create a new kind of great power; it is a method for introducing change in Europe and consequently in the world . . . European unity is not a blueprint, it is not a theory, it is a process that has already begun, of bringing peoples and nations together to adapt themselves jointly to changing circumstances (quoted in Nielsen and Stubb, 1998: 26).

While Delors, in his 1989 address to the College of Europe in Bruges, *contra* Mrs Thatcher's xenophobic rebuttal, dreams of something bigger:

> I find myself dreaming of a Europe . . . which tends its immense cultural heritage so that it bears fruit, a Europe which imprints the mark of solidarity on a world which is far too hard and too forgetful of its underdeveloped regions . . . the perennial values of Europe (quoted in Nielsen and Stubb, 1998: 68).

Equality, fraternity and liberty – no less – as the world project for Europe, are seen also to bind together the member states. This has been the thrust behind European cultural policy in the last decade – promoted by the Commission and the European Parliament to provide a 'fresh boost for culture in the European Community' (Commission, 1987) in order to ease European economic integration.

The EU has been careful to avoid being accused of wanting to manufacture European identity from above. It has sought to stress unity in diversity, that is, to acknowledge and celebrate the unique cultural heritage and trajectory of individual nations and regions (Benoît-Rohmer, 1996; Commission, 1987) at the same time as promoting common attributes. These, for Melissa Pantel (1999), are three-fold: first, a 'shared pluralistic humanism based on democracy, justice and freedom' (Commission, 1987: 5); second, a shared history of peaceful cooperation (with Europe's wars bracketed as the products of 'misjudged interests'); and, finally, a shared interest in responding to the external 'threat to Europe's cultural independence' (Commission, 1987: 13).

Accordingly, since the mid 1980s, EU cultural policy has sought to provide support for cultural exchange and cultural production of a pan-European nature (for example, audio-visual co-production, pan-European broadcasting of national televisual programmes, twinning of towns and schools). Since 1992, the EU has provided for educational exchanges (for example, ERASMUS and SOCRATES), language training, information and research, artistic activities at European level, protection of heritage, translation of European literary works, and other initiatives to promote a sense of European cultural identity beyond local and national affinities (Pantel, 1999). More recent effort has involved the promotion of symbols of European affiliation, such as the EU flag, anthem and passport, and Europe Day on 9 May (who has heard of this date?).

EU cultural policy, and the Idea of Europe in general, has been criticized as an elitist and blunt tool for promoting a sense of 'Europeanness' among its citizens. For example, the EU's own *Eurobarometer* public opinion surveys show that 43 per cent of EU citizens do not feel any kind of European identity (Autumn 1998), a deterioration from the 38 per cent of Spring 1992, while only 11 per cent consider their European identity stronger than their national one (Commission, 1998b and c). Mark Leonard (1998a: 46) comments 'even the 50 per cent who feel "European" cannot give it any definite meaning – it is just something they might feel if confronted with, say, Japanese or American people'. There is thus no Europe-wide equivalent of the myths or stories that make up national identities. And without such stories and myths, 'who will feel', as Anthony Smith asks bluntly (1995: 139) 'European in the depths of their being, and who will willingly sacrifice themselves for so abstract an ideal? In short who will die for Europe?'

Leonard argues (1998b: 7) that European leaders have missed something in not making more of the everyday 'latent legitimacy' that Europe already has 'stored away in holiday snapshots' and 'schemes that allow people to experience Europe more directly'. Cris Shore (1998: 50) agrees that the 'experience of Europe's cultural diversity has become a key dimension of everyday life in myriad ways, from supermarkets and cinemas, to fashion and food':

> Eric Cantona, Jurgen Klinsmann, and Luciano Pavarotti have become household names in Britain. Branches of Benetton and Bata now appear in almost every British high street, while Marks and Spencer have opened up shop in Strasbourg and Brussels. Balsamic vinegar, sun-dried tomatoes, calamata olives, porcini mushrooms, and freshly baked French baguettes are now available in Tesco.

But, unlike Leonard, who does believe in the prospect of a more popular, less ambitious Idea of Europe than that of the founders of European integration, Shore to questions whether the new patterns of consumption amount to the formation of a shared European consciousness. One does not necessitate the other – 'British preference for Indian food or German cars does not inexorably lead to identification with India or Germany', and 'English football fans may worship Eric Cantona and still hate the French' (Shore, 1998: 50).

The Idea of Europe, thus, has gradually softened in recent years, away from Catholic values, Beethoven and lofty enlightenment ideals, towards global solidarity, balsamic vinegar and experience of each other. This said, we should stop to note the desire of Romano Prodi (1999), President of the European Commission, to put Christian humanism back into the centre of the Idea of Europe. He has called for the reawakening of a 'Europe of the spirit', based on a Roman Catholic respect of basic values, including the centrality of the family, free speech, individual rights, legal protection, and the common good. The flame of the holy crusade continues to self-ignite. But, coming back to the new meanings, it is doubtful whether a new banal Europeanness will help cement European unity, and with the same degree of feeling stipulated by Anthony Smith for national identification.

What does seem clear, however, is that both the lofty and the banal vision generalize from partial and relatively fixed, territorially defined cultural identities in Europe. There is a presumed local, national and

European identity, stylized around traditional homeland imaginaries and stereotypes – linguistic purity, blood heritage, reason, Christian values, Beethoven, but also Cantona, sun-dried tomatoes and balsamic vinegar. What do they mean in a Europe of people from non-European backgrounds, who have a weak relationship with an Idea of Europe based on territorial boundaries?

A non-European Europe

A sizeable proportion of the population in a number of member states consists of residents and citizens from a non-European background. The EU unfortunately does not publish data on the ethnic composition or geographical origins of member state citizens, but only the origins of non-nationals (that is, residents who are not citizens of the given member state). These data therefore significantly underestimate the size of the immigrant population by not counting 'non-natives' who are citizens of that state (for example, British Indians or Dutch Surinamese). For example, in Germany, non-nationals are recorded as making up 8.5 per cent of the population, with 74 per cent of them originating from non-EU countries (Commission, 1997a).

A slightly better measure is the proportion of the foreign-born population, which would include who have acquired those citizenship, but not their off-spring born in the host state. In 1994 (Commission, 1998a), the proportion of the foreign-born population in a selection of member states was the following: 9.7 per cent in Belgium, 41 per cent of whom originated from beyond another EU country; 5.3 per cent in Denmark (of whom 74 per cent non-EU); 11 per cent in France (of whom 78 per cent non-EU); 9 per cent in the Netherlands (of whom 88 per cent non-EU); 6.8 per cent in the UK (of whom 71 per cent non-EU); 4.6 per cent in Portugal (of whom 77 per cent non-EU); and 9.9 per cent in Sweden (of whom 60 per cent non-EU). The inclusion of second and third generation citizens of immigrant parents would significantly inflate these figures on the proportion of residents in a country from different ethnic origins (for example, according to the 1991 Census, the non-white population alone in Great Britain was 5.5 per cent).

The outcome of immigration into the EU, together with increased mobility within the EU, is that *de facto* the member states have become multiethnic and multicultural societies. This is no longer a feature of only the ex-colonial nations such as Britain, France, Belgium and the Netherlands, or countries such as Germany which imported cheap migrant labour to fuel economic expansion. It marks also countries such as Sweden, Austria, Italy, Greece and Spain in which recent immigration is related to global poverty and repression. Göran Therborn (1998: 14) summarizes:

> Western Europe has become multicultural, with significant south Asian minorities (in Britain), Blacks from the West Indies and from sub-Saharan Africa (mainly in UK and in France), important populations from North Africa and the Middle East, from Turkey to Iran, spread over the whole continent but concentrated in France and Germany respectively. A large number of mosques have been built, most of them in France, and Britain also has its Hindu temples. Among urban youth a number of life-style sub-cultures are being created, and changed.

Public attitudes in the EU towards immigration from non-EU countries remain ambivalent. In 1997, the European Year Against Racism, the Commission's *Eurobarometer* survey (Commission, 1997b) showed that 21 per cent of EU citizens felt that people from the 'South of the Mediterranean' wishing to work in the Union should not be accepted, 60 per cent felt that they should be accepted only with restrictions, leaving only 13 per cent who were willing to accept them without restrictions. While the Spanish, Finnish, Irish, Italians and Portuguese were the most accepting, more than a quarter of the citizens of Belgium (38 per cent), Greece, France (both 29 per cent), Austria (28 per cent), Germany and Denmark (both 26 per cent) felt that these workers should be rejected.

The attitudes towards foreigners are equally disturbing. The same survey shows that on average 45 per cent of the EU population believe that there are too many foreigners in their country, 40 per cent believe that there are a lot (but not too many), with only 10 per cent believing that there are not a lot. There are large variations in attitudes between member states, similar to the pattern concerning work migrants, with higher levels of tolerance shown in Finland, Ireland, Spain and Portugal, but with a strong feeling of too much foreign presence in Greece (71 per cent), Belgium (60 per cent), Italy (53 per cent), and Germany (52 per cent).

The central question, however, is whether multiethnicity/multinationality is seen to be threatening, and here, the results are counter-intuitive. The 1997 EU survey shows that most Europeans do not personally find the presence of people of another nationality (83 per cent) or race (81 per cent) in their country disturbing. This seems to be the pattern across Europe, with the exception of Denmark, Belgium and Greece where fewer than seven in ten people share this view. In addition, particularly in attitudes towards immigration, the young, the educated, the professional classes, and the unemployed (fearing little to lose?) seem to be least threatened.

The general picture, to summarize, seems to be that, while controls on immigration are seen to be desirable by Europeans, the majority, especially those least wedded to national traditions alone, appear sanguine about the presence of other nationalities and ethnic groups already settled in their country.

Cosmopolitans, traditionalists and racists

How far do these mixed attitudes towards foreigners indicate a changing Idea of Europe? How far do the weak signals of tolerance represent a blurring of the boundaries between 'us' and 'them' in an emerging post-national and multiple sense of European identification? Or is tolerance no more than a recognition of the legitimacy of the 'other' on both sides? Can we indeed speak of tolerance in a Europe in which the felt erosion of once-stable identity and tradition in the face of global cultural mixture, as well as European and other forms of international integration, is provoking new forms of reaction and racism?

It would be too simple to settle for any one of these three views, given the extraordinary variety of, first, national attitudes to Europe and to immigrants, second, government policies towards immigration, assimilation and racism, and, third, ethnic, religious, class generational senses of self and the other. I do want to claim, though, that, if a new Idea of Europe is emerging, it is not one of cultural mixture and hybridity, but one based on the reassertion of difference and in ways which do not correspond to the traditional appeal in the name of common European characteristics.

One – potentially progressive – reading in a Europe of immigrants is that the resulting multiculturalism is consistent with the process of global cosmopolitanization of culture and consumption, now said to be breaking down traditional cultural barriers in any case. Thus, Europe could 'travel light' (Nederveen Pieterse, 1999) as a project of integration based on the multiple identities and multiple senses of territorial identification. A hybrid Europe in continual cultural movement and renewal, an open project, rather than a Europe of overlapping fixed identities and a point of arrival.

This is the Europe claimed by progressive anthropologists or ethnologists trying to make sense of the detraditionalization of communal or local identities under conditions of global cultural exposure and mixture. What if in Europe too – wherever we are – we face the same processes of cultural pluralism and mixture as elsewhere in the world? What if we – all of us – cope with ease with cultural products from all over the world, see ourselves as part of a local community, region, nation and international diaspora of some sort, move socially and geographically without major disruptions of identity and identification, and are not unsettled by others in our midst as we lose our certainty about who is 'us' and what is 'ours'? What if we really have become postmodern? Alberto Melucci is sure that we now live in the age of the 'playing' (1996) or 'multiple self' (1997) characterized by:

> Individuals . . . enmeshed in multiple bonds of belonging created by the proliferation of social positions, associative networks and reference groups. We enter and leave this system much more than we used to in the past. We are migrant animals . . . Thus we are subjected to mounting pressure to change, to transfer, to translate what we were just a moment ago into new codes and new forms of relation (1997: 61) [. . .] Choosing seems now to be our inexorable fate . . . In terms of everyday experience . . . uncertainty has become a stable component in our behaviour (62).

Zygmunt Bauman agrees, asserting that, through the 'overwhelming feeling of uncertainty' and 'ambient fear' (1997: 50) ensuing from such global processes as detraditionalization, deregulation, new world disorder and media play on its indeterminacy, we are seeing the rise of a 'heterophilic age' in which the 'question is no longer how to get rid of the strangers and the strange, but how to live with them – daily and permanently' (88).

Viewed normatively, this interpretation opens the possibility of a heterophilic Europe of multiple and mobile identities and a gradual erosion of the difference between us and them. A Europe – minority and mainstream – moving irreversibly towards the cosmopolitan self, as cultural mixture begins to challenge identification with an essentialized tradition or homogeneous community. A promise of overlapping and weakening boundaries, as people come to develop multiple territorial affiliations (for example, no longer just Italian, but Neapolitan, Italian, and European) and complex geographies of identity formation (for example, I am what I eat, where I shop, where I travel, where I live, what I read, where my family and friends are scattered, and so on).

On the basis of precisely such a reading, Jeremy Waldron (1992) has argued for initiatives that encourage cosmopolitanism. It is an alternative with a very different Idea of Europe from the commonly held one: a project centred less upon the premise of a mosaic of cultures in Europe, than the work of defiant and emerging transnational identities. But, how much does the cosmopolitan alternative confuse process with outcome? How widespread is the feeling of cosmopolitanism? Is there evidence of Europe 'travelling light'? It seems not.

First, let us return to Melucci (1996: 116), for whom the playing or multiple self is far from predisposed automatically to self-mutation and accepting difference:

> there is a profound moral implication: the necessity to keep and to lose, to cope with fears and resistances, but also with the ability of going beyond our given identities ... The possibility of meeting each other needs a big leap in consciousness, to allow people to accept that they exist as separate individual and social groups, but no less that they can *co*-exist and communicate.

Without the 'big leap in consciousness' – which seems unlikely in a Europe of everyday concerns and waning public interest – 'fears and resistances' may well be the dominant response to the perceived erosion of boundaries, leading to heightened feelings of loss of identity and mistrust of others. This is exactly one way of interpreting the contemporary resurgence of regionalism, racism, ethno-communalism, religious fundamentalism and nationalist sentiment in Europe. A Europe without borders – or more accurately without old certainties of belonging – might be seen as producing a fractured self and reactions to difference which are defensive and intolerant.

It is the Europe of 'heterophobia' and tradition rediscovered that I wish to highlight as a more accurate interpretation of contemporary developments associated with multiculturalism. An obvious issue concerns who is described by the model of multicultural hybridity. Jonathan Friedman (1997: 79) does not hesitate to conclude that the discourse of hybridization is the imposition of a small cultural elite – 'post-colonial border-crossers' made up of poets, artists and intellectuals. Similarly, Robin Cohen (1998: 15) pointedly comments on the politics of seeing hybridity everywhere:

> There are those who celebrate the new uncertainty principles, who explore the luxuriant phenomenology of fragmentation and fluidity for their own narcissistic purposes, and fetishize the borderlands as sites of cultural or political transgression; en route the migrant and asylum-seeker, the unemployed and the down-and-out: all those in need of . . . security and safety . . . are often transfigured into a kind of nomadic postmodern hero by those who take all that for granted.

The point here is that the egalitarian language of transgression glosses over the many social worlds which experience very little transgression of a positive nature. These are the worlds of those at the bottom of the social heap, in need of material and social security. Equally, for the 'mainstream' too, integration – in whatever form – encourages a desire to draw sharp boundaries against others, including hybrids.

What of hybrids themselves? In her sensitive book on the lives of six women in Britain of mixed parentage, Jayne Ifekwunigwe (1999) reveals how their everyday life of inescapable *métissage* has involved self-hate, confusion, oscillation between feeling white or black, and above all, derision, isolation and bracketing from not only the white community, but also the black community. Thus, Ruby, travelling in Morocco with her white husband and a white friend, when automatically taken to be the maid, laments how she was made to feel 'that my husband and my White friend were the man and wife, and that the kids were theirs. That was distressing' (80). Similarly, Akoussa concludes from her life experience: 'I think at the end of the day, White society has never accepted me. They see me as a contamination to their stock. Diseased person, and even worse than havin' two black parents, worse than even that. If you come to extermination we would most probably go first' (112). These two experiences are clearly not for generalization, since context, class and colour are likely to make a difference, but what they do show up are the dangers of thoughtlessly celebrating hybridity.

Even light hybridity worn consciously as an identifier has its cultural limits among adherents. To take one example, the anthropologist John Hutnyk (1997: 110), observes at the 1994 Womad World Music festival in Reading, which regularly attracts cultural trangressors from around Europe:

> No one seemed too embarrassed at the irregular dancing of the waif-like hippie woman spiralling trance-circle-ly in sexy rapture in front of the devotional Islamic Qawwals of Hussain and Party; at the same

time, no one seemed to want to join in with her, despite her exhortations to the crowd to 'get up and dance'.

This is not an exceptional but a standard reaction that often accompanies the juxtaposition of difference. We should not be surprised by it. We certainly should not magic it away. Indeed, there is ample evidence to show that multiculturalism is often perceived as a threat – by both dominant and subaltern groups – leading to withdrawal into quite sophisticated imaginaries of tradition, homeland and difference to preserve ethnic and/or national identity (Hall, 1998; Morley and Robins, 1995). Some of the recent history of cultural conflicts in Europe can be seen in these terms, as a reaction to the perceived cultural loss or dilution resulting from integration – from worries about Americanized consumerism, vilification of the Brussels 'bureaucracy' and stereotyping by national tabloids of other member state cultures, to intolerance of immigrants and asylum seekers and the rise of ethnic and other regionalist movements. These are very real and felt reactions, involving closure and recovery of geographical and cultural boundaries, rather than hybridity and plural identification.

Let us take the example of non-white minorities in the EU, beginning with the cultural practices of the ethnic minorities, specifically Muslim groups (estimated at 17 million) for ease of argument. The early sobriety, piety and conformity of first generation Muslims (Werbner, 1996) has produced nothing like Europeans or cosmopolitans among later generations in Britain, France, Germany and other Northern European countries (except, possibly, among mobile, semi-detached, liberal professionals like me). Instead, as Yasmin Alibhai-Brown (1998: 39) puts it:

> Interestingly, young, highly educated Muslims are developing a new sense of superiority through victimhood. Many are attracted to the idea of *intifada* and of an unworkable, though romantic, pan-Islamic identity, and the notion that they can live within their own ideological and religious imaginary territories.

Alibhai-Brown goes on to ask if 'Muslims want to be part *of* Europe or a part *within* Europe' (1998), and concludes that the spectrum of preferences in Britain at least seems to be polarized between those for whom their Islamic identities matters most (with 'integration the last thing on the minds') and young Muslims who see 'themselves as past of a wider movement of other disenfranchised groups seeking a place for themselves in society, (Alibhai-Brown, 1998).[2] Either way, considerations of Europe and Europeanness appear to be remote (perhaps also hostile, as symbols of Christian values) in their attempt to forge strong identities consciously independent from all things nationally 'native'. Like first generation Muslims, they see themselves as different and seek to remain separate from the national community, but unlike their parents and grandparents, they also claim the nation. No longer Muslims in Britain, France and Germany, but British, French and German Muslims, and as much stakeholders in the national community as anybody else.

Among many other Muslims and other ethnic minorities, such alterity is not worn on the sleeve as a strong marker of difference (Rex, 1996). It may not even be a marker, for as Jeff Spinner-Halev (1999: 69) reminds us for some lives across the Atlantic:

> When a devout Sikh serves as a Canadian Mounty, eats hamburgers at home, attends Toronto Blue Jay baseball games on the weekends, and when his children attend the University of Toronto where they partake in their own form of cosmopolitan life, then he and his family are living the cosmopolitan life, one that draws on several cultural traditions.

But, in the majority of cases, ethnic alterity, even when carried lightly, does exist as a source of everyday communal identification, helping to fashion transnational affiliations, special needs and social nourishment. With every step towards national and European cultural assimilation, has grown the demand for denominational schools, recognition of cultural and religious festivals, participation in ethnic cultural associations, travel to the 'homeland' and stories of home, reconstructions of family and diaspora histories and search for solidarity among your 'own' people (Werbner, 1996). These do not necessarily amount to a rejection of the mainstream, or a demand for separation, but they do extress the value of an ethno-cultural dimension in shared affiliations with others.

Good or bad, these are genuine demands for a ethnic minority needs and traditions that have little in common with the territorially defined Europe of Beethoven, Christianity, nationalist sentiment or hybrids. Certainly bad, however, the politics of cultural difference has also played into the hands of fundamentalist demands for a Europe of blood-and-soil based strong nations, without immigrants and 'foreign' cultural influences.

Racism has become a European phenomenon, no longer restricted to individual nations which can be conveniently dismissed as exceptions to an otherwise intact European tradition of equal rights, freedom and solidarity. The naked racism of 20 to 30 years ago against non-white immigrants in Britain, France and Germany, played on the allegedly 'different endowments of human races' (Stolcke, 1995) as a basis for discrimination and violence against particular immigrant ethnic minorities (Turks, Indians, Pakistanis, Afro-Caribbeans, North Africans). Some of this remains – perhaps in less naked form, and among consciously racist individuals and organizations – but it has also spread to countries of more recent immigration. Many of these early horrors have been replicated in Italian responses to immigration from diverse African countries in the 1980s (Melotti, 1997), as well as in Swedish and Danish reactions to liberal asylum policies towards persecuted peoples around the world.

But a new racism, or more accurately a new 'cultural fundamentalism' (Stolcke, 1995) that plays on the legitimacy of cultural difference as a reason for territorial or ethnic separation, has also grown as a pan-European phenomenon, in both old and new countries of immigration (Modood, 1997). While the old form was all about keeping immigrants out, or sending them back as undesirable or ill-fitting aliens, the new phenomenon expresses anxieties about the negative implications – both for 'us' and 'them' of 'having them in our midst'. They and their cultural practices – from worship and ideology to consumption and recreation – will dilute and undermine our sacred traditions and our ethno-national integrity. As Verena Stolcke (1995: 12) summarizes:

> Contemporary cultural fundamentalism unequivocally roots nationality and citizenship in a shared cultural heritage . . . The assumption that the territorial state and its people are founded on a cultural heritage that is bounded, compact, and distinctive is a constitutive part .

Even declared xenophobes and nationalists – now increasingly drawing on all sorts of white–black alliances for their activities – have become cultural relativists alongside ordinary folk, in campaigns across Europe to rescue national or regional cultural heritage and purity. They complain about encroachment from Europe, worry about the threat posed by the rights claims of minorities (for example, special schools, recognition of festivals, holidays and customs, funding for associations) and suggest ways of keeping the ethnic communities separate (from ghettoization to voluntary repatriation and tight immigration controls). The new mood works less on the exclusionary politics of genus, than on one based on loyalty to national cultural stereotypes, with the right of membership possibly spanning across ethnic boundaries (for example, that cricket-loving Indians should support England at a test match against India, or Palestinians gather around Swedish maypoles wild-eyed with enthusiasm on Mayday). Now, perhaps, the requirement is for culture over colour and features, but it is just as exclusionary and just as intolerant of cultural mixture in a Europe without borders.

In summary, the new Europe of porous borders, viewed from below, seems to me to be less a space of happy hybridity, cosmopolitanism, and Enlightenment values, than a space of exclusionary territorial and cultural boundaries in the name of difference.

A Europe of the commons

At stake in an Idea of Europe that assumes mobility, transcience and multicultural presence from around the world is whether what is shared or not, what is seen to be gained or lost, poses a threat to both settled and emerging patterns of identification. If there is no natural current towards cosmopolitanism or popular endorsement of the Idea of Europe, is the politics of difference – both progressive and conservative – the best we can hope for? Like others, I am worried by the fall from grace of modernist aspirations such as equality and universal rights, or that a progressive Idea of Europe without threat to self-and group-identity, might seek harmonized political, social and economic rights and standards available to all residents everywhere in the EU.

A number of commentators on Europe argue that the new cultural fundamentalism draws on much the same politics of difference as progressive arguments in favour of multicultural societies which maximize group autonomy. Kenan Malik (1998), for example, claims that both racist and anti-racist projects rooted in the celebration of cultural difference tend to freeze and essentialize identities around myth and reaction (see also Samad, 1997), instead of allowing the formation of 'identities freely chosen by those communities' (134), thereby allowing 'accomodation to, and exacerbation of . . . inequalities' (125). Slavoj Žižek (1997) is even more direct, and labels even the better of the two projects, namely multiculturalism, as 'a disavowed, inverted, self-referential form of racism' (44). Jeff Spinner-Halev (1999: 65) draws a similarly alarming conclusion:

> A multiculturalism that tries to create a society with several distinctive cultures deeply threatens citizenship. In this kind of multicultural society, people are not interested in citizenship; they are not interested in making the state a better place for all; they care little about how public policies affect most people or about their fellow citizens. Even the term 'fellow citizen' might strike them as strange. What they have are fellow Jews, or fellow blacks, or fellow Muslims, or fellow Sikhs. Citizens, however, are not their fellows.

Spinner-Halev argues that this form of strong multiculturalism can be distinguished from an 'inclusive multiculturalism' that usually enhances citizenship. He has a liberal model of citizenship in mind, distinguished by both the legal requirement that all citizens treat each other in a nondiscriminatory way in public, and the moral requirement that citizens 'are able to talk to one another', 'cooperate with each other', be 'willing to compromise', and look out 'for the public good' (1999: 67). This is a multiculturalism capable of reconciling difference with the common good. I am not convinced that to strike the balance it is necessary for Europe (or its member states) to go so far as to inculcate the virtues of good citizenship – cooperation, listening to others, democratic discussion, scrutiny of policy and politicians, and so on. Moral compulsion of this sort is difficult, possibly also dubious, in any national setting, let alone at the level of Europe, which commands little popular allegiance.

What might help, however, is the offer of universal rights at the level of Europe which are seen to derive material benefits from European citizenship. The different member states discriminate differentially between their own or EU nationals and non-nationals in the offer of rights. They vary in their policies and attitudes towards immigration from beyond the EU. They offer different welfare rights (from health coverage to education and benefits) as well as economic rights (for example, minimum wage, industrial relations, coverage for part-time workers). They vary in their treatment of ethnic minorities (for example, autonomism in Sweden and Netherlands, cultural tolerance in Britain, assimilation into the national imaginary in France). It is hardly surprising that, for example, the Scandinavians fear the Union as a drain on high domestic welfare standards and the British worry about the loss of political freedom, while the Mediterraneans see the Union as a way of enhancing domestic welfare rights, and all the national majorities see immigrants as a further drain on resources.

EU-level universal rights might help to moderate such a politics of envy. But, who should be entitled to the rights? This is a vexed and much debated question, but I am inclined to agree with Yasemin Soysal (1994) that if the interests of immigrants are to be taken seriously, the rights of citizenship should be decoupled from their national constitution and offered, instead, as trans-territorial rights of personhood, based on residence rather than citizenship in the EU. In other words, residents would carry with them a bundle of rights within the EU, and eligibility would no longer depend on national citizenship, the acquisition of which is notoriously difficult for immigrants and varying in rights and duties between member states. As Gerald Delanty (1997: 299) writes:

> If residence is more fully established as the basis of European citizenship, the dimension of inclusion can be enhanced. European citizenship could then become not merely relevant to the some five million citizens of the member states living in other states of the Union, but also to the some 10 to 15 million immigrants.

What kind of rights might be included in an EU-model of postnational citizenship? Soysal has largely human rights in mind, but the coverage can be extended to include other rights – political, economic and social. To my mind, welfare rights are central among these in terms of their offer of immediate material benefits, as well as the chance to become someone or something else through education, shelter, health-care, and so on. Gerald Delanty (1997: 293) argues, 'unless the European Union can reproduce the welfare state on a supranational level . . . there is little point in making pleas for a meaningful kind of European citizenship'. Interestingly, however, the missing words in Delanty's claim are 'a very unlikely prospect', and I am inclined to agree with the view that throughout the history of European integration, national governments have jealously defended their control over welfare decisions as a tool of fiscal and electoral control. But it may now be the case that with increased mobility, immigrant presence, welfare variety (on a downward slide) within the EU, there is stronger popular support for a European welfare state.

I do not intend to go into the details here of which universal rights might be pooled, and which retained at the national level. Instead I wish to make the more basic point that there is much to be gained for multiculturalism and social inclusion in Europe through a new EU model of citizenship based on transnational universal rights. It strikes me as less divisive than attempts to force people to conform to a given Idea of Europe or a given ethno-national mythology, or than strategies of inclusion based on spiralling recognition of group-differentiated citizenship rights to the point of death of the commons. Universals are the basis on which difference can flourish, and along lines of self-development as opposed to identity reaction against the other (Joppke and Lukes, 1999). They might help recognition of, in the words of Bhiku Parekh (1999: 31) 'shared humanity and cultural differences', as well as 'how all cultures share enough in common to make dialogue possible'. There is no in-built conflict between universals and specificities, as Seyla Benhabib (1999: 45) remarks:

> cultures and societies are polyvocal, multilayered, decentred, and fractured systems of action and signification. Politically, the right to cultural self-expression needs to be grounded upon, rather than being considered an alternative to, universally recognized citizenship rights.

A Europe of the commons might indeed, as some observers desire, allow the experimentation with a new model of citizenship, affiliation and identity formation that breaks with the EU's tradition of adopting nation-state based models. Elizabeth Meehan (1996) draws attention to action through EU institutions, states, national and transnational voluntary associations and regional politics. If the trend is towards societies that are increasingly polyvocal and composed of shifting and multiple identities, complex geographies of affiliation and multiple participation, the EU could do something genuinely different and progressive by advancing an Idea of Europe that reflects this change. This will not have the effect of making *EU* residents and citizens participate in European political and cultural projects, or better Europeans and Unionists, but it might make them feel comfortable about not conforming to national and regional stereotypes, and it might legitimate culture as an evolving project. It might help, as Pnina Werbner suggests (1997: 263):

> to remind 'Europe', as it negotiates its internal differences, that the Continent is fundamentally incomplete, a postcolonial locus of multiple diasporas; and by doing so, to 'interrupt' or 'disrupt' singular narratives of nation and supranation.

Afterword

At the moment, there seems little party political interest in advancing the cause of a Europe of the commons enshrined in enhanced welfare rights. Governments too, as I have already indicated, continue to guard jealously their own national standards of provision. And yet, without movement in such a direction, I cannot see how Europe can become a theatre for progressive experimentation with new models of belonging and becoming. A small step in the right direction is the Charter on Fundamental Rights at the level of Europe recently adopted by the European Council in Nice in December 2000.

A Europe of the commons is not an argument, however, for a slow moving Europe of toothless declarations. The threat of racism, for example, is real and prefigering a xenophobic fortress Europe. The member states have joined forces to secure EU agreement on the need to tighten EU borders, on the grounds that excess immigration poses a threat to security ('immigrants are criminals') as well as resources ('they take our jobs and welfare services'). They have managed to gain agreement on this, but progress on effective ways of tackling racism and other forms of cultural fundamentalism has been slower. Since the late 1980s, the European Parliament has produced magnificent declarations against racism in Europe, not ducking from acknowledging its various manifestations and sources. Now, there is slow movement towards member state agreement on the need to tackle racism at the European level. Yet, implementation remains largely in the hands of national governments, which have resisted tough common policies at EU-level in order to use national anti-racist policies for appeasement 'at home' or for vilification of other nations. This is perhaps an overly cynical interpretation of current policy, but then why has the Christian-Enlightenment Idea of Europe not been mobilized as emphatically and effectively against racism as it has been against non-European undesirables?

Notes

1. I am very grateful to Helen Wallace for her comments on an earlier draft.
2. See also Ristilammi (1996) for a compelling account of Muslim alterity constructed through such alliances in Malmö.

References

Alibhai-Brown, Y. (1998) 'Islam and Euro-identity', *Demos. Eurovisions: New Dimensions of European Integration*, 13, pp. 38–40.
Back, L. (1998) 'Inside Out: Racism, Class and Masculinity in the "Inner City" and the English Suburbs', *New Formations*, 33, pp. 59–76.
Bauman, Z. (1997) 'The Making and Unmaking of Strangers', in Werbner, P. and Modood, T. (eds), *Debating Cultural Hybridity* (London: Zed), pp. 46–57.
Benhabib, S. (1999) ' "Nous" et "Les Autres": the Politics of Complex Cultural Dialogue in a Global Civilization' in Joppke, C. and Lukes, S. (eds.) *Multicultural Questions*, (Oxford: Oxford University Press), pp. 44–64.
Benoît-Rohmer, F. (1996) *The Minority Question in Europe* (Strasbourg, Council of Europe).
Cohen, R. (1998) 'Who Needs an Island?', *New Formations*, 33, pp. 11–37.
Commission (1987) *Fresh Boost for Culture in the European Community* (Brussels: European Commission).
Commission (1997a) *Migration Statistics 1996* (Eurostat, Brussels: European Commission).
Commission (1997b) *Standard Eurobarometer 48, Public Opinion on the European Union*, Autumn (Brussels: European Commission).
Commission (1998a) *The Population of Selected European Countries by Country of Birth*, Eurostat (Statistics in Focus), 10 (Brussels: European Commission).
Commission (1998b) *Standard Eurobarometer 49, Public Opinion on the European Union*, Autumn (Brussels: European Commission).
Commission (1998c) *Standard Eurobarometer 50, Public Opinion on the European Union*, Autumn (Brussels: European Commission).
Delanty, G. (1995) *Inventing Europe* (London: Macmillan – now Palgrave).
Delanty, G. (1997) 'Models of Citizenship: Defining European Identity and Citizenship', *Citizenship Studies*, 1 (3), pp. 285–303.
Friedman, J. (1997) 'Global Crises, the Struggle For Cultural Identity and Intellectual Porkbarrelling: Cosmopolitans versus Locals, Ethnics and Nationals in an era of dehegemonisation', in Werbner, P. and Modood, T. (eds), *Depating Cultural Hybridity* (London: Zed), pp. 70–89.
Hall, S. (1998) 'Aspiration and Attitude . . . reflections on Black Britain in the Nineties', *New Formations*, 33, pp. 38–46.
Heater, D. (1992) *The Idea of European Unity* (London: Leicester University Press).
Heffernan, M. (1998) *The Meaning of Europe* (London: Arnold).
Hutnyk, J. (1997) 'Adorno at Womad: South Asian Crossovers and the Limits of Hybridity-talk', in Werbner, P. and Modood, T. (eds), *Debating Cultural Hybridity* (London: Zed), pp. 106–38.
Ifekwunigwe, J. (1999) *Scattered Belongings* (London: Routledge).
Joppke, C. and Lukes, S. (1999) 'Introduction: Multicultural Questions', in Joppke, C. and Lukes, S. (eds), *Multicultural Questions* (Oxford: Oxford University Press), pp. 1–26.
Leonard, M. (1998a) *Making Europe: The Search for European Identity* (London: Demos).
Leonard, M. (1998b) 'Europe's Legitimacy Gap', *Demos. Eurovisons: New Dimensions of European Integration*, 13, pp. 46–7.

Malik, K. (1998) 'Race, Pluralism and the Meaning of Difference', *New Formations*, 33, pp. 125–35.
Meehan, E. (1996) 'The Debate on Citizenship and European Union', in Murray, P. and Rich, P. (eds), *Visions of European Unity* (Boulder: Westview), pp. 201–24.
Melotti, U. (1997) 'International Migration in Europe: Social Projects and Political Cultures', in Modood, T. and Werbner, P. (eds), *The Politics of Multiculturalism in the New Europe* (London: Zed), pp. 73–92.
Melucci, A. (1996) *The Playing Self* (Cambridge: Cambridge University Press).
Melucci, A. (1997) 'Identity and Difference in a Globalized World', in Werbner, P. and Modood, T. (eds), *Debating Cultural Hybridity* (London: Zed), pp. 58–69.
Mikkeli, H. (1998) *Europe as an Idea and Identity* (London: Macmillan – now Palgrave).
Modood, T. (1997) 'Introduction: the Politics of Multiculturalism in the New Europe', in Modood, T. and Werbner, P. (eds), *The Politics of Multiculturalism in the New Europe* (London: Zed), pp. 1–26.
Morley, D. and Robins, K. (1995) *Spaces of Identity* (London: Routledge).
Nederveen Pieterse, J. (1999) 'Europe Travelling Light: Europeanization and Globalization', *The European Legacy*, 4 (3), pp. 3–17.
Nielsen, B. and Stubb, A. (1998) *The European Readings on the Theory and Practice of European Integration* (Basingstoke: Lynne Rienner).
Pantel, M. (1999) 'Unity-in-diversity: Cultural Policy and EU Legitimacy', in Banchoff, T. and Smith, M. P. (eds), *Legitimacy in the European Union* (London: Routledge), 46–65.
Parekh, B. (1999) 'Political Theory and the Multicultural Society', *Radical Philosophy*, 95, pp. 27–32.
Pred, A. (1999) *Even in Sweden*, mimeo (Department of Geography, University of California at Berkeley).
Prodi, R. (1999) *Un' idea dell' Europa* (Bologna: Il Mulino).
Rex, J. (1996) 'National Identity in the Democratic Multi-cultural State', *Sociological Research Online*, 1 (2), pp. 1–12.
Ristilammi, P-M. (1996) 'Alterity in Modern Sweden', in Arvastson, G. and Lindqvist, M. (eds), *The Story of Progress* (Uppsala: Acta Universitatis Upsaliensis), pp. 49–56.
Samad, Y. (1997) 'The Plural Guises of Multiculturalism: Conceptualising a Fragmented Paradigm', in Modood, T. and Werbner, P. (eds), *The Politics of Multiculturalism in the New Europe* (London: Zed), pp. 240–60.
Shore, C. (1998) 'The Myth of a Euro-identity', *Demos. Eurovisions: New Dimensions of European Integration*, 13, pp. 48–50.
Smith, A. (1995) *Nations and Nationalism in a Global Era* (Cambridge: Polity Press).
Soysal, Y. (1994) *Limits to Citizenship* (Chicago: Chicago University Press).
Stolcke, V. (1995) 'Talking Culture: New Boundaries, New Rhetorics of Exclusion in Europe', *Current Anthropology*, 36 (1), pp. 1–13.
Spinner-Halev, J. (1999) 'Cultural Pluralism and Partial Citizenship', in Joppke, C. and Lukes, S. (eds), *Multicultural Questions* (Oxford: Oxford University Press), pp. 65–86.
Therborn, G. (1998) *Multicultural Societies*, [*mimeo*] (Uppsala: Swedish Collegium for Advanced Study in the Social Sciences).

Waldron, J. (1992) 'Minority Cultures and the Cosmopolitan Alternative', *University of Michigan Journal of Law Reform*, 25, pp. 751–93.

Werbner, P. (1996) 'Fun Spaces: On Identity and Social Empowerment Among British Pakistanis', *Theory, Culture and Society*, 13 (4), pp. 53–79.

Werbner, P. (1997) 'Afterword: Writing Multiculturalism and Politics in the New Europe', in Modood, T. and Werbner, P. (eds), *The Politics of Multiculturalism in the New Europe* (London: Zed), pp. 261–7.

Žižek, S. (1997) 'Multiculturalism, or, the Cultural Logic of Multinational Capitalism', *New Left Review*, 225, pp. 28–51.

Part IV
The Scope and Limits of Integration

15
Towards Post-corporatist Concertation in Europe?

Rory O'Donnell

Introduction

In recent years, it has frequently been argued that Europe is witnessing a re-emergence of neo-corporatism through the incorporation of hierarchical interest associations in the policy process. The role of tripartite bargains in the stabilization of many of the European economies in the 1990s, and in aiding the surprising convergence to the Maastricht criteria, are cited in support of this view. Yet there are reasons to be cautious in describing the emerging systems of policy concertation and interest mediation in Europe as neo-corporatist. One is that the current interest in the return of corporatism may just be the latest twist in a debate which has turned several full circles in recent decades. A second is that this return to neo-corporatism has been led by countries, such as Ireland and the Netherlands, which are not easily classified as neo-corporatist. Indeed, the policy process developed in these countries in the 1990s has been understood, by both the actors and analysts, in terms quite different from neo-corporatism. This chapter draws on that understanding to outline some features of what might be called a 'post-corporatist' system of concertation.

The next section describes the system of social partnership in place in Ireland since 1987, and notes the re-emergence of policy concertation in many member states of the European Union (EU) in the 1990s. The main section of the chapter outlines a new interpretation of social partnership, derived from reflection within the policy process in Ireland. This perspective emphasizes deliberation and problem-solving and involves a new view of the nature of a social partner. It seeks a conception of partnership which is consistent with the changing role of the state and the closer link between policy-making, implementation and monitoring. The chapter closes with a brief discussion of whether the conception of social partnership that has emerged in Ireland, and the Netherlands, might also apply to those other EU member states which have relied on concertation in the 1990s.

The emergence of social partnership in Ireland and other member states

Although the Irish economy performed relatively well through most of the 1970s, attempts to maintain growth in the face of international recession involved increased government borrowing during the late-1970s and early 1980s. Ireland joined the European exchange-rate-mechanism (ERM) on its establishment in 1979, hoping to achieve a switch from British to German inflation rates. The period 1980 to 1987 was one of prolonged recession, falling living standards and a dramatic increase in unemployment. Total employment declined by almost 6 per cent and employment in manufacturing by 25 per cent. The length and depth of this depression reflected Ireland's sharp balance of payments and public finance adjustment, yet coincided with increasing public sector deficits and debt. By 1987, the debt/GNP ratio was approaching 130 per cent and real fears of national insolvency emerged. Fifteen years after joining the EC, Ireland's economic and social strategy was in ruins, and its ability to prosper in the international system was in doubt.

In a context of deep despair in Irish society, the social partners, acting in the tripartite National Economic and Social Council (NESC), hammered out an agreed strategy to escape from the vicious circle of real stagnation, rising taxes and exploding debt. The NESC is an advisory body, in which employers, trade unions, farmers and senior civil servants analyse policy issues and seek a consensus. Its *Strategy for Development* (1986) formed the basis upon which a new government and the social partners negotiated the Programme for National Recovery (PNR), to run from 1987 to 1990. This was the first of five agreements that have brought Ireland through more than a decade of negotiated economic and social governance. The negotiation of each social partnership agreement has been preceded by a NESC *Strategy* report, setting out the shared perspective of the social partners on the parameters within which a new programme should be negotiated (NESC, 1990, 1993, 1996).

The social partnership programmes involve agreement between employers, trade unions, farming interests and government on wage levels in both the private and public sectors for a three year period. The first programme enlisted trade union support for a radical correction of the public finances. In return, the government accepted that the value of social welfare payments would be maintained and the tax system reformed. Indeed, the programmes contain agreement on a wide range of economic and social policies – including tax reform, the evolution of welfare payments, trends in health spending, structural adjustment, Ireland's adherence to the narrow band of the ERM and, subsequently, the Maastricht criteria.

While the macroeconomic strategy has been adhered to consistently since 1987, the agreements contain policy initiatives which are worthy of note. Local partnership companies were established – involving the social partners, the community and voluntary sector and state agencies – to explore more coordinated, multi-dimensional, approaches to social exclusion. An Organization for Economic Cooperation and Development (OECD) evaluation of Ireland's local economic development policies considered that the partnership approach constituted an experiment in economic regeneration and participative democracy which is, potentially, of international significance (Sabel, 1996).

An important feature of Irish social partnership has been a concern to widen the partnership process beyond the traditional social partners. A new forum was established and membership of the NESC was gradually widened to include representatives of the community and voluntary sector. Reflecting this, the 1996 programme, Partnership 2000, was negotiated in a new way, involving representatives of the unemployed, women's groups and others that address social exclusion.

The process of policy innovation includes measures to promote partnership at enterprise level and agreement on action to modernize the public service. New institutional arrangements were created to monitor the implementation of the partnership programmes. While partnership began by addressing a critical central issue, looming insolvency and economic collapse, it has since focused more and more on a range of complex supply-side matters. This is reflected in a dense web of working groups, committees and task-forces, which involve the social partners in the design, implementation and monitoring of public policy.

The social partnership approach produced the much-needed economic recovery and has underpinned an unprecedented period of growth since then. Since 1987, employment has grown by an astonishing 34 per cent, and growth of GDP has been the highest in the EU and among the highest in the OECD. Irish growth is based on a combination of inward investment by leading companies – in computers, software, pharmaceuticals and finance – the resurgence of indigenous manufacturing and the emergence of strong Irish enterprises in services. Social partnership also produced a transformation in Ireland's public finances, low and predictable inflation and successful transition to economic and monetary union (EMU).

Elsewhere in Europe, there has been a notable reliance on tri-partite concertation in the 1990s. Compston has shown that there was a significant increase in tri-partite policy concertation in Italy, Denmark, Norway, the Netherlands and Germany, and little change in Austria and Switzerland, where concertation has been the norm (Compston, 1998; Regini, 1998; Regini and Regalia, 1997). Only in Sweden has there been a significant retreat from policy concertation involving unions and business. In addition, Finland, Portugal and Spain have made use of concertation in their adjustment to European integration and preparation for monetary union (Fajertag and Pochet 1997). Indeed, it has been argued that the countries which have been most successful in achieving welfare reform have built a broad consensus for change (Ebbinghaus and Hassel, 1999). These trends raise considerable doubt about the 'decline of corporatism' predicted by some analysts (Gobeyn, 1993; Gerlich, 1992).

Now that the continued, or increased, reliance on policy concertation is recognized, various explanations are being canvassed and explored. These include the idea that the corrosive effect of liberalization has been overrated (Traxler, 1997), an emphasis on the impact of European market and monetary integration (Rhodes, 1998; Grote and Schmitter, 1999), and a focus on the altered content of concertation (Rhodes, 1998; Traxler, 1997).

How should we interpret the emergence and apparent success of social partnership in Ireland and other member states in the 1990s? It is clearly tempting to see it as a return of 'neo-corporatism' and, as noted at the outset, this is an increasingly influential view. But the Irish case, and perhaps also the Dutch case, suggests that there are several difficulties with this view. First, Ireland displays few of the structural characteristics traditionally seen as necessary for successful neo-corporatist 'political exchange' (Hardiman, 1988). Second, the substance of Irish policy under partnership differs from postwar European neo-corporatism (Taylor, 1996; Teague, 1995). Third, the social partners and government have developed a perspective which goes well beyond the categories used to understand and characterize postwar

European neo-corporatism.[1] It is this self-understanding of social partnership which I draw on, in the following section, to suggest an idea of post-corporatist concertation.

Social partnership as post-corporatist concertation

The development of social partnership in Ireland since 1987 has involved a wide range of economic and political actors in a complex process of negotiation and interaction. Detailed, shared, analysis of economic and social problems and policies has been a key aspect of this process. Indeed, that analysis has, for a variety of reasons, focused on the partnership system itself. To assess the applicability of the partnership approach in the new economic context of EMU, it was necessary to assess thoroughly the effects of the centralized system of wage bargaining and the consensual approach to management of the public finances (NESC, 1996). In order to widen partnership successfully beyond the traditional partners it was necessary to thoroughly analyse the nature, purpose and goals of partnership. That examination revealed some severe difficulties in making an inclusive system of partnership work, but also a new view of social partnership.[2] My focus here is on four central arguments that may have a bearing on the way in which the re-emergence of concertation or social partnership in other EU member states should be interpreted.

Beyond bargaining: deliberation and problem-solving

In order to capture the form of concertation that has emerged in Ireland, and possibly in other member states in the past decade, I distinguishing initially between two different conceptions, or dimensions, of partnership:

- functional interdependence, bargaining and deal-making; and
- solidarity, inclusiveness and participation.

It is then argued that while effective partnership involves both of these, there is a third dimension, which transcends these two:

- deliberation, interaction, problem-solving and shared understanding.

The preconditions for this are less stringent than is sometimes believed. In particular, they do not include a pre-existing consensus on the nature, direction or justice of the overall economic and social system.

The first dimension/conception of partnership – which emphasizes functional interdependence, bargaining and deal-making – has always figured in analysis of neo-corporatist political exchange. Its most concrete manifestation is the mutual benefit of a core agreement between business, unions and government. There can be no doubt that this is an important dimension of social partnership. However, for a variety of reasons, this hard-headed view is not adequate on its own to describe or understand the process now. The performance of the economy is not functionally independent of problems of exclusion and unemployment.

The second dimension/conception is that which emphasizes solidarity, inclusiveness and participation. This has been an important theme in many of the key policy reports in Ireland and is reflected in the widening of partnership beyond the traditional partners.

The partnership process, and the policy-oriented discussion of it, combines these two dimensions/conceptions, but cannot be based entirely on either. To rest entirely on the first could be to validate the claim that the process simply reflects the power of the traditional social partners, especially if claims for the unemployed and marginalized are not included in the functional interdependence, and are seen as purely *moral*. To adopt a naive inclusivist view would risk reducing the process to a purely consultative one, in which all interests and groups merely *voiced* their views and demands. Ironically, this would lead, by a different route, to the same end-point; partnership would ultimately be no different from pluralist lobbying, in which the outcome favours those groups with the most resources.

These two dimensions are both present, but even together they are not adequate to explain the process. While functional interdependence is wider than many think, its immediacy and visibility are certainly less present in some problem areas than in others. The absence of a rock-solid affective basis of social solidarity suggests that we resist the temptation to see the partnership model as grounded in some organic characteristic of society.

There is a third dimension of partnership, which transcends the two discussed above. Although the concepts of 'negotiation' and 'bargaining' distinguish social partnership from more liberal and pluralist approaches, in which *consultation* is more prominent, they are not entirely adequate to capture the partnership process. Bargaining describes a process in which each party comes with definite preferences and seeks to maximize its gains. While this is a definite part of social partnership as it has emerged in Ireland and other EU member states, the overall process (including various policy forums) would seem to involve something more. Partnership involves the players in a process of deliberation which has the potential to shape and reshape both their identity and preferences. This idea, that identity is formed in interaction, rather than existing prior to interaction, is important. It is implicit in the description of the process as 'dependent on a shared understanding', and 'characterized by a problem-solving approach designed to produce consensus' (NESC, 1996: 66). This third dimension has to be added to the hard-headed notion of bargaining, (and to the idea of solidarity), to capture the process adequately.

The key to these features of social partnership would seem to be the adoption of 'a problem-solving approach'. A remarkable feature of effective partnership experiments is that the partners do not debate their ultimate social visions. This is not to suggest that partners abandon their social vision. Their action in partnership is definitely informed by, and consistent with, the deep commitments that motivate their work in the public sphere. Indeed, the vision and values that attract people to join the voluntarily associations of social partnership are probably more important now than in the past. Recognition of the prevalence of a problem-solving approach, and the limited debate on ultimate social visions, clarifies what has been said in the previous paragraph. Although the process can go beyond bargaining, and can draw the partners into a process of deliberation and action which can reshape their identity and preferences, not everything is at stake for those who participate.

This suggests that rather than being the *pre-condition* for partnership, consensus and shared understanding are more like an *outcome*. This, in turn, means that the shared understanding cannot be a static, once-off, condition. Indeed, the extension of Irish partnership in recent years has involved the community and voluntary groups *coming to share* the prevailing understanding of the macroeconomic constraints, but simultaneously producing and disseminating a *new* understanding of the policy problem which concerns them most, namely social exclusion and unemployment.

In the right institutional context, skilled actors engage with one another in ways which (temporarily and provisionally) resolve conflicts that are undecidable in more general debate. They can even initiate practical measures of social solidarity and cooperation, for which no one can provide a compelling foundation. These can, in turn, disclose radically new possibilities of social and economic life. If this is correct, then the key task is discovery of the institutional arrangements which can assist this, rather than extended prior discussion of economic and social systems, democracy, solidarity and community. Furthermore, both Irish and international experiences suggest that the discovery of those institutional arrangements is itself an experimental and practical process (Dorf and Sabel, 1999).

It is a remarkable, if not easily understood, fact that deliberation which is problem-solving and practical produces consensus, even where there are underlying conflicts of interest, and even where there was no shared understanding at the outset. It is also a fact that using that approach to produce a consensus in one area, facilitates the same approach in other areas. The key may lie in understanding what kind of consensus is produced when problem-solving deliberation is used. It is generally a provisional consensus to proceed with practical action, as if a certain analytical perspective was correct, while holding open the possibility of a review of goals, means and underlying analysis (see below). This type of agreement certainly involves compromise. But the word compromise is inadequate to describe it. 'Compromise' so often fudges the issues which need to be addressed.

A definite characteristic of successful policy reports is argumentation or reason-giving. In these reports, the social partners and others present the society not with a *deal*, however good, but with the *reasons* why a certain perspective or policy initiative has commanded their agreement. It is to the *problem-solving* and the *reason-giving* that we should attribute whatever success these bodies have had. This contrasts with the view which attributes their influence to their apparent focus on *high level 'strategy'* or *'policy-making'*.

A similar account of the elements and process of concertation has independently emerged in recent work on the 'Dutch miracle' (Visser and Hemerijck, 1997; Visser, 1998a, b). Visser and Hemerijck draw attention to new combinations of centralization and decentralization, and emphasise the combination of interest-group dialogue and expert input which create a common definition of problems. This yielded a 'problem-solving style of joint decision-making', in which participants are 'obliged to explain, give reasons and take responsibility for their decisions and strategies to each other, to their rank and file, and to the general public' (Visser, 1998a: 12). The institutions of concertation work where they facilitate shift from a 'bargaining style' to a 'problem-solving style'. Visser (1998a: 13) considers that 'the most interesting property of social concertation lies in the possibility that interest groups redefine the content of their self-interested strategies in a 'public-regarding' way'.

A new view of what a social partner is now

The second element of the perspective on partnership which has emerged in Ireland is a new view of the nature and role of the social partners themselves. Trade unions, business associations and community groups tend to see themselves as different, each emphasizing the severity of the difficulties they face. Yet extended and robust discussion between them revealed that they all confront the problem of linking national representation to local action and turning participation in national concertation into tangible results. From this there emerged a new definition, or description, of a social partner, emphasizing process rather than structure, and information rather than force.

In international studies of neo-corporatist systems, there is a clear idea of what a social partner is (Cawson, 1986; Schmitter, 1979). This traditional idea is summarized in the left-hand panel of Table 15.1. A key idea is that to be capable of negotiating and delivering, an organization must have 'social closure' or monopoly of representation of a given social group. This monopoly gave them an authorized jurisdiction or charter. A second element was the emphasis on their *functional* roles in the economy. Indeed, many went so far as to say that only *producer* groups were capable of being social partners. The key activity undertaken by organizations with these characteristics was *bargaining*, with each other and with government. In many respects, the logic of that bargaining is summed up in the next characteristic listed in the left-hand box: state intervention in the economy. It was because the state intervened extensively in the economy that it found itself deeply engaged with unions and employers' associations. Finally, each of the organizations which participated was *hierarchically* organized and *concentrated*. This gave them a clear 'peak organization', which was capable of both representing and disciplining a large number of individuals and sub-organizations.

The traditional conception of the nature of a social partner would seem to have lost much of its relevance. An alternative set of characteristics is summarized in the right-hand panel of Table 15.1.

The first is the fact that social partners are continuously mobilizing citizens who have problems that need to be dealt with. Organizations cannot take for granted their role as representatives of a given group, with defined and stable economic or occupational roles. They must offer practical achievements and a vision of a better economy and society. Rather than relying on fixed functional roles, their strength is in coordination: they assist in defining and coordinating functions. Rather than having their base in producer groups, their base is actors in civil society who have to respond to the often unintended consequences of policy, economic change or action by other groups.

While the ultimate role of the traditional social partner was bargaining, and achievement depended on the power resources deployed in bargaining, this is no longer an adequate description. Economic change has fragmented these power resources and shifts in popular opinion have made traditional social partners uncertain about how, and whether, they can deploy them. By contrast, *information* is the key resource which a modern social partner brings to the table. They are needed, precisely because the information is generated within their organizational ambit. They have the links, the capacity, and the contacts with what is really going on in society.

Table 15.1 Traditional and new ideas of a social partner

Traditional idea of a social partner	New characteristics of a social partner
• Monopoly/authorized jurisdiction	• continuous mobilization
• function (economic or regulatory)	• coordination of functions
• producer groups	• actors in civil society
• bargaining	• information as key resource
• state intervention in the economy	• new forms of public advocacy – analysis – dialogue – shared understanding
• hierarchy	• actor, not just voice

In the place of the old form of bargaining, there are new forms of public advocacy. These are summarized in the right-hand panel as *analysis*, *dialogue* and *shared understanding*. It is possible to bargain without discussing, and a lot of traditional bargaining was like that. At the other extreme, it is possible to analyse without putting yourself in the shoes of the actors, and a lot of traditional social and economic science was like that. In between, there is a combination of discussion, analysis and deliberation, which might be called 'negotiated governance'. The new models of social partnership, at their most effective, seem to be moving toward that approach.

The final characteristic is that a new social partner is an actor, not just a voice. Mobilizing, organizing, delivering and solving problems (with others) seem to be features of what makes these social partners effective. Indeed, these might be seen as *conditions* to be an effective social partner. The goals, methods and knowledge of organizations are shaped and reshaped in action. A continuous danger of the partnership approach is the slide to 'talking shops'. Involvement in action, as well as talk, is one prevention against that danger. This feature of a modern social partner is related to a weakening of the traditional distinction between political work, self-help, charity and labour organization.

The importance of action also reflects the limits of representation. One of the effects of the many changes in the economy and society is to qualify further the usefulness of conventional representation. It underlines the increased role of action, and of organizations that create and coordinate action. Furthermore, within that, there is an increased role of *direct* action *by* members, rather than action *for* members, or organization for the purpose of representation.

Many reasons could be offered to explain why the traditional social partner (described in the left-hand panel) has become less relevant in many countries, and is giving way to a new social partner (described in the right-hand panel). These would include the shift from manufacturing to services, technical and organizational change in enterprises, the collapse of unskilled labour, the emergence of new occupational roles and work patterns, new information technology, high unemployment, the emergence of other complex new social problems, the difficulties of large-scale public administration, the development of new social movements and the growth of self-help or empowerment-oriented organizations.

New roles for the centre and national partnership

A further reason why the new examples of concertation should not be seen as a return of neo-corporatism is the changing nature of government and public policy. Across the world, we seem to be witnessing a historical shift in the role of the centre and national government. The complexity, volatility and diversity of economic and social problems, and of social groups, are undermining the capacity of traditional, postwar, legislative and administrative systems. Parliaments find it difficult to pass laws that can accommodate the variety and unpredictability of situations which need to be addressed. Administrative systems, designed for uniform delivery of a predictable range of services, cannot meet the new needs and demands of citizens (Dorf and Sabel, 1999).

It is critical that concertative or partnership arrangements are in tune with the capabilities of government and administration at different levels. This is not easy, since in many countries there is no longer a settled pattern of national, regional, local and sectoral policy-making and institutions. We can, however, paint a provisional picture of the way in which the role of central government is changing. The traditional roles of the centre are summarized in the left-hand panel of Table 15.2. These roles reflect the power, autonomy and effectiveness of central government, as it was understood in most western countries in the postwar period. The democratic legitimacy of central government gave it the ability to allocate public resources, to direct the operation of government departments and agencies, and to administer complex systems of public delivery and scrutiny. In addition, where corporatist-type systems existed, government had the role of underwriting the monopoly representation exercised by business associations and trade unions.

Changes in the economy and society have undermined the effectiveness of central government in many of these roles. This development has drawn attention to the potentially superior effectiveness of regional or local government, and many countries have decentralized significant areas of policy-making and administration. But, for a variety of reasons, central government remains extremely important, and the role of supranational government, such as the EU, is increasing rather than diminishing.

The new roles of central government are summarized, tentatively, in the right-hand panel of Table 15.2. Policy entrepreneurship seems an important characteristic of successful policy at both national and EU level. Governments in EU member states and elsewhere, as well as the European Commission, have in the past decade adopted an experimental approach in many policy areas (Laffan *et al.*, 2000). An emerging role of the centre seems to lie in the authorization, coordination, protection and financing of experimental approaches.

Monitoring is listed as a role of the centre in this emerging system. Yet, the changes noted above suggest that central government would have difficulty in accumulating, checking and interpreting the masses of information necessary to monitor a wide range of public policies

Table 15.2 Traditional and new roles of central government

Traditional central roles	Arena of problem-solving
• allocating • directing • administering • underwriting monopoly representation	• policy entrepreneurship • monitoring (obliging and supporting) • facilitating deliberation • protecting non-statutory organizations • supporting interest group formation

and programmes. A new role for central government then lies in obliging and assisting others in monitoring and benchmarking. This does not mean monitoring in the sense of checking the *implementation* of programmes, the *goals* and *methods* of which are *defined once and for all by central government*. Rather what is pertinent is government's role in setting standards, obliging and assisting monitoring, and in altering both the methods, and sometimes even the goals, of public policy and provision in the light of systematic comparison of successes and failures (Sabel, 1994).

The next new role of the centre listed in the right-hand panel, refers to the role of the centre in facilitating communication and joint action between social interests and organizations. Given the difficulty of directing and administering policy, central government is often more effective when it provides an arena for problem-solving by others. This role is clearly related to partnership, and contrasts sharply with traditional policy and administrative approaches. It involves the systematic organization of deliberation and information-pooling. In identifying the state's role in facilitating deliberation, information pooling and action by other organizations, it is not implied that the state is neutral, or that it comes to issues without an agenda or interests of its own. The state is much more than a referee. Its democratic mandate and resources give it a unique role in the partnership process.

Another emerging role of central government would seem to be protection of non-statutory organizations. An aspect of the exciting policy change of the past decade has been the move from establishing statutory bodies, with a permanent and guaranteed life, to the use of *ad hoc*, or task-oriented, bodies. These seem more flexible and innovative, but are also more vulnerable. Consequently, central government has a role in protecting them in their relations with statutory bodies and heavily-resourced state agencies.

Finally, national governments have the legitimacy and resources to support the formation and development of interest groups. Their willingness to do this depends on whether they believe that the inclusiveness and quality of relationships in society is both a good in itself and is productive. In the partnership process the state sometimes shares some of its authority with social partners; this, of course, involves them in sharing some of its responsibility. In supporting interest groups, it is legitimate for the state to assign certain tasks and favour high standards of openness, democracy, representation *and direct participation*.

National-level concertative or partnership arrangements cannot be effective if they are premised on an outdated view of the power, autonomy and effectiveness of central government. They will not assist in solving problems if they rely on central government to design, direct and administer programmes. Social partnership will not retain its relevance if it relies on the state to underwrite the partners' monopoly of representation of groups of citizens. That legitimacy must be created and recreated in action. A major challenge, discussed at some length among the Irish social partners, is how to refocus partnership arrangements so that they are consistent with the emerging roles of national government. A second challenge is how to redesign public administration itself, so that it is consistent with these emerging roles.

Combining policy-making, implementation and monitoring

What has been argued above suggests that we need not only to *link* policy-making, implementation and monitoring, but to *rethink* them. It may be that these separate spheres of 'policy-making', 'implementation' and 'monitoring' no longer hold good in the conventional sense. Hence, the final element of a new concept of post-corporatist concertation or partnership, concerns the links between policy-making, implementation and monitoring.

The experience of the past decade suggests that national-level partnership focused around national-level *policy-making*, is unlikely to solve the complex and diverse problems which citizens confront. Agreement on a strategic approach, and even on specific policies, means little if these are not implemented effectively. If they cannot be implemented in accord with a central design, then they have to be implemented with local or sectoral discretion. That means little, if we have no way of telling which versions work and which versions fail. In many areas of welfare policy, social policy, labour market policy and industrial policy, how measures are implemented has become crucial, and hence, the ability to monitor pacts is a necessary requirement. In Ireland, it is now recognized that this requires the social partnership system to engage more actively with implementation and monitoring. What is required is examination of the practical successes and failures of policy, so as to provide a basis from which to revise both the *methods* and *goals* of policy. This poses profound challenges to both public organizations and interest associations.

European integration and convergence

I have set out a conception of post-corporatist concertation, based on the experience of the country which has made the most conspicuous, and successful, use of social partnership in the 1990s. Ireland is also a country which has been profoundly and dramatically changed by participation in European integration (O'Donnell, 2000).

There is some evidence, in the work of Visser and Hemerijck (1997), that a similar understanding of social partnership has emerged in the Netherlands, which has also been successful in economic correction and social stabilization.

Further empirical and conceptual work is required to establish whether the ideas apply to the other member states which have used policy concertation in the 1990s. Such work needs to compare both the content of concertation and the process of partnership in various countries – to test whether it is closer to traditional postwar neo-corporatism or to the post-corporatist model set out above. The new system of concertation differs in important respects from the old: it is based on an open economy; it relies less on demand management to deliver its social benefits; it does not guarantee privileged access to the traditional social partners or underwrite their monopoly to the same degree; it involves a different relation between national and firm-level partnership; it relies on direct participation as well as representation; and, most importantly, it is based on deep shared involvement in both deliberation and monitoring. At first glance, the terms used to describe policy concertation across Europe in the 1990s – 'negotiated social pacts', 'supply-side corporatism', 'competitive corporatism', 'cooperative problem-solving', 'macro-economic regulation', 'concertation without political exchange' – suggest a degree of convergence.

While the dominant continental European models – German, French, Scandinavian – are under severe strain, remarkable innovations are emerging in unlikely places and coming from diverse directions. Inside the space of a decade and a half, the EU has created both a new internal market and a new macroeconomic and monetary landscape. It is thus providing the European economy with regulatory and macro-economic instruments made in, and for, the radically new economic and political environment which is emerging. By means of the EU, the countries of Europe can modernize, modify – and in some cases discard – policies and institutions made for the postwar world. Responding to the demand of internationalization, small member states, such as Ireland, Netherlands, Finland and Portugal, seem to be inventing post-corporatist forms of macroeconomic concertation and structural reform which sustain strong economic and employment growth. Under the pressure of integration, Italy is achieving a new combination of strategic policy and microeconomic invention which seems to achieve not only competitive success but also social stabilization. The peripheral countries, so hungry for integration and modernization, are adopting the organizational innovations which were invented in Asia, but which subsequently underpinned the economic regeneration of the US. Furthermore, wherever these innovations in social and economic organization are occurring, the European Commission is to be found as either a catalyst, a partner or a keen observer of the new governance.

Notes

1. Studies of Irish social partnership include: Hardiman (1988, 1992); Roche (1997); O'Donnell (1993); O'Donnell and O'Reardon (1997); O'Donnell and Thomas (1998, 2000); Teague (1995); NESC (1996); NESF (1997); O'Connor (2001).
2. This view of social partnership, upon which the argument of this chapter is based, is set out in a report of the National Economic and Social Forum, NESF (1997).

References

Cawson, A. (1986) *Corporatism and Political Theory* (Oxford: Basil Blackwell).
Compston, H. (1998) 'The End of National Policy Concertation: Western Europe since the Single European Act', *Journal of European Public Policy*, June.
Dorf, M. and Sabel, C. F. (1999) 'A Constitution of Democratic Experimentalism', *Columbia Law Review*, 98 (2), 267–473.
Ebbinghaus, B. and Hassel, A. (1999) 'The Role of Tripartite Concertation in the Reform of the Welfare State', *Transfer*, 5 (1–2), 64–82.
Fajertag, G. and Pochet, P. (eds) (1997) *Social Pacts in Europe* (Brussels: European Trade Union Institute).
Gerlich, P. (1992) 'A Farewell to Corporatism', *West European Politics*, 15, No. 1, January, pp. 132–46.
Grote, J. R. and Schmitter, P. (1999) 'The Renaissance of National Corporatism: Unintended Side-effect of European Economic and Monetary Union or Calculated Response to the Absence of European Social Policy', *Transfer*, 5 (1–2), 34–64.
Gobeyn, M. J. (1993) 'Explaining the Decline of Macro-Corporatist Political Bargaining Structures in Advanced Capitalist Societies', *Governance*, 6, No. 1, January, pp. 3–22.
Hardiman, N. (1988) *Pay, Politics and Economic Performance in Ireland 1970–1987* (Oxford: Clarendon Press), 329–58.
Hardiman, N. (1992) 'The State and Economic Interests; Ireland in a Comparative Perspective', in Goldthorpe, J. and Whelan, C. T. (eds), *The Development of Industrial Society in Ireland* (Oxford: Oxford University Press).
Laffan, B., O'Donnell, R. and Smith, M. (2000) *Europe's Experimental Union: Rethinking Integration* (London: Routledge).

NESC (1986) *A Strategy for Development 1986–1990* (Dublin: National Economic and Social Council).
NESC (1990) *A Strategy for the Nineties: Economic Stability and Structural Change* (Dublin: National Economic and Social Council).
NESC (1993) *A Strategy for Competitiveness, Growth and Employment* (Dublin: National Economic and Social Council).
NESC (1996) *Strategy into the 21st Century* (Dublin: National Economic and Social Council).
NESF (1997) *A Framework for Partnership: Enriching Strategic Consensus through Participation* (Dublin: National Economic and Social Forum).
O'Connor, E. (2001) 'Social Partnership in Ireland; a Historical Perspective', in Compston, H. and Berger, S. (eds), *Social Partnership in Western Europe: A Historical and Comparative Analysis* (forthcoming).
O'Donnell, R. (1993) *Ireland and Europe: Challenges for a New Century* (Dublin: Economic and Social Research Institute).
O'Donnell, R. (2000) 'The New Ireland in the New Europe', in O'Donnell, R. (ed.), *Europe – the Irish Experience* (Dublin: Institute of European Affairs), 161–214.
O'Donnell, R. and O'Reardon, C. (1997) 'Ireland's Experiment in Social Partnership 1987–96', in Fajertag, G. and Pochet, P. (eds), *Social Pacts in Europe* (Brussels: European Trade Union Institute) 79–95.
O' Donnell, R. and Thomas, D. (1998) 'Social Partnership and Policy Making', in Healy, S. and Reynolds, B. (eds), *Social Policy in Ireland; Principles, Practices, Problems* (Dublin: Oak Tree Press), 117–48.
O' Donnell, R. and Thomas, D. (forthcoming) 'Social Partnership in Ireland since 1987', in Compston, H. and Berger, S. (eds), *Social Partnership in Western Europe: A Historical and Comparative Analysis* (Oxford: Berghahn Books).
Regini, M. (1998) 'Still Engaging in Corporatism? Recent Italian Experience in Comparative Perspective', *Industrial Relations Journal*, 3 (3), 259–78.
Regini, M. and Regalia, I. (1997) 'Employers, Unions and The State: The Resurgence of Concertation in Italy', *West European Politics*, 20, 210–30.
Rhodes, M. (1998) 'Globalisation, Labour Markets and Welfare States: A Future of Competitive Corporatism', in Rhodes, M. and Mény, Y. (eds), *The Future of European Welfare* (Basingstoke: Macmillan – now Palgrave).
Roche, W. (1997) 'Pay Determination, The State and the Politics of Industrial Relations', in Murphy, T. V. and Roche, W. (eds), *Irish Industrial Relations in Practice* (Dublin: Oak Tree Press) 126–205.
Sabel, C. F. (1994) 'Learning by Monitoring: the Institutions of Economic Development', in Smelser, N. and Swedeburg, R. (eds), *Handbook of Economic Sociology* (West Sussex: Princeton University Press), 137–65.
Sabel, C. F. (1996) *Ireland: Local Development and Social Innovation* (Paris: OECD).
Schmitter, P. (1979) 'Still the Century of Corporatism?', in Schmitter, P. and Lembruch, G. (eds), *Trends Towards Corporatist Intermediation* (London: Sage), 7–52.
Taylor, G. (1996) 'Labour Market Rigidities, Institutional Impediments and Managerial Constraints: Some Reflections on the Experience of Macro-Political Bargaining in Ireland', *Economic and Social Review*, 27 (3), 253–77.
Teague, P. (1995) 'Pay Determination in the Republic of Ireland: Towards Social Corporatism?', *British Journal of Industrial Relations*, 33 (2).

Traxler, F. (1997) 'The Logic of Social Pacts', in Fajertag, G. and Pochet, P. (eds), *Social Pacts in Europe* (Brussels: European Trade Union Institute), 27–36.

Visser, J. (1998a) 'Concertation – the Art of Making Social Pacts', paper presented at Notre Europe/ETUI seminar on 'National Social Pacts', Brussels, 10 June, 1998.

Visser, J. (1998b) 'Two Cheers for Corporatism, One for the Market: Industrial Relations, Wage Moderation and Job Growth in the Netherlands', *British Journal of Industrial Relations*, 36 (2), 269–92.

Visser, J. and Hemerijck, A. (1997) *A Dutch Miracle: Job Growth, Welfare Reform and Corporatism in the Netherlands* (Amsterdam: Amsterdam University Press).

16
Organizing European Institutions of Governance . . . a Prelude to an Institutional Account of Political Integration

Johan P. Olsen

In search of new forms of political unity

For half a century, Europeans have (again) explored the possibility of new forms of political order and unity. This time change in western Europe has been non-violent and there have been comprehensive and possibly lasting changes in the (west) European institutions of governance. Still, students of European political integration face a partial and emerging polity, with institutions of governance in change and not in a stable equilibrium.

Accounting for the dynamics of political integration requires attention to four questions. First, what is meant by 'political integration', how are such processes to be conceptualized and what are good indicators of changing levels and forms of integration? Second, on what basis is the new polity – the European Union (EU), as a political organization and system of governance – being integrated? Related to this, how much, and what, ties members of the EU together and separates them from non-members? Third, what are the consequences of various levels and forms of integration? What are the most significant effects of changing levels of integration, including implications for the constituent units? Fourth, what are the determinants of political integration and through what processes does change take place? Why are there variations in the levels and forms of integration across institutional spheres and policy sectors? Why are there changes over time?

In particular, what is the integrating power of shifting system performance in terms of efficient problem-solving and service delivery? What is the integrating power of shared, relatively stable constitutive principles, institutions and procedures of good governance?

This chapter is a *prelude* to answering such questions, and only a prelude because it primarily catalogues some issues, controversies and research challenges that need clarification before a coherent theoretical approach to (European) political integration can be developed.[1] The chapter feeds on an institutional perspective. Yet, it does not aspire to document the advantages of this perspective. That is, it does not specify concrete implications that are interesting, non-obvious and disconfirmable. Nor does it document the phenomena that can be better understood within an institutional perspective than within competing accounts of political integration.

The chapter starts with the observation that institutional change is a theme attracting attention from both practitioners and researchers. It argues that a Europe-specific agenda should be closely linked to a more general theoretical agenda. Two complications are addressed: the lack of adequate concepts to capture political integration; and the limited agreement on the nature of existing European institutional arrangements. The focus in what follows is on two types of change that are important for the formation of legitimate democratic governance: the processes through which legal institutions are turned into 'living' institutions; and how incentive-based orders are replaced by orders based on authority and informed consent.

Three frames for understanding institutional change are sketched. In contrast to much conventional wisdom, it is argued that an institutional perspective implies a dynamic, not static, view of political life. Major sources of change are inherent in institutional ideals that are sought, but never reached, and in tensions and collisions caused by competing ideals and principles, built into single institutions and polities. The chapter ends with a metaphor and some remarks about realistic theoretical ambitions.

The relevance of institutions: three agendas

Currently, it is commonplace for practitioners to argue that comprehensive institutional reform is indispensable and should be a top priority for the EU. *The practical-political agenda* refers to:

- the past: European cooperation has been 'deepened' and 'widened'. Formal institutions, it is claimed, are to a large extent the same. They lag behind, due to the stagnation of EU reforms.

- the current situation: the need to respond to the recent (perceived) institutional crisis and restore the credibility of the EU institutions, and
- the future: existing institutions are portrayed as hopelessly inadequate for a Union of 25–30 members. Future enlargements of the EU, with new types of applicants and on a scale never experienced before, require prior institutional reform.

There have been disagreements concerning the scope of reforms, for instance, whether the Intergovernmental Conference in 2000 on institutional reforms should concentrate on the 'leftovers' from Amsterdam, that is, the weighting of votes in the Council, extension of qualified majority voting, and the size and composition of the Commission, or whether 'major surgery' would be needed. Moreover, there is no unanimity when it comes to the methods for preparing institutional reform, such as the use of a small independent committee of experts or intergovernmental diplomacy. There is more agreement that institutional reform requires a long-term process, rather than an *ad hoc*, short-term intervention.[2]

The Europe-specific research agenda portrays the EU polity as *sui generis*. The key question is what competing analytical approaches and interpretations can contribute to a better understanding of the specific EU dynamics and continuities, that is, institutional formation and change in the particular socio-economic and historical–cultural context in Europe.

The intrinsic importance of the emerging European institutions of governance is a sufficient reason for the attention of researchers. However, there is also a more *general theoretical agenda*. This agenda goes beyond understanding the ways in which the EU polity is developing. It aspires to give an account of institutional change and reform that captures developments outside the Union and Europe at large. While the EU system of governance has some unique properties, it also shares important features with other complex polities. For instance, the metaphor that the EU system of multi-level governance is like a 'marble cake' rather than 'layer cake', was used nearly two decades ago to describe inter-governmental relations in the United States (Sharkansky, 1981).

The key issue on the general theoretical agenda is how European studies may help us develop more advanced theories of governance, political organization and institutional change. Taking into account the significance of shifting contexts, are there any general lessons to be learnt about how polities develop, are maintained and change? Are there lessons that require us to revise or to replace basic theoretical ideas, concepts, methods, techniques and normative standards?

A basic assumption of this chapter is that a succesful follow-up of the three agendas is more likely if they are considered together. For instance, all three depend on some serious conceptual homework. The task of analysing the dynamics of European integration is complicated by the limitations of available conceptual tools. The claim that 'despite the seeming importance of the EC institutional components, with few exceptions institutions have played a scant role theoretically in accounts of European integration' has not become obsolete (Caporaso and Keeler, 1995: 49. See, however, Armstrong and Bulmer, 1998; Aspinwall and Schneider, 2000; Bulmer, 1994; Cowles *et al.*, 2000; Jupille and Caporaso, 1999; Olsen, 1996). The next section gives an illustration of some elementary conceptual challenges facing students of European institutions of governance and of political integration in general.

Political integration as institutionalization

In order to talk about differences in the level and form of political integration, as well as institutionalization as an indicator of political integration, we need a metric for political integration and institutionalization. Only then can we recognize possible enduring changes towards a 'higher level of European integration'. Only then can we know whether Europe is moving toward an 'ever closer union', and whether we are facing 'a new stage in the process of European integration'.

'Integration' signifies some measure of the density, intensity and character of the relations among the constitutive elements of a system. Integration may refer to *causal interdependence* among the parts, *consistency* – the degree of coherence and coordination among the parts, and *structural connectedness* – a sociometric or network vision of integration (March, 1999: 134–5). The three aspects of integration are not necessarily strongly correlated, and here political integration is primarily seen as changes in structural connectedness, that is, inter-institutional relations.

Falling back on integration as institutionalization, however, is of limited help, because the concept of 'institution' is also contested. Institutionalized government is 'conducted in the light of some socially standardized and accepted code' (Finer, 1970: 12). Still, institution may refer to an abstract regulatory prescription that is supposed to govern a certain sphere of conduct, and it may also refer to specific less than perfect historical attempts to put such abstract ideas into practice (March and Olsen, 1989).

We may distinguish among three dimensions or processes of institutionalization (March and Olsen, 1995; Olsen, 1997b):

1. *structuration and routinization* – the development of impersonal rules roles and repertoires of standard operating procedures, as well as switching rules between pre-structured responses (March and Simon, 1958: 170). Institutionalization, then, implies routinizing some kinds of change as well as routinizing resistance to others.
2. *standardization, homogenization and authorization of codes of meaning, ways of reasoning and accounts* (March and Simon, 1958: 165). Practices and procedures become valued beyond their technical–functional properties (Eisenstadt, 1964; Selznick, 1957).
3. *binding resources to values and worldviews* (Stinchcombe, 1968: 181–2), that is staff, budgets, buildings and equipment, providing a capability to act and to enforce rules in cases of non-compliance. Authority and power are depersonalized (Weber, 1978: 246).

A perspective on international integration as structural connectedness suggests that a polity has a low level of institutionalization and integration if the constituent units just observe, inform, and adapt to each other through processes of autonomous adjustment (Lindblom, 1965). The level of institutionalization and integration increases as the constitutive units:

- coordinate their policies in an *ad hoc* and pragmatic way, based on self-interest or unit-specific norms;
- remove internal barriers to interaction and exchange, and develop common rules and standards, rights and obligations through inter-unit processes;
- develop distinct supranational institutions of governance and routinized joint decision-making at the system level, allowing various mixes of supranationality, majority voting and veto-power for the basic units;
- develop common administrative and military institutions, with staffs and budgets and therefore capabilities for analysis, planning, decision-making, implementation and enforcement;
- give supranational institutions the right to change their own competence (*kompetenz-kompetenz*); and

- develop a common public space, civic society and institutions able to educate and socialize individuals into informed citizens with a shared political identity and culture.

A caveat is in order. Historically, European political developments have followed complex and varying trajectories (Rokkan, 1999). There is no reason to believe that the list implies a perfect unidimensional or cumulative scale of ascending degrees of structural interconnectedness, or an obligatory pattern of integration and institutionalization. There may be a high level of integration based upon informal codes of conduct, soft law and policy cooperation, without supranational institutions (Wallace, 1999: 13). In addition, supranational formal-legal institutions are no guarantee for strong integration. For instance, establishing formal institutions for a common European security and defence policy without adequate resources may provide less integration than an informal coordination of national defence capabilities. *Ceteris paribus*, however, each step of institutionalization is likely to increase the level of integration. In sum, integrated polities are 'organized around well-defined boundaries, common rules and practices, shared causal and normative understandings, and resources adequate for collective action' (March and Olsen, 1998: 943–4). In this perspective, processes of institutionalization include: (1) reorganizing and rewriting institutional forms, rules, roles and standards; (2) reinterpreting principles and doctrines, frames of understanding and justification, including who is to be accepted as authoritative interpreters of principles, rules and situations; and (3) reallocating resources and changing principles for allocating resources.

A specific measure of institutionalization can be related to changes in the use of coercion and material incentives in regulating human behaviour. An indicator of institutionalization, then, will be the use of less coercion or material incentives in order to make people follow formerly questioned rules and practices. Under some conditions, institutionalization may also be reflected in decreasing demands for participation, as beliefs in the appropriateness of existing structures and political authority are strengthened. This leads to a focus on the normative quality of political orders. In particular, attention is called to how formal-legal institutional arrangements may be turned into 'living institutions'. That is, how organizational 'charts' are translated into collective practices based on legitimate authority, defining appropriate behaviour and ways of reasoning for specific types of actors in specific types of situations.

From legal to 'living' institutions

Analysing the dynamics of European integration is also complicated by the fact that there is limited agreement when it comes to what kind of polity the EU is (Kohler-Koch, 1999; Schmitter 1996). The evolving European political order is often portrayed as difficult to analyse and describe. It is also uncertain what kind of political integration is possible and likely in a multi-cultural and pluralistic region, organized politically on the basis of nation-states.

The architecture of the European polity, that is, its basic institutions, their powers and relationships, has been contested since the original European Community design and throughout subsequent reforms (Wallace, 1996b: 37). The current institutional configuration is complex, ambiguous and changing. It is multi-levelled, multi-structured and multi-centred, characterized by networks across territorial levels of governance, institutions of government, and public–private institutions (Jachtenfuchs and Kohler-Koch, 1996; Kohler-Koch and Eising, 1999).

According to Jacques Delors, the EU is an *'objet politique non-identifié'*. The EU has come a long way from a bargained agreement among nation-states, to a quasi-federal polity (Stone Sweet and Sandholtz, 1998: 1). Still, the EU is not a fully fledged polity (Joerges, 1996: 117; Wallace, 1996b: 39) nor an integrated political community (Mayntz, 1999: 8). Rather, it is an 'experimental union' (Laffan *et al.*, 1999), an 'unfinished polity' and a 'journey to an unknown destination' (Weiler, 1993). The uncertainty of the future is highlighted by the five scenarios in *Europe 2010* developed by the Commissions's Forward Studies Unit (Bertrand *et al.*, 1999).

For behavioural students of governance a challenge is that EU institutions are usually discussed in formal-legal terms, that is, institutional powers formalized in treaties and law. This activates old issues like the relationship between legal and 'living' institutions and the political implications of formal institutions and rules. In the study of political life, legislation – binding for both rulers and ruled – was for a long time believed to be the most striking manifestation of political power (Friedrich, 1950: 268). In this perspective, government is about 'the formation and application of law through public institutions' (Peters, 1999: 5). To understand institutions of government, it was necessary to know their history (Finer, 1999). For instance, understanding western legal institutions required tracing their roots and routes back centuries (Berman, 1983). Furthermore, a legal description of political life, where political institutions are understood by their legal codes and where changes in formal-legal institutions and laws are supposed to change human behaviour, has been seen as 'a typically European way of looking at politics' (Easton, 1964: 154).

The American-led 'behavioural revolution' in political science in the 1950s and 1960s rejected this approach to the study of political life as formalistic, legalistic and old fashioned. There was a need to penetrate the formal surface of constitutional charters, formal governmental institutions and laws, and to describe and explain how politics 'really worked' (Drewry, 1996; Eulau and March, 1969: 15–16). A result was increasing cynicism about the explanatory power of law, constitutions and judicial institutions. In a world of *Realpolitik*, such factors were seen as policy instruments.

Less emphasis was put on law as a distinct method of social control based on the *normative* quality of rules, principles and processes. The main tendency was to ignore law as a revolutionary cultural force in Europe – one that could change concepts, identities and collective understandings. An implication was that behavioural students often ignored historical development where an instrumental view of law as externally imposed order and discipline was supplemented with a theory of law as *justice*. In other words, an interpretation of law as rules with a defensible normative content, defining appropriate behaviour and generating pressure for compliance (Berman, 1983; Habermas, 1996, 1998; Koh, 1997).

In contrast, the EU represents a renewed trust in governance by law and the legal integration of polity and society. While the EU uses a variety of policy modes, it is to a large extent a regulatory polity (Majone, 1996). Therefore, the European context invites students of integration to reconsider the lessons of the behavioural revolution. What are the relationships between, *on the one hand*, formal-legal institutions, legal concepts, categories and ways of reasoning, formal decisions, and legally binding rules, and, *on the other hand*, 'living institutions', rule-implementation, actual political conduct and outcomes? For instance, is it possible to build 'a genuine European political and administrative culture' (Santer) by rewriting treaties and formal institutional designs?[3] What actually happens after the great (formal) bargains are made and the treaties are written (Moravcsik, 1998)?

A key figure in the behavioural revolution maintains that 'most of the basic problems of a country cannot be solved by constitutional design'. The significance of constitutions and institutions – if it really matters whether they are well or badly designed – depends on whether the underlying social and economic conditions are favourable, unfavourable or mixed (Dahl, 1998: 127–8, 139). Some lawyers have also reduced their expectations as to the effectiveness of legislation (Joerges, 1996: 123). Yet, both lawyers and political scientists want to 'analyse the Community constitutional order with particular regard to its living political matrix' (Weiler, 1999: 15, also Armstrong and Shaw, 1998; Craig and de Búrca, 1999; Slaughter *et al.*, 1998).

Weber observed that every system tries to establish and cultivate belief in its legitimacy. Some are more successful than others, and Weber defined the constitution of an organization as 'the empirically existing probability, varying in extent, kind and conditions, that rules . . . will be acceded to' (Weber, 1978: 50). Both legal and other rules present more or less precise binding behavioural claims on more or less specified groups of actors in more or less specified situations.

Rules vary in terms of clarity, pertinence, stringency, adaptability, coherence and consistency (Koh, 1997; Zürn and Joerges, 1999). Furthermore, actors – individuals (Tyler, 1990) as well as states (Checkel, 1999b; Koh, 1997) – sometimes comply with rules and at other times disobey rules. Under some conditions formal-legal institutions have binding authority so that formal and 'living' institutions coincide. Under different conditions the gap between formal-legal arrangements and practices is huge. Actors show great caution in exercising their authority, powers and rights, or they lack the capacity for doing so. There is no straight line from structure to outcome (Caporaso and Keeler, 1995: 47), and institutional continuity and policy change go together well (Eising and Kohler-Koch, 1999; Sverdrup, 1999). Sometimes rules lose their binding authority. They are ignored, contested, changed or replaced. Sometimes legal rules become a 'mask' hiding the political effects of legal integration and a 'shield' insulating legal rules from political influence (Burley and Mattli, 1993).

A staggering feature of the EU has been the rather high level of compliance with rules and the development of legitimacy via judicial processes and legal integration. Therefore, a challenge for students of political integration is to provide a better understanding of the legitimacy and authority of European rules, including the change mechanisms between types of rules and motivations for following them. Which factors affect the probability of acting in accordance with rules of appropriate behaviour? How can we understand variations in compliance across rules, actors and situations? There is no reason to expect simple answers. Rather, a variety of reasons for following and breaking rules can be observed.

Turning incentives into authority

An institutional perspective, as defined here, assumes that rule-following is a more fundamental logic of action than action based on the continuous calculation of expected utility (March and Olsen, 1989, 1995). Still, it is necessary to differentiate between reasons for rule-following. Rules may be obeyed out of habit and 'traditional unreflective reverence for pre-existing authority' (Finer, 1970: 104). Compliance may be governed by rational calculation of the expected utility of alternative behaviours. Rules may also be followed due to an identity-derived internalized feeling of a moral obligation to do so, for example, a law-abiding mentality. Or, compliance may be based on interaction and argumentation. That is, rules are followed because of the causal and normative reasons given for the rules and the processes and institutions by which rules are formed and enforced.

Most of the time, the legitimacy of political institutions is understood in functional – instrumental terms (Finer, 1970: 19; Stinchcombe, 1997). Institutions are purposeful, organized arrangements. Structures and procedures are supposed to promote specific tasks, purposes and goals. Legitimacy and support are based on technical performance, that is, efficiency in problem-solving, service-delivery and the capacity to achieve desired social purposes. Another possibility, however, is to see the legitimacy of a polity as depending on the degree to which structures, procedures and rules conform with societal beliefs about legitimate institutions (Meyer and Rowan, 1977; Scott and Meyer, 1994).

Competing conceptions of political institutions are closely linked to different conceptions of the major institutional impacts (March and Olsen, 1998; Peters, 1999). When institutions are interpreted in functional–instrumental terms, emphasis is usually on policy impacts. Political behaviour is seen as interest-driven and calculative and as externally governed by material incentives and coercion. A supplement is to argue that political institutions constitute, authorize and publicly legitimize actors who are supposed to be pursuing collective goals within a system of rules and due process (Jepperson and Meyer, 1991: 206). Institutions, then, are seen as having the potential to form and transform actors, their mentality and identity and change logics of actions, for example, from expected utility calculation to identity based rule-oriented behaviour.

As a consequence, self-control is added to, or replaces, external controls. Compliance is based on the consent of actors who have internalized the belief that they have a normative obligation to accept certain institutions and policies under certain conditions (Elias, 1982, 1988; Habermas, 1996, 1998; March and Olsen, 1989, 1995; Weber, 1978). Institutional rules are followed because they are accepted as normatively right and not because of a hope to realize pre-determined ends by doing so (Habermas, 1996: 153). Change and continuity are justified by appeals to the moral purpose and inherent value of alternative institutional arrangements and organizing principles, rather than their immediate consequences and functional efficiency (Reus-Smit, 1997: 583). In this perspective, political and economic obligations of EU membership are (eventually) fulfilled because they are seen as reasonable and just.

The latter conception is reflected in an important development in European political history; the gradual subjection of human conduct to due process and the rule of law. Students of international politics, however, have emphasized the difficulty of getting beyond 'anarchy' and cooperation based on calculated alliances and power balances in international relations. While some also see the transformation to legitimacy and authority as 'the essence of governance' in the international context (Ruggie, 1998), the pursuit of justice and virtue is generally not seen as possible in the state's external relations (Curtin, 1997).

This view is also common in the European context, that is, the EU as a 'benign technocracy'. Then, legitimacy and further integration depend on functional performance, comparative problem-solving effectiveness and the ability to satisfy relevant policy interests (Wallace, 1996b: 44). For instance, Scharpf claims that students of European integration have become more aware of some 'lasting limitations' of European political integration. The legitimacy of the EU in the foreseable future will depend on its problem-solving capabilities and its institutional safeguards against the abuse of European power. There is no pre-existing sense of collective identity, and a shared identity is not to be expected, given the lack of a European-wide discourse and an institutional infrastructure that could assure the political accountability of office holders to a European constituence.

Adding new member states from central and eastern Europe will increase heterogeneity and make the development of a common identity even more unlikely (Scharpf, 1999a: 4, 187–8).

Others see European political and legal institutions as having a larger potential for transforming mentalities, identities and logics of action. They argue that processes of opinion- and will-formation, through a communicative logic of argumentation and justification, to some degree can cultivate citizens' character and identities and build solidarity beyond the level of the nation-state (Habermas, 1996: 506; also, Checkel, 1999a; Eriksen, 1999; Habermas, 1998; Risse, 2000). Furthermore, in its self-presentation the EU adheres to several fundamental principles of governance common to the member states and independent of the single policy issue at hand. As formulated in the treaties, the EU is founded on the principles of liberty, democracy, respect for human rights and fundamental freedoms, and the rule of law. A Charter of Fundamental Rights was drafted during 2000 and the principle has been established that decisions are to be taken as openly as possible and as closely as possible to the citizens. The Union, it is argued, should also deepen the solidarity of its peoples, while respecting their history, culture and traditions.

A challenge, then, is to specify the degree to which, and the conditions under which, the main foundation of a polity's legitimacy represents superior functional performance and continuous utility-calculation. Likewise, what is the significance of historically developed and fairly stable internalized codes of appropriate behaviour and principles for living together politically? For instance, to what degree does the effectiveness and legitimacy of legal integration depend on a historic, underlying political culture in western Europe? When and how is the legitimacy-basis of a system of governance transformed from functional performance to internalized codes of appropriateness, or vice versa? What is the explanatory power of discourses and arguments? That is, to what degree, and under what conditions, does legitimacy depend on the defensible normative content of the *Leitidéen*, principles and forms presented in debates over what kind of European order is desirable?

The long-term interaction between, on the one hand, legitimacy based on performance and on normative principles and, on the other hand, institutional forms is not well understood (March and Olsen, 1998). There is no reason to believe that the two are completely independent or perfectly correlated. However, one hypothesis is that, if polities are unable to influence citizens' identity and mentality and instead base their legitimacy on continuous performance, they tend to be unstable. If everyone takes an external calculative approach so that legitimacy is solely based on performance, rewards and punishments, change is driven by shifting distributions of incentives and coercion, and institutions will not last (Habermas, 1996; Weber, 1978).

In comparison, in polities where legitimacy is based on shared political identities, collective understandings and emotions, change is likely to be slow and a result of step-wise reinterpretations or major external shocks. One type of cultural shock is when a polity with a law-abiding culture is extended to countries and groups without a similar respect for law and due process. Possibly, the argument is relevant for some candidates for EU membership. Yet, the effect may be modified, because these new members may emphasize a different legitimacy basis, for example, becoming a part of a modern and democratic Europe. If, however, participation in discourses over the aims and justifications of European institutions and policies is important for awarding the system legitimacy, a possible development is towards an increasing legitimacy gap between those taking part in such discourses and interactions and the bystanders. The bystanders are impacted, but, because they are not taking part in argumentation over the future of Europe, they are less prone to give legitimacy to the new polity.

An institutional perspective assumes that institutional change will depend on both the level of integration and the basis on which a polity is integrated (Brunsson and Olsen, 1998; Olsen, 1998). Other frames for understanding institutional dynamics, in contrast, tend to see institutions as primarily an epiphenomenon, reflecting competitive environments or the will and power of identifiable actors.

Frames for understanding institutional dynamics

The history of the EU is consistent with the view that all political arrangments are contingent and malleable, yet not necessarily in a voluntaristic way (March and Olsen, 1989, 1995). EU developments reflect a history of founding acts and deliberate institution-building, as well as informal and gradual institutional evolution. It is a history where desired policy outcomes and prefered institutional development have not necessarily coincided. It is also a history of different dynamics in different policy areas (Wallace, 1996b: 38–9).

Here, I distinguish between three frames for understanding the determinants of institutional change and the processes through which change takes place: (1) environmental accounts highlighting competitive selection; (2) strategic agency accounts featuring human will, calculations and power; and (3) institutional accounts privileging the significance of institutional structures and histories (March and Olsen, 1989, 1995, 1998; Olsen, 1992).

Environmental accounts start with society and portray institutional change as reflecting shifts in the political institutions' functional or normative environments. Each institutional form has its comparative advantage, in terms of functional performance or how well it 'matches' normative environments. In cases where processes of diffusion and rational adaptation do not secure good 'matches', a process of competitive selection governs which institutional forms evolve, flourish, decay or disappear. Both structures and policies are largely determined by environmental forces. Therefore, tinkering with institutional arrangements will have little independent impact as long as the underlying environmental forces remain constant (Dye, 1975: 20–1).

This view is dominant when European developments are seen as reflecting the imperatives of international competition, technological and economic globalization and mass migration. It is supported by market metaphors emphasizing competitive selection in an increasingly interdependent world.[4] Economic and social integration, in the meaning of causal interdependence among parts, dictate political integration, in the meaning of structural connectedness and institution-building.

One complication is that it is notoriously difficult to specify an optimal political–democratic space (Dahl and Tufte, 1973). Another complication is that environmental accounts seldom specify exactly which changes in institutional forms are required by shifting task environments and through what mechanisms environmental pressure brings about change (Oliver, 1991). For instance, does global competition dictate the size of the European polity? Is territorial enlargement a functional necessity and, if so, which countries have to be included? Do global functional imperatives dictate what Europeans are going to have in common? A single market? Common currency? A defence and security policy? A common defence capability? An integrated public sphere and civic society? A shared language? A collective identity? If a widening and deepening of European cooperation is a functional requirement, through which processes will this happen?

The same questions challenge accounts that assume a necessary adaptation to a normative environment of universally legitimate principles and forms. Here, one task is to explain why some principles and forms in a culture attract attention and get support, while others are ignored or turned down (Risse-Kappen, 1994: 187). For instance, how can we better understand the changing mobilizing power in Europe when it comes to concepts like the market, democracy, welfare state, human rights, civil society, federal state, governance by experts, and so on? Another task is to specify what each principle, or specific combinations, requires in terms of institutional design.

Strategic agency accounts understand institutional change in rational–instrumental terms, as reflecting the will, calculations and power of an identifiable group of actors. Institutional design and choice are solutions to perceived problems (March and Olsen, 1983; Olsen 1997a). This view is shared by intergovernmental interpretations of European institutional developments as the outcome of bargaining between the major member states (Moravcsik, 1998), as well as accounts emphasizing supranational or transnational actors (Sandholtz and Stone Sweet, 1998). Different scholars favour different collective actors, yet, the main focus is on human intention and power.

This is an account that entails two assumptions: On the one hand, that institutional form is a significant determinant of performance, and second, that human choices are important determinants of institutional forms. The former represents a view of institutions as part of modern technology, as illustrated by mechanical methaphors of institutions as 'instruments', 'tools', 'apparatus', and pieces of 'machinery' of democratic governance (Olsen, 1988: 2). The latter conception is supported by a democratic emphasis on having a 'hypothetical attitude' toward existing institutions, so that citizens can choose the institutions under which they want to live together (Habermas, 1996: 468). In this view, democratic politics is an important source for changing long-lasting political relations (Shapiro and Hardin, 1996: 5–6).

For rational–instrumental accounts it is puzzling that reformers are not more efficient in establishing stable institutional arrangements. Institutional reforms do not seem to reduce the demand for future reforms, rather the opposite appears to be the case (Brunsson and Olsen, 1993). Deliberate reform assumes motivation, understanding and social control, prerequisites often missing (among other places) in the context of comprehensive European reforms. In the EU it is often difficult to attribute institutional developments to specific actors. Multiple and conflicting goals are pursued. There is no shared vision of a future Europe and how the EU should be governed, that is, the 'nature and ultimate goals of the integration process' (Majone, 1998). There is no shared understanding of institutional requirements and possibilities, and no single central reorganization authority. A task within this perspective is to specify what actors are trying to make comprehensive reforms, under what conditions they are able to achieve planned organizational change, and under what conditions institutional reforms are producing expected and desired substantive results.

Institutional accounts do not deny that changing environments and reform strategies can be significant for understanding institutional dynamics. Rather, the argument is that processes of competitive selection and rational design are less than perfect, and that change cannot be understood on the basis of knowledge about environments and actors alone. Concepts like 'historical inefficiency' and 'path dependency' suggest that institutional change is not always fast and frictionless. The match between environments, reforms and institutional structure and performance is not automatic, continuous and precise. An institutional account portrays institutions as having lives and deaths of their own, sometimes enduring in the face of apparent inconsistencies with their environments, sometimes collapsing without obvious external cause. Change processes depend to a large extent upon the internal constitutive characteristics of existing institutions. Institutions authorize and enable, as well as constrain, change. Therefore, there is a need for understanding how institutions may transform, modify, redirect and integrate, and not only aggregate, the demands, interests, and powers of societal actors and forces (March and Olsen, 1984, 1989, 1995).[5]

A common criticism of institutional accounts, however, is that they highlight continuity and have little to say about change. To avoid this criticism, institutionalists have to explain 'dramatic and unexpected' changes (Keohane and Hoffmann, 1990: 277), including why major reform agreements sometimes are reached quickly and often to the surprise of even those involved. A recent example is the redefinition of the EU from a 'civilian polity' to placing security and defence high on the common agenda and appointing Javier Solana as 'Mr CFSP' (to project the common foreign and security policy).

More generally, institutionalists have to explain how internal constitutive characteristics of existing institutional arrangements (that is, what integrates a polity) affect the change–continuity mix and the form change takes. Institutionalists have to explain why institutions under some conditions adapt smoothly. There is an incremental modification of internal structures as well as environments (Nystrom and Starbuck, 1981), as institutions codify their changing experience, wisdom and morality. Yet, under other conditions institutions are rigid in spite of changing environments and deliberate reform attempts. Institutions outlive their functional efficiency as well as their normative support. They are outdated, promote superstition and allow exploitation. Then, change may take the form of great leaps, rather than small steps. For instance, as crises have accumulated, there have been critical junctures and exceptional moments in state-building and nation-building processes in Europe (Rokkan, 1970, 1999).

The EU, with its multiple overlapping centres for policy-making, provides a site for studying institutional impacts on institutional change. Developments in the EU system of governance have taken place within a strong nation-state-based order, and not in an institutional vacuum. From an institutional perspective properties of this order – characteristics of the basic units as well as their relations – are assumed to have an impact on institutional dynamics. Such properties are expected to have consequences for both *Europeanization* processes, understood here as the development of new institutions at the European level, and for how the basic units adapt to Europeanization, that is, variations in patterns of change across nation-states and across institutions within the same polity. An institutional perspective also suggests that the relative explanatory power of domestic and European institutions will change with changing levels and forms of European integration and institutionalization.

Therefore, the EU polity is also well suited for studying key issues in political integration: For instance what are the relations between changes in, *on the one hand*, the level and form of polity integration and, *on the other hand*, changes in the component units of the system? Do changes in the number and types of institutional bonds among the component units of a polity depend on how the component units are constituted and how they 'match' each other? What impact do variations in the levels and forms of integration at the polity level have on the component units? Do polities based on different institutional principles make different requirements on their constitutive units (Brunsson and Olsen, 1998; Olsen, 1998)? Do different types of international orders strengthen or weaken different types of states (Ikenberry, 1998: 163, Schmidt, 1999)?

The research task includes exploring the impact of varying levels and forms of state-building and nation-building, producing states with variable internal cohesion, legitimacy and resources (Rokkan, 1999). Given variations in state institutions, traditions and bonds of mutual loyalty and obligations, we should expect different attitudes towards the level and forms of European integration. Moreover, we should expect different patterns of institutional adaptation and not quick and strong convergence in institutional forms. Finally, since the level and form of institutionalization vary across policy sectors, we would expect institutional dynamics – the key actors involved, the patterns of change, and the explanatory power of institutional factors – to vary across policy areas. For instance, patterns of integration can be expected to be different in policy areas like security and defence from in market-building processes. In the latter, supranational institutions have over time won a key role which they are not likely to achieve in the forseable future in, for instance, CFSP. Better specified expectations, however, will depend on detailed knowledge about institutional variations across sectors.

As a further response to the charge that institutional approaches have little to say about change, the next section focuses in more detail on some internal sources of dynamics, often ignored by static conceptions of institutions: the dynamics caused by the fact that institutional orders are never perfectly integrated.

The dynamics of imperfectly integrated political orders

A major historic development in Europe is the emergence of differentiated and partly autonomous institutional spheres with distinct logics of action, meanings and resources. Each sphere legitimizes different participants, issues, and ways of making, implementing and justifying decisions. Weber observed that institutional orders are never perfectly integrated and that modernization inevitably produces imbalances, tensions and collisions between institutional spheres (Gerth and Mills, 1970: 328–57; Weber, 1978; also, Orren and Skowronek, 1994, 1996). An implication is that, in a multi-level, multi-structure and multi-centre polity with partly autonomous sub-systems, a key to understanding institutional dynamics may be to study how institutions relate, balance, collide and penetrate each other. If integration, seen as coherence among the parts, is never perfect, *striving* for coordination also becomes a potential source of institutional change, at least in political cultures favouring consistency and order.

The French institutionalist Georges Renard observed that institutions are built around foundational principles and organizing ideas that provide *'themes of development'* (Broderick, 1970: xxiii). Institutions strive to achieve ideals without ever being able to reach them, that is, there is a potential for change because there are always discrepancies between ideal abstract regulatory prescriptions and actual implementation. In addition, this potential increases, because single institutions, as well as institutional orders, are less than perfectly integrated. Institutions have built-in competing and conflicting organizing principles, imperfections and conflicts (Broderick, 1970).

All this suggests a dynamic, not a static, concept of institutions. In general, it is difficult to keep institutions constant by deliberately reproducing and sustaining patterns of appropriate behaviour. There are continuous interpretations and reinterpretations of what the rules of appropriate behaviour are, how concrete situations are to be understood, and how to map rules on to individual cases. Change may follow as rules are differently understood and as resources are reallocated so that actors become able to follow rules differently. Here attention is focused on processes of reinterpretation.

Under some conditions, change results from 'a reality test' and a process of rational learning. For instance, Europeans may learn about international interdependencies and the loss of national 'fate control'. If so, they may avoid wishful thinking and concentrate on alternatives effective under current international interdependencies. Improved knowledge may also make them reconsider the balance between, and justification of, the maximization of market competition and other social and political goals. Furthermore, actors may adapt collective aspiration levels, internalize dependencies and the interest of other member states. As consequence, they may – in the very long run – develop a European 'we-feeling' (Scharpf, 1999b: 283–6). In brief, according to Scharpf, Europeans may come together to cope with common practical problems, in search for common gains. Yet, the process may foster a sense of community.

This view is consistent with the idea that identity formation has a strong cognitive component (March and Simon, 1958). But learning processes are not necessarily rational and interpretations of history are seldom inherent in the events themselves. Interpretations and their effects are influenced by institutional contexts (March and Olsen, 1995: 44). Most of the time, learning in densely institutionalized contexts produces step-wise reinterpretations. Still, in polities encompassing a large repertoire of institutional forms, forms are typically attended to sequentially or separately, rather than simultaneously and in a coordinated way (Cyert and March, 1963). Shifting attention among forms, or a focus on their relations, may therefore also trigger major change. In polities where legitimacy is largely based on habit and unreflected tradition, processes of reflection and consciousness-raising can also produce sudden, dramatic and unexpected change.

In the EU, generalized institutional forms shared by member states compete with each other and with forms of governance and organization particular to each nation (Andersen, 1999). Which of several legitimate forms are appealed to and evoked has significant implications. For instance, an emphasis on the freedoms derived from the market-building project, compared to a focus on 'a shared commitment to freedom based on human rights, democratic institutions and the rule of law' (European Council, Tampere, 1999), legitimizes and activates different participants and arguments, problems and solutions, and institutional forms. Therefore, they 'bias' decision-making processes differently. The dynamics of change will also depend on how proposals are framed, typically an institution-dependent process. For instance, a suggested transition of the EU to a democratically constituted federal state, where German federalism 'might not be the worst model' (Habermas, 1998: 161), can be discussed in terms of the system's problem-solving capability (Scharpf, 1999a, b). It can also be discussed in a power context; the future of the realm of the political and majority institutions, and the power implications of winning popular elections in democratic societies (Rokkan, 1966). Furthermore, the proposal can be discussed in terms of the development of democratic beliefs and practices, public deliberation and decision-making based on the best argument (Habermas, 1996, 1998). While all are legitimate standards of assessment, they typically suggest different institutional designs.

Change and stability are linked to definitions of the self and the situation (March and Olsen, 1998: 959), and Union enlargement has been related to a normative, and not only functional, definition of the EU. By formulating its policy toward the central and east European countries (CEECs), the EU has developed the constitutive normative principles of the European political order. By defining the fundamental norms and operational criteria of eligibility for membership, or eligibility for assistance programmes, the EU has discovered or defined important aspects of its self-image and collective identity. Likewise, EU policy-makers have developed a specific role, identity and rules of appropriate behaviour for the EU towards the CEECs. Examples are the notion of an EU responsibility for the integration of the CEECs, the attempts to delegitimize (or limit) narrowly self-interested behaviour towards the CEECs, and the duty to accommodate the interests of the CEECs in EU policy (Schimmelfennig, 1999; Sedelmeier, 1998, 1999).[6]

A step-by-step commitment to enlargement as a moral obligation has taken place – in spite of vigorous opposition and hard bargaining over the distribution of costs, yet with no thorough debate about the EU interests involved or detailed cost–benefit analysis (Schimmelfennig, 1999; Sedelmeier, 1999). EU policy-makers have been afraid that current institutions will not be elastic enough for a major enlargement, but they have not developed shared expectations about the institutional requirements of enlargement. It is often argued that the EU will work better with a small number of willing and similar members (Wallace, 1996b: 65). On the other hand, enlargement to 12 members set in motion processes that strengthened Community institutions (Keohane and Hoffmann, 1990: 277). The lesson of history is also uncertain, because several of the new candidates are different from the former ones, for instance in terms of inadequate institutional capabilities of action, including a capacity for deliberate institutional reform (Nakrosis, 1999). One possibility is that the EU, facing candidate states without, or with weak, democratic state traditions, will be more able to demand institutional reforms than it has been able to do so far in relation to current member states.

Most of the time, institutional actors take each other into account. They routinely observe formal or tacit boundaries of their legitimacy and an established institutional balance. What happens, then, when the ideals and the rival conceptions of political order embedded in different institutional spheres come into conflict with one another (Broderick, 1970: xv–xvi)? Such *institutional collisions* may, for instance, take place when institutional striving leads to 'overstretching' one ideal and imposing principles and codes outside their traditional legitimate sphere of activity.

The European context provides a laboratory for studies of institutional collisions. This is so because the EU represents a new type of combinations of institutions, with no dominant centre of authority and power (Jachtenfuchs and Kohler-Koch, 1996; Sand, 1998: 285; Wallace, 1996a, b). Therefore, imbalances, collisions and dynamics are likely. First, they are likely because of the lack of agreement on the fundamental normative principles and ends according to which the European polity is to be integrated and governed. Second, they are likely due to the lack of a clear and stable allocation of powers between levels of governance and institutions (Curtin, 1997; Kirchhof, 1999; Weiler, 1999). For instance, the EU is a polity where functional performance depends heavily on national agencies, budgets and staffs (Wallace, 1999). Tensions between levels of governance, as well as between territorial integration and functional integration that do not overlap with territorial boundaries, are also built into the major European institutions. The EU provides a meeting-place for actors with different institutional affiliations interacting within a variety of institutional contexts, emphasizing territorial and functional concerns differently (Egeberg, 1999).

Is the Westphalian system of spatial organization then seriously challenged by European functional organization? The dilemma is well known in organizational research. As each part of an organization adapts to its specific task environment, there is an increasing demand for coordination across functional sectors. At the same time, functional differentiation and integration, makes such coordination difficult (Brunsson and Olsen, 1998). Functional specialization and differentiation and institutional 'fusion' between levels of governance make coordination difficult at both the European and the domestic level (Rometsch and Wessels, 1996). So far, however, there is no agreement that EU functional networks have produced territorial disintegration, making the nation-state less unitary, weakening the power of majority-based institutions, as well as of coordinating agencies (Knodt, 1998; Lange, 1998).

Institutional collisions, including the relations between legal and 'living' institutions, can be better understood through studies of how institutions, after they are formally and legally established, learn their place in an institutional order. For example, the European Court of Auditors, as a new institution, had to 'chart the difficult waters of inter-institutional relations' (Laffan, 1999: 255). Defining its tasks, methods and organizational forms was an important part of the learning process. It had to establish its credentials, discover opportunity structures, define ground rules for interactions with other key institutions, and establish trust and appropriate relations. Search and learning processes took place in a changing normative and cognitive climate, with increasing concern for financial management and fraud, and changing formal institutional responsibilities, legal status and resources. Learning its place, finally, meant coping with the dependence on the resources of national audit offices and the need to develop cooperation and partnership with domestic institutions jealous of their independence (Laffan, 1999: 256-8, 265).

The likelihood and consequences of institutional collisions depend on properties of the polity. In tightly integrated polities, characterized by high causal interdependence, by coordination and consistency among the parts and by structural connectedness, collisions may not be very likely. However, if an external shock causes collisions, change in one part of the system produces fast and precise changes in other parts. In loosely integrated polities, with modest causal interdependence, separation of tasks, powers and responsibilities, and with slack resources buffering the various parts (Cyert and March, 1963), consequences tend to be local, with system impacts more modest and less precise.[7]

The Treaty of Rome and San Pietro in Vatican

Historically, Europe has been a key site of innovation when it comes to forms of governance and political organization (Finer, 1999: 14). Now, the region is again experiencing a period of political experimentation, innovation and transformation. Building European institutions of governance may be compared to building San Pietro in Vatican – Saint Peter's Basilica. Some trace its history nearly two thousand years back, and even the current (new) Basilica took generations to build. There have been many builders, architects, and popes, as well as artists and workers. Plans have been made, modified and rejected. There have been conflicts over designs and over the use of resources. There have been shifting economic and political conditions and changing cultural norms, including religious beliefs and fashions of architecture. Such factors have affected both the motivation and ability to develop the Basilica. Yet, as parts have been added, modified and even demolished, the project has had dynamics of its own, constraining the physical development, the use, and the meaning of, the Basilica.

I ask for mercy from those who know the history in detail. The point of using the metaphor is simply to suggest that the processes underlying European integration are not well understood. Furthermore, it may simply not be possible to develop a single, coherent theory of a complex historical phenomenon like the EU. As has often been the case historically (Rokkan, 1999), change in the European political order seems to be an artefact of a complex ecology of processes and trajectories, rather than the result of a single dominant process. Again, it may be concluded that 'the historical processes by which international political orders develop are complex enough to make any simple theory of them unsatisfactory' (March and Olsen, 1998: 968).

Still, the evolving European polity provides great empirical opportunities for those interested in political development. Studies of the EU may help us understand political integration and disintegration as universal phenomena unfolding somewhat differently in different territorial, historical-cultural and socio-economic contexts. Studies of a polity with some special features, like the EU, may improve our ability to differentiate between forms of political organization and their key dimensions and characteristics. They may also make it easier to *compare* political and governmental structures. In addition, such studies may shed light on the consequences of institutional form. That is, whether, under what conditions, how and through what mechanisms institutional form matters. For instance, when and how do institutions fashion agency, so that constitutive institutional principles and identities make actors follow a rule-driven logic of appropriateness? When and how do institutions have an impact upon policies, performance, power-relations, and the democratic quality of governance? Inquiries into the co-evolving processes of institution formation and adaptation at the European and the domestic level may also improve our understanding of institutional continuity and change. They may help us understand shifts between periods of radical change and stability and, thus, the shifting basis for periodization of political development. They may also shed light on variations in developmental trajectories. Under what conditions do institutions (and actors) gain and lose legitimacy and support, or see their legitimacy-basis change? Under what conditions are existing institutions overwhelmed by environmental forces, for example shifting social and economic interdependencies? Under what conditions are different types of actors able deliberately to form and reform institutions and to achieve desired and intended results? And the key issue of an institutional approach: under what conditions do institutions, and different levels and forms of political unity, modify the change potential of environmental forces and reform strategies?

This chapter is a prelude to answering such questions. Exploiting the research potentials of the changing European polity may contribute to more interesting theories of governance, political organization and institutional change. In turn, such theories may give a better understanding of the significance of Europe as a specific context for political integration and disintegration.

Notes

1. Earlier versions of this chapter were presented at the Workshop on *Research Directions in Relation to Governance and Citizenship in a Changing Europe*, European Commission, DG Research, Brussels 8–9 September 1999 and the ARENA Annual Conference in Oslo 17 November 1999. A previous version was published as an ARENA Working Paper in 2000. I want to thank the participants and in particular Svein S. Andersen, Morten Egeberg, Beate Kohler-Koch, Ulrich Sedelmeier and Helen Wallace, for constructive questions and suggestions. Thanks also to Peggy Brønn, Jeffrey Checkel, B. Guy Peters and Ulf I. Sverdrup and to James G. March, with whom I have worked on theories of formal organizations and political institutions for more than 30 years.
2. For an overview of this debate, see *Bulletin Quotidien Europe*. Also, Dehaene, von Weizsäcker and Simon (1999). The Commission's *Reform Strategy Programme*, 'embarking on a process of fundamental reform' was published

in February 2000 (http://europa.eu.int/rapid/start/cgi/gue...on.gettxt=gt& doc= IP/99/769|0|RAPID&lg=EN).
3. Jacques Santer 1999–03–03 (http://europa.eu.int/rapid/start/gue...on.gettxt= gt&doc=IP/99/143|0|RAPID&lg=en).
4. Ruggie claims, with a reference to Etzioni (1966), that 'the boldest variant of functionalism actually posits the existence of evolutionary trends: that in reacting and adapting to its environment, humanity will build for itself ever-higher forms of socio-political organization, from tribes to baronies, from national states to global authorities' (Ruggie, 1998: 46).
5. In attempts to typologize institutional approaches, this interpretation is often placed together with 'the new institutionalism' in organizational sociology. Such typologies overlook that the two take opposite views when it comes to the importance of internal factors. The latter argues that: 'Most of the institutional change now occuring in any given polity can be predicted more readily from knowledge of the wider world environment than from an understanding of internal structure' (Jepperson and Meyer, 1991: 226). This approach, emphasizing the spread of a general world culture, is closer to Weberian ideas of a general rationalization and 'disenchantment of the world' (Gerth and Mills, 1970: 41).
6. Thanks to Ulrich Sedelmeier and Helen Wallace for helping me formulate this point.
7. Thelen suggests that collisions are likely to be most consequential when they interfere with the reproduction mechanisms of institutions (1999: 400).

References

Andersen, S. A. (1999) 'Hvordan er EU mulig?', MS (Oslo: ARENA).
Armstrong, K. A. and Bulmer, S. J. (1998) *The Governance of the Single European Market* (Manchester: Manchester University Press).
Armstrong, K. A. and Shaw, J. (eds) (1998) 'Integrating Law', *Journal of Common Market Studies*, 36 (2) (Special Issue).
Aspinwall, M. and Schneider, G. (eds) (2000) *The Rules of Integration: The Institutionalist Approach to European Studies* (Manchester: University of Manchester Press).
Berman, H. J. (1983) *Law and Revolution. The Formation of the Western Legal Tradition* (Cambridge MA: Harvard University Press).
Bertrand, G., Michalski, A. and Pemch, L. R. (1999) *Scenarios Europe 2010. Five Possible Futures for Europe* (Brussels: European Commission, Forward Studies Unit Working Paper).
Broderick A. (1970) 'Preface', in Broderick, A. (ed.), *The French Institutionalists. Maurice Hauriou, Georges Renard, Joseph T. Delos* (Cambridge, MA: Harvard University Press), pp. xiii–xxv.
Brunsson, N. and Olsen, J. P. (1993) *The Reforming Organization* (London: Routledge) reprinted 1997 (Bergen: Fagbokforlaget).
Brunsson, N. and Olsen, J. P. (1998) 'Organization theory: Thirty Years of Dismantling, and Then . . .?', in Brunsson, N. and Olsen, J. P. (eds), *Organizing Organizations* (Bergen: Fagbokforlaget), pp. 13–43.

Bulmer, S. J. (1994) 'The Governance of the European Union: A New Institutionalist Approach', *Journal of Public Policy*, 13 (4), pp. 351–80.

Burley, A-M. and Mattli, W. (1993) 'Europe Before the Court: A Political Theory of Legal Integration', *International Organization*, 47 (1), pp. 41–76.

Caporaso, J. A. and Keeler, J. T. S. (1995) 'The European Union and Regional Integration Theory', in Rhodes, C. and Mazey, S. (eds), *The State of The European Union. Vol. 3: Building a European Polity?* (Harlow: Lynne Rienner), 29–62.

Checkel, J. T. (1999a) 'Social Construction and Integration', *Journal of European Public Policy*, 6 (4), pp. 545–60.

Checkel, J. T. (1999b) 'Why Comply? Constructivism, Social Norms and the Study of International Institutions' (Oslo: ARENA Working Paper 24).

Cowles, M. G., Caporaso, J. A. and Risse, T. (eds) (2000) *Transforming Europe: Europeanization and Domestic Change* (Ithaca, NY: Cornell University Press).

Craig, P. and de Búrca, G. (eds) (1999) *The Evolution of EU Law* (Oxford: Oxford University Press).

Curtin, D. M. (1997) *Postnational Democracy. The European Union in Search of a Political Philosophy* (The Hague: Kluwer).

Cyert, R. M. and March, J. G. (1963) *A Behavioural Theory of the Firm* (Englewood Cliffs, NJ: Prentice-Hall) second edition (1992) (Cambridge, MA: Blackwell).

Dahl, R. A. (1998) *On Democracy* (New Haven: Yale University Press).

Dahl, R. A. and Tufte, E. R. (1973) *Size and Democracy* (Stanford CA: Stanford University Press).

Dehaene, J. L., von Weizsäcker, R. and Simon, D. (1999) 'The Institutional Implications of Enlargement' (Brussels: Report to the European Commission).

Drewry, G. (1996) 'Political Institutions: Legal Perspectives', in Goodin, R. E. and Kingemann, H. D. (eds), *A New Handbook of Political Science* (Oxford: Oxford University Press).

Dye, T. R. (1975) *Understanding Public Policy*, 2nd edn (Englewood Cliffs, NJ: Prentice Hall).

Easton, D. (1964) *The Political System* (New York: Alfred A. Knopf).

Egeberg, M. (1999) 'Transcending Intergovernmentalism? Identity and Role Perceptions of National Officials in EU Decision-making', *Journal of European Public Policy*, 6 (3), pp. 456–74.

Eisenstadt, S. N. (1964) 'Institutionalization and Change', *American Sociological Review*, 29, pp. 235–47.

Eising, R. and Kohler-Koch, B. (1999) 'Governance in the European Union: a Comparative Assessment', in Kohler-Koch, B. and Eising, R. (eds), *The Transformation of Governance in the European Union* (London: Routledge).

Elias, N. (1982) (first published 1939) *The Civilizing Process: State Formation and Civilization* (Oxford: Basil Blackwell).

Elias, N. (1988) 'Violence and Civilization: The state monopoly of physical violence and its infringement', in Keane, J. (ed.), *Civil Society and the State* (London: Verso).

Eriksen, E. O. (1999) 'Towards a Logic of Justification. On the Possibility of Postnational Solidarity', in Egeberg, M. and Lægreid, P. (eds), *Organizing Political Institutions* (Oslo: Scandinavian University Press).

Etzioni, A. (1966) *Political Unification. A Comparative Study of Leaders and Forces* (New York: Holt, Rinehart & Winston).

Eulau, H. and March, J. G. (1969) *Political Science* (Englewood Cliffs, NJ: Prentice Hall).
European Council, Tampere (1999) *Presidency Conclusions*, 15 and 16 October (Brussels: SI) 800.
Finer, S. E. (1970) *Comparative Government* (Harmondsworth: Penguin).
Finer, S. E. (1999) (paperback edition) *The History of Government* (Vol. I–III Oxford: Oxford University Press).
Friedrich, C. J. (1950) (revised edn) *Constitutional Government and Democracy. Theory and Practice in Europe and America* (Boston: Ginn & Company).
Gerth, H. H. and Wright Mills, C. (1970) (paperback edition) *From Max Weber* (London: Routledge and Kegan Paul).
Habermas, J. (1996) *Between Facts and Norms* (Cambridge MA: The MIT Press).
Habermas, J. (1998) *The Inclusion of the Other. Studies in Political Theory* (Cambridge, MA: The MIT Press).
Ikenberry, G. J. (1998) 'Constitutional Politics in International Relations', *European Journal of International Relations*, 4 (2), pp. 147–77.
Jachtenfuchs, M. and Kohler-Koch, B. (eds) (1996) *Europäische Integration* (Opladen: Leske & Budrich).
Jepperson, R. L. and Meyer, J. W. (1991) 'The Public Order and the Construction of Formal Organizations', in Powell, W. W. and Di Maggio, P. J. (eds), *The New Institutionalism in Organizational Analysis* (Chicago: University of Chicago Press).
Joerges, C. (1996) 'Taking the Law Seriously: On Political Science and the Role of Law in the Process of Integration', *European Law Journal*, 2 (2), pp. 105–35.
Jupille, J. and Caporaso, J. A. (1999) 'Institutionalism and the European Union: Beyond International Relations and Comparative Politics', *Annual Review of Political Science*, 2, pp. 429–44.
Keohane, R. O. and Hoffman, S. (1990) 'Conclusions: Community Politics and Institutional Change', in Wallace, W. (ed.), *The Dynamics of European Integration* (London: Pinter).
Keohane, R. O., and Krasner, S. D. (eds) (1999) *Exploration and Contestation in the Study of World Politics* (Cambridge, MA: The MIT Press).
Kirchhof, P. (1999) 'The Balance of Powers Between National and European Institutions', *European Law Journal*, 5 (3), pp. 225–42.
Knodt, M. (1998) *Tiefenwirkung europäischer Politik: Eigensinn oder Anpassung regionalen Regierens?* (Baden-Baden: Nomos).
Koh, H. H. (1997) 'Why Do Nations Obey International Law?', *The Yale Law Journal*, 106 (8), pp. 2599–659.
Kohler-Koch, B. (1999) 'The Evolution and Transformation of European Governance', in Kohler-Koch, B. and Eising, R. (eds), *The Transformation of Governance in the European Union* (London: Routledge).
Kohler-Koch, B. and Eising, R. (eds) (1999) *The Transformation of Governance in the European Union* (London: Routledge).
Laffan, B. (1999) 'Becoming a "Living Institution": The Evolution of the European Court of Auditors', *Journal of Common Market Studies*, 37 (2), pp. 251–68.
Laffan, B., O'Donnell, R. and Smith, M. (1999) *Europe's Experimental Union. Rethinking Integration* (London: Routledge).

Lange, N. (1998) *Zwischen Regionalismus und europäscher Integration: Wirtschaftsinteressen in regionalistischen Konflikten* (Baden-Baden: Nomos).

Lindblom, Ch. E. (1965) *The Intelligence of Democracy* (New York: Free Press).

Majone, G. (1996) *Regulating Europe* (London: Routledge).

Majone, G. (1998) 'Europe's "Democratic Deficit": The Question of Standards', *European Law Journal*, 4 (1), pp. 5–28.

March, J. G. (1999) 'A Learning Perspective on the Network Dynamics of Institutional Integration', in Egeberg, M. and Lægreid, P. (eds), *Organizing Political Institutions* (Oslo: Scandinavian University Press).

March, J. G. and Olsen, J. P. (1983) 'Organizing Political Life: What Administrative Reorganization Tells Us About Government', *American Political Science Review*, 77 (2), pp. 281–96.

March, J. G. and Olsen, J. P. (1984) 'The New Institutionalism: Organizational Factors in Political Life', *American Political Science Review*, 78, pp. 734–49.

March, J. G. and Olsen, J. P. (1989) *Rediscovering Institutions* (New York: Free Press).

March, J. G. and Olsen, J. P. (1995) *Democratic Governance* (New York: Free Press).

March, J. G. and Olsen, J. P. (1998) 'The Institutional Dynamics of International Political Orders', *International Organization*, 52 (4), pp. 943–69. Reprinted in Katzenstein, P. J., Keohane, R. O and Krasner, S. D. (eds) 1999, *Exploration and Contestation in the Study of World Politics*: (Cambridge, MA: The MIT Press, pp. 303–321.)

March, J. G. and Simon, H. A. (1958) *Organizations* (New York: Wiley; 2nd edn, Cambridge, MA: Blackwell, 1993).

Mayntz, R. (1999) 'Multi-level Governance: German Federalism and the European Union. Cologne, Max Planck Institute for the Study of Society'. Paper presented at the AICGS Workshop 'Governing Beyond the Nation State: Global Public Policy, Regionalism, or Going Local?'.

Meyer, J. W. and Rowan, B. (1977) 'Institutionalized Organizations: Formal Structure as Myth and Ceremony', *American Journal of Sociology*, 83, pp. 340–63.

Moravcsik, A. (1998) *The Choice for Europe: Social Purposes and State Power from Messina to Maastricht* (London: UCL Press).

Nakrosis, V. (1999) 'Assessing Governmental Capacity to Manage European Affairs: The Case of Lithuania, (Florence: European University Institute: EUI Working Papers RSC No. 2000/58).

Nystrom, P. C. and Starbuck, W. H. (eds) (1981) *Handbook of Organizational Design* (1,2) (Oxford: Oxford University Press).

Oliver, C. (1991) 'Strategic Responses to Institutional Processes', *Academy of Management Review*, 16 (1), pp. 145–79.

Olsen, J. P. (1988) 'The Modernization of Public Administration in the Nordic Countries: Some Research Questions', *Administrative Studies (Hallinon Tutkimus)*, 7 (1), pp. 2–17.

Olsen, J. P. (1992) 'Analyzing Institutional Dynamics', *Staatswissen-schaften und Staatspraxis*, 2, pp. 247–71.

Olsen, J. P. (1996) 'Europeanization and Nation-state Dynamics', in Gustavsson, S. and Lewin, J. (eds), *The Future of the Nation-State* (London: Routledge).

Olsen, J. P. (1997a) 'Institutional Design in Democratic Contexts', *Journal of Political Philosophy*, 5 (3), pp. 203–229.

Olsen, J. P. (1997b) 'The Changing Political Organization of Europe: An Institutional Perspective on the Role of Comprehensive Reform Efforts', in Hesse, J. J. and Thoonen, T. A. J. (eds), *The Yearbook of Comparative Government and Public Administration*. Vol. II 1955 (Baden-Baden: Nomos).

Olsen, J. P. (1998) 'The New European Experiment in Political Organization', Oslo, ARENA: Paper presented at the conference 'Samples of the Future', SCANCOR, Stanford University.

Orren, K. and Skowronek, S. (1994) 'Beyond the Iconography of Order: Notes for a "New" Institutionalism', in Dodd, L. and Jillson, C. (eds), *The Dynamics of American Politics: Approaches and Interpretations* (Boulder, CO: Westview).

Orren, K., and Skowronek. S. (1996) 'Institutions and Intercurrence: Theory Building in the Fullness of Time', in Shapiro, I. and Hardin, R. (eds), *Political Order* (*Nomos* XXXVIII) (New York: New York University Press), pp. 111–46.

Peters, B. G. (1999) *Institutional Theory in Political Science. The New Institutionalism* (London: Pinter).

Reus-Smit, C. (1997) 'The Constitutional Structure of International Society and the Nature of Fundamental Institutions', *International Organization*, 51 (4), pp. 555–89.

Risse, T. (2000) 'Let's Argue. Communicative Action in World Politics', *International Organization*, 54 (1) Winter 2000, pp. 1–39.

Risse-Kappen, T. (1994) 'Ideas do not Float Freely: Transnational Coalitions, Domestic Structures, and the End of the Cold War', *International Organizations*, 48 (2), pp. 185–214.

Rokkan, S. (1966) 'Norway: Numerical Democracy and Corporate Pluralism', in Dahl, R. A. (ed.), *Political Oppositions in Western Democracies* (New Haven: Yale University Press).

Rokkan, S. (1970) 'Nation-Building, Cleavage Formation and the Structuring of Mass Politics', in Rokkan, S. *et al.* (eds), *Citizens, Elections and Parties: Approaches to the Comparative Study of the Processes of Development* (Bergen: Universitetsforlaget).

Rokkan, S. (1999) (Flora, P. [eds] with Kuhnle, S. and Urwin, D.) *State Formation, Nation-Building and Mass Politics in Europe: The Theory of Stein Rokkan* (Oxford: Oxford University Press).

Rometsch, D. and Wessels, W. (eds) (1996) *The European Union and Member States. Towards Institutional Fusion?* (Manchester: Manchester University Press).

Ruggie, J. G. (1998) *Constructing the World Polity. Essays on International Institutionalization* (London: Routledge).

Sand, I. J. (1998) 'Understanding the New Forms of Governance: Mutually Interdependent, Reflexive, Destabilised and Competing Institutions', *European Law Journal*, 4 (3), pp. 271–93.

Sandholtz, W. and Stone Sweet, A. (eds) (1998) *European Integration and Supranational Governance* (Oxford: Oxford University Press).

Scharpf, F. W. (1999a) *Governing in Europe. Effective and Democratic?* (Oxford: Oxford University Press).

Scharpf, F. W. (1999b) 'Legitimacy in the Multi-actor European Polity', in Egeberg, M. and Lægreid, P. (eds), *Organizing Political Institutions* (Oslo: Scandinavian University Press).

Schimmelfennig, F. (1999) 'The Double Puzzle of EU Enlargement. Liberal Norms, Rhetorical Action, and the Decision to Expand to the East' (Oslo: ARENA Working Paper no. 15 1999).

Schmidt, V. A. (1999) 'National Patterns of Governance Under Siege. The impact of European Integration', in Kohler-Koch, B. and Eising, R. (eds), *The Transformation of Governance in the European Union* (London: Routledge).

Schmitter, P. C. (1996) 'Examining the Present Euro-polity with the Help of Past Theories', in Marks, G. *et al.* (eds), *Governance in the European Union* (London: Sage), pp. 1–14.

Scott, W. R. and Meyer, J. W. and Associates (1994) *Institutional Environments and Organizations* (Thousand Oaks, CA: Sage).

Sedelmeier, U. (1998) 'The European Union's Association Policy Towards the Countries of Central and Eastern Europe'. Collective EU identity and policy paradigms in a composite policy. Brighton: University of Sussex: DPhil Thesis.

Sedelmeier, U. (2000) 'Eastern Enlargement: Risk, Rationality and Role-compliance', in Cowles, M. G., and Smith, M. (eds), *The State of the European Union. Risks, Reforms, Resistance and Revival*, 5 (Oxford: Oxford University Press).

Selznick, P. (1957) *Leadership in Administration* (New York: Harper & Row).

Shapiro, I. and Hardin, R. (1996) 'Introduction', in Shapiro, I. and Hardin, R. (eds), *Political Order* (New York: New York University Press).

Sharkansky, I. (1981) 'Intergovernmental Relations', in Nystrom, P. C. and Starbuck, W. H. (eds), *Handbook of Organizational Design. Vol. 1* (Oxford: Oxford University Press).

Slaughter, A-M., Stone Sweet, A. and Weiler, J. H. H. (eds) (1998) *The European Courts and National Courts. Doctrine and Jurisprudence* (Oxford: Hart).

Stinchcombe, A. L. (1968) *Constructing Social Theories* (New York: Harcourt, Brace & World).

Stinchcombe, A. L. (1997) 'On the Virtues of the Old Institutionalism', *Annual Review of Sociology*, 23, pp. 1–18.

Stone Sweet, A. and Sandholtz, W. (1998) 'Integration, Supranational Governance and the Institutionalization of the European Polity', in Sandholtz, W. and Stone Sweet, A. (eds), *European Integration and Supranational Governance* (Oxford: Oxford University Press).

Sverdrup, U. I. (1999) 'Ambiguity and Adaptation. Europeanization of Administrative Institutions as Loosely Coupled Processes', MS (Oslo, ARENA).

Thelen, K. (1999) 'Historical Institutionalism in Comparative Politics', *Annual Review of Political Science*, 2, pp. 369–404.

Tyler, T. R. (1990) *Why People Obey the Law* (New Haven: Yale University Press).

Wallace, H. (1996a) 'Politics and Policy in the EU: The Challenge of Governance', in Wallace, H. and Wallace, W. (eds), *Policy-Making in the European Union* (Oxford: Oxford University Press).

Wallace, H. (1996b) 'The Institutions of the EU: Experience and Experiments', in Wallace, H., and Wallace, W. (eds), *Policy-Making in the European Union* (Oxford: Oxford University Press).

Wallace, H. (1999) 'The Domestication of Europe: Contrasting Experiences of EU Membership and Non-membership'. Leiden: The University of Leiden, Department of Political Science: Sixth Daalder Lecture.

Weber, M. (1978) *Economy and Society* (Berkeley CA: University of California Press).
Weiler, J. H. H. (1993) 'Journey to an Unknown Destination: A Retrospective and Prospective of the European Court of Justice in the Arena of Political Integration', *Journal of Common Market Studies*, 31 (4), pp. 417–46.
Weiler, J. H. H. (1997) 'The Reformation of European Constitutionalism', *Journal of Common Market Studies*, 35 (1), pp. 97–131.
Weiler, J. H. H. (1999) *The Constitution of Europe* (Cambridge: Cambridge University Press).
Zürn, M. and Joerges, C. (1999) 'The Study of Compliance: A Framework', Bremen: Paper presented at the ECPR 27th Joint Session of Workshops, Universität Mannheim.

Index

Accession Partnerships 152
acquis communautaire 153
actors, network 58–60
administrative capacity 161–8
affiliation 5–6, 8–11, 19–20
EU citizenship and pan-Europeanism 263–79
European identity and national identity in CEE 247–62
Idea of Europe 280–301
imagining the union 233–46
nationalism and deep integration 236–9
African, Caribbean and Pacific (ACP) states 39–40
Agenda 2000 152–3, 199–200
agglomeration 124, 131, 134
Ahtisaari/Talbott/Chernomyrdin mission 205
alliance capitalism 56–7
Allianztreue (alliance loyalty) 203–4
Amsterdam, Treaty of 8, 104, 115, 116, 270
anti-Americanism 98
anti-communism 9
Arab countries 35–6
Asia 96, 98
Asia-Europe Meeting (ASEM) 38
asylum-seekers 109–10, 115–16, 119
Austria 109, 308
authority 332–5

Balkans 109, 111
banal Europeanism 240–3
banal nationalism 238
Barcelona Agreement 116–17
bargaining 309–12, 313, 314
behavioural revolution 330–1
Berlin 196
Berlin Wall 87
Berlusconi, S. 258
Bibo, I. 247–8

bifurcated models 146–50
Bonn 196
borders 7, 108, 118
changing 110–13
democracy and 87–8
Bosnia 222, 225
budget, EU 199–200
Bundesbank 183, 188, 207–8

Canada 54
capitalism 56–7, 125–6, 220–1
Carnogursky, J. 257
causal interdependence 326
central and eastern Europe (CEE) 342–3
economic growth 129
European identity and national identity 247–62
Europeanization of local and regional governance 145–78
GDP *per capita* 127, 128
industrial networks 46, 47–54, 60–2;
industrial upgrading 50–4
migration 111–13, 119
and *Modell Deutschland* 190–1
regional capacity 137
transnationalism and multilateralism 11
see also enlargement; *and under individual countries*
central government *see* national governments
Charter of Fundamental Rights 298, 334
Chechnya 89, 227
Chile 36, 38
Christianity 281–2
citizenship 263–79
civil society, national ties and supranational bonds 275–7
cultural differences 267–72

355

356 Index

citizenship *continued*
    differences in the material bases
        for participation 264–7
    implications of diversity for EU
        policy 272–5
    implications of socio-economic
        indicators of unequal
        citizenship 266–7
    migration and 106–7, 115, 118
    universal rights 295–7
civic nationalism 256–7
civil society 269–72, 275–7
civilian power 203, 205
Clinton, W. 226
clustering 124, 131, 134
cohesion policy 74, 273–4
cold war 217, 218–19
collective forgetting 239–43
Commission on Global Governance
    73
Committee of the Regions (CoR)
    148
commodity chains 133, 138, 139
common agricultural policy (CAP)
    29
Common Foreign and Security Policy
    (CFSP) 99, 206, 338
commonality 267–9
    values of 272–3
commons, Europe of the 294–8
communist local government 154–5
community 96–7
    European identity and 233–5,
        238
compliance 332–5
concertation 305–22
    European integration and
        convergence 318–20
    social partnership as post-
        corporatist concertation
        309–18
conditionality 221
    Europeanization of governance
        150–3, 172–3
consciousness, national 237
Consultative Council of Regional
    and Local Authorities 148
consumption-led migration 109
containment 218

convergence
    economic growth 129–30
    national identity 260–1
    social partnership and
        concertation 318–20
Copenhagen criteria 151
cosmopolitanism 287–94
Cotonou Agreement 40
Council of Europe 254
cross-national production networks
    (CNPNs) 49–50
    see also industrial networks
culture
    cultural differences 267–72
    cultural fundamentalism 293–4
    Idea of Europe 280–301
Cyprus 35
Czech Republic 93, 153, 156,
    160–1, 168, 221
Czechoslovakia 248, 256–8

decentralization 149, 155
deep integration 5, 10, 46, 61, 145
    characterizing 12–15
    nationalism and territory, function
        and affiliation in 236–9
defence 224–6
    see also security
deliberate power 185, 207
deliberation 309–12, 317
Delors, J. 282, 329
democracy 220
    and borders 87–8
    identity in the politics of democratic
        transformation 247–60
democratizing reforms 164
Denmark 270, 308
détente 218
Deutsch, K. W. 2, 5, 233, 234,
    236–9 *passim*, 240, 241–2
Dienstbier, J. 256
diffused power 56
Directorates General (DGs) 78–9
divergence 260–1
diversity 272–5
domestication
    of the EU 239–43
    of Europe within national
        politics 15–18

Index 357

economic inequalities 264–5
  dynamics over time 129–30
  national 126–7
  regional 127–9, 264–5
  regional trajectories and uneven development 122–44
economic and monetary union (EMU) 106, 188, 308
education 265–6
elites, local 168–71, 172, 173, 174
enlargement of the EU 104, 105
  civil society and 276–7
  conditionality 150–3
  and EU *per capita* GDP 124–5
  institutions and 342–3
  and migration 112–13
  and regionalization 145–78
  Russian attitudes 95–8, 99–100
Estonia 153, 158–9, 162, 166–7, 172
ethnic minorities 291–2
ethnic nationalism 250, 256–8
Euro-Mediterranean Agreements (EMAs) 35–6, 37
Euro-Mediterranean partnership 116–17, 119
Europe Agreements (EAs) 34–5, 151–2
Europe of the commons 294–8
Europe of the Regions 74, 123, 146
Europe-specific research agenda 325
'Europe of the spirit' 284
European Coal and Steel Community (ECSC) 69, 234
European Commission 71, 129, 152–3
  Commission's Opinions 152, 153, 162
European Communities (EC) 68–9
European Court of Auditors 344
European Economic Area (EEA) 34
European Economic Community 105–6
European Free Trade Area (EFTA) 254
European identity 233–46, 283, 341
  mapping indicators of 241

and national identity in CEE 247–62
European integration 1–22
  affiliational dimension 5–6, 8–11, 19–20
  characterizing deep integration 12–15
  contrasting legacies in central and eastern Europe 11
  functional dimension 5–6, 6–7, 10–11, 18–19
  institutions 20
  macro and micro 46–7
  perceptions of and nationalism 233–46
  policy concertation 318–20
  politics of individual countries 15–18
  territorial dimension 5–6, 7–8, 10–11, 19
European security *see* security
European Security and Defence Identity (ESDI) 3, 224–6
European Union (EU) 254
  budget 199–200
  citizenship *see* citizenship
  enlargement *see* enlargement of the EU
  Germany and 187–90, 199–202
  institutions of governance and political integration 324–6, 329–40, 341–4
  local elites in CEE countries and 169–70, 171, 173, 174
  and migration *see* migration
  multi-level governance and globalization 73–81
  nature of polity 329
  normalization of 239–43
  provision of security 221–3
  Russian attitudes to 95–8, 99–100
  trade policy 25–44
  see also west European integration
Europeanization 233, 339
  as conditionality 150–3
  local elites and 168–71, 172, 173, 174
  regionalization and in CEE 154–61

exchange-rate-mechanism (ERM) 306
exclusion
   immigrants and social exclusion 114
   Russia and 90–3

federalism 273
Finland 17, 308
firms
   and industrial networks 57, 59
   relations with regional institutions 131–2
   role in regional development 131
   TNCs 51, 55, 59, 123
Fischer, J. 4, 204, 205
Fischer Peace Plan 205
foreign direct investment (FDI) 48, 55, 137
foreign multinationals 59
foreign policy 27
forgetting, collective 239–43
'fortress Europe' 87, 112–13, 115
Forza Italia 258
fragmentation
   local government in CEE countries 156–7
   migration space 104–10, 117
France 224–5, 271
Freedom Party 258
frontiers 110–13
   see also borders
function 5–6, 6–7, 10–11, 18–19
   deep integration and nationalism 236–9
   EU trade policy 25–44
   pan-European industrial networks 45–67
   see also functions/levels question
functional independence 309–12
functions/levels question 68–84
   Europe, multi-level governance and globalization 73–7
   globalization 71–3
   governing globalization 77–81
   theory 69–71

GDP *per capita* 47, 124–5, 126–9, 264–5

General Agreement on Tariffs and Trade (GATT) 38
Generalized System of Preferences (GSP) 32–4
generational change 196
genetically modified organisms (GMOs) 29–30
Geneva Convention 116
Germany 17, 109, 179–214
   after 1989 181–6
   delayed normalization 197–207
   and EU 187–90, 199–202
   European security and 218, 219
   Kosovo conflict 196, 202–7
   multilateralism between domestic politics and transnational governance 186–93
   reflexive multilateralism 193–7
   social partnership 271, 308
global networks 57–8
   see also industrial networks
globalization 15–16, 122–6, 135–6
   Europe, territorial inequality and 122–3
   Germany, multilateralism and transnational governance 186–93
   governance and 71–81; Europe and multi-level governance 73–7; governing globalization 77–81
industrial networks 45–6, 57
   and migration 119
   and regional transformations 123–6
governance
   commodity chains 138, 139
   EU 12–13; multi-level governance 73–7
   functions/levels question 68–84
   institutions of 323–53
   local and regional governance in the CEE countries 145–78
great power, Russia as 91–2
Greece 111
Group of Eight 227

growth
  convergence and divergence between east and west Europe 129
  GDP *per capita* 47, 124–5, 126–9, 264–5
  industrial networks and 50, 51, 52–3
  Ireland 307–8
  Gulf War 222, 223, 225

Haider, J. 258
Havel, V. 256
hegemony 190–1
Helsinki agreement 104, 105
Hemerijck, A. 312
homogeneity 272–3
hot nationalism 238
human rights 227
humanitarian intervention 204, 205
Hungary 60, 93, 153, 172, 221
  local government 156, 157–8
  national identity and 'returning to Europe' 258–60
  opening of border with Austria 109
  proto-regional government 162, 165–6
Hungarian Socialist Party 259
Hurd, D. 198
hybridity, multicultural 285–94

Iberian migration 111
Iceland 114
Idea of Europe 280–301
  Europe of the commons 294–8
  history of 281–5
  non-European Europe 285–94
  ideational legacy 194–6
identity
  double identification 269
  European *see* European identity
  national *see* national identity
  politics of and democratic transformation 247–60
illegal immigration 107–8
immigrants 285–94
  see also migration
  implementation 318

incentives, material 328, 332–5
'indigenous way of life' 249–50
industrial districts 131
industrial networks 45–67
  alignment of networks 57–8, 62
  industrial organization and political economy perspectives 54–6
  and industrial upgrading 50–4
  multi-level factors 56–7
  network actors and linkages 58–60
  in the wider Europe 47–54
industrial organization 54–6
industrial upgrading 50–4
industrialization 125
institutional collisions 343–4
institutional pluralism 186–8, 201–2
institutional power 186, 188–9, 208
institutionalism 335, 337–40
institutionalization 326–8
institutions 20, 323–53
  deep integration 12–13
  dynamics of imperfectly integrated political orders 340–4
  frames for understanding institutional dynamics 335–40
  Germany's influence on European 191–3
  incentives and authority 332–5
  legal and living 329–31
  lock-in 80
  political culture and civil society 269–72
  regional and firms 131–2
  relevance of 324–6
intellectuals 255–60
interest groups 317
internal security 217
internalization 55
international migration *see* migration
Iraq (Gulf War) 222, 223, 225
Ireland 17, 268
  National Economic and Social Council (NESC) 306, 307
  social partnership 306–9, 318–19

Iron Curtain   87
Israel   35
Italy   110, 308, 319–20

Klaus, V.   258
Kohl, H.   200
Kosovo conflict   225
  Germany and   196, 202–7
  Russia and   92, 93, 99

labour   132–3
language   267–9
learning   240, 341
legal institutions   329–31
legitimacy   332–5
less-developed countries (LDCs)   33
levels   *see* functions/levels question
local elites   168–71, 172, 173, 174
local governance   145–78
  bifurcated models   146–50
  communist local government   154–5
  country cases   157–61
  post-communist local government   155–7
local networks   57–8
lock-in   80
Lomé Convention   39–40

Maastricht Treaty on European Union   8, 26, 104, 114–15, 115–16, 260
Malta   35
mandates, product   54
manufacturing   30–1
material incentives   328, 332–5
McDonagh, B.   273
Meciar, V.   258
Mercosur   36, 38
Mexico   36, 38
migration   103–21, 204, 298
  changing borders and frontiers   110–13
  Europeanization of migration space   113–17
  extra-EU migrants   106–7
  fragmented European migration space   104–10, 117
  impact of immigrants on society   285–94
  intra-EU migration   105–6
  retirement migration   109
  temporary migrants   108
military force
  Germany and use of in Kosovo   196, 202–7
  Russia and use abroad   92–3
minorities law   259
Modell Deutschland   190–1
money laundering   89
monitoring   316–17, 318
Monnet, J.   234, 282
Morocco   35
most-favoured nation (mfn) trade policy   28–31
multiculturalism   285–94, 295
multiethnicity/multinationality   285–94
multilateralism, Germany's   179–80, 181–5
  between domestic politics and transnational governance   186–93
  reflexive   193–7
multilateralization   206–7
multi-level governance (MLG)   73–7
multiple self   288, 289
Muslims   291–2

nation state   123, 124, 259
national character   182, 184
national consciousness   237
national governments   79–80
  internationalization and 'new regionalism'   135
  new roles   315–18
national identity   241–2
  civil society and supranational bonds   275–7
  European identity and in CEE   247–62
  Germany   195
  Russia   95–6
  and state-building   234–5
national interests   198
  Germany   199–202
national networks   57–8

National Programme for the
  Adoption of the *Acquis* (NPAA)
  153
national self-determination 247–9
nationalism 235
  civic nationalism 256–7
  ethnic nationalism 250, 256–8
  territory, function and affiliation
    in deep integration 236–9
nationality laws 274–5
NATO 3, 7, 10, 254
  bombing of Yugoslavia 92, 93,
    94, 95, 99, 222, 259–60
  European security 217, 218–19,
    220, 221–3, 227
  Germany and 184, 185
  Hungary and 259–60
  NATO–Russian Cooperation
    Council 227
  Partnerships for Peace 88
  Russian attitudes to 93–5, 98,
    99–100, 227
neo-corporatism 305, 308–9
neo-functionalism 71
neo-liberalism 105–6
Netherlands 308, 319
network organizers 58–60
networks 208
  alignment of 57–8, 62
  industrial *see* industrial
    networks
new states 249–50
normalization
  of the EU 239–43
  Germany and delayed 197–207;
    EU 197–202; Kosovo 202–7
North American Free Trade Area
  (NAFTA) 38
Norway 114, 308
nuclear armaments 184
NUTS system 163

Organization for Security and
  Cooperation in Europe (OSCE)
  220

partnership
  Russia and 88–90
  social *see* social partnership

Partnership and Cooperation
  Agreements 88
Partnerships for Peace 88
party politics 258–9
path dependence 80
perestroika 97
Phare Programme 152, 272
Pithart, P. 256
Poland 93, 153, 172, 221, 255, 256
  immigration 112
  local government 157
  national identity 252–3
  proto-regional government 162,
    164–5
policy
  combining policy-making,
    implementation and
    monitoring 318
  concertation *see* concertation
  diversity and EU policy 272–5
  EU trade policy 25–44
  policy entrepreneurship 316
  policy incoherence 187–8
  political culture 269–72
  political economy 54–6
  political integration Chapter 1
    passim, 323–53
    imperfect 340–4
    as institutionalization 326–8
    new forms of political unity
      323–4
  politics of identity 247–60
  populism 255
  Portugal 111, 308
  post-communism 145
  regional and local governance
    149–50, 155–6
  security in Europe 219–21
power
  diffused 56
  facets of 185–6, 207–8
  Germany's power in Europe
    179–214
  strategic agency 336–7
pre-accession strategy 151–2
preferential trade policy 31–40
  GSP 32–4
  relations with ACP states 39–40
  RTAs 32, 34–9

protection of non-statutory
    organizations 317
Putin, V. 227

racism 115, 287–94, 298
rapid reaction force 225–6
rational-instrumentalism 336–7
rational learning 341
realism 216
realist (deliberate) power 185, 207
recentralization 149–50, 156
reciprocal trade arrangements (RTAs)
    32, 34–9
reflexive multilateralism 193–7
refugees 109–10, 115–16, 119
regional development 122–44,
    270–1
  beyond the 'new regionalism'
    130–8
  globalization and regional
    transformations 123–6
  regional economic disparities
    127–9, 264–5
Regional Economic Partnership
    Agreements (REPAs) 40
regional fallacy 70
regional governance 145–78
  bifurcated models 146–50
  proto-regional government in CEE
    161–8
regionalization
  and Europeanization in CEE
    154–61
  and globalization 73–81;
    governing globalization
    77–81; multi-level governance
    73–7
Regular Reports 153, 162, 163
'returning to Europe' 250–60
rights
  EU-level universal rights 295–8
  human rights 227
  international migrants 114–15
Roma ethnic group 259
Rome, Treaty of 26, 104, 115, 345–6
routinization 327
Russia 37, 41, 87–102
  EU and its enlargement 95–8,
    99–100

  and European security 226–7
  and NATO 93–5, 98, 99–100, 227
  and partnership 88–90
  perceived as excluded 90–3
  see also Soviet Union

Scharping, R. 204
Schaukelpolitik (see–saw policy)
    182–3
Schengen Agreement 110, 112,
    113, 115, 118, 270
Schröder, G. 200–2, 203–4
security, European 215–30
  European security and defence
    initiative 224–6
  meaning of 215–18
  NATO and 217, 218–19, 220,
    221–3, 227
  in post-communist Europe
    219–21
  provision by EU 221–3
  and Russia 226–7
Serbia see Yugoslavia
shallow integration 45, 61
Slovak nationalism 256–8
Slovakia 258
  Movement for a Democratic
    Slovakia 258
Slovenia 111, 153, 159–60, 167–8,
    172
social commonality 267–9
social constructivism 194–5
social exclusion 114
social learning 240
social partnership 271, 305–22
  emergence in Ireland and other
    member states 306–9
  European integration and
    convergence 318–20
  as post-corporatist concertation
    309–18; combining policy-
    making, implementation and
    monitoring 318; deliberation
    and problem-solving
    309–12; new roles for centre
    and national partnership
    315–18; new view of social
    partners 313–15
social problems 216–17

socio-economic modernization   9
Solana, J.   206, 338
solidarity   309–12
South Africa   36, 38, 39
southern frontier   110–11
sovereignty   86–8, 201–2
Soviet Union   218–19, 248
   see also Russia
Spain   111, 308
specialization   48
'spirit of the age'   249–50
stability   37
Stability Pact for Southeast Europe   205
standardization   272, 327
state   see nation state; national governments
strategic agency   335, 336–7
structural funds   148
Structured Dialogue   152
subsidiarity   13, 80–1, 148
supranational bonds   275–7
   see also European identity
Suzuki   60
Sweden   308
Switzerland   308
systemic turbulence   109–10

Tampere European Council   116, 117
territorial inequalities   122–44
   beyond the 'new regionalism'   130–8
   dynamics of territorial trajectories   126–30; over time   129–30; national economic disparities   126–7; regional economic disparities   127–9
   globalization, Europe and   122–3
   globalization and regional transformations   123–6
territory   5–6, 7–8, 10–11, 19, 236
   European security   215–30
   Germany's power in Europe   179–214
   local and regional governance in CEE countries   145–78
   migration   see migration

Russian attitudes towards Europe   87–102
Thatcher, M.   198, 199
third way   134–5
trade   47, 183, 184–5
trade policy, EU   25–44
   most-favoured nation policy   28–31
   policy process   26–8
   preferential trade policy   31–40; ACP states   39–40; GSP   32–4; RTAs   32, 34–9
trade unions   132–3, 271
traditionalism   287–94
transnational corporations (TNCs)   51, 55, 59, 123
transnational networks   208
   industrial   see industrial networks
Treaty on European Union   8, 26, 104, 114–15, 115–16, 260
Tunisia   35
Turkey   7, 35, 118

Ukraine   37, 41
unemployment   266
uneven development   122–44
United Kingdom (UK)   113–14, 198, 224–5, 271, 275–6
United Nations (UN)   225
United States (USA)   98, 184, 185
   European security and   218–19, 224–6
universal rights   295–8
upgrading, industrial   50–4

value chains   133, 138, 139
values   8, 272–3
Verheugen, G.   201

Waigel, T.   200
Warsaw Pact   94, 217, 218–19, 220
welfare rights   296
west European integration   3–11, 16–17, 18, 20
   affiliational dimension   5–6, 8–11
   deep integration   12–15

west European integration *continued*
  functional dimension   5–6, 6–7,
    10–11
  territorial dimension   5–6, 7–8,
    10–11
Western European Union (WEU)   3,
  7, 206, 224
World Trade Organization (WTO)
  28, 30, 33, 40

World War II   257

Yeltsin, B.   91
Yugoslavia   223, 248
  NATO bombing   222, 259–60;
    Russia and   92, 93, 94, 95,
    99
  refugees following break-up   109,
    111